A Brief History
of Iraq

A BRIEF HISTORY OF IRAQ

HALA FATTAH
WITH FRANK CASO

Facts On File
An imprint of Infobase Publishing

Facts On File, Inc.
An imprint of Infobase Publishing
132 West 31st Street
New York NY 10001

Library of Congress Cataloging-in-Publication Data
Fattah, Hala Mundhir, 1950–
    A brief history of Iraq / Hala Fattah with Frank Caso.
        p. cm.—(Brief history)
    Includes bibliographical references and index.
    ISBN-13:978-0-8160-5767-2
    ISBN-10:0-8160-5767-2
    1. Iraq—History. 2. Iraq—Civilization. I. Caso, Frank. II. Title.
DS70.9.F38 2008
956.7—dc22   2008008451

Facts On File books are available at special discounts when purchased in bulk quantities for businesses, associations, institutions, or sales promotions. Please call our Special Sales Department in New York at (212) 967-8800 or (800) 322-8755.

You can find Facts On File on the World Wide Web at http://www.factsonfile.com

Text design by Joan M. McEvoy
Cover design by Semadar Megged / Jooyoung An
Maps by Dale Williams

Printed in the United States of America

This book is printed on acid-free paper and contains 30 percent postconsumer recycled content.

To Muna, Tala, Alia, and Raya(tuni), so that they may learn about their mother's homeland.

CONTENTS

LIST OF ILLUSTRATIONS

LIST OF MAPS

ACKNOWLEDGMENTS

I wish to acknowledge the help of Dr. Lamia Al-Gailani Werr, who read and commented on the first chapter, and that of Professor Matthew Gordon, who critiqued chapters 3 and 4. I thank them for their time and effort, and they are, of course, absolved of any errors of commission or omission, which are mine alone.

I also wish to thank Frank Caso, who wrote chapters 2 and 10 and added material to chapter 9 and elsewhere. This book would literally not have been completed without his assistance. Even though Frank and I have distinctive viewpoints with regard to Iraq's historical developments, I think the book benefits from our different perspectives. Finally, I salute the patience and professionalism of my editor, Claudia Schaab, who helped see the manuscript into its final stages. Thanks are also due to the combined efforts of the editorial team at Facts On File.

INTRODUCTION

Any book on Iraq's history from the pre-Islamic era to the present must address important paradigms that continue to vex the historian in her or his research. One of these is the notion of the "artificiality" of Iraq, a thesis that continues to be propounded by Western as well as Arab policy makers, without it actually meaning very much. Greatly in vogue these days, this particular theory has as its starting point the idea that the British "cobbled" together Iraq in 1920 and then proceeded to rule its "mosaic" of ethnicities and sects in the full face of separatist sentiment and schisms of religion and sect. After the "creation," adherents of the thesis maintain, the country's main groups, which shared little by way of history or culture, continued their contentious existence until they were forcibly taken in hand by the Baathist-influenced regime of Saddam Hussein and made to conform to a militantly ideological variant of Arab national socialism. Before the war of 2003, Iraq was seen as a potential Yugoslavia, a nation that was not really one nation but several, all shackled together by a coercive state undergirded by a brutal military-ideological machine.

This thesis has always been an outsider's vision of Iraq. It has very little actual resonance in Iraq today. Even after 35 years of wars, the brutal suppression of minority rights, and the continued assault on civil society, the majority of Iraqis still consider themselves Iraqis first, and Shia or Sunni or Turkoman or Yazidi or Chaldo-Assyrian second. To be sure, during the war, ethnic and sectarian identities have been strongly reasserted into the national fabric, and this for a number of reasons, among the most important having to do with the particular way that the United States and the United Kingdom configured the representation of the first interim ruling bodies. Kurdish aspirations, in particular, have taken on a life of their own, and many Kurds are on record that they wish to form their own nation-state. Until that time, however, the Iraqi Kurdish leadership has expressed a willingness to enter into a federal union with the rest of Iraq.

But the "artificiality" thesis also has serious flaws on an academic level. Ever since political scientist Benedict Anderson propounded his famous thesis on "imagined" nations (Anderson 1990), the "nation" has been seen as an ideological construct that varies over time and, of course, over space. In this sense, Iraq is an "idea" in the same way that other nation-states are "ideas," including those in the West. And because these "ideas" spring from a particular geographical, ecological, religious, civic, and political bedrock, nations are neither more nor less artificial than others; they are just constructed and imagined differently. Of course, in Iraq's case, and as a result of its colonialist experience, the unitary state that emerged as a result of the post–World War I climate had an important role in shaping the nation. Nonetheless, it is important to remember that it was the collective visions, desires, and aspirations of the Iraqi people that gave the new nation-state its internal logic and specific makeup.

In fact, the term *Iraq* has been part of the mental, ideological, geographic, and economic mind-set of the people and societies that lived in that particular region for a very long time. In the ninth century, when geography was considered an Islamic science, the geographer Yaqut al-Hamawi believed the name *Iraq* to connote the lowland region next to Kufa and Basra (which were called al-Iraqan, or the "two Iraqs," as a result) that was traditionally part of Ard Babil, the "land of Babylon" (al-Jundi 1990, 106). The term *Iraq* also referred to the alluvial south-central part of the country, at times referred to as ard al-Sawad ("the black earth," because it was fertile ground). The point is, the name existed even before the Islamic conquests, and it referred to a particular region and was equated with a particular culture, which was that of Iraq, no matter how loose or vague the association. Any examination, however superficial, of the premodern historiography of Iraq will unearth hundreds of similar references to the term *al-Iraq* by journeying scholars or government officials. While it is undoubtedly correct to note that the term itself did not in any way reflect a politicized reality, it nonetheless connoted an association with home, however limited or circumscribed that notion was in premodern Iraq. It therefore possesses a flavor and an immediacy that merits recognition, if only en passant, of the historical continuum that ties present-day Iraq to its illustrious past.

This said, it behooves us to understand the different phases of Iraq's history in order to appreciate the problematics of its modern-day formation. The thousands of years of civilization and evolution that mark this new-old nation saw the first cities and agricultural systems built in recorded history, the establishment of the first empires, and the rise and fall of dynasties, tribes, and principalities (chapter 1). Chapter 2 takes the story up to the Sassanian and Byzantine Empires. Traditionally,

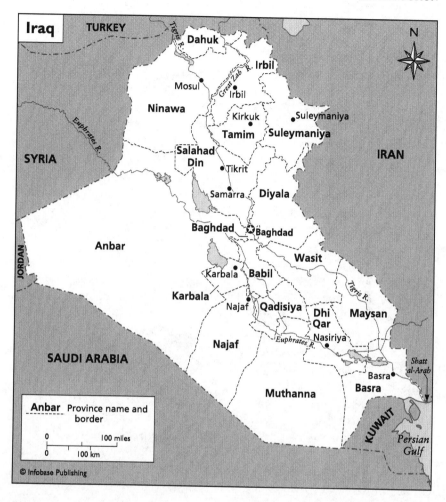

historians have insisted on far too radical a separation between the ancient world and the rise of Islam; in this book, I have tried to make an effort, however small, to connect the pre-Islamic period with the more mature development of a faith-based civilization that emerged out of Arabia to revolutionize all of the known world. Because the first monotheists bridged the gap between ancient and Islamic Iraq, making Iraq one of the important regions for the spread of unitary religions, it seemed important to dwell on the underpinnings of faith and urbanity in the first Islamic centuries; a discussion carried out in chapter 3. Under the Umayyad dynasty, Iraq became a secondary outpost of the Islamic empire, where religious, literary, and chiliastic movements developed in near obscurity, only flaring into flash points of rebellion when the more "secular" Umayyad rulers came into brief but violent contact with developing Alid (later Shia) groups (chapter 3).

I then proceed to discuss the quintessential Islamic civilization, that of the Baghdad-based Abbasid Empire and its formulation of an Islamic universalistic ethos that drew inspiration from the cultural, economic, and military energies of the farthest, as well as nearest, provinces of the realm (chapter 4). After the last Abbasid ruler's demise under the hoofs of Mongol horses, the Turkic era began, bringing with it hundreds of years of Turko-Mongol domination of the central Islamic lands and the marginalization of the once all-powerful imperial capital, Baghdad (chapter 5). A Turkic dynasty, later to create the Ottoman Empire, having established its hold on geographic Iraq (Baghdad, Mosul, Shahrizor, and Basra) in the early to mid-17th century, then proceeded to rule the country until its defeat by the British in World War I (chapter 6).

After the British occupation of Iraq and the establishment of the modern state, the Iraqi monarchy flourished for 37 years; in 1958, the last monarch of Iraq, King Faisal II, was massacred alongside the rest of his family, and the first republican regime, that of Brigadier General Abdul-Karim Qasim, was established (chapter 7). The republican regimes continued to follow one another in short order until the second Baathist government came to power in 1968. From 1968 onward, at first ruling in the shadows but eventually becoming second to none, Saddam Hussein rose to power in Iraq, bringing with him the trappings of a strong centralized state, a powerful security apparatus, a large army, and overweening ambitions to become the Bismarck of the Arab/Islamic worlds (chapter 8). The Iran-Iraq War, in which military offensives took place against a background of forced deportations of ethnic and sectarian groups, the collapse of a once robust economy, and the creation of chauvinist ideologies pitting Arab against Iranian, made way for the unilateral invasion of Kuwait in 1990. After the defeat of Iraq by a combined coalition force led by the United States and United Kingdom, a 13-year sanctions regime took its toll on Iraqi society (chapter 9). The war in 2003 finally overthrew the Baathist regime of Saddam Hussein, and a new but fragile Iraq was reconstituted under U.S. and U.K. auspices (chapter 10).

Finally, a conclusion attempts to reconfigure Iraq's future with an eye to the past. What elements in Iraq's society reemerge, time after time, to make a lasting imprint on the cities, empires, and states in this self-same region over the course of centuries? Is it really true that Iraq's diverse and complex social ties are stronger than those predicted by foreign and local potentates alike, and that quite unlike Yugoslavia,

Iraq's cohesiveness will endure despite the odds? What is the true "core" of Iraqi society, and what are the foundational myths, principles, and traditions that Iraqis recognize as vital to their "nationness"? And finally, what are the lessons to be drawn by U.S. and British commanders from Iraq's history as they wrestle with this discordant but ultimately dynamic nation-state of 23 million people, each with her or his sectarian, confessional, ethnic, and linguistic traditions, and yet all inclusively Iraqi in yearnings and desires?

1

IRAQ, THE FIRST SOCIETY
(PREHISTORY TO 539 B.C.E.)

Historically, Iraqi society boasts a number of firsts: Ancient Mesopotamia was the site of the world's first cities, first irrigation systems, first states, first empires, first writing, first monuments, and first recorded religions. The archaeological sites that dot Iraq's landscape—and those still buried under telltale mounds all over the country—are witness to great, but often brutal, civilizations that organized men and women into hierarchies, groups, and classes and created order out of chaos, instilling meaning where there was none and devotion and piety in place of an existential void. Sumerians, Akkadians, Babylonians, and Assyrians built and rebuilt large, well-organized civilizations whose cultural underpinnings were so novel and yet at the same time so enduring that they still link Eastern to Western civilization today and give meaning and structure to the way we see our past and, of course, ourselves.

Cultural Unity in Ancient Iraq

The term *Iraq* is used in this book to define a territory that corresponds to the Tigris-Euphrates valley, the region once called Mesopotamia, most of which encompassed what is now modern-day Iraq but which at various times also stretched into present-day Syria, Iran, and Turkey. Fluid borders are one of the striking features of the region, so much so that it is estimated that in certain periods, ancient Iraq even included parts of the Arabian Peninsula. Paradoxically, while Iraq's shifting territorial frontiers were one facet of its historical development, the other was its inherent unity. The notion that ancient Iraq was unified culturally and economically, if not always politically, over most of its history has staunch supporters in academic circles. Georges Roux, one of the pioneers of the history of this ancient land, states that the region "forms a large, coherent, well-defined, geographical, historical and cultural unit" (Roux 1992, xvii). McGuire Gibson, of the University of Chicago, asserts that although political unity was rare and more often than not imposed by centralized empires, shared cultural, economic, and social features continued to mark the region even after the collapse of political dynasties (in Inati 2003, 26–30). For instance, trade routes continued to thrive and prosper, and "southern" artistic genres survived and were refined for northern tastes. At the same time, religious customs and rituals in both the north (Assyria) and the south (Babylonia) developed broad similarities, and administrative methods traveled to where they found the best reception, which was often at the courts of rival dynasts. Cultural unity took on added force with the discovery of writing. Unlike those of other cultures, the clay tablets created in ancient Iraq were durable and long lasting. Thus hundreds of thousands of Mesopotamian texts have survived into this century, and the great variety and complexity of the works produced in ancient Iraq have been a boon to archaeologists, art historians, anthropologists, and historians alike.

Prehistory

No culture throughout the long span of history has arrived prepackaged, least of all the first civilization on earth. The prehistory of Iraq is in some ways intimately tied into the prehistory of southwest Asia as a whole, and especially to the advance of the two other great river civilizations, that of the Indus and Nile Valleys. Continuities in culture and technology, religious rites, and social structure tied these subregions together, as did language codes based on symbols and signs. Regional customs and variations traveled far and wide and made their mark on different societies. For example, historians have theorized that the Sumerian language, considered to be the first language in the world, was itself nourished by other, unrecorded languages over millennia, enriching Sumerian vocabulary and deepening its structure. Moreover, precisely because the region's absorbent borders were never sealed, a constant wave of immigrants bringing new ideas and technologies poured into ancient Iraq and contributed to its economic growth, architectural heritage, and overall culture. Arguably, however, the larger unities that drew Iraq within the Asian orbit seem to have converged on the domestication of plants and animals and their distribution, along with the technologies and systems that propagated their growth all over the region. These wider patterns of social change and economic development ultimately led to the agricultural revolution that gradually began to change the organization of work, the patterns of human consumption, and the relationship of humans to the environment.

During the Pleistocene era, which began about 2 million years ago and ended in 1000 B.C.E., the reconfiguration of the region's physical, economic, and technological features began to take shape. During this period, a radical transformation of Iraq's climate and geography took place, a change so eventful that it eventually led to the emergence of the first human settlements in Iraq's agricultural northern belt and along its southern riverbanks. In or around 7000 B.C.E., agricultural settlements were established in northern Iraq, where clusters of stone houses have been uncovered, littered with flint utensils and obsidian tools. In good years, a combination of rain-fed agriculture and plentiful game allowed those villages to flourish. Jarmo, in what is now Iraqi Kurdistan, was one of the largest agricultural villages in the region. Jarmo's inhabitants lived in solid, many-roomed mud houses; ate with spoons made of animal bone; possessed spindles to weave flax and wool; domesticated sheep, cattle, pigs, and dogs; and even made necklaces and bracelets of stone. Besides hunting for meat, Jarmo's inhabitants also grew wheat, barley, lentils, peas, and acorns. The most noticeable feature of the village was its organized character: Its population had learned to live together as a community, banding together to defend their land, and working together to harvest the crops. Even though individual farms seemed to have been the norm, the evidence suggests that Jarmo's inhabitants were not averse to joining together in small communes, where sociability and ties of kinship cemented neighborly relations, and survival depended on group cohesion.

Meanwhile, the combination of water and good alluvial soil brought forth similar settlements in the southernmost tip of the country, the land called Sumer. Although still an influential thesis, the notion that the earliest cities arose in the alluvial mud left by desiccated rivers is now coming under question (Postgate 1994, 20–21). Nonetheless, some scholars still believe that around 14,000 B.C.E. the Tigris and Euphrates Rivers formed two broad waterways that flowed directly into the Gulf, depositing a large amount of silt on the riverbanks. During the last ice age (20,000 to 15,000 B.C.E.), the sea level changed. Global warming dried up the Gulf bed, leading some scholars to theorize that the flatlands thereby created inspired early humans to experiment with the growing of crops in marshlands or districts bordering the sea. Irrigation agriculture, the mainstay of southern Iraq, had drawn immigrants from the north, who founded several villages in marshy areas of the Euphrates, invented the plow and the stone-wheeled carriage, and built the first reed ships. Eventually, the aridity of the climate led to the desiccation of the tributaries of the Euphrates River, and the need to do more with very little forced the organization of the first settlements. The scarcity of fertile land and the necessity to redistribute precious water in turn led to the emergence of planned and fortified communities, a centralized government structure, organized religion, and bureaucracies. And so it was that over the thousands of years that preceded the development of the first cities, archaeological evidence suggests that the model for all later civilizations had already begun to make its mark in the rudimentary settlements of southern Iraq that were dependent on subsistence agriculture as well as hunting and fishing.

The Ubaid period (ca. 5000 B.C.E.), which takes its name from the Sumerian-speaking peoples that inhabited the area of Tell al-Ubaid, near Ur, is the first record of human settlement in southern Iraq. Even though not much is known about the Ubaid colony, what we do know throws into relief certain features that were shared by all of the succeeding settlements in the region. The Ubaid constellation of villages set the tone for the settlements that came afterward: They were differentiated by size and number, grouped around each other for self-defense, and set apart by the fact that many of their inhabitants carried out specialized nonagricultural occupations. The Ubaid period is remarkable because it is the first link in the chain of civilization, which in all probability was early Sumerian. Seemingly arriving full blown in southern Iraq (although there is evidence that religious and architectural currents from Samarra, in the northeast, had partly influenced their development), the most famous Ubaid villages were situated on the banks of the Euphrates. They were built of reeds and mud bricks and concentrated around a temple, with characteristic pottery that set them apart from other, northern cultures, even though they had interacted with them for millennia.

Sumerian Cities (ca. 3500–2334 B.C.E.)

It is not until the fourth millennium that cities in the modern sense—that is, large settlements built around a central focus, usually a shrine, and inhabited by groups of people cooperating with one another in some form of a centralized administration—developed. The prototype city of the period, Uruk (now known as Warka, about 150 miles southwest of Baghdad), was a city not only because it was large but also because it was fortified; it had a wall, which most villages did not. Uruk was influenced by the settlement at Ubaid. In fact, Ubaid paved the way for the more developed society of Uruk to the point where the latter's temple was built on the remains of the former's own shrine complex (Postgate 1994, 24). Although the tip of southern Iraq has not been excavated to the degree necessary to draw analytic comparisons with settlements in the north, Uruk is one site that has received fairly extensive attention, enough to merit a detailed study (Van de Mieroop 2004, 20). Archaeological digs have uncovered an urban blueprint of shrines and temples, artistic tableaux inscribed on cylinder seals and written records that depict a highly sophisticated society. Uruk's prosperity (derived in large part from agriculture) funded a class of craftsmen that turned out a distinctive form of pottery, including a quintessential article, "the so-called beveled-rim bowl"

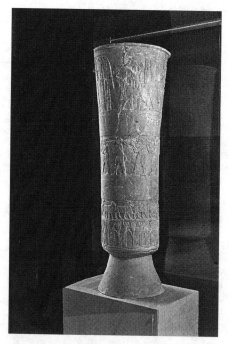

The Warka vase, ca. 3500–3000 B.C.E., stolen from the Iraqi National Museum at the beginning of the 2003 war but soon recovered, depicts an offering to the fertility goddess Innin. (Scala/Art Resource, NY)

(Van de Mieroop 2004, 204). One of the most precious objects to have been discovered by present-day archaeologists at Uruk was an alabaster vase that was carved with an intricate scene depicting, among other figures, the goddess Inanna. The Uruk, or under its better-known name, Warka, vase was looted during the war in April 2003 but was miraculously restored almost intact to the Iraqi Museum several months later.

Uruk's other innovation was its differentiated class-based society, in which people were known by their occupations. Tax records uncovered by historians point to a chain of command in which priest-kings were at the top, peasants at the bottom, and in between were landowners, temple officials, scribes, and merchants. Uruk was not, of course, the only city of note in southern Iraq. There was also Jamdat Nasr, a later development. Much that we know of Sumer's earliest city-states is conserved in two documents of the period, the Temple Hymns and the Sumerian King List. Composed in the Akkadian period, after the fall of Sumer, they refer to 35 different cities, the most important of them being Lagash, Larsa, Kish, Ur, Nippur, Eridu, and Sippar. The mystery of their origins is best explained by Assyriologist A. Leo Oppenheim, who speculates that in Sumer, "a spontaneous urbanization took place . . . [and that] nowhere do we find such an agglomeration of urban settlements as in southern Babylon" (Oppenheim 1977, 110–111).

For him, as for other scholars, the city is the only construct that made sense at the time: Arising out of fortuitous circumstances of soil, climate, water, and people, it catered to the needs of a large and settled population and hewed to an inclusive ideology built on the principles of equality and individuality. Its citizens were not democratic in the strict sense of the word but followed a more patriarchal code built on consensus and collective justice. The most important buildings were the temples and, only later on, the palace, which managed to coexist with the corporate-minded landowners in the city, who may have instituted large, private farms worked by kinfolk and foreign laborers. A balance in power between the king, high priests, and landowners may have resulted in a more or less harmonious existence, in which economic and social tensions were muted.

Economy of the Early Cities

Ancient Iraq's economy was largely based on agriculture, although trade in livestock products and the weaving of textiles were known. Cereal production was the mainstay of the agricultural economy, complemented by sheep, cattle, and pig herding. Cuneiform tablets also describe long-distance trade, with merchants traveling to and from Anatolia and Iran. Agriculture was time consuming because in the south it depended on the steady maintenance of irrigation canals, which were prone to heavy silting caused by the mud deposits carried by the rivers. Farmers in antiquity knew that while the river waters were a boon to agriculture, they also spelled trouble if not kept under tight surveillance. Because of the constant need to supervise the work carried out on irrigation channels, a centralized system was established whereby a class of people, for the most part overseers employed by higher patrons, were hired to keep the peasants in check and to see that the system of irrigation agriculture was fully carried out. Historians theorize that people in southern Iraq developed complex forms of social organization based on group participation necessary to build and maintain canals and to keep rival groups away from their sources of water and stores of food. Eventually, this central administration was to culminate in a tightly organized, highly differentiated class system.

The Invention of Writing

It has been claimed, "while [ancient Iraq's] true singularity may lie in the complexity of social organization, the two most striking characteristics of early Mesopotamia are its literacy and urbanization" (Postgate 1994, 73). In or about 3300 B.C.E., and at Uruk itself, the Sumerians invented writing. At first, writing was a specialist's art, and not everyone was qualified in its use. Before the invention of cuneiform, scribes "wrote" the first tablets by using pictographs or primitive art to represent objects and people, which were then inscribed on fired clay tablets with a reed "pen," or stylus. Because there were more than 700 signs used in the pictograph system, writing remained a cumbersome project until a new script, cuneiform, was invented. Basically, cuneiform used wedge-shaped signs and symbols, as well as sounds, to convey ideas and meaning, speeding up the process of communication and making it much more of a flexible medium. Cuneiform was used for thousands of years, influencing many different civilizations, such as the Assyrians and the Persians.

Although writing originated as a means to record commercial transactions, it quickly became a tool for less official communication. For instance, religious lore pertaining to the later Sumerians was noted

In common usage by the second millennium B.C.E., cuneiform script was used for ancient Babylonian private as well as ceremonial communication. (Michael Fuery/Shutterstock)

down for posterity; among the thousands of clay tablets that survive are also funerary orations, which Oppenheim calls "ceremonial writing," in reference to the often private messages written by Sumerian and Babylonian kings to gods and goddesses. The personal letter, considered to be the archetypal modern communication, was also widely used in the post-Sumerian world. For example, it is known that other than the letters describing official business sent by royal families or merchants or ambassadors, private communication on health issues, communal welfare, and even gossip made the rounds in the ancient world.

In the second millennium, cuneiform became a commonly used script, used by many different language groups. Other than Sumerian, which underwent a period of renaissance in Babylonia, the language most often used in the region "can now be identified as a separate dialect of Akkadian; [it] was used almost everywhere by native speakers of other languages (Amorite, Hurrian, Elamite) who also adopted the southern writing style and spellings" (Van de Mieroop 2004, 81). Only in Ashur, the heartland of what was to become the Assyrian Empire, was Old Assyrian, another dialect of Akkadian, used.

The *Epic of Gilgamesh*

One of the most remarkable stories that has come down to us from Sumerian tradition is the much-discussed *Epic of Gilgamesh,* the tale of the one-quarter mortal, three-quarters divine Gilgamesh. The central character in the story, Gilgamesh, is the powerful and arrogant king of the Sumerian city of Uruk. A man with little respect for the inhabitants of the city he rules, nor for their wives or daughters, he is confronted with his earthly opposite, Enkidu, whom the gods create to teach Gilgamesh about life, death, and the meaning of it all. After becoming boon companions, they embark on various adventures. Enkidu dies, bringing sorrow to his friend and teaching Gilgamesh about the inevitability of death. In a quest for everlasting life, Gilgamesh braces himself for a harrowing journey through the Underworld. There, he confronts his own mortality and realizes that life is not a perennial adventure but a journey with a beginning and an end. And because there is no permanence to life on earth, its sole meaning emerges from the way that it is lived. After this transformative experience, Gilgamesh returns to Uruk a much wiser, if sadder, man and contemplates the story of humanity high on the walls of his city, to which he adds an engraved brick detailing his epic journey. Exhibiting a fluent and gripping style, the *Epic of Gilgamesh* is an amazing document that is as fresh as if it were written yesterday. A joy to read, it tackles with remarkable depth the existential questions that perplex humans in any age.

Religions of Ancient Iraq

A deeply religious people, the Mesopotamians derived their ideas of God and the universe from the land in which they lived. Mesopotamian religions were not attached to a particular dynasty or ruling family; rather, notions of the divine developed out of ancient Iraq's natural surroundings—the changing seasons, the pull of the ocean tides, the abundance of the harvests, the radiance of the Moon, and the heat of the Sun. The Mesopotamians held their gods in very high esteem, building large temples and shrines for them that were administered by a class of priests and bureaucrats whose functions at first were to make offerings to the gods and, later on, to regulate the affairs of the city and the countryside.

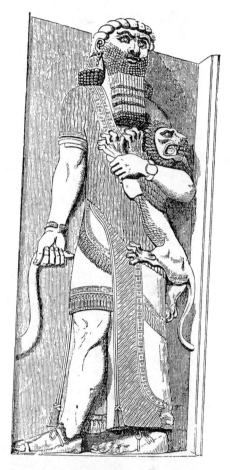

A depiction of Gilgamesh, eponymous hero-king of the Sumerian epic, whose adventures and travels to the Underworld provide a philosophical underpinning to the meaning of life (Bonomi, Nineveh and Its Palaces, 1875 [after Botta])

The pantheon of Mesopotamian gods ranged from the three superior male gods, Anu, Enlil, and Enki, to the lowest deities, evil spirits and demons. There was also a group of goddesses, the most famous of which was Inanna, who personified carnality and temptation. There were close to 3,000 names of gods and goddesses in the Sumerian-Akkadian world, depicting young gods and older ones. Marduk, the god of Babylon; Nabu, the deity attached to Borsippa (and Marduk's son); and Samas, the sun god, were especially revered.

Several creation epics, most notably that of Gilgamesh, attest to the fact that gods were the prime instruments in the making of the world. It is unclear, however, what role religion played in everyday life. One of the most respected scholars in the field, Oppenheim, queried the standard by which archaeologists and art historians of ancient Iraq built up the notion of a Mesopotamian religion. According to him, the material available to construct a valid theory of Mesopotamian religion is too meager, and most of what we refer to as religion is really myth, created by a literary and artistic class of Mesopotamian scribes. He concluded that religion in ancient Iraq was an elite practice, confined to kings and priests, and only superficially affected the masses. His assumption that religion was more of a literary paradigm than a social ritual is still controversial today.

The Akkadian Empire (2334–2154 B.C.E.)

The rise of Akkad was an immense conceptual shift in the early history of Iraq that gave rise to a different power formation—the empire. The shift to empire did not entirely do away with the city-state, which reemerged in rather spectacular fashion with the rise of the Third Dynasty of Ur some 200 years later; however, once rooted, the idea of empire continued to have a great impact on the region's political, military, and economic calculations thereafter. The location of the Akkadian Empire was in northern Babylonia, close to present-day Baghdad. The first ruler was Sargon of Akkad (r. ca. 2334–2279 B.C.E.), a military commander who measured success in territorial conquest and perpetual war. A Semitic people who migrated north from Arabia, the Akkadians easily defeated the Sumerian city-states in southern Babylonia and, much later on, conquered vast stretches of territory that extended all the way from the Upper Euphrates River to Lebanon, on the Mediterranean coast.

Sargon of Akkad based his empire in the city of Akkad. He and his descendants helped produce a new language, Akkadian, that was of Semitic origins but written in the cuneiform script invented by the Sumerians. Eventually, Akkadian became the language of administration, while Sumerian remained the language of the people. Even so, evidence of Sumerian translations of Akkadian texts exists, lending credence to the theory that neither cultural tradition was entirely divorced from the other but continued to coexist, albeit in a new political formation. In fact, it has been claimed by more than one historian that the primary difference between Sumerians and Akkadians was not

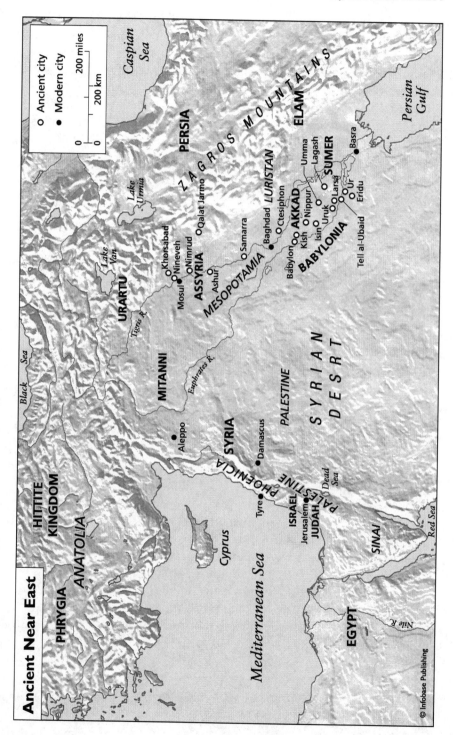

Ancient Near East

o Ancient city
• Modern city

0   200 km

0   200 miles

Caspian Sea

PERSIA

ZAGROS MOUNTAINS

ELAM

Persian Gulf

Basra

Lake Urmia

LURISTAN

Umma

Lagash

SUMER

Qalat Jarmo

Ctesiphon

AKKAD

Ur

Khorsabad

Nineveh

Nimrud

Baghdad

Nippur

Larsa

Eridu

Mosul

Samarra

Kish

Isin

Uruk

ASSYRIA

Ashur

MESOPOTAMIA

Babylon

BABYLONIA

Tell al-Ubaid

URARTU

Lake Van

Tigris R.

MITANNI

Euphrates R.

SYRIAN DESERT

Black Sea

PALESTINE

PALESTINE

Aleppo

SYRIA

Damascus

HITTITE KINGDOM

ANATOLIA

PHOENICIA

Dead Sea

Tyre

ISRAEL

Jerusalem

JUDAH

PHRYGIA

Cyprus

Mediterranean Sea

SINAI

Red Sea

EGYPT

Nile R.

© Infobase Publishing

race but language, and neither physical nor cultural features served to distinguish one set of peoples from another. The foremost distinction was a philological or linguistic one, a peculiarity usually glossed over by scholars interested in making a questionable case for ethnic differences between Sumerians and Akkadians.

Sargon of Akkad is known primarily for his creation of a superior army; his military pursuits ranged from northern Iraq to Syria (and Lebanon), Iran, and Anatolia. At the same time that the borders of his state were stretched to incorporate new territories, Sargon established unities in administrative practice and religious thought that he hoped would instill a wider Akkad-based identity. He sowed the seeds for the creation of a centralized bureaucracy in the region. After defeating the Sumerian cities, Sargon created a well-oiled palace organization in which Akkadians took on the title and functions of *ensis,* or governors; administrative records duly mentioned the names of the Akkadian king and his descendants; lands were confiscated from Sumerian landholders and parceled out to Sargon's chief military and civilian retainers; and beginning a tradition that was to last throughout the Akkadian period, Sargon's daughter was installed as a high priestess of the moon god Nanna in the city of Ur, taking on a Sumerian name in the process. Finally, the palace was financed by taxes from overland trade, and in keeping with the empire's methodical organization of almost every aspect in the imperial domain, the king of Akkad also centralized the classification of weights and measures in his empire "into a single logical system which remained the standard for a thousand years and more" (Postgate 1994, 41).

It is important to relate that not all of these inventions were completely novel. For instance, the word *ensi,* or "governor," was of Sumerian derivation, and though the Akkadian kings claimed that many of the new governors were Akkadians, there is some evidence that Sargon retained some of the original Sumerian rulers in place. Akkadian culture, consciously promoted by Sargon to suit his ideological needs, was never entirely an autonomous phenomenon; Sumer, with its complex history, flourishing urbanity, and religious heritage, was in large part the background from which the kings of Akkad drew their inspiration, just as they assimilated other influences throughout their long rule. Despite Sumer's decline, the waning of Sumerian culture and language was slow and gradual; even in its nadir, it was being propagated in communities as far afield as Syria, Anatolia, and Palestine, which adopted Sumerian script and myths.

At the same time, Sargon and his descendants deployed a large military organization to subjugate various districts and regions throughout the ancient Middle East. The borders of the Akkadian Empire stretched and contracted with each military defeat or victory. At one point, Sargon began to refer to himself as "king of the world," later amending it to "king of the entire inhabited world" (Van de Mieroop 2004, 64). The broad principles underlying ancient Iraq's history are once more apparent in the existence of regional unities with fluid borders and the reality of cultural diffusion and adaptation even in times of war. The Akkadians, a Semitic peoples originating from the Arabian Peninsula, carved out the first empire in ancient Iraq by force of arms, certainly, but also by assimilating to cultural forms already entrenched in the land called Sumer; and in turn, they became the conduits for a Sumerian-Akkadian synthesis of mores and traditions in the course of their own world dominion.

The Third Dynasty of Ur (2112–2004 B.C.E.)

The memory of Sumer among the people of the south engendered resentment and hostility against Akkadian power. Rather than succumb to its internal enemies, however, the Akkadian Empire seems to have been defeated by the Gutians, about whom historians know very little but who seem to have been foreigners who first mounted raids then concerted military campaigns against Akkad, which eventually destroyed the dynasty altogether. After close to 100 years of Gutian supremacy, a longer-lasting, and certainly more organized, city-state formation came to the fore. A successful counterattack against the last Gutian leader was finally mounted by a governor of Ur, Ur-Nammu (r. ca. 2112–2095 B.C.E.). This period is frequently referred to as the Neo-Sumerian period because Sumerian culture, language, and traditions were revived under the kings of the Third Dynasty of Ur (Ur III), who ruled for more than a century. But the Ur dynasty is also important because it continued to be an arena for a broadly based movement of fusion and transmission between Sumerian and Akkadian cultures. As we have seen, even during Sargon's centralized rule, the two societies had overlapped; but after the establishment of the Ur dynasty, they became united in name as well, as Ur-Nammu took on a new title, "king of Sumer and Akkad."

The Third Dynasty of Ur is unusual because of the vast corpus of texts and documents it left behind. Historians know more about this era than many others because of this large archive. For the most part, it consists of records of state economic activity relating to the agricultural, commercial, and manufacturing sectors of Ur. Despite the pro-state bias of much of this material, historians have been able to decipher the larger workings of the Ur dynasty through a careful sifting of the records. Several conclusions emerge. One, "the Ur III state was indeed of a different character than its predecessors [ancient Sumer]: geographically more restricted in size, but internally more centrally organized" (Van de Mieroop 2004, 73). Two, it consisted of the core territories of Sumer and Akkad, with a military zone between the Tigris River and Zagros Mountains.

The state was divided into 20 provinces, ruled by civilian governors (ensis) on behalf of the king. Usually from the highest families of the land, the ensis formed a hereditary caste; property was inherited from the father and passed on to the sons. These governors also acted as judges and supervisors of the irrigation works of the country. Paralleled by army generals who were not native born but selected by the king from among a cadre of "outsiders" (perhaps Akkadian in origin), these administrators oversaw the state taxation system and dispensed justice where necessary. Altogether, the Third Dynasty of Ur was a highly centralized state in which urbanization was high; royal works (irrigation, the building of temples, and so on) were undertaken by laborers either forced or recruited to work by state administrators; and some regions were, at different periods, governed by military fiat. Finally, agricultural prosperity and wealth from trade were central imperatives of the state.

While there is more documentation on Ur-Nammu's successors than on Ur-Nammu himself, he did leave a number of clay tablets recording his achievements that, taken as a whole, point to an unusually capable leader. Ur-Nammu waged war against bandits and rebels, and either he or his son Shulgi (r. ca. 2094–2047 B.C.E.) may have been responsible for dictating the first law code in the world, more than 100 years before Hammurabi, who has gone down in history as the first ruler to have promulgated a legal framework for society. Ur-Nammu or Shulgi's law code was all the more remarkable because it stressed compensation, not physical punishment, for murders or wrongful deaths. Ur-Nammu also invested in agriculture and had his laborers dig a number of ditches and canals, and he fortified Ur's walls, as well as the walls of the other cities (Uruk, Eridu, and Nippur) that came under his authority. But the king's main claim to fame rests with his adaptation of the distinctive Mesopotamian temple towers, staged towers called ziggurats, which he built in Ur, Uruk, Eridu, and Nippur, among other cities in his realm.

The ziggurat was uniquely Mesopotamian. Built on platforms that rested on terraces, these towers were of enameled brick and plaster, with the highest floors reserved for the temple and its sanctuary. Some ziggurats rose up to 300 feet and had seven floors (Bertman 2003, 194).

THE CONTROVERSY OVER CLIMATE CHANGE AS A FACTOR IN THE COLLAPSE OF DYNASTIES IN THE LATE THIRD MILLENNIUM B.C.E.

From the middle of the 1990s onward, an archaeologist named Harvey Weiss and his colleagues began publishing several articles on climate change and its impact on the agriculture of ancient Iraq. Weiss argued that as of 2200 B.C.E. and continuing for about 200 to 300 years, this sudden climatic change resulted in "major aridification, a radical increase in airborne dust, cooling, forest removal, land degradation . . . possible alterations in seasonality, as well as flow reductions in the area's four major river systems due to reduced or displaced Mediterranean westerlies and Indian monsoons" (Zettler 2003, 17). Drought led to the neglect of agricultural lands and massive population flight and may have brought about the breakdown of the Akkadian Empire (because the accumulated changes sapped its economy) so that when the Gutians invaded, some parts of the Akkadian Empire were ripe for the plucking. Even though there was a reconsolidation of agriculture under the Third Dynasty of Ur, irrigation agriculture remained forever at the whims of nature, and economic crises leading to the reappearance of major aridity zones were never entirely ruled out. This plus the important attacks of the northern peoples caused problems with the food supply on which the cities of ancient Iraq relied and may have fatally weakened the economic bases of Mesopotamian society.

There are problems, however, with this theory, which have been pointed out by several scholars of the region. The first concerns Weiss's literal translations of the Sumerian texts and his claim that the historians of ancient Iraq are much too insistent on interpreting hard evidence as "poetic metaphor" (Zettler 2003, 18). Then there is Weiss's chronology; scholars of ancient Iraq are still grappling with how to "read" the decades and centuries in terms of calendar years. There are standard chronologies that many archaeologists and historians rely on, "more out of convenience than conviction" (Zettler 2003, 20), but these are not necessarily the most accurate. Finally, archaeologist Richard Zettler has pointed out that Weiss has not taken into account the vast amount of grain sent down from the north to the south to rescue the southern cities of the Akkadian Empire and has placed too much emphasis on climatic changes as a single factor, leading to a radical explanation for the decline of both Akkadian and Third Dynasty cities.

Steps leading to the top of the ziggurat of the ancient city of Ur Kasdim. The ziggurat was a uniquely Mesopotamian structure. (Shutterstock)

The famous ziggurat of Ur, the best-preserved temple in southern Iraq, was built of unbaked as well as baked brick and was crisscrossed with flights of stairs reaching to the top, on which it is presumed, a small shrine stood (there is little evidence for this argument, even though it seems the most logical explanation). And yet, as characteristic of ancient Iraqi architecture as they were, until today, the ziggurat's overall function has not been completely deciphered. Other than the theory that the highest floor of the building housed the temple complex, what

ARCHITECTURE IN ANCIENT IRAQ

Ancient Iraq was marked by a number of different architectural forms. Other than the ziggurats, Mesopotamia also boasted palaces, temples, public buildings for various purposes, and perhaps even "headmen's houses" (Crawford 2002, 79). The important feature of these structures was their versatility of function. None of them seem to have served as a building imbued with a single rationale. All of them, except possibly the headmen's houses (which were to be found mostly in northern Iraq), combined religious aspects with political and administrative functions.

The most characteristic structure associated with ancient Iraq was the temple. Temples usually were built in the center of the city and were distinguished by intricate decorations and an altar. The priests of certain temples were responsible for managing the temple's properties (such as granaries and workshops) and the ceremonial contributions of food and beverages to the shrine. J. N. Postgate makes the point that while temples may have played the part of economic institutions, they were, first and foremost, markers of communal identity. The "social conscience" of the priestly class turned the temple into a sanctuary for the poor and homeless, while the temple's storage of wealth functioned as "inviolable capital" that could ransom villagers from bondage or "buy" unwanted children and afford them priestly protection (Postgate 1992, 135–136).

was the ziggurat built for? The explanations are as numerous as they are fanciful. One of the most interesting theories rests on the notion that the uppermost floor of the temple was the scene of a ritual or sacred marriage between gods and mortals. Such ceremonies are known to have been performed in that location because they were the closest staging place to the sky and the divine order. On a more prosaic level, coalition aircraft bombed the ziggurat at Ur during the Gulf War of 1991, as they bombed other, less exalted monuments (Cotter 2003).

The Isin-Larsa Period (2025–1763 B.C.E.)

As with many of the city-states and empires in ancient Iraq, the breakdown of the Third Dynasty of Ur may have come at the hands of nomadic tribes, the most important of which were the Hurrians and especially the Amorites. This interregnum between empires saw the emergence of various small states, the most important of them being the Amorite states of Isin and Larsa (Larsa was founded in 2025 B.C.E. and Isin in 2017 B.C.E.) in southern Iraq; the Amorite state of Babylon (1894–1595 B.C.E.); and the Assyrian state of Ashur under King Shamsi-Adad I (r. ca. 1813–1781 B.C.E.), who later became the unrivalled master of northern Iraq, from the Zagros Mountains to Carchemish on the Euphrates (near the present-day Syrian-Turkish borders).

For more than two centuries, Isin and Larsa dominated the area. Initially, Isin laid claim as successor of the Third Dynasty of Ur, and Larsa was a vassal city. Isin's decline coincided with the rise of Larsa and commenced during the reign of the usurper Ur-Ninurta (r. 1923–1896 B.C.E.). Wars against Bedouin attackers and fights over the domination of water resources taxed the state's means, and in 1896 B.C.E., an army led by King Abe-Sare of Larsa defeated Isin and killed Ur-Ninurta. The two city-states coexisted, but Abe-Sare's descendants were able to pick off Isin territory until, in 1793 B.C.E., Rim-Sin attacked and conquered Isin itself. Larsa was only able to enjoy its "empire" for another 30 years. In 1763 B.C.E., Hammurabi conquered southern Babylonia, which included Isin and Larsa.

During the Isin-Larsa period, the cultural currents so reminiscent of Sumerian influences continued to thrive. Although the Sumerian language had begun its long decline, giving way to the Akkadian tongue (itself an early amalgam of Sumerian and other dialects), Akkadian became the lingua franca of the "wild" Amorites-turned-settlers, as well as of the various nomad-based states neighboring Isin and Larsa, long after the power of the Akkadian Empire had subsided.

First Dynasty of Babylon (Old Babylonia) (1894–1595 B.C.E.)

Around 1894 B.C.E., Babylon was taken over by Amorite kings, one of whom built a large wall around the city. When the Amorite ruler Hammurabi, sixth to head the dynasty, came to power in Babylon (r. 1848–1806 B.C.E.), it was still a mid-sized city-state whose claim to fame rested on the fact that its inhabitants had built at least two temples dedicated to the gods. The city was hemmed in on practically all sides by rival dynasties, especially that of Shamsi-Adad in Ashur, that of Isin-Larsa, as well as those of other rulers in northern Syria. Hammurabi had to wait for close to 29 years to expand his hold of the region. In the meantime, he dedicated himself to the internal affairs of his state, to which he finally brought peace and stability. Then, sensing that his enemies were weakening, he attacked them and conquered southern Babylonia, inheriting the kingdom of Sumer and Akkad in the process. Eventually his many conquests, with none more dramatic than that of the Assyrian state, unified the whole of ancient Iraq (Assyria and Babylon) into one empire, with Babylon as his capital.

The Assyro-Babylonian Empire formed a Semitic state built on a Sumerian foundation. Under Hammurabi, Babylon became the most significant city in the region and held its own as a cultural, and often political, capital for close to 1,500 years, down to the time of Alexander the Great. Hammurabi promoted the cult of the god Marduk, the deity of Babylon, and himself as supreme master of southern Mesopotamia along with Marduk. Cities far and wide had to acknowledge the supremacy of both ruler and deity in everything from ceremonial rituals to everyday affairs. Assyrologist Stephanie Dalley notes that the greeting sent from one provincial ruler to another in Hammurabi's time began with the customary, "May Shamash and Marduk grant you long life," signifying the by-now standard insertion of Marduk among the Mesopotamian pantheon of gods (Dalley 2002, 44). Such was the solidity of the state built by Hammurabi that the five kings who succeeded him each ruled for no less than 20 years, a "situation that is usually indicative of political stability" (Van De Mieroop 2004, 111). The dynasty came to an end, however, in 1595 B.C.E. when Hittites from Anatolia (central Turkey) under King Mursili sacked Babylon.

Hammurabi the Lawgiver

Although built on earlier precedents, the law codes published under Hammurabi are forever associated with his name. In his 42nd year, Hammurabi had his judgments immortalized by publishing them as a set of codes inspired by Shamash, the sun god, a copy of which was found in Susiana (in what is now Iran) and transported to the Louvre Museum in Paris at the turn of the 20th century. It is important to understand that Hammurabi's codes were not law statutes but grew out of day-to-day regulations adopted by the king while adjusting previous edicts to new socioeconomic realities. In this way, they should be seen as practical instructions, not as fully worked out laws ensuring universal application. And yet, they have not only achieved worldwide acclaim but influenced all modern law up to our day.

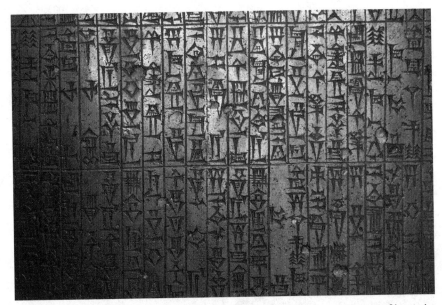

Detail of the stela on which is inscribed the *Code of Hammurabi*, the ancient set of law judgments that has influenced modern law (John Said/Shutterstock)

Consisting of 282 laws engraved on a basalt stela (stone slab or pillar used for commemorative purposes), the Code of Hammurabi dealt with various crimes, as well as with trade, family law, property, agricultural issues, and even the buying of slaves. The codes describe three classes in society: free men, *mushkenu* (perhaps military men attached to the state by land grants or other forms of service), and slaves (Roux 1992, 204). According to Roux, the principal change in the codes was the de-emphasis on compensation in cash or tribute, which was part of the Sumerian penal code, and the stress laid on "death, mutilation or corporal punishment" (Roux 1992, 205). Thus, if a surgeon killed his patient, his hand would be cut off; if a house collapsed, its architect would be put to death; if a slave were killed when the house collapsed on him, the builder of the house would compensate the slave's owner with another slave. But there was leniency, too. For instance, an adulterous woman's sentence was to be put to death, but she could also be pardoned by her husband. If a man was determined to divorce his wife because she had not given birth to sons, then he had to compensate her with the full amount of the dowry or bride wealth given to her by her father. According to Roux, the advances made in Hammurabi's codes are innumerable; chiefly, however, ". . . it remains unique by its length, by the elegance and precision of its style and by the light it throws on the rough, yet highly civilized society of the period" (Roux 1992, 206).

The Dark Ages (1595–1200 B.C.E.)

The subsequent era until about 1200 B.C.E. is usually referred to as the Dark Ages because fewer texts were written, thus providing less information for historians to work with. From the fall of the first Babylonian empire to the conquest of Babylon by the Assyrians, raids and counter-raids characterized the period, and although lesser dynasties emerged, such as the Hittites and the Kassites, no one nation or people were strong enough to gain the upper hand and take control of the ultimate prize, Babylonia. Even though in certain epochs Assyrian commanders were able to defeat the lightly armed tribes decisively, submission to one ruler meant very little in the unstable politics of the time. While tribal leaders paid an arranged tribute to signify their obeisance, the minute the Assyrian commanders wheeled around to return home, the tribes went back to their established ways.

The Assyrian Empire (1170–612 B.C.E.)

The Assyrians were Semitic peoples who lived through a turbulent history, first as a small kingdom at the mercy of pillaging tribes and then as subjects of the Babylonians. But in about 1350 B.C.E., Ashuruballit I founded the independent state of Assyria, and a few centuries later, this state metamorphosed into the supreme masters of ancient Iraq. Throughout their long history of empire-building, the Assyrians were known as fierce fighters, invading and controlling large swaths of land formerly belonging to their traditional enemies, the Babylonians and the mountain tribes, as well as inhabitants of Mediterranean countries far beyond their borders. Under a succession of able military commanders and rulers and over a period of several centuries, the Assyrians began to expand across the entire known world. Under Tiglath-pileser (r. ca. 1113–1075 B.C.E.), and especially Ashurnasirpal II (r. 883–859 B.C.E.) and his son Shalmaneser III (r. 858–824 B.C.E.), the countries of the eastern Mediterranean fell under Assyrian sway, and for all intents and purposes, the Mediterranean became an Assyrian lake (ca. 853 B.C.E.).

One of the recurrent themes of Assyrian history, then, is perpetual expansion; even when military setbacks occurred, as they often did, the memory of earlier successful raids created a momentum that was not easily forgotten. One of the first actions normally undertaken by a reigning Assyrian king was to step up military offensives to recover

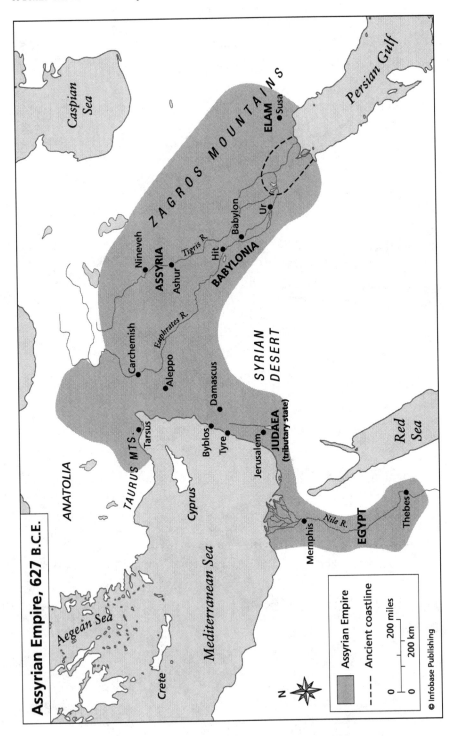

Assyrian Empire, 627 B.C.E.

Caspian Sea

Persian Gulf

ZAGROS MOUNTAINS

ELAM
• Susa

Nineveh •
ASSYRIA
Ashur •
Tigris R.
Hit •
Babylon •
BABYLONIA
Ur •

Carchemish •
Euphrates R.
Aleppo •

Damascus •

SYRIAN DESERT

Tarsus •
TAURUS MTS.

Byblos •
Tyre •
Jerusalem •
JUDAEA
(tributary state)

ANATOLIA

Cyprus

Red Sea

Thebes •

Nile R.
EGYPT

Memphis •

Mediterranean Sea

Aegean Sea

Crete

N

Assyrian Empire

- - - Ancient coastline

200 miles

200 km

0

0

© Infobase Publishing

lands lost, either in the south or the west. Oppenheim has made a provocative case for the relentless Assyrian compulsion to go to war. He believes that the Assyrians periodically created and re-created "ephemeral empires" (Oppenheim 1977, 167) that rarely outlasted a particular Assyrian king's reign because of two main reasons: the instability of the Assyrian system of government and the collapse of the economic revenues available to Assyrian rulers within the core territories. Certainly, evidence suggests that the tightly centralized inner domain (Ashur) was always under pressure to produce a surplus to meet taxes. Obviously, one of the calculations of Assyrian generals was that a wider empire would extend revenue flows. But Oppenheim speculates that the almost automatic imperative to "restore" the greater empire may also have sprung from protonationalist ideals on the part of a select Assyrian ruling clique who wanted to enlarge the homeland for ideological (that is, religious) reasons. In other words, in order to appease the gods as well as to actualize an "Assyrian" identity, more tribute-bearing lands would have to be joined to the Assyrian center. Of course, on a more mundane level, it is undeniable that the Assyrian campaigns were also launched as defensive wars, to secure the always troublesome outermost borders of the empire and to keep open vital trade routes from northern Iraq to Syria, Anatolia, Iran, and the Gulf.

Alongside issues of war and peace, the Assyrians may also have innovated mass deportation campaigns. History relates that Tiglath-pileser III (r. 744–727 B.C.E.) was particularly well known for employing this strategy. According to Roux, "[W]hole towns and districts were emptied of their inhabitants, who were resettled in distant regions and replaced by people brought in force from other countries. In 742 and 741 B.C.E., for instance, 30,000 Syrians from the region of Hama were sent to the Zagros mountains, while 18,000 Arameans from the left bank of the Tigris were transferred to northern Syria" (Roux 1992, 307).

The other famous example is that of Sargon II (r. 721–705 B.C.E.), who vigorously dispersed the Hebrews after the conquest of the northern kingdom of Israel (after having made them pay taxes, as Assyrian kings did with all occupied peoples). Referred to as the dispersion of the Ten Lost Tribes of Israel, this mass deportation was perfectly in line with Assyrian practice (deportation measures were carried out as far south as Arabia). Deportations occurred for a number of reasons. Assyrian commanders, always anxious to maximize imperial gain, either transported farmers and laborers from one overpopulated area to a less productive district and made the deportees grow crops deemed necessary for the empire or pressed the deportees in the army, or even forced them to relocate to less-developed areas where crafts and industries were absent. The point, crudely made by these forced migrations, was that Assyrian authorities would not rest until Greater Assyria became completely self-sufficient in terms of people and resources, and the internal distribution of specializations and services was rationalized to create a rough equity, if not for the Assyrians at large, then at least for the elite that ran the empire.

In sum, even though the Assyrians followed the tradition of earlier civilizations and built institutions that influenced the region for centuries to come, their innovations and adaptations are always deemed secondary to the more celebrated exploits of boots on the ground. And yet, most Assyrian kings, for example, were avid builders: Ashurnasirpal II constructed a great palace complex close to the Tigris River and Upper Zab tributary in northern Iraq; eventually the site took on the name of Nimrud (originally, Kalkh). Nimrud, south of present-day Mosul, has been the scene of excavations for more than 150 years by the British, Poles, Italians, Americans, and of course, Iraqis. Its site is now so well known that archaeologists can confidently list four important palaces, three smaller ones, "perhaps five temples, three gates, a ziggurat or temple tower of Ninurta, the patron god of the city, and six townhouses, all dating to the period of the Assyrian Empire" (Paley 2003, 1). After the coalition attack on Baghdad in 2003, a National Geographic team drained the underground floors of a Baghdad bank to find the vast treasure of one of Ashurnasirpal's palaces. The bank's vaults had been plunged underwater in the war's chaotic aftermath.

The ruler Sargon II, who succeeded Ashurnasirpal II, built an entire town in Khorsabad (Dar-Shrukin). Khorsabad had a square plan and was defended by statues of bull-men erected at the seven major gates. The palace, situated in the inner sanctum of the city, was built on a raised platform and had 300 rooms and 30 courtyards and a ziggurat of many different hues. But Sargon did not live long enough to take pleasure in his new town: One year after Khorsabad was completed, he was killed in battle, after which the Assyrian ruling house retreated to Nineveh, ancient capital of Ashur.

Even Sennacherib (r. 705–681 B.C.E.), famous for destroying Babylon, built temples and palaces and started massive public works to restore agricultural prosperity to the empire. Nineveh became the spacious, fortified capital of the Assyrian Empire with a great exterior wall, the remains of which still occupy the left bank of the Tigris, opposite present-day Mosul. A splendid palace guarded by statues of bronze lions and surrounded by a landscaped garden, watered by an aqueduct built specially for that purpose, completed the lavish picture. Esarhaddon (r. 680–669 B.C.E.), Sennacherib's son, rebuilt Babylon, which his father had razed to the ground because of Babylonian "perfidy," and by 669 B.C.E., Assyria's southern province had taken on all the magnificence of the old.

The Spread of Tribal Movements

The cities and empires that ruled Iraq and battled each other for domination also constantly fought to extend their sway over the nomadic peoples who lived on the margins of urban settlements and whose histories are, for the most part, unwritten (except by their enemies) and therefore all the more obscure. Geography truly determined destiny in ancient Iraq; the same patterns were repeated over and over again for thousands of years and all the way into the premodern era, with the eruption of nomadic pastoralists emerging out of the Arabian Peninsula, the settlement of tribal peoples on the fringes of civilization in Iraq, Syria, and Yemen, and their eventual defeat and incorporation into the larger empires. The fact that city folk were once nomadic pastoralists or seminomads themselves only tends to blur the boundaries between cities, empires, and tribes. The cycle of nomads settling down to form or join already established cities and then blending into larger formations such as empires, only to return to a pastoralist mode once these larger formations disappear, is a familiar one in the Middle East. It is best described by a 14th-century Muslim historian, Ibn Khaldun, the famous author of *al-Muqadimma* (*Prolegomena*). In that work, Ibn Khaldun described the "natural life of empires" as having three stages, basically corresponding to generations in which the nomadic (or, for modern empires, rural) life gives way to the settled, or urban, life. In the final stage, the nomadic life is completely forgotten, and decadence sets in.

The domestication of the camel (2000–1300 B.C.E.), allowed the Arabs to become more mobile, and they started to penetrate into the more prosperous regions of the Middle East. In the ninth century B.C.E., we first begin to hear of the Arabs, a term usually glossed over by archaeologists and historians until the dawn of the Islamic era. And yet, 15 centuries before the rise of Islam, the word *Arab* appears on clay tablets in the Assyrian period, starting from the reign of Shalmaneser III onward (Gailani and Alusi 1999, 9–14). Referring both to the Arabian Peninsula, as well as to a distinct category of people under a variety of names, such as *Arubu* or *Amel-Ur-bi,* the term has generally been suspended in favor of broader categories, such as "the Semites," which came to include not only the Arabs but the Aramaeans and Canaanites as well.

Of nomadic origins but from different regions of the eastern Mediterranean, both the Aramaeans and the Arabs turned to trade once they had crossed into greener Syrian pastures, while the Canaanites, the best-known traders of the region, made Palestine their home. In north Syria, the largest group, the Aramaeans overwhelmed earlier civilizations and took over their cities, eventually subordinating the megalopolis of Aram-Damascus to their growing empire. Equally important was another community, the Chaldeans, who lived in the marshes of southernmost Iraq. The Chaldeans spoke a dialect of Aramaic but they were a distinct group of peoples. Like the Aramaeans and Arabs at an earlier stage, the Chaldeans were divided into several different regions, each ruled by a tribal chief. They grew dates, subsisted on fishing, and bred horses. The Chaldeans, just like the Arabs and the Arameans, profited from the overland trade passing by way of Arabia to northern Syria. Fortune was only to smile on the former group, in 626 B.C.E., when the fluctuating military and political developments of the period brought forth the Neo-Babylonian Empire.

The Neo-Babylonian Empire (625–539 B.C.E.)

After several centuries of eclipse, the Babylonian dynasty rose again. Under the Chaldean Nabu-apla-usur (Nabopolassar, r. ca. 625–605 B.C.E.), Babylonia invaded and conquered the provinces of the Assyrian Empire from the Mediterranean Sea to the Arabian Gulf. The three main Assyrian cities, Ashur, Nineveh, and Nimrud, were devastated by fire and were left in ruins. Assyria was obliterated from the map. After the decline of Assyria, Babylonia and Egypt were the only large empires facing each other in Syria-Palestine. The Babylonian troops were commanded by Nebuchadnezzar II (r. 604–562 B.C.E.), who was married to Amyitis, the daughter of the king of the powerful Medes, located in what is now northern Iraq, and thus Babylonia was protected by its alliance with the Medes against the forces beyond the kingdom. After the death of his father, Nabu-apla-usur, Nebuchadnezzar became king and began a long war to conquer the kingdom of Judah and its capital, Jerusalem. In 586 B.C.E., the city fell. When Nebuchadnezzar's appointee in Jerusalem, Zedekiah, tried to turn the tables on his master and make himself the actual ruler of the province, the Babylonian king used the time-honored tactic

Detail of the reconstructed Ishtar Gate at the Pergamon Museum, in Berlin. The gate to Babylon's inner city was constructed ca. 575 B.C.E., during the reign of Nebuchadnezzar II, who conquered the kingdom of Judah and brought the Jews to Babylon in exile. (Martina I. Meyer/Shutterstock)

of deporting approximately 3,000 of Judah's Jews as punishment. Zedekiah attempted a revolt but was defeated; he was brought before Nebuchadnezzar and, after witnessing the execution of his sons, had his eyes gouged out.

After Nebuchadnezzar's death, Babylonia experienced a period of misrule and assassination. Three kings ruled during the next six years (one for only nine months) until a commoner named Nabonidus (r. ca. 556–539 B.C.E.) became king. He is reported to have angered the Babylonian priestly hierarchy by demoting their supreme god, Marduk, and replacing him with a non-Babylonian moon god, Sin. Furthermore, Nabonidus sojourned for 10 years at the oasis of Teima (in present-day Saudi Arabia), this forcing the cancellation of the new year's festival of Akitu, during which the king and the high priest played important roles. Eventually, his reconsolidated state, resting on the laurels of Old Babylonia, came to an end when another king, Cyrus of Persia, moved into the capital without encountering resistance.

Conclusion

This chapter has traced the history of ancient Iraq over a course of some 30 centuries, and what scintillating centuries they were. Even though archaeologists, historians, and philologists are still far from knowing the details of each and every century, let alone decade (and there are huge stretches of time for which there are no records at all), the overriding theme that emerges when studying those 30 centuries is cultural unity despite constantly shifting borders. Permanent features of this period are, first, a lack of fixed borders and the constant spread of peoples and cultures throughout the region and, second, the assimilation and integration of languages, cultures, and civilizations in an unending search for new technologies and methodologies, commercial exchange, and, not least of all, meanings in this life and the next. The permeability of borders and the diffusion and absorption of languages and cultures reinforced one another; as mutually supporting trends of state and society, they gave impetus to the spread of novel ways of understanding the world, worshipping the gods, the growing of new crops, and the organization of fiscal, legal, and educational regimes.

Let us conclude with a description of the broad reception accorded to Sargon's rule in Sumer-Akkad. His impact was felt in regions far and wide, not simply because of Sargon's many conquests and achievements but also perhaps because he was adopting modes of thought and organization long current in the region that made appeal to all cultures and traditions. Oppenheim states:

> Sargon remained a semi-mythical king throughout much of the second millennium. The story of his birth and exposure, his rescue from a basket floating down the Euphrates, his rise to power, and last but not least, his campaigns, adventures, victories, and reverses and his conquest of the West was read in Amarna in Egypt, in Hattusa in Anatolia and even translated into Hurrian and Hittite (Oppenheim 1977, 151).

2

FROM THE PERSIAN EMPIRE TO THE SASSANIANS (539 B.C.E.–651 C.E.)

In the succeeding millennium, Mesopotamia, or ancient Iraq, continued to be a focus for invasion and conquest. Up to this period, all overlords of Mesopotamia, with the probable exception of the Sumerians, had been Semitic, but now, the conquerors came not from nearby regions but from farther afield. They not only brought a further intermingling of cultures in the alluvial plains of the Tigris and Euphrates but relegated the area to a mere region of their far-flung conquests. Under the Persian, Macedonian-Greek, Parthian, Roman, and Sassanian Empires, the Assyro-Babylonian cities ceased to be great capitals in their own right (although Babylon was still held in highest regard even in the time of Alexander the Great); in fact, many were destroyed in the conquests.

These empires left their marks on the land in many ways. With the exception of the Romans, who only held portions of Mesopotamia, each succeeding imperial dynasty contributed to the cultural history of ancient Iraq, not simply its political and military histories. Art, architecture, religion, literature, law, and financial institutions were all redefined and expanded during this long period of struggle and takeover.

The Persian Empire (554–330 B.C.E.)

According to Greek sources, which, along with Neo-Babylonian documents, are frequently the only material available to trace the history of the Persians, the latter hailed from southwest Iran and were led by a man called Achaemenes, after which the Achaemenid dynasty takes its name. Initially vassals of the Medes, the Persians, under Cyrus the Great (r. 559–530 B.C.E.), defeated the Medes in about 550 B.C.E. and captured

29

their king, Astyages. Cyrus thereupon assumed the kingship of the Medes as well, absorbing them and the territory they controlled into an empire that would rapidly expand during the next 20 years. The Persians, at least in the beginning, ruled in an almost indistinguishable style from the Medes, so much so that the Greeks referred to them as Medes (Van de Mieroop 2004, 268). There may also have been other reasons for that. According to Greek historian Herodotus, Cyrus's mother was actually a daughter of Astyages, thus making Cyrus in part a member of the tribe. Another ancient Greek historian, Ctesias of Cnidus, who stayed at the Persian court around 400 B.C.E. and wrote several histories of the Persian Empire, claimed that it was Cyrus who had married one of Astyages's daughters. If either or both of these accounts is legendary, they may have been propagated to justify Persian rule over the Medes and their lands. Further contributing to their legendary aspect is an account by the third-century B.C.E. Babylonian priest Berrossus, who placed Astyages at the beginning of the Chaldean period (Sack 1991, 7).

During the course of the next 20 years, Cyrus overran Greek-speaking Anatolia (the Asian part of Turkey), eastern Iran, parts of Central Asia, and the Neo-Babylonian Empire, which controlled much of the Fertile Crescent, an arc-like area stretching from the Persian Gulf through Mesopotamia and into Upper Egypt. In 539 B.C.E., Cyrus defeated the army of the last Babylonian king, Nabonidus (r. 556–539 B.C.E.), and made his son, Cambyses, king of Babylon. Historians have speculated that Cyrus, aware of the power of the priestly hierarchy, made Cambyses king to ensure the proper continuation of the Akitu festival since Cyrus, himself, would be gone for long periods on the battlefield. Like his Chaldean predecessors, Cyrus (as well as later Achaemenid emperors) held Babylon in high esteem as the cultural center of the ancient Near East. Not only did he preserve the city, but in an echo of the rationalization used to justify his triumph over the Medes, the royal inscription on what has become known as the Cyrus Cylinder, a cylindrical clay tablet, has it that the Babylonian high god, Marduk, chose Cyrus to reign over the empire. The Cyrus legend extends further. Biblical accounts (among others) describe that the year after Cyrus occupied Babylon, he allowed the Jews to return to Judah after their nearly 50-year exile, begun during the reign of the Babylonian king Nebuchadnezzar II. However, this is not confirmed by the Cyrus Cylinder. According to ancient historical texts, Cyrus led military expeditions as far east as India.

In 530 B.C.E., Cambyses (r. ca. 530–522 B.C.E.) inherited the throne of the Persian Empire and five years later, conquered Egypt, becoming its

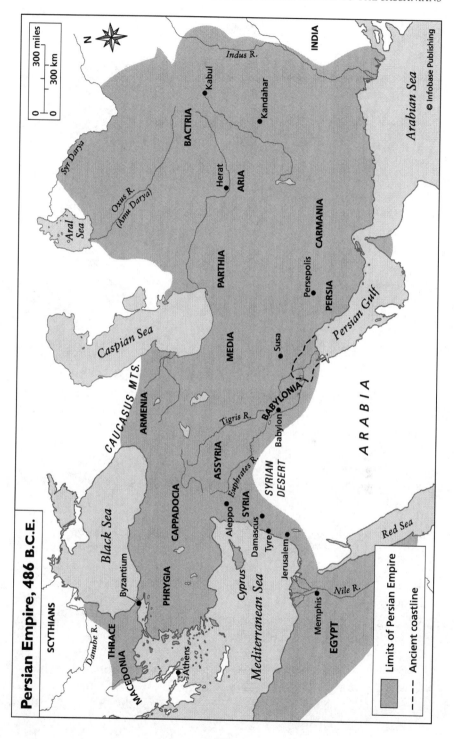

Persian Empire, 486 B.C.E.

SCYTHIANS

N

300 miles

300 km

INDIA

Arabian Sea

© Infobase Publishing

Indus R.

Kabul

Kandahar

BACTRIA

Syr Darya

Oxus R. (Amu Darya)

Herat

ARIA

°Aral Sea

CARMANIA

PARTHIA

Persepolis

PERSIA

Caspian Sea

Persian Gulf

MEDIA

Susa

CAUCASUS MTS.

ARMENIA

BABYLONIA

Tigris R.

Babylon

ASSYRIA

ARABIA

Euphrates R.

SYRIAN DESERT

CAPPADOCIA

Black Sea

Aleppo

SYRIA

Damascus

Tyre

Red Sea

Byzantium

PHRYGIA

Jerusalem

Cyprus

Mediterranean Sea

Nile R.

Danube R.

THRACE

Memphis

MACEDONIA

Athens

EGYPT

Limits of Persian Empire

- - - - Ancient coastline

The Cyrus Cylinder, upon which is inscribed the Persian king's conquest of Babylon at the behest of Marduk, the Babylonian high god (HIP/Art Resource, NY)

king. Cambyses remained in Egypt until 522 B.C.E., when he returned to Babylon to oust a usurper of his throne (here the historical record is unclear): either the magian (an expert in religious traditions) Gaumata or his own brother Smerdis. Some accounts declare that Cambyses had had Smerdis secretly murdered and that Gaumata assumed the throne as the dead brother, while most claim that Smerdis briefly held power. Soon after his return to Babylonia, Cambyses died—whether of natural causes, suicide, or at the hand of another is unclear—before removing the usurper. That task was left to the man who became the next Persian ruler, Darius I (r. 521–486 B.C.E.), also referred to as Darius the Great.

Darius was not a direct member of the royal line but claimed Achaemenid kinship through his father, Hystaspes. The first years of Darius's reign were marked by civil war throughout the empire. The first region to rebel was Babylonia, where a local leader "called Nidintu-Bêl recruited an army by declaring that he was 'Nebuchadnezzar, son of Nabonidus' and seized kingship in Babylon" (Roux 1980, 376). Darius led an army against Nebuchadnezzar III (who ruled Babylon for approximately two months) before destroying his army and executing him in Babylon. The following year, yet another claimant to the throne appeared, naming himself Nebuchadnezzar, but he met the same fate as his predecessor. The unrest spread to other parts of the empire as local tribes sought to take advantage of the disarray in Babylon. By 518 B.C.E., however, Darius had secured control over the empire. He then set about expanding it, overwhelming parts of Africa, including Libya, and annexing western India. Darius also set his sights westward where the Hellenic city-states, just beyond the empire's border, were the next logical step. Part of Darius's (and his successor Xerxes') strategy in the area was to pit the Greek city-states against one another, for "having watched the Iraqi cities hack one another to pieces and so make their conquest easy, Darius and Xerxes tried to apply the Iraqi lesson to Greece. In one of the great turning points of history, they failed . . ." (Polk 2005, 32). Darius was twice thwarted in his attempt at Greek conquest: first, when a Persian fleet was destroyed in a storm in 492 B.C.E. and then, when his army was defeated by an Athenian army at the Battle of Marathon in 490 B.C.E., which halted the Persian advance in its tracks. Thereafter, the goal of conquering the whole of Greece became one of the defining visions of the Persian rulers, attempted by practically every one of them after Darius.

By the end of Darius's reign, the Persian Empire stretched over thousands of miles, from the Aegean Sea eastward to the Indus River, and from Armenia in the north to Lower Egypt. Its rulers governed a multitude of men and women and coexisted with several different religions and cultures. The Persian Empire exerted influence on its contemporaries as well as its successors; for example, its lingering effects were evident on the Sassanian Empire that followed in its wake, which contributed to world civilization through its emphasis on the divine rule of kings and the construction of imperial authority.

The Persian Empire under the Achaemenids was famous for its building activities. In much the same vein as all the rulers and dynasts that preceded them, the Persians built magnificent administrative capitals, such as Persepolis (begun in 518 B.C.E.) and Susa, which consisted of several palaces and large gardens. The most celebrated tradition associated with some, if not all the rulers of the Persian Empire, however, was the policy of toleration for all ethnic, religious, and social groups. According to historian Marc Van de Mieroop, "it was the first empire that acknowledged the fact that its inhabitants had a variety of cultures, spoke different languages, and were politically organized in various ways" (Van de Mieroop 2004, 274). The Persians' keen interest in promoting efficient government allowed them to retain the administrative languages used by different peoples so as to be able to use them in local affairs; as well, the inscriptions on the walls of temples or on monuments were in several different languages, testimony to the diversity of the empire, which at its height contained more than 70 ethnic groups.

Ruins of the ancient Persian capital of Persepolis, built in the late sixth–early fifth century B.C.E., located approximately 45 miles north of Shiraz, Iran (Steba/Shutterstock)

Imperial expansion aside, Darius left his mark on the empire through its internal reorganization. Van de Mieroop theorizes that as a result of the civil war and provincial uprisings, "Darius regularized control once he was fully in charge. . . . [T]he empire was turned into a uniform structure of about 20 provinces" (Van De Mieroop 2004, 272). The provinces, or satrapies, were each ruled by a satrap, or governor. Over time, those satraps became rival contenders for power because some of them developed their own local power bases. Meanwhile, Babylonian revolts and Egyptian insurrections strained the empire's resources and ate into its revenue. Equally significant was the outsourcing of the army, which went from a relatively professional organization to a body composed almost entirely of mercenary troops, some of whose members were Greek. Ultimately, the empire was too large to be controlled exclusively by one dynasty, and in the end, it was a case of the middle nibbling at the edges. By the end of the fourth century B.C.E., this deterioration made the Persian Empire ripe for conquest.

In the rough and rude environment of Macedonia (northern Greece), a ruling family emerged that threatened the Persian Empire's hold on power. Taking a leaf from the Achaemenids' book, Alexander of Macedon, who became king in 336 B.C.E., started his long march toward the formation of yet another sprawling empire, this time joining Persian administrative experience to Hellenistic traditions. Reverting to local legacies of imperial rule, he made Babylon his capital and restored the temple of Marduk, Babylon's reigning god. His practice of melding local institutions with imperial rule, entirely in keeping with ancient precedent, marks him as yet another proponent of the cultural unity of the region, of which ancient Iraq, with its fluctuating frontiers but its vastly absorptive civilization, was perhaps a notable example.

Alexander the Great (r. 336–323 B.C.E.)

Alexander was born in Pella in 356 B.C.E., the son of the Macedonian king Philip II, who had seized power just three years earlier. Alexander's mother, Olympias, was also of royal blood, being the daughter of the king of Epirus. As a young man, Alexander was a student of Aristotle and by the age of 16 was standing in for his father as leader of Macedonia when Philip was off fighting against Byzantium. At age 18, Alexander was a commander in his father's army and played an important role in Philip's victory in the Battle of Chaeronea, in which the Macedonians defeated an alliance of Greek city-states led by Athens and Thebes. Following the victory, Philip founded the Corinthian League, named for the city where representatives of the city-states met with the Macedonians to unite Greece. The exception to the league was Sparta, which rejected the terms imposed on the city-states by the victor. The true purpose of the Corinthian League was to make war on the Persian Empire.

In 337 B.C.E., Philip divorced Olympias; during the feast celebrating his father's new marriage, Alexander and Philip quarreled so violently that the former and his mother sought refuge in her family homeland of Epirus. Alexander also traveled to Illyria during this sojourn. The enmity between father and son ended soon enough, although Alexander's position was less secure than it had been. In 336 B.C.E., Philip sent an army of approximately 10,000 men, led by his general, Parmenion, to capture the Greek cities in Anatolia under Persian control. At the time, the Persian Empire was undergoing its death throes. Not only had the satrapies of Babylonia and Egypt revolted, but assassination had made the throne of Cyrus and Darius unstable. Before Philip could join his army and lead it in conquest, he was assassinated by his guard. Alexander, at age 20 and with the backing of the army, ascended to the throne as Alexander III.

Alexander spent the next few years securing his hold on the kingship by forming alliances with important generals, including Antipater, who became the second most powerful man in the kingdom, and Parmenion, who still commanded the forces in Anatolia. He also made war on recalcitrant Greek city-states. By 334 B.C.E., he was ready to turn eastward and continue the war against Persia. No sooner had Alexander begun his long quest for glory than the great king of Persia, Darius III Codomannus, tried to make peace, but Alexander preferred to have the Persian Empire. His first battle pitted his army against a Persian army made up largely of Greek mercenaries. Alexander's victory at the Granicus (Kocabas) River resulted in the slaughter of many of the mercenaries, and those who managed to survive the defeat were sent to Macedonia as prisoners and subsequently slaves. Over the course of the next two years, Alexander battled in and conquered western and west-central Anatolia (Phrygia). Then, in 333 B.C.E., he defeated the Persians at the Battle of Issus, nearly capturing Darius III in the process. By fleeing the battlefield (and sacrificing his family to be captured), Darius brought humiliation upon himself, as later ancient Greek historians depicted his action as cowardice. However, his action preserved the Persian Empire (at least for a few more years), which would not have been the case had he been captured or killed. Darius even tried to ransom his family at one point, offering to Alexander all satrapies west of the Euphrates River. In a famous anecdote, Parmenion is quoted as saying, "I would accept [this offer] were I Alexander." Alexander replied, "I too if I were Parmenion."

Alexander then proceeded to pick off Persia's Mediterranean satrapies: Syria, Phoenicia (modern Lebanon), and Egypt all fell to his army over the next two years. In Egypt, he founded the city of Alexandria. In 331 B.C.E., with the eastern Mediterranean seacoast firmly under Macedonian control, Alexander headed for Mesopotamia.

The decisive battle of Gaugamela took place on October 1, 331 B.C.E. When it was over, it "opened for Alexander the road to Babylonia and Persia" (Roux 1980, 381). Prior to the battle, Alexander had the option of marching straight to Babylon, engaging a Persian army under the Babylonian satrap Mazeus, or turning north to engage Darius in Assyria. He chose the third option. Although the Macedonian army was numerically inferior to the well-supplied Persian forces, they again won the battle. How the battle was fought was unclear. Greek accounts say that Darius fled the battlefield once again, while the Babylonian account lays the blame on the Persian soldiers for having deserted the king. At any rate, the Macedonians were free to take Babylon and the entire satrapy of Babylonia, the wealthiest province in the empire. One of the unintended consequences of Alexander's marching into Babylon

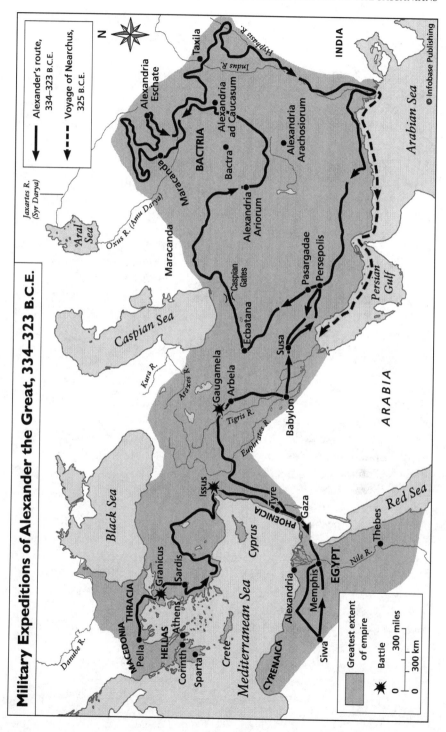

Military Expeditions of Alexander the Great, 334–323 B.C.E.

Alexander's route, 334–323 B.C.E.

Voyage of Nearchus, 325 B.C.E.

Greatest extent of empire

Battle

0   300 miles
0   300 km

© Infobase Publishing

was the discovery of Babylonian astronomical tables that were more accurate than those the Greeks used, forcing the latter to revise their calendar.

According to the classical Greek historians, Alexander was hailed as a liberator by the Babylonians, who only a few years earlier, had had their own revolt put down by the Persians. Yet, as Van de Mieroop points out, these accounts are "to a great extent Macedonian propaganda . . . and most people probably saw little difference between the old and new regimes" (Van De Mieroop 2004, 279). Possibly one of the reasons for this was because Alexander retained Mazeus as satrap of Babylonia. Nevertheless, Alexander followed Cyrus's lead in gaining favor with Babylon's aristocracy, especially the religious elites, so as to make his kingship more acceptable to the people. He especially paid homage to the Babylonian supreme god, Marduk, by undertaking the rebuilding of the temple dedicated to that god. Alexander remained in Babylon for approximately one month, before turning toward Persia itself.

Alexander's campaign into Persia marked (at least superficially) a departure from what had preceded it. Whereas the dismantling of the Persian Empire in Anatolia, Egypt, and Babylonia had been under the guise of liberation, the same could not be said of Persia. Though they were no longer fighting against mercenaries or overlords but against people whose sole aim now was to protect their homeland, the Macedonian army was invincible. One by one the great cities fell: Persepolis, Susa, and Pasargadae (Cyrus's capital, founded near the site of his victorious battle against the Medes and where all subsequent Persian kings were invested). Persepolis, in particular, was laid to waste, presumably in retribution for the Persian attack on Athens. Despite these successes, Alexander had not managed to capture Darius, who was king of the Persians in name only.

His base of power nonexistent, Darius fled eastward, where he was eventually held captive by the satrap of Bactria, Bessus; however, before Bessus could bargain with Alexander, the Macedonians attacked, in July 330 B.C.E. Darius was killed during the ensuing battle, most likely by his captors. This worked to Alexander's advantage as he was able not only to give Darius a state funeral but to legitimately—from his perspective—claim the crown. For the next six years, Alexander continued his eastward campaign, reaching as far as the Indus River. His conquests were brought to a halt not by a superior army but by his own soldiers, who in 324 B.C.E., refused to continue making war. Far away from their homeland and exhausted by more than 10 years of conquest and putting down revolts among already conquered peoples, the Macedonians revolted against Alexander, essentially forcing him to turn back. He reached Susa later that year and married two Achaemenid princesses so as to cement his claim to the throne. Meanwhile, the Macedonians were becoming alarmed as Alexander increasingly assumed the trappings of the Persians.

Early in 323 B.C.E., Alexander returned to Babylon, which he decided to make his capital. Following a night of heavy drinking, Alexander fell ill; he died a few days later, on June 11, 323 B.C.E. Although it has never been proven, historians lean to the theory that Alexander was murdered, most likely by disenchanted comrades, although he had made enemies among the so-called religious elite of Babylon, too. Whatever the truth, Alexander's death spared Arabia from Macedonian conquest; Alexander had been eager to begin a campaign in that region.

Alexander's empire was the first spread of Hellenistic culture outside of western Anatolia and the Mediterranean area. However, the farther from Macedonia it expanded, the weaker it became—and this was seen after Alexander's death—which was probably Alexander's main reason for deciding to make Babylon his capital. One of the world's great cultural cities, Babylon would remain important for nearly another millennium. The claim that the Macedonian conquests helped invigorate the ancient Near East has come under revision in the past 20 years. Some historians have gone so far to regard this notion as "an example of, and justification for, nineteenth-century European colonial enterprise in regions that had known a glorious past but had not modernized" (Van De Mieroop 2004, 280). Still, Alexander did not pursue only warfare and conquest; he was a founder of cities.

Alexander's death left the empire without a clear successor, and the Macedonian generals immediately conferred in hopes of coming up with an amicable solution. They were unsuccessful. The result was not only civil war but revolt in the eastern satrapies. From the time of Alexander's death until the end of the fourth century B.C.E., the Diadochi, or "successors," engaged in four wars: in 322, 318, 314, and 307 B.C.E. By 320 B.C.E., the various Macedonian factions had briefly exhausted themselves and met at Triparadisus (in Syria) to hash out an agreement as to how the empire should be divided, with each of the various generals reigning as satraps. While many areas were parceled out to various generals, essentially Antipater became regent for Alexander's young son, Alexander IV, and would control Macedonia and Greece. Meanwhile, Ptolemy was to get Egypt, where he established a dynasty that lasted until the late first century B.C.E., when the last of the Ptolemaic rulers, Cleopatra, committed suicide and Egypt became a Roman province. Antigonus controlled Syria. And the final prize, Babylon, went to Seleucus, who would himself establish a dynasty and empire.

Seleucid Empire (312–64 B.C.E.)

The division of Alexander's erstwhile empire was harder on Babylonia (and Syria) than the conquest had been. Historian Amélie Kuhrt has observed that "the worst consequence for Babylonia of the Macedonian conquest was undoubtedly the long-drawn-out and disastrous wars between the Diadochi in which Babylonia . . . was frequently the central arena" (Kuhrt in Kuhrt and Sherwin-White 1987, 51). The warfare that followed was strictly between the Macedonian satraps; the Babylonians themselves accepted a Macedonian overlord. As historian Susan Sherwin-White notes, Babylonian Chronicle Number 10 "does not question the validity of, or regard as illegal Seleucus's position as satrap, which is simply accepted by the author" (Sherwin-White in Kuhrt and Sherwin-White 1987, 15). By 316 B.C.E., Seleucus was at war with Antigonus, the satrap of Phrygia. Antigonus briefly gained the upper hand, forcing Seleucus to flee to Egypt, where Ptolemy was firmly lodged. (Ptolemy, in fact, chose Egypt as his share of the division because of its remoteness, thus, in the years just after Alexander's death at least, making it less susceptible to the constant warfare that plagued the other satrapies of the empire.) In 312 B.C.E., Seleucus regained Babylonia and once again ruled from Babylon. The Seleucid dynasty is measured from this date. In time, the empire that Seleucus (r. 312–281 B.C.E.) and his successors forged became the largest of the successor states to Alexander's empire. During the next decade, Seleucus managed to place himself on equal footing with Ptolemy by expanding his empire. A détente with Antigonus, who, himself was looking westward to Athens, combined with earlier victories over Demetrios and other satraps under Antigonus, allowed Seleucus to turn his army east, whereupon he conquered what had been the Iranian satrapies. By 305 B.C.E., he, like the other Macedonian satraps, declared himself king and ruled not from Babylon but from Seleucia, a city he founded on the Tigris River south of Babylon. Seleucia was not a capital in the classical sense; as historian John D. Grainger points out, "the kings were peripatetic in the first century or so of the [Seleucid] kingdom's life" (Grainger 1990, 122). Seleucus had forsaken Babylon (he would later forsake Seleucia) as an administrative center, and this required that many Babylonians relocate to the new city. Despite the fact that Chaldean astrologers remained, the legendary city began its slow decline. Still, in Seleucid times, Babylon was a somewhat autonomous city locally ruled by, to quote historian R. J. van der Spek, "the ☒atammu (the chief administrator of the temple [Esagila]) and the board called 'the Babylonians, (of) the council of Esaghila'" (van der Spek in Kuhrt and Sherwin-White 1987, 61).

As had Cyrus and Alexander before him, the "peripatetic" Seleucus campaigned in India, but to less success. First, he came up against the Mauryan Empire, whose king, Chandragupta, had taken over Alexander's Indian possessions. Then, Seleucus was forced to return to Mesopotamia to join the alliance against Antigonus and Demetrios in the Fourth Diadochi War. Seleucus's entering the fray tipped the scales against Antigonus. Seleucus defeated and killed him in the Battle of Ipsus in 301 B.C.E. and took Syria as his prize. By then, his title was Seleucus I Nikator (Conqueror). Seleucus eventually moved his capital from Seleucia to Antioch on the Orontes River in Syria, and it was clear that Seleucus hoped to reunite Alexander's empire with himself as king. Intrigues and interdynastic marriages, as well as city foundings and the organizing and administrating of his empire, occupied him for most of the rest of his life, but in 281 B.C.E., he invaded the territory of his former ally, Lysistratus, northwest of Syria. Having defeated Lysistratus, who died in the battle, Seleucus entered Europe, with plans to march to Macedonia, but he was assassinated (in 281 B.C.E.) before achieving his goal.

In many ways, it appears that the Babylonians were content to remain a satrapy under the Seleucids, even as to forsaking the capital of the empire to Syria. The Seleucids, even in the later stages of the empire, ruled Babylonia in the spirit of Alexander. While Babylon's decline can be traced to the transfer of the imperial capital and the widespread diffusion of Hellenic culture throughout the territories of the former Persian Empire, some historians contend that Babylon, itself, did not decline under the Seleucids. However, one of the later kings, Antiochus IV Epiphanes, hoped to populate the city with Europeans. That aside, Sherwin-White has noted that the formal administrative functions of the satrapy were conducted not just in Greek but also in Aramaic and Akkadian (Sherwin-White in Kuhrt and Sherwin-White 1987, 23–24). This is corroborated through various documents of the period, including taxation documents as required by the reorganization of the imperial taxation system under Antiochus I, Seleucus's successor. In this and other cultural aspects (such as temple building), as Sherwin-White contends, the Seleucid kings acclimated their rule to Babylonia.

SELEUCUS THE CITY BUILDER

Seleucus was one of history's more prolific imperial city builders and/or expanders. His reasons for doing so no doubt were primarily for security, but it also can be said that he wished to place a Hellenic stamp upon his empire, which, after all, was based far away from his home country. To that end, after defeating Antigonus at the Battle of Ipsus and acquiring the satrapy of Syria into his growing empire, he set about transferring his capital from Seleucia to Antioch. Once in Syria, he formulated a plan for 10 cities, which Grainger has characterized as "the central event in the urban history of Syria" (Grainger, *Cities* 1990, 91). There were other Syrian cities, but these 10 were the most important.

Some of the cities were actually built prior to Seleucus's time, but Seleucus expanded them and Hellenized them to a certain extent. (After the demise of the Seleucid Empire, they discarded in varying degrees their Hellenistic traditions.) In addition to Antioch, Seleucus's cities are Seleucia-in-Pieria (this is distinguished from the prior Seleucid capital, located in Babylonia, known by scholars as Seleucia-on-the-Tigris), Apamea, Laodikea-ad-Mare, Kyrrhos, Chalkis, Beroia, Seleukeia-Zeugma, the island city of Aradnos, and "its mainland suburb Marathos" (Grainger, *Cities* 1990, 93). The first four were considered major cities, while the second quartet were second-level cities. Of the last two cities, Marathos was actually larger but in Seleucid times took second status because of the strategic importance of Aradnos's port. Grainger points out that all of these cities were built or expanded upon with an eye toward geographic placement so as to allow Seleucus and presumably his successors to maintain control over Syria. Half the cities of the group of 10 already existed—Apamea (Niya), Aradnos (Arvad), Beroia (Halab), Chalkis (Quinnesrin), and Marathos (possibly called Marathus)—so that Seleucus built his strategic urban plan around them. Though the cities he built were the larger of the group, the ones that were already in place suggest the possibility that Persia may have had an eye toward geographic expansion in Syria as well.

For the Macedonian Seleucus, Babylonia, and indeed all of Mesopotamia, was a satrapy too far from the homeland to consider maintaining as the capital province. In a way, this is ironic because not only had he claimed Babylonia as his "inheritance" after the death of Alexander, but he expanded his empire with hopes of reunifying most of what Alexander had conquered. Yet, he chose not to keep his capital in the more central province.

Example of Seleucid artwork—an odalisque or, perhaps, a goddess—now in the Louvre Museum, Paris, France (Erich Lessing/Art Resource, NY)

This acclimation and Babylonian acceptance of the Seleucids was made easier by tradition: By the time of Alexander's arrival in Mesopotamia, the Babylonians opposed Persian suzerainty, and thus, the Macedonian conquest of Babylonia was spared a protracted war. After Alexander's defeat of Darius, Babylon, as some historians believe, exercised an old right to sue for its own peace, which saved the city from destruction (Kuhrt in Kuhrt and Sherwin-White 1987, 49). Apparently, a similar procedure had been followed 200 years earlier, when Cyrus defeated the last Babylonian king, Nabonidus. By the time Seleucus established his rule in Babylonia, the Macedonians had already been firmly in place for eight years.

The empire had achieved its greatest territorial gains under Seleucus. Over the next 220 years, in fits and starts, it would lose territory and face pressure from both the east and the west. In the east, the first satrapy to revolt against Seleucid rule was Bactria in the 240s B.C.E. Nearly simultaneous to this was the settlement of the Parni in Parthia, who would eventually spell the end of the Seleucids. Some of the lost territory was regained by Antiochus III the Great (r. 222–187 B.C.E.), especially in the final decade of the third century B.C.E., when Antiochus engaged in a series of wars that have come to be known as the Syrian Wars. Essentially, these were the Diadochi Wars fought all over again with the essential difference that the Seleucid Empire and Egypt were now antagonists. In 200 B.C.E., Antiochus wrested Palestine from Egypt. However, when he attempted to push westward into Europe, he came up against Rome, which soundly defeated the Seleucids in 192–188 B.C.E., despite their assistance from Carthage. Rome further weakened the Seleucid Empire by encouraging the Maccabean Revolt in Palestine (165–152 B.C.E.). But it was the Parthians, not the Romans, who would cause the Seleucid decline.

The Parthian Empire (ca. 125 B.C.E.–224 C.E.)

Parthia, located in what is now northeastern Iran, had been a satrapy of the Persian Empire, but previous to that it had, like Achaemenid Persia, been a vassal state of the Medes. Parthia was one of the satrapies that revolted from the Persian Empire—joining the Medes—upon the ascension to the throne by Darius I. But the revolt was short lived; Darius reconquered the region and brought it back under Persian overlordship in 521 B.C.E. From then until the end of the empire, the Parthians were loyal and valued members of the Persian army, gaining fame as excellent horsemen. They fought the Greeks under Xerxes and under Darius III fought against the Macedonians led by Alexander the Great. Parthia surrendered to Alexander in 330 B.C.E. As part of his new "Persian" policy (as the Macedonians thought), Alexander reappointed Phrataphernes as satrap of Parthia even though Phrataphernes, as was custom, had led the Parthian forces against the Macedonians. After the death of Alexander, Parthia became a satrapy of the Seleucid Empire.

As forceful as these Parthians were, however, the catalysts of what was to become the Parthian Empire were the Parni (also known as Aparni). A seminomadic tribe that had moved south from the area east of the Caspian Sea into Parthia during the time of Seleucid rule, the Parni, under their leader, Arsaces (Arshak in Parthian, r. 247–? B.C.E.), came to power in Parthia in an elaborate way. War in the west in the mid-240s B.C.E. provided the occasion for the satrapy, along with that of Bactria, to revolt from Seleucid authority. In 238 B.C.E., when the Seleucids were defeated by invading Celts at the Battle of Ancyra, Arsaces, as ancient history scholar Malcolm A. R. Colledge notes, was able "to eject [the Parthian satrap Andragoras] and occupy the province of Parthia" (Colledge 1967, 25). Arsaces' successor was his brother, also Arsaces (also known as Arsaces Tiridates, r. ?–211 B.C.E.). Much like *Caesar* in Rome, the name *Arsaces* was used as a title by the first 19 kings of Parthia, the majority of whom retained their personal names, and the dynasty is referred to as the Arsacid. Arsaces II made a treaty with the satrap of the neighboring and still rebellious province of Bactria, allowing him to consolidate his authority and pursue expansion.

Parthian expansion was at the expense of the Seleucid Empire, as Arsaces II and the next three of his successors methodically picked off territory from the eastern satrapies. However, they were unable to defeat Seleucid power outright, especially during the reign of Antiochus the Great. During this period, Parthia was an autonomous state within the Seleucid Empire. It was the sixth Parthian king whom historians have credited with creating the Parthian Empire. Arsaces VI Mithridates (also known as Mithridates I and Mithridates the Great, r. ca. 171–138 B.C.E.), the younger brother of his predecessor, Arsaces V Phraates, came to power at a conspicuous time in history as "one by one the provinces of Iran were lost to the Seleucids, and became a series of independent monarchies" (Colledge 1967, 28). Nevertheless, Mithridates bode his time for almost 11 years. In 160 B.C.E., the Parthians overran Tapiura and Traxiane to the east, formerly Bactrian territory. He then turned westward, and by 147 B.C.E., the Parthians occupied the ever-rebellious kingdom of Media. A few years later, Mithridates took a step that signaled Parthian independence from Seleucid rule: He became the first Parthian king to issue coinage.

The record next becomes somewhat hazy, but Mithridates returned east, "perhaps on account of an attack on his borders" (Colledge 1967, 29). After further eastern conquest, he turned westward again with the intention of taking Babylonia as well as a few kingdoms, such as Elam and Armenia. This he swiftly accomplished, in 141 B.C.E., but once again had to repel an invasion in the east—this time from Bactria. The Seleucid king, Demetrius II, took advantage of Mithridates' preoccupation in the east to mount a counterattack to regain his lost territory. But Mithridates defeated the Bactrians, turned west for the third time, and defeated Demetrius, taking the Seleucid king prisoner. Demetrius thereupon forsook his throne but reclaimed it ca. 129 B.C.E. and held it for another four years after that. Nevertheless, the Seleucid Empire was at a virtual end; the dynasty continued to rule until 64 B.C.E. but had long since fallen back on Syria as its final domain, where it served as a buffer state between the Parthian and the Roman Empires. Mithridates died in 138 B.C.E., but the empire he founded continued to expand. By 113 B.C.E., during the reign of Arsaces XI Mithridates (c. 124–87 B.C.E.), upper Mesopotamia fell under Parthian sovereignty. This was the furthest west the Parthians would push. From then on, the focus of the Parthian kings shifted from conquest to maintaining and governing their possessions. This era, dating approximately from the accession of Mithridates the Great to the throne of Parthia in 171 B.C.E. to 10 B.C.E., is known as the phil-Hellenistic period because many of the provinces of the empire had retained their Greek qualities, especially language and culture, and the Parthians utilized them, though individual regional characteristics were preserved.

One characteristic of the Parthians that the kings themselves maintained was their nomadic urge. The kings built or occupied numerous cities as their capitals, the most important being Ctesiphon on the Tigris River, which they built from the ancient town of Opis. The Parthian monarchs shuffled their courts between these capital cities, though Babylon does not seem to have been one of them. Possibly as a result of all that movement, comparatively few official records from the Parthian Empire have survived, but this may be due in part to Sassanian hostility (Colledge 1967, 174). Dura Europos (Syria), Susa (Iran), and Nisa (Turkmenistan) seem to be the main repositories of Parthian documents and inscriptions, further suggesting the decline of Babylon under the Parthians. Despite such decline, Babylonia on the whole fared well under Arsacid rule: "Minority languages of the Empire included the living and defunct tongues of Babylonia still written in cuneiform script until, at least, 6 B.C., and of course Hebrew" (Colledge 1967, 71). Colledge also makes the point that Babylonian law also survived as it "underlies the parchment contract of 121 A.D. from Dura" (Colledge 1967, 73), near the end of Parthian rule.

Art and Religion under the Parthians

Greek culture underlay the Parthian Empire; this is most evident in surviving artwork and less so in architecture, the latter being more diffuse in style. However, it took more than a century before classical Greek artistic styles began to influence Parthian artists. A late date for such influence can be partially attributed to the degree of political autonomy that Parthia enjoyed under the Seleucids. In addition, there was a "new Hellenic style . . . [a] variation between oriental and Greek style" (Colledge 1967, 143). One of the major Greek influences was the positioning of figures in reliefs. Ancient Near East artists positioned figures in profile, usually in rows, and the Parthians were no exception. When Greek influence finally arrived, spreading eastward—and the Parthians are considered the first Eastern artists whose work was transformed by Hellenic culture—Parthian artists began positioning figures frontally. This new style fairly quickly became the norm for Parthian artists. Frescoes, reliefs, and statuary survive from the later period of the empire (especially in Dura) that show Parthian adaptation of Greek influence. Another aspect of Parthian art was that it was less imperial than either Achaemenid or Sassanian art and in this sense resembled Seleucid art.

A second and perhaps more important aspect of Parthian rule is the influence of imported religions in Babylonia and Mesopotamia. During the empires of the Achaemenids and Seleucids, the ancient religions managed to survive and, indeed, were actively promoted by the dynasties. But during the Parthian period, the ancient religions of Mesopotamia became extinct (though worship of Shamash continued), replaced at first by Greek and Persian religions—the latter reintroducing and/or reinforcing Zoroastrianism—then by Jewish monotheism, to which the royal family of the semiautonomous kingdom of Atiabene (in Assyria) converted. Christianity also spread into Mesopotamia and Babylonia during the first two centuries C.E., especially the Gnostic variety. Lastly, there is evidence in Dura Europos of Roman cults where the legions had been stationed. The death of the old religions and cults and the fact that the newer ones vied with each other and were never able to gain deep-rooted stability across Mesopotamia made it easier for Islam to supplant other religions in the region in later centuries. Lastly, this influx of new religious ideas in the last centuries B.C.E. and the first of the common era contributed to the further decline of Babylon, as its god, Marduk, was abandoned.

The Fall of the Parthian Empire

The fall of the Parthian Empire was a process that was drawn out over more than two centuries. In its latter decades, it was weakened by dynastic struggles, which exacerbated problems both east and west in an empire that was largely decentralized. In the west, the Parthian problems were directly linked to the demise of the Seleucids, who the Parthians, ironically, helped eradicate in conjunction with Rome.

After their defeat by the Parthians, the Seleucids retreated to Syria where they maintained a rump empire. In the meantime, further west, Rome was on the ascendant, having extinguished Carthage in the Third Punic War, in 146 B.C.E. Thus, simultaneous with the expansion of Parthian power in the ancient Near East was that of Rome in the western Mediterranean area. However, with Seleucid Syria in the middle to buffer its territory from Rome, the Parthian Empire was seemingly impregnable. To the east, China and Parthia had developed a cordial relationship, including representatives of each kingdom traveling to their counterparts. In fact, by the mid-first century B.C.E., Parthia had control of the Silk Route, from which its treasury derived a great deal of wealth. Then it made a drastic strategic error.

In 69 B.C.E., Parthia entered into an alliance with Rome to attack what was left of the Seleucid Empire. At a time when Parthia's dynastic struggles were sapping its energy, Parthia and Rome agreed upon the Euphrates River as the western border of the Parthian Empire with Seleucid Syria. However, in 63 B.C.E., the Roman general Pompey the Great conquered the Seleucids once and for all, putting Roman legions on the border of Parthian territory. The situation in the west remained that way for almost 10 years until the Roman general Crassus invaded the Parthian Empire in 53 B.C.E. The Roman incursion was turned back, but the Romans continued intermittently to pursue their goal of eastern conquest over more than two centuries. Parthia's wars with Rome abated only during times of Roman political instability, such as the civil wars between the partisans of Pompey and those of Julius Caesar and the one that emerged after the assassination of Caesar, and the Pax Romana.

After 150 years of intermittent warfare between the two empires, most often fought over the strategically important territory of Armenia, Roman emperor Trajan (r. 98–117 C.E.) invaded Parthia in 114 C.E. The reasons for Trajan's invasion of Parthia have been debated since ancient times. Fame, the reason provided by Cassius Dio, is most often put forth, but modern historians have also asserted that the war was actually started for economic reasons. F. A. Lepper presented French historian J. Guey's opinion that "Trajan's real objective in going to war with Parthia was the securing of the overland trade-routes through Mesopotamia" (Lepper 1948, 158). Whatever the reason, the Roman pretext for war with Parthia was, as usual, a squabble over Armenia; the Parthian emperor had deposed the Armenian king without permission from Rome. Trajan, a former general who led his legions, marched into Armenia virtually unopposed. He then set about conquering upper Mesopotamia and Babylonia. (It is said that when Trajan arrived in Babylon, where he had gone to see the room where Alexander the Great had died, he was disappointed on the pitiable ruin of the city.) In fact, he marched his army to what is now the Persian Gulf.

In 116 C.E., Osroes launched a counterattack and regained some of the territory, while rebellion against the Romans broke out in other provinces. Trajan, in turn, was able to recover Armenia and Mesopotamia, though he lost Assyria. Babylonia was given to Parthamaspates (r. 116 C.E.), a Parthian prince, who served at Trajan's behest. Thus, for a brief time there were three kings of Parthia. After Trajan's death in Anatolia (Asia Minor) in 117 C.E., Hadrian (r. 117–138 C.E.), ascended to the emperor's throne in Rome. He returned Roman policy to one of peaceful coexistence with Parthia. He also returned the territory Trajan had won to the Parthians.

During the next 50 years, Parthia was at peace with Rome, but its dynastic struggles continued. Nevertheless, in 161 C.E., Vologases IV (r. 148–192 C.E.) took advantage of a temporary dynastic problem in Rome to seize Armenia (which had remained under Roman suzerainty). Under co-emperors Marcus Aurelius (r. 161–180) and Lucius Verus (r. 161–168), the Romans not only regained Armenia but invaded Ctesiphon. And this time, when they took Mesopotamia, they kept it. In 193 C.E., another Roman civil war emboldened yet another Parthian monarch, Vologases V, who sought to recapture Mesopotamia. But when the Roman succession question was settled with the accession of Septimus Severus (r. 193–211 C.E.), Parthia's days were numbered. Severus sacked Ctesiphon in 198 C.E. and returned to Rome with a legendary hoard of gold and silver. Parthia was impoverished and no match for Rome, but it was not the successors of Septimus Severus who put an end to Parthian rule. Just as Parthia had revolted against Seleucid rule and in time overtook their master, so did the Iranian petty king Ardashir I (r. 208–241 C.E.) attack the weakened Parthian dynasty from his home base of Persis. The army of Ardashir fought victoriously over the Parthians in 224 C.E. Thereupon, Ardashir easily took Ctesiphon and installed himself as king over what remained of the Parthian Empire and those areas he had conquered beforehand. The new empire became known as the Sassanian Empire, named for the dynasty descended from the Zoroastrian priest Sasan, an ancestor of Ardashir. However, the Sassanians, themselves, "called their empire Eranshahr, the kingdom of the Aryans; perhaps the Parthians did likewise" (Colledge 1967, 57). Historians have also referred to the Sassanian Empire as the Neo-Persian Empire.

The Sassanian, or Neo-Persian, Empire (224–651)

The Sassanians were the last native dynasty in Iran and the last Indo-European overlords of Iraq. Upon taking control of the Parthian Empire, the dynasty moved its capital from Istakhr, near Persepolis, to

Ctesiphon in order to take advantage of whatever structure and trappings of empire remained. Unlike its predecessor, the Sassanian state was a highly centralized bureaucracy based on a hierarchical system of administration. This centralization accounted for greater stability than under the Parthians throughout most of the empire's history and allowed it to resist first Roman, then Byzantine intrusions in the west. Like their Parthian predecessors and the Achaemenids, the Sassanian monarchs bore the title "king of kings."

The Sassanians, in fact, felt a close kinship with the Achaemenids. One of their more important decrees upon taking over in Ctesiphon was the restoration of Zoroastrianism (also known as Mazdaism), which became the state religion (Hourani 1991, 9). Zoroastrianism had been the religion of at least the early Achaemenid kings. Under the Sassanians, Zoroastrianism not only became the official religion, but nonbelievers were often persecuted. However, the Zoroastrianism of the Sassanians differed from that of the Achaemenids. In the religion's earlier incarnation, the god Ahuramazda (Wise Lord) was much like the Hebrew Yahweh, the creator of all things. By the time of the Sassanians, indeed even during the time of the Persian Empire, Ahuramazda was considered the creator of all things good, while the origins of Angra Mainyu, the god of evil, had been reinterpreted. In the reinterpretation, which bears a resemblance to ancient Greek mythology, the two gods were twin sons of Zurvan, the god of time; hence, the religion had ceased to be monotheistic.

Sassanian Expansion

The first Sassanian war with Rome began in 231 C.E., during the reign of Ardashir. But it was under Ardashir's son and successor, Shapur I (r. 241–272), that the Sassanians really began to flex their military muscle. Shapur's most important victory in the West was fought at the Battle of Edessa in 260, when he defeated and captured the Roman emperor Valerian (r. 253–260). Rome's ill fortune gradually reversed as the century wound down so that long after Shapur I was dead, under Narseh (r. 293–303), the Sassanians, in 298, signed a treaty with Rome that restored much territory to the latter in northern Mesopotamia. The Sassanians were also victorious in the East. They defeated the Kushans, who controlled Gandara, which had been a satrapy of the Achaemenid Persian Empire but was nevertheless Indian and not Persian. In doing so, they looted the capital of Peshawar (in modern-day Pakistan). Legend has it that one of the objects taken was Buddha's begging bowl. The tight governmental structure of the Sassanians meant not only that the plunder from Antioch and Peshawar went to the royal treasury but that the provincial governors had to answer directly to the monarch. The dynasty financed city- and road-building (whereas in the past, generals or satraps would have done so), expanded agriculture, and even instituted a financial system. This tight control also accelerated the spread of Pahlavi as the language of the empire, whereas the Parthians throughout most of their imperial history had had no lingua franca until the emergence of Parthian in the final century or so of the empire's existence.

The Sassanian Empire was dominated in the fourth century by one man, Shapur II (r. 309–379). Technically, he ruled from the moment of his birth, though a regent actually governed the empire until 325. Shapur II, like his namesake, was driven to expand the empire, and like Shapur I, he did so by attacking Rome's holdings in Mesopotamia and Armenia in 337. This war went back and forth for the next 13 years and basically was fought to a standstill. But the war had a serious effect on Shapur's domestic policy. By 337, the Roman Empire had become Christianized, and with hostilities between the two empires on the increase, the numerous Christians in the Sassanian Empire suddenly became suspect. An empire-wide policy of persecution and forced conversion of Christians was put into place sometime after the beginning of the new war with Rome, which lasted throughout the reign of Shapur II, and even during the eight years when there was relative peace between the two empires. The long and costly conflict with the Roman and later the Byzantine Empire and a succession of short-lived kings seriously weakened the Sassanian Empire and made it ripe for takeover by Muslim Arabs to the south.

The year 634 marked the first clashes between Arabs and Sassanian Persians in Iraq. After early defeats that resulted in the loss of the fertile area along the Euphrates' right bank, the Persians routed the Arabs in the Battle of the Bridge. However, in 637, the Arabs attacked again achieving a major victory that allowed them to seize and sack Ctesiphon. By 638, they had conquered nearly all of Iraq, and the final Sassanian king, Yazdgard III (r. 632–651) fled to the ancestral homeland. Three years later, the Arabs invaded Iran. When Yazdgard was killed in 651, the Sassanian Empire ceased to exist. By then, however, Iraq was already a province of the Muslim caliphate.

Trade in the Sassanian Empire

Although the Sassanian economy was based on agriculture, trade played an important role in keeping the empire vital and extending its influence beyond it political boundaries. China, via the Silk Route, was a prominent trading partner but by no means the sole one in the East. Evidence of Sassanian trade in what is now Vietnam and the Indochinese peninsula has been uncovered in the form of caches of Sassanian coins. Shahab Setudeh-Nejad points out that after the fourth century, "Sassanians monopolized the maritime trade of the Far Eastern routes," capitalizing on "technological innovation in the shipbuilding industry of the Persian Gulf" that had begun in the previous century (Setudeh-Nejad). A good deal of Sassanian trade eastward was sparked by the rivalry with the Byzantine Empire. When a war over the satrapy of Armenia threatened the Silk Route, both empires took to the sea to reach the Far East. For the Sassanians, the war also prodded trade to the south, in the Arabian Peninsula. "The Sassanians," as historian Touraj Daryaee has noted, "were competing with the Romans and disputing trade concessions as far as Sri Lanka, and it appears there was even a Sassanian colony in Malaysia. . . . Persian horses were shipped to Ceylon [Sri Lanka], and a colony was established on that island where ships came from Persia" (Daryaee 2003, 8–9). Archaeological evidence has shown that Sassanian merchants established ports in various parts of the Persian Gulf, the Arabian Sea, and beyond.

A melding of cultures along the Silk Route: This Tang dynasty plaster camel carries an ewer in the Sassanian form and a monster mask, it is now located at the Idemitsu Museum of Art in Tokyo. (Werner Forman/Art Resource, NY)

Another important trade route for Sassanian merchants was to the north, with the Ugric peoples of what is now northwestern Russia. Historian Richard N. Frye, in a paper discussing Sassanian trade in the north, contended that "Iranians in the towns of south Russia acted as middlemen in the trade between the Sassanian Empire in the south and the Ugrian-speaking peoples of northern Russia" (Frye 1972, 265). While Sassanian coins have been discovered in abundance as far to the northwest as Scandinavia, they are usually accompanied by Islamic coins, but Frye noted "the large number of Sassanian silver bowls of the fifth to eighth centuries" found in the Kama-Perm region of northwestern Russia as evidence that significant Sassanian trade took place prior to Islamic times (Frye 1972, 265). The silver objects were used in religious worship. What the Sassanians may have received in return was "fish, hides, wax, honey, amber, and walrus and mammoth ivory," which were more prized than elephant ivory (Frye 1972, 266).

Conclusion

The wealth and geographical situation of ancient Iraq made it a point of contention for external dynasties for more than 1,000 years. As each dynasty succumbed to what seems an almost inevitable collapse—following a cycle of empowerment, growth, and decadence—it was succeeded by a hungrier group. The Persians were drawn by the wealth and mystery of Babylon, for example, and the Macedonians by that and its role as the cultural capital of the ancient Near East and the centrality of it geographical position—Alexander the Great planned to make it the capital of his far-flung empire.

Even when Babylon's glory had faded, ancient Iraq had something to offer. Much like the Low Countries of Europe in the 20th century, it was easy to conquer, but unlike them, its conquerors tended to remain, for much the same reasons that Alexander intended to stay. Even the Romans understood the region's importance as the link between the Mediterranean and the Far East. What is remarkable about this period of Iraq's history is not so much the amount of warfare and cities seized and retaken over and over but that for more than 1,100 years the area was ruled by and large by only four empires, each of which played its part on the Mesopotamian stage before receding into history.

3

IRAQ UNDER THE UMAYYAD DYNASTY (651–750)

Traditionally, the emergence of the Islamic empire has been seen as a disruption of a historic trend in which the rise of city-states and empires increasingly confined nomadic life to the periphery. The Islamic realm, in that perspective, is seen as nomadic in outlook and tribal in structure and thus as reversing that trend. Recent research faults this paradigm and assigns the Islamic empire a more productive role in bringing the classical world into modernity. It argues that while Islam emerged in a society largely tribal in structure, the term *tribe* encapsulates a number of occupational, economic, and social groups, not all of which rely on camel pastoralism or the trade in livestock. Furthermore, the state and society that Islam inspired was not nomadic in outlook but urban and mercantile.

Islamic society was heir to a number of diverse cultural and political developments already characteristic of earlier societies. To its credit, it served as "a positive continuator" for the heritage of past civilizations (Hodgson 1974, 1977, 104), while displacing the old with the new only after a complex synthesis had been achieved, which took place following several decades after its emergence on the world scene. Quite naturally, the social, political, economic, and religious climate in which Islam was born and the early genesis of what was to become a major world civilization can only be understood against a backdrop of what had gone on before. Yet, the Islamization of Iraq and the fusion of the region's heretofore distinctive cultural features (Sassanian administrative traditions, imperial authority, and the divine right of kings) with a rigorously monotheistic and rough-and-ready egalitarianism cannot be seen as merely the wholesale adoption of previous traditions or the rapid acculturation of a society that was bereft of guiding principles of its own. The story of the Islamic conquests and the setting up of the new state had as much to do with the application of the particular moral vision of the new holistic order in the making as it had to do with the religious and cultural traditions already embedded in the region by past civilizations.

The End of One Era and the Beginning of Another

In the hundreds of years that preceded the rise of Islam, the agricultural and trade potential of both Iraq and the greater zone that encompassed it continued to serve the cities and the countryside of what has been termed the Nile to Oxus region, that is, the area between North Africa, the Iranian highlands, the northern Gulf, and the eastern Mediterranean. Although agriculture was not a widespread activity because of the excessive aridity of the region, overland and seaborne trade flourished, acting as the major link between cities, markets, and the greater countryside. The most important commodities traded were spices.

Possibly the more interesting aspects of this region had to do with two almost parallel developments: the rise of monotheistic religions and the construction of culturally specific civilizations. The one drew its élan from the thousands of years of spirituality and religious syncretism innate to the region, the other from the widespread use of language (Aramaic being one of the most important). Thus, even before the rise of the three monotheistic traditions—Judaism, Christianity and Islam—there already existed charismatic preachers calling for spiritual regeneration and the introduction of codes of morality among men and women. Two important movements preaching a more spiritual cosmic order were those that grew up around Zoroaster, in Sassanian Iran, and Mani, in Iraq. Roughly parallel to these two developing traditions, Judaism and Christianity began to make their mark on the region as well.

Historian Marshall Hodgson explains the difference between these new religions and what had come before:

> By the early centuries of the Christian era were thus established ... organized religious traditions which, in contrast to most of the previous religious traditions, made not tribal or civic but primarily personal demands. They looked to individual personal adherence to (or "confession" of) an explicit and often self-sufficient body of moral and cosmological belief (and sometimes adherence to the lay community formed of such believers); belief which was embodied in a corpus of sacred scriptures,

55

claiming universal validity for all men and promising a compre-
hensive solution of human problems in terms which involved a
world beyond death (Hodgson 1974, 125).

Further, what made these religious traditions persevere and develop was their close connection to a particular state. Zoroastrianism functioned in some ways as a state religion and as an ideological legitimator of the Sassanian Empire, while Christianity had become so intertwined with the Roman Empire after the reign of Constantine I that it became the official creed of the state. While Abrahamic (exclusively monotheistic) and Mazdean (Hodgson's term for traditions usually originating in Iran, mixing monotheism with polytheism and a dualistic vision of the world) traditions are usually seen as irreconcilable, at some point, they began to influence each other to a considerable degree and to hew to certain fundamental principles that characterized them all. Eventually, however, the Abrahamic communities (Judaism and Christianity) became the more dominant. With their concentration on "justice in history through community" (Hodgson 1974, 130) and their belief that an individual was answerable for his or her actions in the world, the Abrahamic vision bore witness that God was one, man or woman bore ultimate responsibility for his or her fate, and the notion of an ethical God was kept alive by a community of men and women upholding morality and social justice.

As the first of the monotheistic traditions, Judaism was a significant influence in parts of Iraq in the fourth century (Berkey 2003, 10–13). Through migration and conversion (initially very important in the early period), the religion spread rapidly in Iraq, to the point where the number of adherents outstripped the Jewish population of Palestine. Other important stimuli on Islam derived from Christianity. It is estimated that by the late sixth century, Christians constituted the largest faith-based community in pre-Islamic Iraq. Christianity was divided into a welter of sects and confessions, of which the Nestorians were probably the most important. The dissension between the Christian sects was so sharp that it is considered to have paved the way for the later Islamic conquests, so much so that in the eyes of some Christians, "God permitted the Arabs to triumph as a punishment for Christian disunity" (Berkey 2003, 26). On the eve of the prophet Muhammad's birth, then, Iraq had imbibed and assimilated a number of monotheistic traditions that paved the way for (in Muslim eyes, at least) the last of the great unitary religions in the region and the development of one of the most enduring and resourceful civilizations on earth.

The Birth of Islam

Arabia at the end of the sixth and beginning of the seventh centuries consisted of a complex of tribes—either nomadic, seminomadic, or settled—and an urban society along the coasts whose rich merchants traded with the nomadic interior and engaged in political relations with its tribal chieftains. Mecca, the trading capital of the western peninsula, was linked to Yemen in the south; Palestine, Syria, and Egypt in the west; and Iraq in the east. Its chief monopoly was in the trade of slaves and spices. The town was also the seat of an important pilgrimage site centered on the sacred area (haram) of the Kaaba, a key center for worship for tribal migrants and pilgrims from inside and outside the city. A group of wealthy merchants, some of whom belonged to Mecca's most important tribe, the Quraysh, controlled the city, where growing wealth vied for recognition alongside more traditional tribal identity. The many opportunities in Mecca attracted tribesmen and settlers from other areas. Power grabs by Byzantine and Sassanian rulers succeeded only temporarily in deflecting Mecca's trade away from Qurayshi control. By the time of Muhammad's birth in 571, the Quraysh tribe had reverted to a near-monopoly of Mecca's economy and control of the land and pilgrimage routes into the city (Ibrahim 1982, 343–358).

Muhammad was born into an economically disadvantaged clan of the ruling Quraysh tribe of Mecca, the Banu Hashim. It has often been said that whereas other religions emerged in eras before recorded history, Islam was born in the full light of day. Unlike other prophets and men of God who had appeared before him, details of the prophet Muhammad's life were well established in his own time, especially from the time he was 40 and beginning to receive divine revelation, which were later collected in the Qur'an. Benefiting from his home city's renown as a center of East-West trade, Muhammad became a merchant and quickly earned the title of *al-amin* (the trustworthy one) because of his honesty and scruples. As noted, Mecca was an urban haven for businessmen as well as pilgrims; long-distance traders, of whom Muhammad was one, were the lifeblood of the economy. Having become the business agent of a rich 40-year-old widow, Khadija, he gained her trust and admiration, eventually making her his first wife.

The Clash with Mecca, the Flight to Medina, and Ultimate Victory

The Prophet's preaching gained him a number of followers, some from his immediate family. After his wife, Khadija bint Khuwaylid, and cousins Ali and Jaafar submitted to Islam, a wise and highly respected companion of the Prophet, Abu Bakr converted as well. The Prophet's first challenge was preaching the sacred message to his tribe, the powerful Quraysh. Although they listened to him at first, the tribe's leaders soon became angry by his insistence on forsaking idols and praying to the one God. Their worry centered on their position as the aristocracy of the commercial elite in Mecca. If pilgrims and traders converging on Mecca at the time of the annual pilgrimage were to hear that their traditional gods were being attacked, and that the attacker was none other than a member of the Quraysh, they would stop coming. Having approached the Prophet's uncle, Abu Talib, to ask him to stop his nephew from attacking the traditional gods in Mecca and been sent away empty-handed, they now resolved to guard against the new religion by posting men at the entrance to Mecca denouncing Muhammad as a sorcerer and liar. However, by the time of the pilgrimage, Islam had already influenced a number of smaller clans and families in and around Mecca. In particular, the Prophet's reputation as a mediator and evenhanded diplomat had reached the warring clans of Yathrib, some distance away from Mecca, who came together just long enough to ask the Prophet for counsel and advice.

In Islamic tradition, Muhammad's flight to Medina (the former Yathrib) along with several of his most loyal followers marks the beginning of a new calendar, the *hijri*. In Islam, *hijra*, or "flight," is considered to be both a positive as well as negative occurrence, because the Muslim who flees to a more secure country or region where he can practice his faith in a protected environment is understood to be making the only choice left to him. In a broad sense, the Hijra (Hegira), the Prophet's escape to Medina, is considered both a beginning and an end: a beginning because it led to the phenomenal rise of the last monotheistic religion to pervade the Arab and Middle Eastern region and an end because it brought to a close an era often based on pagan injustice and oppression (Hourani 1991, 17).

As soon as he had settled down in Medina, the Prophet started to make plans to challenge the Quraysh. Meccans were jealous of Medina's commercial prosperity, and any move to establish a secondary trade center so close to Mecca itself would have been seen as a dangerous signal. The fact that Muhammad was not only advocating better trade terms for his new hometown but a whole revolution in religious and social practices made his authority in Medina doubly threatening. It was one thing to go to war against a commercial rival and another thing altogether to do battle with an opponent who held up the standard of religious legitimacy and promoted the message of the one true God.

Muhammad's followers began to attack Meccan caravans and to inflict serious losses on Mecca's trade. They gained their first military victory in the Battle of Badr in 624, which was fought against a much larger Meccan army. The Battle of Uhud in 625 ended in a draw, with both sides retreating to count their losses. The Battle of the Ditch (al-Khandaq) in 627 again resulted in defeat for Mecca, and it showed the Qurayshi leadership that their days were numbered. For the Muslims, Mecca's eventual surrender in 630 was the worthiest prize of all; but even in peace, the Prophet had to tread carefully. He did not try to humiliate the Meccans but immediately set down terms to include them within the *umma* (Muslim community of believers), knowing full well that strength lay in numbers. And, in fact, Mecca's submission opened the door to the whole of Arabia. Delegations from all the powerful tribes in Arabia began to arrive at Medina to reach agreements with the Prophet. The Muslims had grown from a small band of loyalists to become the basis for a new community of believers in the one God and the followers of his messenger, a brand new distinction for which there was little precedent in seventh-century Arabia.

The Death of the Prophet Muhammad

Muhammad died suddenly in 632 after a brief illness, leaving the question of succession unresolved. He had pacified an unruly region of nomadic and semi-settled tribes, large towns, and small oases; brought social justice to the poor and oppressed; and told men that they were all brothers in Islam. But his achievements had to be followed through in order to reach a wider audience. And they had to last. The question of who would succeed Muhammad would prove to be the most dangerous fault line in the early history of Islam and would eventually tear the young community apart. There was no real authority to decide once and for all how the mantle of leadership would pass down from the Prophet to his successors. One thing, however, was agreed upon, and it was that there would be no prophet after Muhammad. He was the Seal of the Prophets (Khatim al-Anbiyya), and none could replace him. Upon the urging of a close companion, Umar ibn al-Khattab, Abu Bakr Muhammad's closest friend and father-in-law (father of Aisha, whom Muhammed married after Khadija's death), became the successor (*khalifa*; r. 632–634) of the Messenger of God, an institution that is virtually without parallel outside of the Islamic world. While the *khilafa*, or Islamic leadership (caliphate, in English), lasted for centuries, it was to change many times, bringing with it countless disturbances in its wake.

However, it remained a potent symbol for Muslims everywhere, as the ultimate contract between rulers and ruled. So long as the ruler was just and followed the principles laid down by the Prophet and in the holy book of the Qur'an, his subjects were satisfied. The problem lay with obedience to an unjust ruler, an issue that would trouble Muslims throughout their long history.

The Genesis of Empire

Immediately after the Prophet's death, all the powerful tribes in the Arabian Peninsula that had come to a security agreement with him broke away. The Muslim armies saw this as a declaration of war and began the Apostasy Wars of reconquest (called the Ridda wars in Arabic). One of the most interesting aspects of these wars is how much the whole concept of power had changed in the region. The tribal rebellions in the peninsula, while carried out by pagan leaders eager to restore their independence in their home regions, were seen by the Muslim camp, and justifiably so, as the renunciation of these tribes' contract with the Prophet himself. But they were carried out in a novel fashion. Four of the six tribal leaders who broke away from the Muslims actually declared that they were prophets of God, thus proving how deeply Muhammad's message had penetrated the furthest reaches of Arabia. Abu Bakr, in his new role as commander-in-chief of the Muslim troops, sent brilliant but mercurial generals, such as Khalid ibn al-Walid, to force these tribes to submit once more.

The Expansion into Iraq

Even while the Apostasy Wars were continuing in the Arabian Peninsula, Abu Bakr began other offensives in the region. Relying on the general Muslim consensus to wage wars both against the Sassanian and Byzantine Empires, he sent armies northward to enforce the caliph's authority. Abu Bakr died but two years after the Prophet. His successor, Umar ibn al-Khattab (r. 634–644), took up the challenge. Again the maverick general Khalid ibn al-Walid was responsible for the first victories in Iraq. In 634, thousands of Arab tribesmen did battle with the occupying Sassanian force, whose soldiers were exhausted from their all-out wars against the Byzantines. The Sassanians fought badly, and the Muslim armies won the first round. In 636, the most important battle of the Iraq campaign took place at Qadisiyya, near Najaf, where the Muslims won an overwhelming victory, despite the

THE APOSTASY WARS (632–634)

The rebellion against the authority of the first caliph, Abu Bakr, began with Yemenite tribes, who claimed their oath to Muhammad was intended only for the Prophet. That aside, four other important reasons for the rebellion have been identified. These include disgruntlement that the caliph would only come from Medina or Mecca; refusal to send money to Medina that had been previously collected by the Prophet; the Bedouin tribes' attraction to the force of Muhammad's personality, not his teaching; and Roman, Sassanian, and Abyssinian influence on the border tribes. The rebellion was not confined to Yemen; it included Nejd (the central highland of modern-day Saudi Arabia), Oman, Bahrain, and Mahra in present-day eastern Yemen. The caliph made peaceful overtures but when they failed to bring the rebellious back into the fold, sent armies to do so by force.

Perhaps the most dangerous of the rebellious leaders was Musaylimah of the Banu Hanifa tribe, one of the largest in Arabia. It was against this tribe that Abu Bakr sent his general Khalid ibn al-Walid in command of an army of 4,000 men, Musaylimah having defeated the first two smaller armies sent against him. Khalid defeated Musaylimah at the Battle of Yamama in the eastern Nejd in about 632, where the latter was killed. The defeat brought the Banu Hanifa back into the fold. Musaylimah was one of those who claimed to be a prophet after Muhammed's death and was subsequently declared a false prophet. He is also often referred to as al-kadhab (the Liar).

Although Musaylimah's defeat and death was the most important event in the Ridda wars, it took approximately two more years before the apostates in all the regions were finally defeated.

heavy odds. In 637, the Arab armies occupied the Sassanian capital of Ctesiphon in Iraq and established the first mosque in the country. And in 642, the "Victory of Victories" at Nahavand brought to an end the Sassanian hold over Iran proper. Iraq and Iran were now under Muslim rule.

The Islamic conquest was made easier because the Sassanian Empire was on its last legs, and a weakened Byzantine Empire would prove unable to hold Syria. Furthermore, the native populations, who chafed under their imperial misadministration, had little to lose and quite a lot to gain by cooperating with the Muslim armies. It has been argued that both tribesman and townsman had no real interest in who ruled them, so long as they were taxed fairly and lived in security (Hourani 1991, 24). However, a change in power may also have been in the interest of the local Christians and Jews, who may have hoped to benefit from a new army and administration open to new philosophies and methods of rule and whose legal and religious codes were still receptive to change. In addition, Islamic law strictly prohibited attacks against civilians and noncombatants, and Muslim warriors must have thus seemed lenient in comparison to other foreign occupiers that had ravaged both Iraq and Syria-Egypt. Finally, the Muslims realized that the land was for the taking; they were not going to damage property that had become theirs through war.

Umar ibn al-Khattab

The Muslim administrations of Iraq, Iran, Syria, and North Africa followed a certain system worked out at the very beginning of the invasions. This system was conditioned by the prevailing ideology at the time. Islamic society was roughly structured into four classes: These were the House of the Prophet (Al al-Bayt), meaning the wives of the Prophet and his immediate family; the Companions (al-sahaba), who were the first people to accept Islam and the prophecy of Muhammad and many of whom had made the Hijra and fought alongside him; the Muslim Arabs who formed the bulk of the army and the upper echelons of the administration; and the "clients," or *mawali*, non-Arabs who became Muslim by means of attaching themselves to certain Arab tribes as clients and paid taxes to the Islamic treasury. The treasury (*bayt al-mal*) paid out stipends to the first three classes in descending order of importance, while the *mawali* partly financed the state.

The man most responsible for the administration of the early empire was the able Umar ibn al-Khattab. He has largely gone down in history as the second caliph in Islam, but he may also have been the real founder of the Islamic state. A sober, powerfully built man with a resonant voice, he was at first an enemy of the prophet Muhammad, but upon converting to Islam, Umar became one of the staunchest followers of the faith, and the one person (after the Prophet's cousin Ali and his closest companion, Abu Bakr) whom the Prophet relied upon for counsel and advice. Umar is also known as a reformer, having introduced a number of legislative and religious changes within the Islamic body politic that had far-reaching effects. Among these were legal prohibitions against drinking wine; the introduction of night prayers (*tarawih*) in the month of Ramadan; and the call, repeatedly made, for a definitive collection of the text of the Qur'an (which remained in oral form for a long time, memorized by men and women until the time of the caliph Uthman, Umar's successor). Finally, Umar was for free-market reforms and the prohibition of trade monopolies (*ihtikar*).

Umar's prowess in battle was equaled by his genius for military strategy, and he was a confident leader when it came to deciding which of his generals to dispatch to any given battlefront. For instance, he plucked Khalid ibn al-Walid out of Iraq just as he had secured his greatest victory and dispatched him to Syria to further secure that province from Byzantine attack. Under his command, expansion was waged on three fronts: Iraq-Iran, Syria, and Egypt and North Africa.

Among Umar's notable achievements as an administrator was the establishment of several garrison cities that later developed into major trade and religious centers. Of these, the most important were Basra and Kufa in Iraq and Fustat in Egypt. Kufa became the first capital of Iraq, and Basra, its main port. Traditionally, historians believed that these cities were designed as military cantons, meant to segregate and keep "pure" the Arab tribesmen who made up the first wave of Islamic armies. However, some scholars have made the argument that these garrison cities were designed to attract a whole host of social forces, from the transient merchant to the Greek-speaking scribe. They, in fact, became the advance cities of the embryonic Islamic state. Rather than conquering the older, traditional centers of learning and trade instituted by the Byzantine and Sassanian Empires, Umar's experiment led to the creation of an alternative urban experience, which may have contributed to the slow but sure Islamization of the native population of Iraq, Iran, Syria, and North Africa.

By far the most important of Umar's innovations was the financial system and the implementation of fiscal responsibility. The state was divided into provinces governed by a military commander, assisted by a fledgling bureaucracy. All state officials received salaries, including the caliph. This was not only to keep them honest (and Umar judged himself as severely, if not more so, as other Muslim commanders) but also to grant them the freedom to govern their province without worrying about gaining a livelihood. Besides the commander, each province was entitled to an imam, or prayer leader; a *qadi*, or judge; and an official to oversee the *bayt al-mal* (treasury). Another office, the *diwan*, or registry, originally a Sassanian office, was assigned the task of keeping track of the troops and their dependents, for each fighter had a salary com-

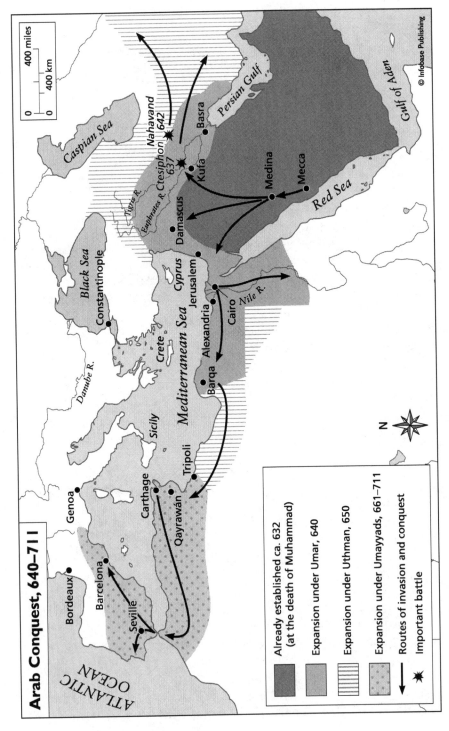

Arab Conquest, 640–711

mensurate to the level he had reached in the army. The office started tracking each fighter from the time he had joined the army and noted at which juncture of the expansion of the Islamic state he had declared his submission to Islam. Women and children received a fixed income, the Prophet's wives and family receiving the highest stipends of all.

Umar ordered that the fertile and well-watered lands originally part of the Sassanian domain were to be held in perpetuity by the state. This entitled the inhabitants of these agricultural lands to collect the harvest, a portion of which was allotted to the state in the form of the *kharaj* tax and then distributed to the military and the rest of the population. This was to ensure a rough equality in economic resources for all Muslims, although field commanders were granted more discretion in the administration of their plots of land than others were. Meanwhile, a poll tax was imposed on minorities called the *jizya*, signifying that these people were regarded as *dhimmis*, or "protected" minorities; in a sense, they were to pay for their protection by the Islamic state. A large proportion of the inhabitants of Iraq were Christians or Jews at the time of the Islamic conquest and chafing under the misadministration of the Sassanians. Despite this tax burden, many non-Muslims deserted the Sassanians early on in the battle for Iraq and chose instead to live in peace under their new Muslim rulers by paying the *jizya*.

The Settlement of Iraq

How did these changes affect the newly conquered province of Iraq? When the Arabic-speaking Muslim invaders spread out across the region, they discovered that the social, religious, ethnic, and cultural diversity of Iraq made for a number of different mores, customs, and traditions, not all of them immediately comprehensible. Linguistically, most of the inhabitants of Iraq either spoke a dialect of Aramaic (a Semitic language close to Hebrew and Arabic) or a form of Persian (the written form of which was called Pahlavi). Indians and Africans, who spoke a variety of languages quite possibly unknown in Arabia, congregated in southern Iraqi ports. The main religions in Iraq were Judaism and Christianity (with Nestorian Christians the majority), while a small but still powerful minority of Persian upper-class officials espoused Zoroastrianism, the state religion of Sassanian Persia. Finally, Arabic-speaking tribesmen were present in Iraq even before the Islamic conquest, although more of them seemed to have settled in the northern regions than the central or southern ones. In fact, Arab tribes had been moving back and forth between Arabia and Iraq for millennia; all that the Islamic expansion did was to throw the gates wide open to districts that had been proscribed in the past because they were under the control of a foreign dynasty (the Sassanian). Thus, some of the migrating Arab tribes, far from being foreigners, were at home in Iraq, because the transregional impulse of tribes had already allowed for the relocation and resettlement in Iraq of several clans and subdivisions originally from Arabia.

Central and southern Iraq formed two military fronts in the Islamic campaign against the Sassanian state, while operating independently of each other under different commanders. Those men who joined the Islamic armies on their way to fight the Sassanians and Byzantines were not from a single tribe; rather, most of them were volunteers from many different tribal clans and subsections. Both fronts were manned by volunteers from Medina, tribesmen who joined to fight alongside the Muslim armies on their way to Iraq, and tribal sections from the large Banu Shayban, Tayy, and Asad tribes. They were also part of a select few. Noted Islamic scholar Fred Donner estimates that the tribal armies that fought in Iraq numbered no more than 4,000 men (Donner 1981, 221). They were able to join as a formidable military force because they were tightly organized, with tribal chieftains coming under the military command of representatives from the settled Muslim ruling elite from Mecca, Medina, and the oasis of al-Taif, who were supremely loyal to the Islamic state.

Saad ibn Abi Waqqas, the commander in Iraq, moved from his initial settlement of al-Madain (the former Sassanian capital of Ctesiphon) to the new *misr*, or military camp, of Kufa, where the first temporary houses were built of dried reeds. According to Arab chroniclers of the conquests, Kufa was partly chosen as the "capital" of the new army because it offered good pasture for sheep and camels, the former providing milk and milk products, and the latter, transport. There is evidence that Kufa was a planned community, for alongside the customary mosque were headquarters for military commanders and tribal residences built around a communal courtyard. Its population was estimated at anywhere between 10,000 to 20,000 men. By around 640, Kufa was settled not only by Arab Muslims, but by at least one Persian division that had fought alongside the Arab soldiers, and some sections of the town had Jewish inhabitants, expelled from Arabia (Donner 1981, 236).

Like Kufa, Basra, Iraq's main seaport, was also built as a tribal encampment. Although there is not as much information on Basra, we know that a very large number of tribesmen settled there and that it merited some attention from Iraq's new rulers. In the wake of the Islamic

THE RISE AND FALL OF NESTORIANISM

At the time of the Islamic conquest of Iraq, the main Christian element in the area belonged to what was considered in the West the heretical cult of Nestorianism. The cult was inaccurately named for Nestorius, a fifth-century heresiarch (the originator and/or leader of a heretical movement) from Syria whom Byzantine emperor Theodosius II chose to be patriarch of Constantinople in 428. As patriarch, Nestorius, himself, punished heretics, so it was ironic that he, too, should be stamped as one. Essentially, he like others from the Antioch school, taught that within the person of Christ there was a unity between the God and the man. Nestorius also decried the term *theotokos* (literally, "God-bearer"), used to identify Jesus's mother, Mary, as the Mother of God. These teachings, somewhat misinterpreted by others, led to the denunciations of Nestorius. In 431, the Council of Ephesus condemned Nestorius as a heretic; he was also condemned by the Council of Chalcedon in 451, the year of his death in Egypt. Ironically, the latter council accepted what Nestorius had taught early on but after two decades of condemnation could not accept the man.

Though no longer patriarch of Constantinople, the church did not excommunicate Nestorius. In fact, he held ecclesiastical authority in Antioch and northern Africa and died trying to defend his orthodoxy. His teachings attracted a fair number of followers, especially in Persia and Iraq, where the church in Rome held less influence. Nestorianism came to be defined as a split between the human and divine principles within Christ, with emphasis on the human. The term *theotokos,* they believed, ought to be replaced by the term *Christotokos* (Christ-bearer), thus making Jesus a man inspired by God rather than God.

In the West, the Catholic and Orthodox Churches managed to stop the Nestorian movement in its tracks, but from Iran, Nestorianism moved eastward into China and Mongolia, with less success, and India, with more success. The latter group came to be known as the Malabar Christians. Western Christians called the Near East Nestorians Chaldean Christians. *Chaldean Christians* is now used to define former Nestorians whose churches, usually in Islamic countries, were reconciled with the Roman Catholic Church. Small groups of Nestorians continue to exist in the Near East and South America.

conquests, it became apparent that agriculture had been neglected in the region, so the first thing that Arab commanders ordered was the planting of palm trees in Basra and the drainage of marshlands. In fact, land reclamation became an important activity, undertaken by military governors as well as tribal shaykhs. Investment in land, however, was slow due to a variety of factors, one of which related to the uneasiness of Arab troops to commandeer lands that had not completely fallen under an Islamic regime (Donner 1981, 243–244).

The Split between Sunni and Shia

As noted earlier, very early in the history of the religion, the Islamic elite had strong disagreements concerning grave issues affecting the *umma*. Among the most bitter, and certainly the longest lasting, was the rupture that occurred over the political succession to the Prophet. What came to be known as the Sunni-Shia split was a result of the different claims to the leadership of political Islam and developed over a period of decades; the rift took place for the most part in Iraq. But the Sunni-Shia issue was not the only bone of contention among the nascent Muslim elite, for jealousy and resentment among those who had been the earliest converts and companions of the Prophet (*al-sahaba*) and those who had joined the faith much later on (mostly elders of the Quraysh tribe) threatened to tear apart the earlier consensus. The people of Medina looked askance at the inhabitants of Mecca, while movements of incipient rebellion stalked the new settlements in Iraq.

Without question, the most serious issue the young community had to face after the Prophet's death was who to appoint as successor and on what basis was the succession to be guaranteed. One group believed that the Prophet had already designated a successor, and that man was Ali ibn Abu Talib, the cousin and son-in-law of Muhammad. According to this faction, a few weeks before his death, the Prophet had stopped at a place called Ghadir Khumm and uttered the momentous words "He for whom I was the master, should hence have Ali as his master" (Enayat 1982, 4). Further, this same group reinforced their support for Ali by arguing that only the most knowledgeable should rule, and who was better versed and better informed of the true spirit and import of Qur'anic teachings than the Prophet's closest relative? Finally, Ali's partisans believed that only the persons who were intimately associated with the Prophet possessed the attribute of *isma* (infallibility and purity), a belief that was later to grant the imam Ali and his line near-divine status.

This party of Ali supporters was in the minority, however. The majority prevailed and came to be known as the Sunnis (because they adhered to the *sunna,* or prophetic tradition). This bloc believed that rather than attaching the office to a certain family line, the community of Muslims should choose the person best suited as political leader. The key for the Sunni party was *ijma,* or the consensus of the community, signified by the *baya,* or oath of allegiance (sealed by the clasping of hands) to signify loyalty to the new leaders. While the overwhelming majority eventually followed what came to be known as the Sunni position, the strains introduced among the community by the first public disagreement between fellow Muslims continued to rankle, especially among those people for whom Ali had become a political cause of the highest significance.

But it was only after Uthman ibn Affan (r. 644–656) was proclaimed the third caliph, following Abu Bakr and Umar, that the simmering hostility between Ali's supporters and the Umayyad branch of the Quraysh tribe came out in the open. Members of the Quraysh, although the Prophet's tribe, were late converts to Islam and thus their sincerity to the Islamic cause was sometimes questioned by other Muslims. Although Uthman was a member of the Umayyad clan of the Quraysh, he was one of the most fervent supporters of the Prophet's mission and had become a Muslim early. Ultimately, it was not the strength of his conviction that brought him down but his nepotism and the corruption of his government. Uthman's overdeveloped sense of family obligations and the promotion of his Umayyad relatives over more capable people, plus the liberal distribution of land grants to favorites, eventually brought upon him the wrath of his subjects and a group of rebels assassinated him in 656.

Ali ibn Abu Talib (r. 656–661), who had been passed over three times, finally succeeded to the caliphate, becoming the fourth and last of the Rightly Guided Caliphs (*al-rashidun*), original companions of the Prophet named leaders of the community after his death. Almost immediately, Ali's succession became a point of contention with Uthman's very ambitious nephew Muawiya ibn Abi Sufyan, the governor of Syria. The tribal code of justice, still honored by the Arab inhabitants of the newly settled regions of Iraq and Syria, required vengeance for Uthman's death. Because some of Ali's supporters were implicated in Uthman's murder, the responsibility was placed on Ali by Muawiya to find and prosecute the killers (Morony 1984, 485). As a result, Ali was forced to rule first in Medina and then in Kufa under the shadow of an unresolved murder, and even though he was able to defeat other mutinies to his rule (including one in which the Prophet's last and favorite wife, Aisha, was an active participant), Muawiya's challenge was too formidable to ignore.

The Battle of Siffin, Ali's Death, and the Martyrdom of Husayn

The two finally met on the plains of Siffin, in Syria, where after a desultory battle, Muawiya's troops resorted to the stunning tactic of placing their Qur'ans on their spears, signifying their readiness to accept divine justice. When Ali chose to accept human mediation, he lost the support of the Khawarij (those who go out); upon seeing him resort to mediators to solve his political claim to the caliphate, they were furious. "Judgment belongs only to God!" they shouted and immediately deserted Ali's camp. And so it was that after the Battle of Siffin, the Khawarij became yet another political group to oppose the Islamic state as it was being constituted at this very dramatic juncture of its fortunes.

The Khawarij deserve more than a passing mention because they embodied a radical but very significant strain among the Muslim *umma*. The Khawarij were austere, fanatically devoted to the Qur'an and sunna, fiercely egalitarian and democratic in their relations with one another as well as with Christians and *mawali*, and adamantly opposed to the easy living of the settler cities in Iraq. They demanded financial equality for all Muslims in the distribution of the spoils of war, as well as in the disbursement of funds from the treasury. More to the point, they regarded themselves as "the only true Muslims" (Morony 1982, 471) and consigned all non-Khawarij Muslims to perdition. Their attacks against legitimate authority continued throughout the seventh and eighth centuries, embodying an absolute and uncompromising tradition that persisted wherever social injustice and economic inequality existed.

Ali's caliphate did not last long, for he too was assassinated—in Kufa in 661 by a member of the Khawarij. Muawiya was now absolute ruler, and under him, the Umayyad dynasty, with its capital in Damascus, Syria, began a long period of monarchic absolutism, leaving Iraq a mass of discordant voices and even more confused fealties. Kufa and Basra, the two garrison cities of Iraq, each with their rebellious traditions, were now leaderless: Kufa had lost its imam, Ali ibn Abu Talib, and Basra, its chief insurrectionists, Talha and Zubayr, two early Companions of the Prophet who had met their deaths earlier at the hands of Ali's supporters as they were struggling to seize power for themselves and their associates.

Mosque in Damascus, Syria, constructed 706–715 (Styve Reineck/Shutterstock)

Nonetheless, the struggle for succession to Ali, pursued by *shiat ali* (the party of Ali, whence comes the term *Shia*) continued unabated. Some of Ali's supporters at Kufa tried to carry on with the fight but were repulsed by Umayyad commanders. After the Umayyad caliph Muawiya's death in 680, a group of Kufan community leaders asked Ali's son Husayn to pick up Ali's fallen banner and lead the Shia movement against "the usurpers." Husayn agreed, provided the Kufans were sincere. In a fateful move, he sent his agent to Kufa to meet with the notables in that city and prepare for battle. By some accounts, Husayn received pledges of loyalty from 18,000 Kufans. The plot, however, was discovered, Husayn's agent was killed, and the governor of the city forbade the Kufans from joining Husayn's campaign. Left with scant supporters and besieged on all sides, Husayn, his immediate family, and supporters were massacred by the forces of Yazid ibn Muawiya, son and successor of Umayyad caliph Muawiya, on September 28, 680.

The assassination of Husayn on the plain of Karbala, a few miles from Kufa, marks the beginning of a powerful Shia tradition of martyrdom that has developed over the centuries into a full-fledged movement of protest. Ever since his death in the late seventh century, the Shia leadership has taken up Husayn's call and militated for social justice for the Shia community. But it was to take a further 90 years to crystallize the

71

disparate teachings of various Shia jurisprudents and community leaders into a doctrine of the imamate, the chief Shia institution.

Iraq Under the Umayyad Empire

Of the four Rightly Guided Caliphs, three died through assassination; only Abu Bakr, the first *khalifa*, died a natural death. Besides the violent blows directed against the leadership of the *umma* after the Prophet's death, there were other, equally fierce struggles for power that drove a wedge between Muslims and embittered relations between them.

For instance, problems quickly developed as a result of the distinctions made between Arab and non-Arab Muslims. Particularly in Iraq, how did cultural, religious, and linguistic diversity give way to the adherence to one religion, Islam, and one language, Arabic? The process of Islamization was so gradual that most historians date the beginning of mass-scale conversions only to the 10th or 11th centuries. Because Muslim administrators initially categorized their subjects into Arab Muslims and *mawali* and discouraged large-scale conversions to Islam for fear of losing their exclusive status, the process of adaptation to the new faith was deliberately slow. The *mawali* deemed this unfair and complained, with some justification, that they risked their lives every day for the Islamic cause and yet were still seen as second-class Muslims. Those *mawali* were to be found, for the most part, in Iraq and the eastern parts of the Islamic empire, particularly in Khurasan, where resentment at their treatment by the Arab elite soon developed into a political platform.

Schismatic movements and political discord were not all that happened in the first couple of centuries of Islam. Much larger and far more significant developments took place that testified to the growing linkages between groups and classes from Medina to Herat. Solid advances were made in theology, law, the economy, culture, and politics that transformed the lives of many Muslims as they went from a partly nomadic society to a multilingual, multiethnic, and progressively inclusive empire. Under the Umayyad dynasty in Damascus, the Arabs in Iraq and many of the newly conquered regions of the Islamic empire saw a slow but steady diffusion of Persian administrative traditions that transformed the caliphate; financial organization, such as an early form of banking; agricultural expertise, such as canal building and irrigation at which the people of Mesopotamia excelled; and cultural practices, in part inherited from Sassanian and Hellenistic sources, in part native born, experimental, and often brash. Although the Arab military elite had marched into Iraq (and Iran, Syria, Afghanistan, and North Africa as well) determined to hold on to their language and customs, eventually even the most unyielding let down their guard and began to assimilate into the more developed urbanity of the land between the two rivers and its rich and polyglot culture.

Very early on, then, and despite the political and military turmoil all around them, the Muslims of Iraq, whether new or late converts, settled down to make sense of their new surroundings and to participate in the building of their new society. And because the Qur'an, the revered and holy book for all Muslims, had made such an immediate impact on their lives, it was natural that the first literate communities would try to draw lessons from it and generalize those lessons into standards by which to judge the new state and society that had emerged in Islam's wake. In Basra and Kufa in Iraq, as well as in other towns across the empire, men, young and old, began to discuss and debate the structure of the Arabic language, poetry, law, Islamic mysticism, theology, and history. Whereas the population of the new settlements fused tribal and pre-Islamic oral tradition with the new emphasis on Qur'anic interpretation and recitation, state leaders in Medina and later on, in Damascus,

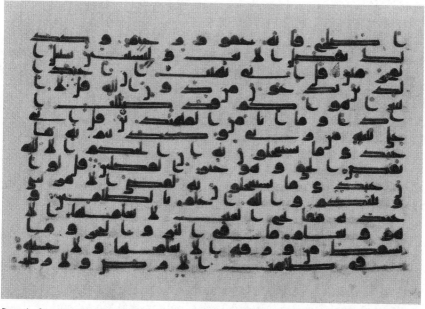

Detail of an eighth- or ninth-century Qur'an written in Kufic script, which fused with tribal and pre-Islamic oral tradition in the newer settlements of Iraq during the nascent Islamic period (Victoria and Albert Museum, London/Art Resource, NY)

created a courtly literature that integrated Arab motifs with Sassanian or Byzantine authority symbols. Such, for instance, was the practice of addressing the caliph as *khalifat allah* (the deputy of God), which was unheard of in the early Islamic period (Lapidus 1988, 85).

In mid-eighth century Basra, a whole school of thought evolved based on grammar, lexicography, and the hermeneutics of the Arabic language. While recording the oral poetry of the nomadic and half-settled tribes of Arabia, the scholars of Basra and Kufa also began to collect the oral histories of the men who had known the Prophet and the elders of mid-seventh century Arabia. Eventually that lore, scrupulously checked and rechecked through hundreds of interviews, formed the basis for the compilation of the Prophet's sayings in the Hadith (*al-ahadith al-nabawiyya*), which is the second source, after the Qur'an, to be used by Muslims as a guide to live the exemplary life, modeled after that of the Prophet's.

Meanwhile, in the eighth century, Persian-influenced ideas of absolute monarchy, social hierarchy, and rigid class structure began to permeate the way that Arab caliphs saw themselves, and principles of a rough egalitarianism began to give way to notions of imperial autocracy. In this period, too, Persian literature, Sanskrit religious texts, and translations from Greek of works by authors such as Aristotle, Plato, Galen, and Hippocrates began to transform the Arabs' ideas of the world. Various philological schools, located mainly in Baghdad but also in other cultural centers such as Basra, gained scholarly acceptance so that by the mid-ninth century, "the output of the translators was prodigious, and the editors achieved excellence in the preparation of accurate and reliable editions" (Lapidus 1988, 94). Geographers and astronomers sought to retrace the footsteps of the ancients and discover the principles of the universe.

Eventually, schools of law were established, in which the sharia, or law derived from the Qur'an and Hadith, gained ground and in due course began to influence both state and society. These schools of law, fluid as they were in their composition and their teachings, began to formulate the beginnings of a Sunni position on everything from family law to the nature of authority. Meanwhile, at the very same moment that the religion of Islam was being interpreted and codified by groups of pious Muslims in the new settlements, the state was starting to use it as an instrument of legitimization and imperial authority. In fact, even during the period of the Umayyad state (which came to an end in 750), religion, theology, philosophy, and law became the battleground for different interpretations, with the caliphs attempting to gain primacy over religious scholars by means of imperial fiat. Conversely, as Lapidus notes, the "Umayyads also sponsored formal debates among Muslims and Christians which led to the absorption of Hellenistic concepts into Muslim theology" (Lapidus 1988, 82). While the struggle over who was to be the custodian of Islam came to a peak much later, during the Abbasid period, it is important here to underline the tensions between the centralizing Umayyad state in Damascus and the scholars of law and theology that largely lived in Kufa and Basra in Iraq.

Conclusion

Iraq's history throughout the seventh and up to the mid-eighth centuries was one of rapid conquest, a more or less orderly transition from tribal encampment to urban heterogeneity, and the adaptation of Muslims to the diversity of the Iraqi experience. If there is a central thread of Iraqi history in this period, however, it is the spillover of intellectual thought into political activity and the creation in Iraq of zones of contention and disputation in which local groups such as the pro-Ali Shia parties centered in Kufa (and later, Karbala); the new solidarity among Sunni Qur'an readers and reciters in both Kufa and Basra; the claimants to the caliphate converged in Basra; and the Khawarij, who were everywhere, created the first Islamic communities separate from the state. The latter, in its Umayyad incarnation, mounted several military campaigns to do battle against those heterodox elements but could not completely wipe out the most radical among them. Iraq was to remain a political tinderbox throughout the Umayyad period and for many decades to come after that.

4

ABBASID AND POST-ABBASID IRAQ (750–1258)

The Abbasid dynasty began surreptitiously as an underground revolt in the far-away province of Khurasan, a region between Iran and Afghanistan and continued until it had amassed enough men and arms to overthrow the entire Umayyad ruling family in Damascus bar one, the famous Abdul-Rahman who made his way to Spain and eventually installed a dynasty of his own. Like the Alids, the descendants of Ali, who was the last of the Rightly Guided Caliphs, the Abbasids were descended from an uncle of Muhammad, al-Abbas. However, "their immediate claim to the Caliphate rested upon the allegation that a great-grandson of Ali, Abu Hashim, had bequeathed them leadership of the family" (Lapidus 1988, 65). The Abbasids were supported by Abu Muslim (728–755), a brilliant strategist who soon became the leader of the revolution in all but name. They also drew on the support of the *mawali* (the non-Arab Muslim "client" population in the Islamic empire). Although the old landed Iranian aristocracy had assimilated quickly in Khurasan and lands further east, the Iranian converts were still discriminated against and had to form patron-client relationships with Arab tribes in order to achieve some form of parity in the new society. Many came to believe that their status as second-class citizens was unfair and utterly unworthy of the Islamic ideology of the empire. Joined to those grievances were those of the former Arab warrior class, "who had been promised tax reform by the Umayyads and had been betrayed" (Lapidus 1988, 76). They had become settled farmers in Khurasan; burdened by taxes and yet denied relief, they took up arms against the Umayyad in a last-ditch effort to strike a better bargain for themselves and their families.

The Abbasid revolution has gone down in history as one of the best-organized rebellions in the annals of early Islam and one that was of central importance to the reorientation of the Islamic empire to the east, Iran in particular. In the latter stages of the campaign, eschatological prophecies were reproduced to announce the coming of the impending revolution, and black banners, which had already acquired messianic overtones because of their connotations with past rebellions, were unfurled once more, this time as the Abbasids' symbol. All those signs and portents of a looming battle were widely circulated to create a base for revolutionary hopes and millennial expectations (Shaban 1971, 183). The call to arms was accompanied by the vivid reenactment of the martyrdom of Ali's son, Husayn, at the hands of the Umayyad ruler, Yazid, and the promise of justice and retribution once the Abbasids had come to power. When, after months of secret and intense preparation, the revolution finally broke out in Merv (present-day Turkmenistan) in 747, close to 10,000 people joined Abu Muslim's command. In 750, Kufa fell, and the first spiritual leader of the Abbasid forces, Abu al-Abbas (r. 750-754), became the Commander of the Faithful (*amir al-muminin*). Four years later, he was succeeded on the throne by his stronger and more charismatic brother, Abu Jaafar al-Mansur (r. 754–775); by that time, the last of the Umayyad family, Marwan II (r. 744–750), had been defeated, and the new dynasty, reflecting a wider mix of Arab and non-Arab Muslim, Jewish, Christian, and even Buddhist populations, was well on its way to bursting onto the world stage.

The Building of Baghdad

Abu Jaafar al-Mansur, the second caliph of the Abbasid Empire, decided to build a new capital as a symbol of a new beginning. The building of Baghdad is one of those highly symbolic moments in history that was fortunately captured by Muslim historians either contemporary to or living somewhat later than al-Mansur. One summer day in 762, it is recounted, the caliph surveyed the spot on which his new capital was to be erected and proclaimed it to be excellent. After praying the afternoon prayer, he spent the night in a nearby church, "passing the sweetest and gentlest night on earth" (quoted in Hourani 1991, 33). The next day al-Mansur was further impressed by the commercial opportunities offered by the Tigris and Euphrates Rivers that tied Iraq to lands east and west, as well as the immense potential for the provisioning and resupply of his large land army. And so he is supposed to have ordered the immediate building of his new capital on that very morning. After calling for God's mercy on himself and his subjects, he initiated the project by laying the first brick by hand.

Continuing with an ancient Iraqi tradition of constructing new cities outside the traditional population centers in the empire and in so doing, underlying the shift from the old to the new, Baghdad was built on a concentric plan in which the centers of power, such as the palace, the military barracks, and the bureaucracy, were situated in the inner core while the markets and residential quarters were located outside. Reflecting its structure, foreign observers referred to the new capital as the "Round City." However, for the Abbasid caliph who built it and for all the Muslim chroniclers who recorded its development and transmitted that lore over centuries, the city retained its original title, Madinat al-Salam (the City of Peace). The name that ultimately stuck, Baghdad, is the name of the village that previously existed on the site. In addition to the palace-administrative complex, Baghdad spawned two large city quarters, that of the Harbiyya (where the troops were situated), and al-Karkh, the suburb where the builders and workmen lived and where workshops, industries, and markets testified to the bustling activity generated by the ongoing building of the city.

After its inception, Baghdad went from strength to strength. From the eighth to the 12th centuries, it was one of the most sophisticated cities in the world, a multicultural hub of economic opportunity, intellectual brilliance, and expanding social horizons. As al-Mansur had so aptly prophesied, Baghdad became a thriving center of trade: it was not only a major international transit point for goods but produced a number of valuable products of its own, such as textiles, leather, and paper. Moreover, the city was thronged by people from all over the known world—Christians, Jews, Persians, Arabs, Syrians, Africans, and people from *ma wara al-nahr* ("what is beyond the river," the Arab name for Transoxania or Central Asia)—many of whom settled in Baghdad and took up occupations that further added to the capital's prospects. In the words of a famous historian,

> *Baghdad, then, was the product of upheavals, population movements, economic changes, and conversions of the previous century: the home of a new Middle Eastern society, heterogeneous and cosmopolitan, embracing numerous Arab and non-Arab elements, now integrated in a single society under the auspices of the Arab empire and the Islamic religion. Baghdad provided the wealth and manpower to govern a vast empire: it crystallized the culture which became Islamic civilization (Lapidus 1988, 70).*

ELEVENTH-CENTURY BAGHDAD, AS DESCRIBED BY A HISTORIAN WHO CALLED IT HOME

Yaqut al-Hamawi was an Islamic geographer of Greek origin who traveled all over the Islamic Middle East, temporarily calling Baghdad home. Originally, he sold books; later on, he wrote them. In his great work the *Dictionary of Nations (Mu'jam al-Buldan)*, completed in 1228, Yaqut wrote a historical geography of the Arab-Islamic world that is still considered to be one of the best references written on the towns, districts, and regions he visited. One of the accounts he related concerned the almost magical properties attributed to Baghdad under the Abbasids. The legend had it that because a reigning caliph had built the city, no Abbasid ruler would ever die in it. Yaqut confirms this by writing a remarkable postscript to the story:

> And one of the strangest [of the strange things that happened] is that Al-Mansur died as a hajji [a religious pilgrim on his way to Mecca]; his son Al-Mahdi went out to the mountain districts and died . . . in Radh; Mahdi's son Al-Hadi died in the village of 'Isabad, east of Baghdad; while [yet another son] Al-Rasheed died in Tus [Persia]; Al-Amin [Al-Rasheed's son] was killed . . . on the eastern front; Al-Mamun [Amin's brother] died in Badhandoun . . . in Syria; and Al-Mu'tasim, Al-Wathiq, Al-Mutawakil and Al-Muntaser, and the rest of the Abbasid Caliphs died in Samarra [a town north of Baghdad].

Source: Shihab Al-Din Abi Abdullah (Yaqut bin Abdullah al-Baghadi 1990, 546) Al-Rumi Al-Baghdadi. *Mu'jam Al-Buldan* (The dictionary of nations). Edited by Farid Abdul-Aziz Al-Jundi. Vol. I. Beirut: Dar Al-Kutub Al-Ilmiyya, 1990, p. 546.

The Structures of Power in Abbasid Iraq

Under the Abbasids, a number of changes occurred in the political and administrative structures of the empire. Among the most important were those that underlined the transformation of the caliphate from an Arab monarchy to an Islamic empire. While the Umayyads had relied on the old Arab military and civilian elite, the Abbasids flung open the doors of their empire to people from every ethnicity and sect. As a result of the concerted effort to diversify the structures of state and society in keeping with the pluralistic character of the new imperial government, recruits from all over the empire were brought in to staff the provincial administrations of the extended state. Even so, and as with any state determined to succeed in a region prone to endemic instability, there was a deliberate effort to create a new set of loyalties to the Abbasid dynasty by creating fresh constituencies in key provinces. Formerly marginalized groups such as the Khurasanis, made up of a mix of Persian and Arab settlers, were now placed in highly sensitive government positions. Nestorian Christians and Jews were also granted opportunities in the new Islamic empire; as were the Shia, or partisans of Ali, who had provided the Abbasids with their early ideological legitimization. The very multiplicity of the new governing group buttressed the cosmopolitanism of Abbasid Islam and reinforced the empire's wide latitude for social distinctions and differences.

In Baghdad itself, government became more efficient as an elaborate bureaucracy grew around the caliph. The offices of the *qadi* (judge), the controller of state finances, and the *barid* (courier) expanded as their functions became more complex. An entirely new post—that of the *wazir*, or chief minister—came into existence to execute the instructions of the caliph; eventually, this position, which may well have been adapted from Sassanian example, was to become the most powerful in the Abbasid state. Nurturing this newly installed administrative tradition was the use of Arabic as the lingua franca of the empire (replacing Persian in former Sassanian territories), which created incentive to write instruction booklets and other how-to manuals important for the development of the bureaucratic class. The wide usage of Arabic also allowed a new form of literature to emerge in the Abbasid realm that drew from several cultural traditions within the larger empire. Finally, military reorganization followed in the wake of this administrative shake-up, as the caliph dismissed the Arab regiments that had been the mainstay of the Umayyad caliphate and relied instead on the Khurasani troops that had brought him and his family to power.

For an example of the changes in administration under the Abbasid state, a look at Syria, the home region of the defeated Umayyad, is relevant. On the provincial level, the shift from Damascus to Baghdad was accompanied quite naturally by a diminution of the power of Syrian Arab notables. In their place, however, the caliphs in Baghdad either appointed younger Arab kinsmen, who, while capable governors, did not enjoy the same legitimacy as the Abbasid ruling family and therefore could not inspire revolts against the center, or military men from Khurasan, the heartland of the Abbasid revolt. Syria was divided into five administrative sections *(ajnad)*, namely, Palestine (Filastin), Jordan (al-Urdunn), Damascus (Dimashq), Homs, and Quinnesrin (Cobb 2001, 11). Whereas under Umayyad rule Damascus had been the hub of the universe, under the Abbasids, Jerusalem took on more importance because of its association with the Muslim pilgrimage and its holy sites.

Because the Muslims were locked in perpetual hostilities with the Byzantine Empire to the west, the frontier in Syria became central to Abbasid strategy: border districts demarcating Syria from the Byzantine territories were heavily defended by Abbasid troops. Those fluctuating borders, called *al-awasim* or *al-thughur* by Muslim historians, were a central theme of Islamic history and were given considerable attention by the Muslim chroniclers of the medieval period. Finally, as in most other Abbasid provinces, the governor of Syria was sometimes also the chief tax collector, as well as the prayer leader on Fridays, the chief judge, and overall military commander.

Syria, like Iraq, Egypt, and Iran, was directly governed. After the first flush of conquest had begun to make way for a more complex administration, a cadre of provincial officials, of which the governor was not always the longest serving, gradually took the reins of power. As the empire became more bureaucratic, posts became more specialized, and a division of functions occurred so that provincial bureaus of taxation, the judiciary, and the military commander began to make their appearance.

Try as it might, however, the Abbasid state was not able to control all the provinces under its rule with equal efficiency. Distant provinces, such as those in Central Asia and in North Africa, fell back on local family rule. For example, as early as the mid-ninth century, a local dynasty, the Tahirids, began to govern the important province of Khurasan. Meanwhile, regions of Central Asia came under the rule of the Samanids in the same period. In North Africa, Tripolitania (now in Libya) and regions that are now in Morocco, Algeria, and Tunisia threw out their Arab commanders and formed new, sometimes short-lived dynasties with the support of non-Arab, Berber tribes; significantly, some of these states adopted forms of the Khawarij or pro-Shia positions, which were by then completely inimical to Abbasid interests. Faced with the reality of local warlords taking over the reins of power, the Abbasids acquiesced in their rule, so long as the required taxes to the empire were paid. While the warning signs of an overstretched empire crumbling at the edges were all but ignored for the sake of realpolitik considerations, mutinies and rebellions rumbled on, particularly those mounted by religious-political parties, such as the Khawarij and Shia. By the beginning of the ninth century, and as a result of the vicious civil war between two sons of the fifth caliph, Harun al-Rashid (r. 786–809), al-Mamun and al-Amin, the caliphate had become a shell of its former self, relying almost totally on foreign councillors and armies and facing prolonged revolts against central authority.

Trade and Agriculture under the Abbasids

Prior to the civil war, during the reign of al-Rashid, Abbasid prosperity reached such heights that the real motors of imperial expansion may not have been as much military and political in nature as they were economic. Starting from the late eighth century onward, trade and agriculture connected the empire with the entire known world through networks of land and sea routes. By the 13th century, it is estimated that empire-wide trade had become the vital linchpin of a world system, tying the eastern Mediterranean to the Indian Ocean and both of them to China. The Abbasid Empire, a key player in world trade, was at the heart of this world system, if not its chief conduit, as Muslim, Christian, and Jewish merchants operating under its patronage bartered, bought, and used credit to ship textiles, food products, and livestock all over the empire and far beyond. Among the first items to be traded were wood, metal, sugar, and paper.

One of the chief reasons for the efficiency and success of long-distance trade, whether by land or sea, was the unity imposed by Islamic rule. That unity was established from the very first outpouring of Muslim troops into the fertile and cultivable lands of the East Mediterranean and North Africa. Later on, Umayyad and then Abbasid control of the Mediterranean Sea and Indian Ocean created a clearly defined and homogeneous area for transempire trade, unified by Islamic customs and mores and tied by the Arabic language. However, historians have pointed out that while the Abbasid Empire at its height controlled a large proportion of the known world, there were at least two other economic zones that cooperated as well as came into conflict with the Muslim realm, and those were China and the yet-to-be unified and largely underdeveloped European states.

Sociologist Janet Abu Lughod has written that there were striking similarities between economic systems in Asia, the Islamic world, and the West, and that contrary to the belief that capitalism or a money-driven economy only developed in Europe, both the Islamic empire and China

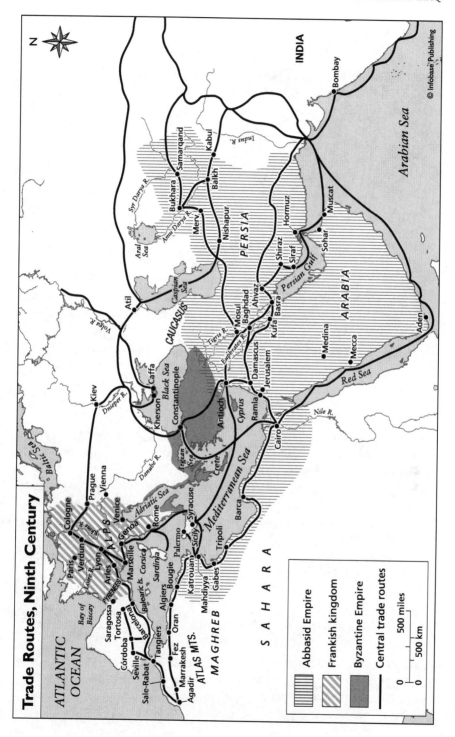

Trade Routes, Ninth Century

An Abbasid-era dirham, the unit of currency, from Baghdad ca. 786–809 (Kenneth V. Pilon/Shutterstock)

had created capital-intensive economies that competed fairly well with each other (Abu Lughod 1989, 15–18). The Abbasids and, later on, the Italian merchant city-states minted coins in their rulers' names; in China, paper money was introduced in the early ninth century. Credit was widely available so that traders could buy in one place and guarantee payment in another. Banking appeared initially in the Islamic world and was later copied by Europeans: members of merchant families worked for family firms in disparate regions of the world and guaranteed long-term credit and cash payments in a premodern system of family banking. As a result, Muslim traders were able to establish trading posts as far away as India, the Philippines, Malaya, the East Indies, and China. Abu Lughod also shows that even in small Islamic city-states, there was a controlling oligarchy at the head that monopolized trade and organized traders.

According to historian K. N. Chaudhuri, there were four great Asian commodities bought and exchanged in medieval times: silk, porcelain, sandalwood, and black pepper (Chaudhuri 1985, 39). Other products complemented transregional trade, such as shipments of horses from the Gulf; incense from southern Arabia; and ivory, cloth, and metal. There were many important port cities that facilitated this regional trade. Until the advent of the Abbasid Empire, trade was mostly land based and carried out by camel caravans passing from ports such as Jeddah (western Arabia) to Egypt and Yemen. After the conquest of the eastern Mediterranean and the Indian Ocean, Abbasid merchants were able to use the sea to great effect. New port towns developed or, in some cases, were redeveloped from small coastal communities to large trading emporia. For instance, Basra in southern Iraq, although built as a garrison town for Islamic troops, quickly became a major trans-shipment route for goods from Syria, Baghdad, and the coastal Gulf islands to India. Until the 20th century, Basra remained the main port of shipment to Bombay (present-day Mumbai) and other cities in western India. Other famous commercial centers in the Abbasid era were Siraf, a short distance away from Basra on the Persian side of the Gulf, Hormuz at the tip, Sohar in Oman, and Aden in Yemen. There were also the famous East African ports of Kilwa and Mombasa, from which sailors traveled across the Indian Ocean in ships that had been constructed without the use of a single nail.

Cultural and Intellectual Developments

The political and socioeconomic achievements of the Abbasid state were accompanied by riveting developments in the spread of human knowledge and the growth of the sciences, which came to be seen as the determining features of the far-flung Abbasid Empire. The sophistication of its literate elites, the mass appeal of its educational establishments, the systematization of its legal and societal structures, and the receptivity to the world are what underpinned the true Abbasid revolution.

The Question of Legitimacy

From 759 to 874, among the thorniest issues bedeviling the Abbasid caliphate was its relationship with the two main strains in Islam, Sunnism and Shiism. By the eighth century, the split between both had led to several wars, or *fitnas,* as well as polemical and doctrinal arguments, which were later to be incorporated in each community's traditions and bequeathed to later generations. At this initial stage, those religious-political currents had not yet gelled into hard-and-fast ideologies; they were more or less rival interpretations of certain crucial events in early Islam (such as the succession question or the issue of salvation) that, while inspiring political revolts throughout the empire, were not yet adequately supported by a systematic body of doctrine.

The Abbasids came to power promoting what was essentially a Shii message: They emphasized revenge for the death of the Prophet's grandson Husayn, who had been killed in piteous circumstances by Yazid, the son of the first Umayyad caliph, Muawiya ibn Abi Sufyan. The problem for the early Abbasids, however, lay in the fact that by propagating the martyrdom of Husayn, they were helping to endorse the legitimacy of the family of Ali ibn Abu Talib, the father of Husayn and son-in-law of the Prophet. The Alids, as some Western scholars call the family of the imam Ali (in Arabic, the Alids are referred to as Al al-Bayt, or the Family of the House of the Prophet), were revered by the Khurasanis and other Muslim settlers in the eastern parts of the empire, who fully expected an Alid descendant to become imam, or ruler, of the new Abbasid Empire.

The Abbasids were therefore involved in an ideological struggle with the Alids from the very beginning, with the Abbasids attempting to buttress their claim to be the most legitimate of the Prophet's descendants in a variety of ways. One surefire method was to maintain, on the basis of assorted hadith, or sayings of the Prophet or his Companions, that "the Prophet had a special regard for the Abbasids' ancestor al-Abbas and [to encourage] various prophecies foretelling the Abbasid accession" (Buckley 2002, 135). Because these claims did not prove legitimacy to the Alids and the substantial majority was in favor of the Alids, the second Abbasid caliph, al-Mansur, eventually had two pro-Alids, Abu Salama and Abu Muslim, the celebrated leader of the Abbasid revolt, executed.

Meanwhile, al-Mansur's shaky relationship with the imam Jaafar al-Sadiq, the sixth imam (descendant of the House of the Prophet through Ali and the charismatic leader of the Shia community), grew shakier as the years went on. Finally, on December 4, 765, Jaafar al-Sadiq died under suspicious circumstances in Medina, widely thought by his followers to have been poisoned by the caliph.

Jaafar al-Sadiq is a very important figure in Shii lore because it was he who formulated the doctrine of the imamate, that is, the notion of the charismatic leader who would lead the Shii community in times of travail. After his death, the Alid, or Shii, party split over the identity of the Mahdi, a messianic belief in a savior who will reappear on earth to bring social justice. One faction believed that al-Sadiq was the Mahdi, whereas another group forwarded Jaafar's son Musa al-Kazim as a candidate for the role of the Mahdi. Yet a third group proclaimed two other descendants of Jaafar al-Sadiq, his son Ismail, who died in 760 five years before Jaafar, and then Ismail's son Muhammad as the Awaited Ones. However, it was only in 874 that the three Shii factions crystallized into different, definitive schools of thought to which the preponderant majority of Shiis adhere until the present day. After the death of the 11th imam without an heir, the theory of the Greater Occultation (ghayba) was developed, which stressed that the hidden 12th imam was not dead but in seclusion until the time when he was to reappear as Mahdi to rescue his flock. The two schools of thought most associated with this philosophy were the Twelvers (ithna ashariyun, in Arabic; so called because they believed that it was the 12th imam who disappeared) and the Ismailis who believed that it was Jaafar al-Sadiq's son Ismail who was to return as the Mahdi. The third school of thought,

Zaydism, was not as widely subscribed to; therefore, it posed lesser problems to the Abbasids.

The dilemma posed to the Abbasid caliphs by the growing Shii movement thus involved not only legitimacy or ideological "cover" for an increasingly secular state but, worse, the persistence of political claims to the leadership of the Muslim community that the Abbasids believed settled with their accession to power. To control the imamate, the caliph al-Mamun even tried to bring it within the direct orbit of the caliphate by designating Musa al-Kazim's son Ali al-Ridha as his successor, only to witness his death a few years later, in 817. Suffice it to say that until the end of their caliphate, no real solution was found by the Abbasids to the Shii challenge, which continued as an underground tradition throughout the major part of the Abbasid era.

Sunni Law and the Development of Sufism

By the middle of the ninth century, a similar process of self-definition was taking place in what was soon to be called the Sunni community. The evolving Sunni consensus centered on the study of the Qur'an and Hadith and the developing system of *fiqh,* or the inferences and precedents of Islamic law. The latter was used most often in matters of personal or family status, such as marriages, divorces, and inheritance. The creation of Sunni law was the work of a professional elite of religious scholars and professors of law and theology, but the legal system also developed as a result of strong Abbasid support. Nevertheless, just as Shiism had developed splits in religious interpretation and political alignments, so too, at times, did Sunnism.

One of the largest differences between Muslims as a whole concerned the path to salvation. In Sunni Islam, in particular, this took two forms: a literal and prescriptive reading of the Qur'an and sunna, which led to the formulation of the principles of Islamic law, or sharia; and a mystical, transcendent, deeply individual interpretation of Islam's holy book called Sufism. From the dawn of Islam, there were two types of men: those who read the Qur'an and Hadith in order to draw out from them an orderly, rational, legal structure and those who read the Qur'an in order to grasp its immediacy and power. The first, the *ulama,* became the leaders of the Sunni religious community; the second, the mystics, were the traveling men of God who searched for an experience of the divine that was not bound by cold, formal logic. The mystics, or *sufis,* in Arabic, believed that they could experience a direct union with God through the pursuit of rigid self-discipline, poverty, spirituality, and the renunciation of human desire, and that, rather than subscribe to the literal meaning of the Qur'an, the true Sufi could arrive at a deeper, more allegorical meaning of God's unity through a closer and more emotive reading.

By the early 10th century, Sufi brotherhoods were beginning to initiate followers in the way, or *tariqa,* by which they could directly experience God's Oneness. The late scholar Albert Hourani continues with the story:

> There was a process of initiation into an order: the taking of an oath of allegiance to the shaykh, the receiving from him of a special cloak, the communication by him of a secret prayer . . . the central act of the tariqa and the characteristic that marked it off from others [was] the dhikr or repetition of the name of God, with the intention of turning the soul away from all the distractions of the world and freeing it for the flight towards union with Him (Hourani 1991, 154–155).

However, after some time, Sufism, with its more esoteric knowledge of the divine, began to create enemies among the more orthodox Sunni scholarly establishment, and a serious rift developed between the *ulama* and the mystics of Islam. This rift was only resolved by the great Islamic scholar al-Ghazali (1058–1111), whose synthesis of Islamic learning won over both the Abbasid ruler of the time and the more disaffected scholarly circles in the empire. In various texts, al-Ghazali set out his treatise that "Muslims should observe the laws derived from the Will of God as expressed in Quran and Hadith . . . to abandon them was to be lost in a world of undirected human will and speculation" (Hourani 1991, 168).

The Islamic Sciences and the Translation Movement

Unlike scientific inquiry in the West, what fell under the rubric of the Islamic sciences (alchemy, astronomy, mathematics, medicine, and so on) grew out of a religious outlook and was not "secularized" until the 19th century. From the very first, scientific investigation was permeated by the ideas of God, nature, and the universe. The essential doctrine of unity—that there is no God but God, and Muhammad is his Messenger—allowed Muslims to conceive of all creation as God given so that any endeavor to understand the principles of the natural world was to be, first and foremost, an exercise in understanding the beliefs and directives of Islam. For instance, astronomy became a key subject under the Abbasids because the marvels of the universe occupied much of the Qur'an. Meanwhile, geography originally grew out of the Qur'anic concentration on nature. Finally, because of the attentiveness given in Islam to studying the unity of humans and their surroundings, the Islamic sciences were, by their very nature, comprehensive and meant to embody universal lessons, useful primarily because they reconciled religion with the world. As a result of this philosophy of knowledge, the Arab scientist's greatest aim was to be a generalist in all things; in the larger sense of the term, this meant that while he may have been best known for his pioneering studies in astronomy or medicine, he could also combine the specialties of music, literature, and mathematics. Much like the famous universalists of the 14th-century European Renaissance, who were directly influenced by Arab-Muslim translations of Greek philosophy and science, the Muslim scholar in Abbasid times aspired to be well versed in every type of cultural and intellectual discipline.

From the ninth to 13th centuries, the Abbasids and their successors patronized a scientific and literary movement that had few parallels in history. The genuine scientific interest of some of the reigning caliphs in Baghdad as well as the independent inquiry of a number of brilliant scholars in the city and throughout the empire, coalesced in a vast translation movement that created the momentum for further research and discovery. In the early ninth century, the caliph al-Mamun established the research university Bayt al-Hikma (House of Wisdom) in Baghdad, which spurred on the translation of many Greek, Sanskrit, and Old Persian manuscripts into the Arabic language. Bayt al-Hikma's library was only one of the 36 libraries built in Baghdad; much later on, the library at the famous al-Mustansiriya University (dating from around 1227) was to grow to include 80,000 books. Meanwhile, schools of astronomy and medicine were founded; and teaching hospitals such as the Bamiristan al-Adadi in west Baghdad were instituted. There, a cadre of doctors watched over a stream of patients and compiled meticulous records, which, in the case of the celebrated physician Abu Bakr al-Razi (d. 932) served as invaluable research for his world-famous medical encyclopedia, *al-Hawi* (Inati 2004, 39). Some of these great universities, including the Mustansiriya and al-Nizamiyya (11th century) in Baghdad, were created decades before European institutes of higher learning were even thought of.

Among scholars of Baghdad, the great Arab philosopher, mathematician, astronomer, and musical theorist al-Kindi (d. 873) was employed by al-Mutasim and tutored the caliph's son. Because astronomy was much in favor at the caliph's court, Baghdad was the seat of numerous observatories, the most famous of which was built by al-Mamun. Al-Khwarizmi (d. 847) concerned himself with the study of "celestial

This 13th-century miniature by Maqama of Hadjr-al-Yamana, located at the Institute of Oriental Studies in St. Petersburg, Russia, depicts a physician drawing blood. Islamic science first blossomed under the Abbasids. (Erich Lessing/Art Resource, NY)

objects" (Inati 2004, 40), pioneering the use of the astrolabe, an instrument designed to measure the positions of the stars in the sky. Other great names in Islamic philosophy such as al-Farabi (873–950), who wrote *al-Madina al-Fadila* (*The Ideas of the Citizens of the Virtuous City*), and Ibn Sina (known as Avicenna in the West; 980–1037), came from afar to make Baghdad their second home. Ibn Sina's thinking, in particular, exerted great influence on Islamic culture.

Abbasid culture and science was the result of a multicultural society. For instance, the Christian contributions to Islamic science have been noted in different ways. On one level, a steady stream of Christian philosophers and scientists made an active contribution to world culture by translating Greek texts into Arabic, and under Abbasid patrons such as Caliph al-Mamun in Baghdad, they wrote a great many medical and technical compilations of their own. On the other, in monastic communities in eighth-century Abbasid-era Palestine, monks began writing ecclesiastical histories, not in Syriac or Aramaic, languages of the Bible, but in Arabic. It may well be that the use of Arabic was a conscious decision on the part of the monastic translation movement to spread its liturgical and theological principles to regions distant from Palestine-Syria (Griffith 1999, 25–28). Whatever the reason, Syriac scholar Sidney Griffith has shown that even the strictest Christian authors were so immersed in Arab culture that they had a tendency to use the Arabic of the Qur'an in their general correspondence.

Samarra and the Creation of a Turkish Army

The death of al-Mamun in Tarsus and the accession to the caliphate of his half brother, al-Mutasim (r. ca. 834–847), marked a change in attitude between the caliph and his subjects, particularly the citizens of Baghdad, that is signified by the building of Samarra. The traditional explanation for the creation of Samarra is that al-Mutasim, whose own mother was a Turk, felt uncomfortable in Baghdad. Both he and his Turkish troops were seen as unwelcome in that city, having been dominated for so long by his more forceful half brother, al-Mamun. Whatever the reasons—and they must have been many to leave a capital city so well entrenched in Abbasid tradition—al-Mutasim decided to move out of Baghdad (which remained the cultural and commercial capital) into a newly established city further north, called Samarra. Samarra's name is usually seen as a play on the Arabic words *surra ma raa* (pleased is he who sees it), and al-Mutasim's city fulfilled that expectation very well. It was extremely large, spectacular in terms of architectural design, and took several decades to complete (Robinson 2001, 9–20). The building of the city drew on exorbitant sums from the Abbasid treasury, but it was to last as a breakaway capital only until 892, somewhat less than 60 years. Still, its very establishment was indicative of important trends that were to manifest themselves throughout the century.

The first trend had to do with the so-called Turkish component of the new governing and military elite. The introduction of Turkic-speaking tribes from Central Asia into the armies of the Islamic caliphate is recognized as having begun with the early Umayyad period; Turkish soldiers were fairly prominent in al-Mamun's reign, but it was only in the later Abbasid era that those nomadic tribesmen became a central factor in the empire as a whole. However, as historian Matthew Gordon has noted, the somewhat one-dimensional term *Turk* does not begin to do justice to the complexity and nuances of their objective reality (Gordon in Robinson 2001, 123). There were at least three different groups under that term: a small elite of Turkish families originally from Khurasan (eastern Iran, and the original source of Abbasid influence); Turkish slaves from Central Asia who were bought from families residing in Baghdad; and Turks bought in Central Asia proper. Most of those Turks became Muslim. Eventually, it was the Central Asian Turks who made up the bulk of al-Mutasim's troops, while the first two groups made up the military and administrative command and were partly compensated by land grants in and around Samarra, as well as in outlying provinces.

The Abbasid caliph's relationship with the Turks was not always ideal; in fact, one of al-Mutasim's successors, Caliph al-Mutawakkil (r. 847–861), was murdered by his Turkish generals in 861, and the Samarran episode was frequently marred by friction between the Abbasid family and the various military regiments in the city. The turmoil in the city grew into anarchy from 861 to 870 when most of Samarra's Turkish commanders were murdered by a mob composed of formerly loyal troops. The city nearly fell apart under the hammer blows of the subsequent Turkish insurrectionary movement. Finally, a general economic decline, including less income from trade and agriculture in the empire as a whole, and military-political entanglements forced a return of the caliphate to Baghdad in 892.

The second and perhaps more important trend had to do with the very real divisions in the Abbasid Empire that no new capital could paper over. Various administrative changes had crippled the power of the central government to function properly. Essentially, the changes led to factionalism within the bureaucracy, because many of the high-level bureaucrats treated their departments as personal fiefdoms to serve their personal gain. In this, they were assisted by their staffs, which mostly consisted of family, close friends, and followers. The factionalism extended to the military as well. As noted above, al-Mutasim's initial move to Samarra is sometimes attributed to his desire to shield both himself and his troops from local jealousies and intrigue in Baghdad. Whatever the real reasons for Samarra's inception, its demise reflects the same set of circumstances that led to caliphal flight from Baghdad in the first place. The Turkish commanders, grown from loyal servitors to near competitors of the caliphs, wrested influence away from the nominal rulers at times and murdered a number of them. Although they were never able to make themselves complete masters of the Islamic empire, their violent overthrow of the titular authority as well as the factional fighting that ensued as a result of intra-Turkish struggles led to a chaotic period lasting about a decade, that further sapped the Abbasid Empire's power. Notwithstanding the restoration of Abbasid authority in 870 under the generalship of al-Muwaffaq, the empire's fortunes never really improved after the caliphate's return to Baghdad.

A Populist Revolt: The Zanj Movement

Al-Muwaffaq was the brother of al-Mutamid who had become caliph in 870, but for all intents and purposes, al-Muwaffaq was the real power behind the throne. Although he never became caliph himself, his stout defense of the empire eventually allowed his son al-Mutadid (r. 892–902) to become ruler. Al-Muwaffaq's resolve was put to the test in the 870s and early 880s by the formidable Zanj insurrection in Basra, southern Iraq, and he has largely gone down in history as the commander that broke the back of that revolt in 883.

In southern Iraq, slaves from East Africa had been brought to work in the clearing of salt pans in the lower Shatt al-Arab region. Those plantation slaves came to be known as the Zanj. Their miserable conditions were such that they attracted the attention of a charismatic leader, Ali ibn Muhammad, virtually unknown before the Zanj revolt but identified later on as an Arab brought up in Iran and a self-described descendant of the imam Ali ibn Abu Talib. By virtue of his Shia origins, his religious ideology incorporated both Shii and Khariji symbols, even though his main claims to leadership of the revolt rested on racial equality and the fair distribution of wealth.

Arab historians of the period see the Zanj revolt as highly significant because it was no ordinary rebellion. Begun in 869, it lasted almost 15 years, and at the high point of their insurrection, the Zanj reportedly had built up an army, a navy, and six well-established towns, the most important of which was al-Mukhtara. One of the most interesting aspects of the Zanj revolt was the diversity of its base; the Zanj were supported by Shii Arabs, *mawalis,* semi-settled tribesmen, as well as local peasants and African troops who deserted the caliph's army. More important still is the composition of the leadership; the controversial Ali ibn Muhammad is thought to have been joined at various stages of the rebellion by East African as well as Arab merchants from the Gulf whose interests in protecting long-distance trade must have intersected with his.

Distracted by numerous revolts in the larger empire, the Abbasids were not to confront seriously Ali ibn Muhammad until 10 years after the initial Zanj revolt in 869. In the intervening decade, the revolt not only succeeded in freeing the slaves but in 872, inflicted a major military defeat on the caliph's troops led by al-Muwaffaq himself. Prior to the full-fledged Abbasid attack on the Zanj, the government had imposed an outrageous 20 percent tax on imports into the empire, which threatened to bankrupt merchants throughout the Abbasid realm; the permutations of that hasty decision roiled long-distance trade and affected the empire's economic base, contributing perhaps to the government's inability to confront the rebellion militarily. However, the increase in taxation on Abbasid merchants could also have been a ploy by the government to break the trade monopolies imposed by southern merchants who used Basra, the Zanj base, as a shipment point for goods coming from various areas of the empire. Once the Abbasids began a full-blown military campaign against the Zanj, they fought pitched battles with Ali ibn Muhammad's troops; despite the offers of amnesties, Ali ibn Muhammad continued fighting. In 883, al-Muwaf-faq, with Egyptian assistance, finally crushed the Zanj rebellion and brought back Ali ibn Muhammad's head to Baghdad in triumph. Many of the former slaves who accepted amnesty were incorporated (or in some cases reincorporated) into the caliph's army to fight their former comrades and thus spared execution.

The Zanj revolt has inspired numerous present-day writers to frame the episode in political, economic, and social terms. Marxist writers tend to view it as a movement for egalitarianism and social justice. Others see it as a purely economic revolt, with Ali ibn Muhammad replacing the Abbasids as master of the plantation, eager to control the trade and agricultural revenues made possible by African slave labor. Still others see it in racial terms, as an all-African movement for eman-cipation. Whatever its actual nature, it is important to realize that at its outset, the Zanj revolt inspired the widespread defection of African troops in the Abbasid army, surely as emblematic a move as any in soli-darity with the enslaved Africans in southern Iraq.

The Breakup of the Abbasid Empire and the Eclipse of the Caliphate

By the middle of the 10th century, popular revolts, economic decline, and sheer imperial inertia had begun to make vast inroads in the empire's fabric. Sectarian divisions on the part of the Shia and the Ismailis, both rival claimants to Muslim legitimacy, instigated empire-wide resistance that was put down only with great difficulty. To make matters worse, various caliphs took to depleting the central treasury through luxurious living and disregarded investment in irrigation agriculture, the mainstay of Iraq's prosperity, bringing about depopulation, excessive salination of farmlands, and widespread poverty. Once the most prosperous of Middle Eastern regions, Iraq now became a backwater and easy prey for outsiders.

In 945, the Buyids (Buwayhids), a Shii dynasty under the leadership of Muizz al-Dawla (r. 945–967), established a military regime in Iraq and Iran. From the time of the Buyid occupation of Baghdad until its sack by the Mongols in 1258, the Abbasid caliphate was transformed into a ceremonial post. Under the Buyids, Shiism emerged in the open, because it was afforded protection by the rulers of the moment. It is then that Shii hadith, or the orally transmitted traditions of Imam Ali and the later imams, were collected and began to form the body of Shii law. The two most important scholars associated with the compilation of law are al-Kulayni (d. 925) and al-Tusi (d. 1067).

After this Shii interregnum, the Seljuk Turks, fresh from their conquest of Iran, invaded Iraq and defeated the Buyid dynasty in 1055. There is some indication that the Seljuks had been invited to take over Baghdad by the much weakened Abbasid caliph, al-Qaim bi-Amr-Allah (r. 1031–75), whose more pressing concern was whether to offer resistance to a more immediate enemy, the commander of the Turkish troops in Baghdad, al-Basasiri. The latter, it was suspected, was not only ready to crush the Abbasid dynasty altogether but to take over the capital in the name of the Fatimid rulers of Egypt, who followed the esoteric Ismaili sect, which was total anathema to the Sunni caliph. As a result, when the Seljuk sultan Tughrul Bey and his army entered Baghdad, they were welcomed as saviors, and Tughrul's name was immediately associated with the caliph's in the Friday prayers, the ultimate recognition of leadership in the Islamic world. The caliph's gratitude was such that he married Tughrul's niece. And when Sultan Tughrul finally defeated and killed al-Basasiri in 1059, the caliph's cup overflowed with such appreciation that he

Late-Abbasid-era tomb of Zumurrud Khatun (ca. 1193), wife of Caliph al-Rashid and mother of Caliph al-Nasr, located in Baghdad's al-Karkh neighborhood (Library of Congress)

awarded the Seljuk leader the title of "Sultan of the East and the West" (Hassanein 1983, 48–50).

The Seljuks spoke a variation of the Turkish language and were nomadic troops that had arrived from the Central Asian steppes. Originally pagan, they became Muslim upon entering the Islamic Middle East, following the Sunni path of the caliph. They thus shored up the dwindling fortunes of the Sunni caliphate, once deemed under threat in the Shii Buyid era. The Seljuks were also the first to take on the title of sultan for their leaders, which derives from the Arabic word, *sulta*, or "power," and connotes a more secular vision of authority than that associated with the caliph, whose influence was, in theory, more spiritual than worldly. Adopting the Buyid model of allowing the caliph to remain the titular sovereign of Iraq, Tughrul Bey was careful not to intrude in the caliph's religious domain, but he allowed himself a free hand in the administration of Iraq's revenues, going so far as to expropriate the caliph's private lands. Tughrul Bey was followed in Iraq by a number of strong rulers, one of whom, Malikshah, set new standards for the courtly patronage of all aspects of learning in Baghdad by establishing universities and theological schools.

Under the Seljuks Iran-Afghanistan, Iraq, Armenia, and Anatolia were ruled by one Sunni Muslim Turkic dynasty. The Seljuk sultanate continued as a unified polity until 1157 when, after the death of the Sultan Ahmad Sanjar, the Seljuk territories broke up into several lesser states. Finally, the Ilkhanid Mongols invaded and took over the Middle East, bringing Seljuk rule to an end. The sack of Baghdad in 1258 by the Mongols opens up a completely different episode in the history of medieval Iraq. With the death of the last Abbasid caliph, the tottering Islamic realm of which he had been titular head, collapsed. The Mongols shifted trade back to Asia, and Baghdad and its dependencies fell into rack and ruin, its inhabitants having only incorporated into the Mongol world empire through the sword. The once magnificent Abbasid courts in Baghdad and Samarra, the propagation of an Islamic ideology that tied one corner of the diverse empire to another, the vast trade links with China and Europe, and the well-oiled administrative machinery of state had begun to falter. Under the Mongol and Timurid impact, all those varied features of the Abbasid experience failed at one point or another and were only partially resurrected by the advent of Turkic tribal states in the 13th and 14th centuries.

Conclusion

Prior to its complete destruction by the Mongols, Baghdad, the capital of the Abbasid Empire, was above all, an Islamic city, but it was a city that was thronged by native-born Jews and Christians, Persians, Indians, Greeks, and people from Central Asia. Abbasid culture and science, therefore, were not the monopoly of one or two religious or sectarian or ethnic groups; they literally were the contribution of a pluralistic, polyglot, and even international culture. That, then, is the true Abbasid contribution to history; a city and, at times, an empire that spoke in different tongues and believed in distinctive creeds but ultimately worked for and shared in the ideals of Islamic universalism.

For centuries after the sack of Baghdad, the lure of the city lived on in the memories of men. There is an interesting postscript to the destruction of Baghdad at the hands of Hulegu Khan (1217–65), the Mongol conqueror, and grandson of Genghis (Chinggis) Khan. It is related that Hulegu pondered long and hard before he took the decision to conquer Baghdad and that he asked for advice from both his astrologers and his chief minister, Nasir al-Din Tusi, as to whether he should enter the city. Hulegu's astrologers warned him it was not a propitious time to capture Baghdad, on the grounds that the city had been built by a caliph and given the symbolic name of the City of Peace and that it had been foretold that no Abbasid caliph would die there. Tusi, on the other hand, encouraged his master to override the concerns of his astrologers and to forge ahead in his plans. After the horrific onslaught on Baghdad had begun and the last Abbasid caliph was killed, it was revealed that Tusi had agreed with Hulegu to rescue 400,000 scientific manuscripts (for the most part, relating to astronomy) prior to the pillage and to store them in an Islamic observatory in the city of Maragha, in northwest Iran. Tusi then brought together under his auspices the best team of astronomers of the period and commanded them to initiate an exhaustive research project on Islamic astronomy. His hidden agenda, it is claimed, was to create an alternative to the still important tradition of Greek astronomy. Eventually, two of the mathematical theorems produced by Tusi's scientists "made their way into the works of Copernicus, the father of European Renaissance astronomy, and by extension [into] modern science" (Saliba 2003, 111). Thus did Abbasid science live on to serve the exalted aims of its very own destroyers.

5

TURKISH TRIBAL MIGRATIONS AND THE EARLY OTTOMAN STATE (1256–1638)

The era from the end of the 11th century onward was character-ized by the relentless expansion of Turkish-Mongol tribal move-ments from inner Asia that crossed the Oxus River, steadily moving westward, bringing in their wake military onslaughts on settled society, political upheavals, and brief eras of stability and prosperity under Turco-Mongol regimes. Close to a century after the 1258 Mongol attack against Abbasid Baghdad, a tribal chieftain by the name of Osman rose to power in Anatolia (sometimes called Asia Minor by European writers) and eventually consolidated his hold on the Turkish frontier state that was later to bear his name, an event that was to have wide repercussions on both the Middle East and the West. That frontier state, headed by a *ghazi*, or Muslim warrior battling for the faith, was to meta-morphose into the longest-lived, as well as one of the most complex, states the Islamic world had ever seen—the Ottoman Empire. Built on the fringes of the crumbling Byzantine Empire at the very end of the 13th century, the expanding Ottoman polity eventually spread out from Anatolia into Europe and the Arab-Islamic region. In Iran, however, the sultan of the Ottoman Empire encountered stiff resistance to both his imperial and ideological objectives by the Safavids. Eventually, the Ottoman-Safavid rivalry developed into military, political, and religious clashes that extended over several centuries. In that rivalry, Iraq was a central prize. Long after the Ottomans wrested Baghdad from the Safavids in 1638, the Ottoman Empire's frontiers to the east remained those maintained and defended in Iraq.

The Coming of the Mongols

There is probably no single event, in the early medieval period at least, that has consumed Islamic historians and litterateurs more than the sack of Baghdad by Hulegu Khan (1217–65) and his Mongol armies. It has gone down in the history books as the epitome of the clash between high civilization and barbarity, an episode so horrific that it dwarfs all the pillage and mayhem that followed in succeeding generations. But to read the laments of 13th-century historians is to understand only one part of the Mongols' history, albeit the most notorious part. Like all peoples with a recorded past (even if that past was sometimes outrageously fabricated by their enemies), the Mongols had a known history. Earlier scholars and students of the Mongol period usually identified them as nomadic pastoralist groups with a common ethnic or linguistic origin. However, while the Mongols associated with the redoubtable Genghis Khan (ca. 1162–1227) eventually did begin to speak a form of Turkish (descending from the Altaic language group, with an alphabet based on the Uighur script) and adhered to clans descended from a common ancestor, they were not monolingual, nor did they base themselves on a single culture. In fact, the Mongols, like other steppe peoples, were linked by many things, including geography, tribal ties, or political loyalty to a khan, or leader.

Painting of Mongol leader Genghis Khan. At its peak, the Mongol Empire spread from China to Europe. (Courtesy of the National Palace Museum, Taipei)

One of a long line of nomadic pastoralist groups that arose in the steppes of inner Asia, and along the northern and eastern borders of Central Asia, the Mongols, just like other Turkish-speaking nomads before them, conquered (and sometimes destroyed) established states in the Islamic world, only to become pillars of the state in the end. Originally a confederation of tribal horsemen from Central Asia united and led by the formidable warrior Genghis Khan, the Mongol Empire was eventually to conquer most of the known world, bringing, within a few decades, all of Eurasia from central Europe to the Pacific under its rule (Lapidus 1988, 276).

The Mongol invasion of Iraq and Iran did not arise without warning; it had been in the making for several decades. Inspired by dreams of world conquest, Genghis Khan began a march into China as early as 1206; his successes there encouraged even greater military campaigns farther south. Beginning with campaigns against the great Central Asian markets and intellectual capitals of Bukhara—Samarqand, Balkh, and Khiva (1219–21)—the Mongol armies next devastated the Oxus River region—laying waste to Nesa, Herat, and Hamadan—and finally began their military offensive against the Khwarizm shahs, who were rulers on the borders of present-day Iran and Afghanistan. News of Mongol atrocities stunned the Irano-Islamic world; many leaders, fearing for themselves and their subjects, strove to make peace with the new conquerors, only to be killed at their hands and their capitals razed to the ground. At the high point of the Mongol conquest, Genghis died, reportedly leaving close to 100 sons and grandsons. His empire divided into four regions, each ruled by a son of the khan, who often squabbled with one another. It was left up to Hulegu, one of Genghis's grandsons, to oversee the sack of Baghdad, just as earlier Mongol armies had laid waste to Iran and Transoxiana.

Besieging Baghdad in 1258 with a huge army, composed chiefly of Mongols but also of Christians from Georgia and Armenia, Hulegu pressured the last Abbasid caliph to negotiate or surrender altogether. When close to 3,000 of Baghdad's notables finally met with the khan to discuss ways of ending the conflict, they were murdered. Baghdad was now open to the conquering armies. Hulegu Khan's onslaught on Baghdad brought about the end of the 500-year Abbasid caliphate, the last ruler of which was savagely trampled to death under the hooves of Mongol horses.

But it is the descriptions of Baghdad after the Mongol invasion that have stayed with us down through the centuries, especially the wanton cruelty of the invaders and the appalling loss of life in the city as well as its environs if one considers, for example, the claims of the late 12th- early 13th-century Muslim historian Ibn al-Athir, who noted that it was Mongol practice to slaughter men, women, and children ruthlessly, even ripping up the abdomens of pregnant women. As to the sack of Baghdad, another historian, Ibn Kathir, claims that after the Mongol onslaught on the Abbasid capital, dead bodies were piled in the streets in heaps, "as high as a ridge." After it rained, the corpses decomposed, their stench filling the air, resulting in a huge epidemic that spread as far away as Syria. Baghdad's great libraries, universities, and observatories

Depiction of the siege of Baghdad in 1258 by the Mongols, led by Hulegu, grandson of
Genghis Khan, which ended the Abbasid caliphate (Courtesy Staatsbibliothek zu Berlin—
Preussischer Kulturbesitz Orientabteilung)

were pillaged, their holdings burned or, as legend had it, thrown in the
river (Elbendary 2003). Altogether, it is speculated by the Indo-Persian
historian Juzjani that up to 800,000 people were killed as a result of the
Mongol sack of Baghdad (Saunders 1971, 231).

QUESTIONS CONCERNING THE SACK OF BAGHDAD

Historians continue to debate the particulars surrounding the siege and subsequent sack of Baghdad by Mongol forces in 1258. The Mongol invasion accelerated what had been a gradual decline of the Abbasid capital. Not until the 20th century would Baghdad reemerge as an important center in the Middle East. By the time of the Mongol invasion, the power of the Abbasid caliphate had been greatly reduced by prior invasion, internal strife, crop failure, and famine. Yet Baghdad, like Babylon in the days of Alexander, was seen as the center of culture. Some historians argue that prior to the Mongol siege, the great khan Mongke had ordered the caliphate be spared if it submitted to Mongol authority. But historian J. J. Saunders contends that "the continued existence of a sovereign like the Caliph, who claimed a vague authority over millions, was an affront to [the Mongol sky-god] Tengri and the Great Khan, who brooked no rival on earth" (Saunders 1971, 109). In either case, historians agree on the caliph's arrogance and his lack of preparation for the defense of the city.

Lastly, there is some argument over the amount of destruction. That it was great, and that the loss of life was uncountable has never been debated. That the Mongols destroyed the canal system is not debatable either, but there is contention that toward the end of their reign, the Abbasids had not kept the canals in good working order. Also, it is argued that Baghdad's agriculture continued to suffer in the wake of the destruction because of soil salination.

Contrary to Islamic historians of the time, modern-day historians tend to downplay the devastation engendered by the Mongols. A leading scholar on the Mongols, Wilhelm Barthold, drily observed that, "the results of the Mongol invasions were less annihilating than is supposed" (quoted in Saunders 1971, 6). However, even though the figures for casualties may have been inflated by local historians, there is ample proof for Mongol havoc in other sectors of Iraq's society. In addition to the great loss of life as a direct result of the military conquest, the city population contracted in no small part because of the ruin of its urban infrastructure, as a result of which many parts of the city became near desert. Iraq's great irrigation system was smashed. Channels that had been dug to bring water to the city fell into disrepair, agriculture declined, and people left once prosperous city quarters to move closer to the Tigris River, where they could more easily fetch water. Habitation became confined, for the most part, to the eastern part of the capital, where sanctuary was more abundant. Iraqis were left to forage for food and water as best they could, their world shattered, their faith sorely tested (Rauf 2002, 57–67). Interestingly, the legend of the murderous Mongol persists until today and has so infiltrated popular memory that even nowadays, ordinary Arabs and Muslims use it as a yardstick with which to measure all present-day massacres and catastrophes. Rightly or wrongly, the U.S. invasion and occupation of Baghdad in April 2003, which gave rise to days of looting and pillage of museums, libraries, and government ministries by angry mobs, has been compared to the destruction of Baghdad under Hulegu the Mongol (Hanley 2003).

Pax Mongolica and Trade

Janet Abu Lughod has argued that the 13th century witnessed the rise and eventual demise of a world system based on transcontinental trade (Abu-Lughod 1989, 3–40). The middle passage consisted of "the three routes to the east," namely the northern route passing from Constantinople (later Istanbul) to Central Asia; the central route connecting the Mediterranean with the Indian Ocean by means of Baghdad, Basra, and the Gulf; and the southern route, tying Cairo and Alexandria to the Red Sea, Arabian Sea, and Indian Ocean. The northern passage became the monopoly of the Mongols and, later on, the Turkish dynasties that arose in their wake.

According to Abu Lughod, "[T]he thirteenth century Mongols offered neither strategic crossroads location, unique industrial productive capacity, nor transport functions to the world economy. Rather, their contribution was to create an environment that facilitated land transit with less risk and lower protective rent" (Abu Lughod 1989, 154). The Mongol genius lay in transforming the barren and inhospitable wastes of Central Asia into a central trade thoroughfare by means of the construction of caravansaries (traveler resthouses), warehouses for merchants' goods, and armed frontier posts, which greatly contributed to the overall security of the region. Moreover, "protection" costs, which entailed paying tribes or transport agents a fluctuating rate so as to travel in relative security, were reduced under Mongol administrations. Because the Mongol Empire was unified under one overarching family system over a large expanse of territory, and because it provided a climate favorable to long-distance trade, the northern route attracted traders from Iran, India, Anatolia, and, eventually, Genoa. In fact, as a result of European-led voyages of exploration into China (Marco Polo's voyage to Cathay in 1260–71 comes to mind), Europeans began to learn of these mysterious people and to engage with them in a commercial as well as cultural spirit. The great caravan meeting point was Samarqand, in Central Asia, where traders from India met those coming from the Islamic lands. The prized commodity that attracted them all was silk. Chinese silk was so important that it trumped Iranian silk in Western markets, even though Iran was closer to home and, from an overall perspective, less unwelcoming terrain than the large expanse of the Mongol Empire.

The Il-khanids and Timurids (1256–1405)

After the sack of Baghdad, the Il-khanate, a Mongol successor state, rose to govern both Iraq and Iran, as well as parts of Armenia, Anatolia, northern India, and Afghanistan. (The title of Il-khan referred to the state being subordinated to the great khan.) After having kept it at arm's length for the duration of a generation, the Il-khanid governors finally submitted to Islam and gave up on their fruitless campaign to promote Buddhism in the Irano-Islamic region. Under one of their ablest leaders, Ghazan (r. 1295–1304), the Il-khanids also began to repair the damage wrought by the Mongols' earlier depredations, rebuilding irrigation works, reconstructing cities, and opening trade. They made alliances with the local notability in the region and began to rely on former administrators for assistance in local government. As security returned, so did the revival of artistic influences and literary and scientific inquiry. The Chinese influence in art (especially pottery) became particularly important in this period. These influences included lotus and peony motifs and depictions of clouds and dragons. In addition, the writing of history became a critical and well-rewarded endeavor. For instance, an influential Mongol adviser, Ata Malik al-Juvaini (1226–83), who was the Farsi-speaking author of *The History of the World Conqueror* (which depicted the rise and rule of Genghis Khan), was employed as governor of Baghdad in 1260. Meanwhile, another famous historian, Rashid al-Din (1247–1318), wrote a compendia of historical works, using a variety of sources, including Chinese, Indian, European, Muslim, and Mongol (Lapidus 1988, 279).

The Il-khanids are best remembered for their trade policies, which made Tabriz (western Iran) one of the most important commercial

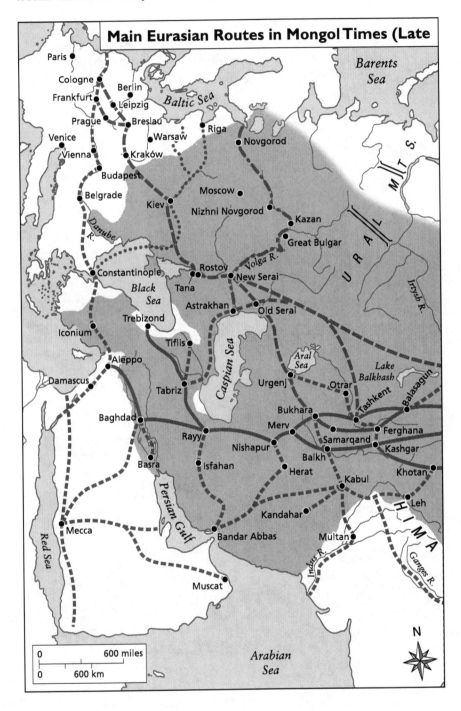

Main Eurasian Routes in Mongol Times (Late

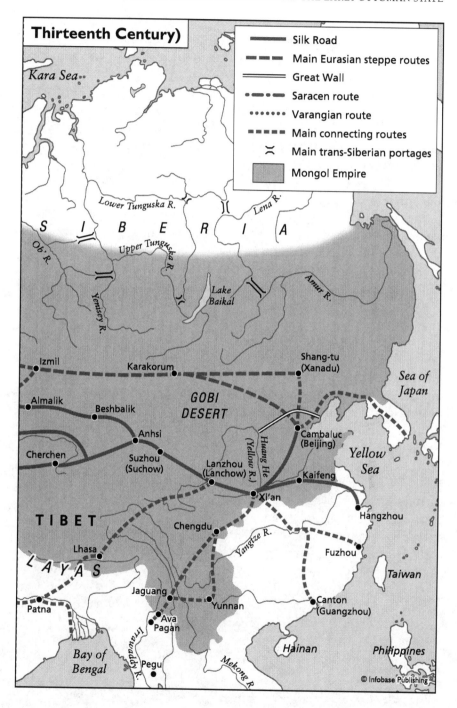

Thirteenth Century)

Silk Road
Main Eurasian steppe routes
Great Wall
Saracen route
Varangian route
Main connecting routes
Main trans-Siberian portages
Mongol Empire

Kara Sea

Lower Tunguska R.   Lena R.

S I B E R I A

Ob' R.

Upper Tunguska R.

Yenisey R.

Lake Baikal

Amur R.

Izmil   Karakorum   Shang-tu (Xanadu)

Sea of Japan

Almalik   Beshbalik   GOBI DESERT

Anhsi   Cambaluc (Beijing)

Cherchen   Suzhou (Suchow)   Huang He (Yellow R.)   Yellow Sea

Lanzhou (Lanchow)   Kaifeng

Xi'an

TIBET   Hangzhou

Chengdu

Lhasa   Yangtze R.   Fuzhou

LAYAS   Taiwan

Jaguang   Canton (Guangzhou)

Patna   Yunnan

Ava Pagan

Irrawaddy R.

Bay of Bengal   Pegu   Mekong R.   Hainan   Philippines

© Infobase Publishing

capitals of the 13th century. Benefiting from the Pax Mongolica instituted in the aftermath of the Mongol invasions, Tabriz became the
center of a trilateral trade network, between the Mediterranean Sea,
the Black Sea, and the Gulf and Arabia. Italian (Genoese and Venetian)
merchants were especially important in Tabriz, exchanging "European
cloth and linen for silk and other eastern wares" (Mathee 1991, 16).
The rise of this commercial center underlined the shift away from
Baghdad and Cairo and the growth of an alternate market in Anatolia
and the Black Sea ports.

In 1336, beset by internal problems and the fact that it was fighting on far too many fronts, the Il-khanid state, which had long
broken up into smaller states, saw its vast territories assimilated by
conquest into the growing empire of a Central Asian warrior from
the east, Tamerlane, (Timur; 1336–1405). Although he claimed the
mantle of Genghis Khan, Tamerlane was not, strictly speaking, a
descendant of the Mongol warlord but a Mongol only by marriage.
Nonetheless, he replicated the Mongol system to a fault by embark-
ing on a ferocious campaign of world conquest, invading and occupying Iran, northern India, Anatolia, and northern Syria. Like the
Mongols before him, he again swept into Iraq and destroyed a society
just beginning to recover from the wholesale onslaughts of Hulegu's
troops 98 years earlier. Unlike Hulegu, however, Tamerlane's empire
was strictly Muslim, although only formally so. The religious climate
at Tamerlane's court in Samarqand (now in Uzbekistan) was characterized by the overwhelming contribution of Islamic brotherhoods,
or *tariqas*, composed of Sufis (Muslim mystics), who were to wield
far more influence over the populace than the more orthodox, sharia-
inspired Muslim clergy.

While Tamerlane followed the Turco-Mongol practice of encouraging long-distance trade with friend and foe, even writing letters to
King Henry IV of England, inviting him to pursue commercial interests
with the Timurid Empire, his invasion of Anatolia and his capture of
the seaport of Izmir in 1402 dealt a death blow to Tabriz's fortunes
(Knobler 2001, 102–103). The trade of Asia, which had benefited from
Mongol protection and encouragement, now suffered as overland merchants, both Asian and European, deserted this newly insecure trade
route and focused on finding an alternative route to ship their goods.
At Tamerlane's death in 1405, just as he was reportedly on the point of
marching on China, the instability of the Timurid Empire had become
evident.

The Black Sheep and White Sheep Dynasties (1378–1508)

In the post-Timurid period, several Turkmen tribal federations divided up northern Iraq, Azerbaijan, and eastern Anatolia; among the most famous were the Ak Koyunlu (White Sheep) and the Kara Koyunlu (Black Sheep) dynasties. They fought over the pasturelands and farmlands of the region from 1378 to 1508. In an era in which legitimacy depended on a strong patron, intermarriage with Byzantine princesses cemented the Turkmens' hold on regional alliances, as did their canny leadership in times of war. One of the Ak Koyunlu commanders, Uzun Hassan (r. 1452–78), was even able to rally his tribal armies to capture Baghdad, southern Iraq, and eastern Iran, in the process creating a formidable threat to the Ottomans, who had by then grown from a small Turkish principality founded by Osman I (r. 1281–1326) to an empire centered on Constantinople, the former Byzantine capital. The Ottomans were intent on occupying those same districts conquered by Uzun Hassan, and by 1473, they were able to inflict a resounding defeat on the Ak Koyunlu tribes.

The Rise of Osman and the Genesis of the Ottoman Empire

Cemal Kafadar, a historian of the Ottoman Empire teaching at Harvard, begins his study of the early empire with these words: "Osman is to the Ottomans what Romulus is to the Romans, the eponymous founding figure of a remarkably successful political community in a land where he was not . . . one of the indigenous people" (Kafadar 1995, 1). In its broad outlines, Kafadar's statement is true, with the exception that Osman was not a mythical persona but very much a historic figure (a fact noted by Kafadar elsewhere in his book). Born in 1258, Osman was one of the many Turkish tribal leaders who settled in Bithynia (Anatolia), on the constantly fluctuating frontiers of the Byzantine Empire. His ancestors had arrived in the region in the second great mass migration of Turkish nomads from Central Asia. The region was then a fluid center of power, characterized by constantly shifting alliances between Turkish nomads, Armenian princes, crusading knights, and Byzantine generals. Drawn into the no-man's (or everyman's) land on the unstable Byzantine frontier, Turkish warriors skirmished and sometimes entered into military agreements with a host of adventurers and interlopers of every conceivable political, religious, and linguistic stripe. Before the arrival of the Ottomans as an organized political unit, two large Turkish tribal confederacies held sway: the family group that revolved around the legendary warrior Melik Danishmend and the Seljuks of Rum, a nomadic pastoralist cluster that eventually formed a state (*Rum* was yet another term used for the Byzantine, or Eastern Roman, Empire).

The *ghazi* state, of which Osman's was one, was not just a military formation but a militant one as well. And the militancy of that state rested upon its Islamic component, which itself was an amalgam of the shamanistic and spiritualist vestiges of a Turkic nomadic past with the holy war tradition in Islam. *Ghazis* were, for the most part, warrior Sufis who raided the lands of *dar al-harb* ("the abode of war," the name given by Muslims to non-Muslim districts), in the process opening up the Byzantine-Anatolian borderlands to Islam. It was the *ghazi* ethos that was to shape Ottoman societies from the very beginning, in its insistence on "a dynamic conquests policy, basic military structure and the predominance of the military class within an empire that successfully accommodated disparate religious, cultural and ethnic elements" (Inalcik and Quataert 1994, 11). Osman's state was only one of the many contending polities that struggled for ascendancy in that period, but his state-building venture was to outshine and outlast all the polities that had existed before. According to tradition, in 1299, Osman, taking advantage of a perceived power vacuum in Anatolia, declared his principality's independence from the Seljuk Turks, who, in any case, ruled the area for only eight more years. This tradition has it that Osman's declaration of independence is the beginning of the Ottoman Empire.

An exceptional commander and an even better administrator, Osman's chieftaincy became an enduring state only gradually. In 1326, just prior to Osman's death, the Ottomans, led by Osman's son Orhan, captured Bursa (located in what is now northwestern Turkey) from the Byzantine Empire and made it their capital. After Orhan (r. 1326–62) succeeded his father as *bey*, he named his brother Alaeddin as vizier, the ruler's most trusted adviser. In 1328, Orhan began a three-year siege of Nicaea (modern Iznik) that ended with that city's surrender in 1331. The capture of Nicomedia (modern Izmit) in 1337 and the defeat of the principality of Karasi placed all of northwestern Anatolia in Ottoman hands. Together Orhan, who was the first Ottoman to bear the title of sultan, and Alaeddin forged the basis of the empire. Instead of simply conquering and moving on as had many of their predecessors, the Ottomans worked to assimilate conquered territory into their (Anatolian) empire. This period of consolidation was aided by Ottoman-Byzantine peace for approximately 20 years and by the marriage of Orhan to Theodora,

The mausoleums of Osman I, for whom the Ottoman Empire was named, and his son Orhan at Bursa in northwestern Turkey (Library of Congress)

daughter of Byzantine emperor John VI Kantakouzenos (r. 1347–54), whom Orhan had assisted in gaining the throne.

Orhan was succeeded by his son Murad I (r. 1362–89). During Murad's reign, the Ottoman Empire, with the assistance of the *ghazi* warriors and using Gallipoli as a base, expanded into Byzantine territory, making vast inroads in northern Greece, Macedonia, and Bulgaria which bypassing Constantinople. Murad's administration of the conquered European territory differed from his father's Anatolian plan of assimilation but nevertheless proved successful, as the Ottomans maintained suzerainty over their European vassal states.

However, after these impressive gains of the Ottoman state in the Balkans and Anatolia, Bayezid (r. 1389–1402), Murad's successor, was defeated in 1402 at Ankara by Tamerlane, who then turned eastward to resume his conquest of India. His excursion into Anatolia was to restore the Turkish princes, including some Ottomans, to their thrones, thus dividing Anatolia and making it less likely to pose a threat on his own western flank. In this, Tamerlane was temporarily successful.

Under Murad II (r. 1421–44, 1446–51), the Ottomans took up their mission once more, expanding even farther into Europe by taking over Serbia and threatening the gates of Vienna. In the most spectacular coup of all, Constantinople, the Byzantine capital, fell to the troops of Mehmed II (known as "the Conqueror"; r. 1444–46, 1451–81) in 1453. Thereafter, it was named Istanbul and became the seat of the Porte, the administrative and political heart of the empire. In the words of Turkish scholar Halil Inalcik, "Mehmet the Conqueror was the true founder of the Ottoman Empire [because] he established an empire in Europe and Asia with its capital at Istanbul, which was to remain the nucleus of the Ottoman Empire for four centuries" (Inalcik 1973, 1995, 29).

After a century and a half of Ottoman expansion into eastern Europe, the new rulers next turned their attention to the Arab region and North Africa. But while they were able to sweep through the Mediterranean lands and North Africa with relative ease, they met obstacles in the East and finally had to come to grips with their most stubborn rivals, the Safavid dynasty in Iran. The Safavids, originally a mystic brotherhood that all but deified their ruler as a descendant of the House of the Prophet, were to stand in the way of total Ottoman control of the East. For more than four centuries, the enmity between the Ottomans and Safavids and their successor states remained a feature of the historic struggle between two competing strands of Islam and two loci of power. The struggle between the two great world empires invariably took its highest (or most violent) form in Bilad Wadi al-Rafidain (Mesopotamia, in Arabic).

The Emergence of the Safavid Empire (1501–1736)

Much like the White Sheep and Black Sheep dynasties of an earlier generation, the Turkmen tribes that had established dynasties in Anatolia and northern Iraq were zealously anti-Ottoman and *sufi* (mystic) in their beliefs. A member of the Turkmen Shaykhly dynasty from Ardabil (now in northwest Iran), one Ismail Safavi consolidated his hold on eastern Anatolia, Azerbaijan, and Iran in 1500 and prepared to do battle with the Ottomans to regain what he claimed to be the Turkmens' ancestral homeland, the whole of Anatolia. In 1501, Shah Ismail (r. 1501–24) ascended to the throne of Iran as the first ruler of the Safavid dynasty. Originally a mystic brotherhood called the Safawiyya, whose leadership believed in "a militant commitment to holy war and also a potent mix of Sufi and shamanistic doctrine" (Berkey 2003, 266), the order attracted thousands of fervent Turkmen supporters; distinguished by their red hats, they were accordingly called Kizilbash ("redhead,"

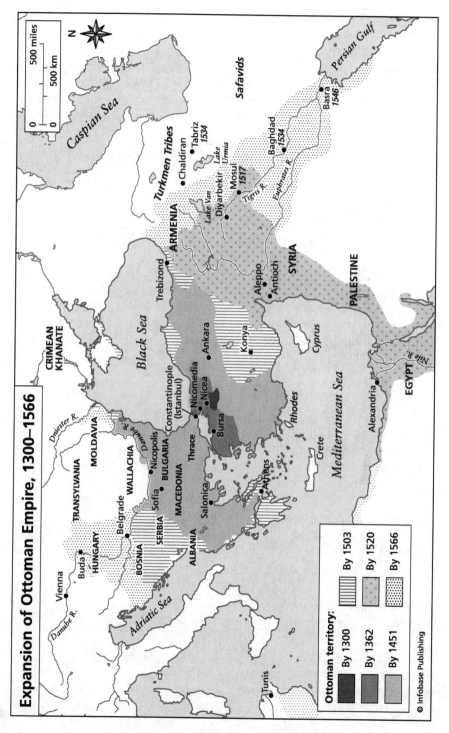

Expansion of Ottoman Empire, 1300–1566

© Infobase Publishing

in Turkish). The Kizilbash tribesmen retained their special status as devotees of the Safavid monarchy for a very long time, even though the latter began to recruit Georgian slave soldiers into their army some years later.

Very early on, Shah Ismail and his successors began an aggressive campaign to convert Iran's mostly Sunni population to Twelver Shiism, a transformation so radical that it may safely be considered as one of the foremost developments of the 16th century. The development had wide ramifications not only in Iran itself but throughout the Arab-Islamic world. However, contrary to the received wisdom that Iran's Shiism formed an impenetrable block against the Ottoman advance, there was far more interaction between the Safavid state and the surrounding region than envisaged by the older histories on the subject, especially where Safavid influence coincided with support of Shii communities in Iraq, Lebanon, Syria, and Anatolia (Cole 2002, 16–30). Yet in some periods of history, the establishment of a Shii state so close to Ottoman territories indeed posed a very great challenge.

To be sure, Sunni-Shia polemics contributed a great deal to the friction between the two "orthodoxies," the staunchly Sunni Ottomans and the unfalteringly Shii Safavids. As explained by the late Hamid Enayat, a scholar of Islamic political thought, those polemics have not changed for hundreds of years. The anti-Sunni polemics basically emerged out of the quarrel over the succession to the Prophet, which, over the centuries, had "[taken] on an increasingly scurrilous tone, and were eventually institutionalized into the practices of *sabb* (vilification) and *rafd* (repudiation of the legitimacy) of the first three Caliphs" (Enayat 1982, 33). The Shii persistence in cursing the first three Rashidun caliphs as well as Aisha, the wife of the Prophet, infuriated and still infuriates Sunnis. The Sunnis countered with anti-Shia polemics of their own. Basically set down by Ibn Taymiyyah, a 14th-century scholar, the Sunnis claim that the imamate cannot become a "pillar" of Islam, the idea of Ali's succession is illogical, and the doctrine of *ilm,* or special knowledge, which Imam Ali and his descendants are supposed to have been endowed with, is untenable (Enayat 1982, 34–37). The Ottomans reserved their most severe hostility for the Shii sects they deemed to be the most extreme, such as the Kizilbash. Frequent massacres of the latter were the result; Ottoman jurists even declared them beyond the pale and therefore expendable. As Juan Cole has shown, however, much of the Ottoman antagonism for the Kizilbash nomadic pastoralists stemmed from the Kizilbash's total and unswerving dedication to the Safavid shahs (Cole 2002, 18).

Ottoman Expansion in Iraq

By the first half of the 16th century, the Ottomans had begun their expansion in the Arab lands. Syria and Egypt fell in 1516, the Ottoman armies were perched to take over Basra in 1546, Yemen succumbed to Ottoman rule two years later, and Ottoman forces reached Morocco in the same period. Iraq was not conquered at once; in fact, the earlier campaigns focused on Mosul and Kurdistan, the latter, on Baghdad and Basra. Still, it is imperative to understand that what was conquered was not immediately integrated; for instance, the first Ottoman occupation of Baghdad was quickly followed by a countervailing Safavid attack, which in turn led to a second and more permanent Ottoman occupation. A similar development took place in Basra, where the Ottomans were able to wrest the province from nominal Portuguese control, only to have it hijacked later on by local tribal leaders. There was a constant back and forth between the Ottomans and Safavids in the first wave of conquests of the Iraqi provinces.

The Ottoman Incorporation of Mosul (Northern Iraq)

One of the first confrontations between the Ottomans and Safavids took place in 1514 at the epic battle at Chaldiran in eastern Turkey that ended in defeat for the Safavid shah Ismail. The Ottoman sultan Selim I (r. 1512–20) next marched against Safavid forces in Armenia and Azerbaijan. After several pitched battles against the troops of the shah, the Ottoman armies found themselves sweeping through northern Iraq in pursuit of their foe. Following the fall of Mardin and Diyarbakr (both in what is now southern Turkey) to the Ottomans, the al-Jazeera plain was now within easy reach. The al-Jazeera district was strategically important both for its linkages to southern Anatolia and central Iraq and because it contained the ancient city of Mosul, which had been the regional capital of Arab dynasts throughout the 11th and 12th centuries. Situated on the Euphrates River with direct access to Baghdad and Basra by water and the mountains and villages of Kurdistan by land, the city was an asset for any conqueror. Although it was undergoing a temporary eclipse in that period, Mosul's renown in medieval times still harked back to a more prosperous past that could be revitalized under the proper attention.

The Ottoman occupation of northern Iraq also resulted in assimilation of Shahrizor (Kurdistan), which, after Mosul, Baghdad, and Basra, became the fourth Ottoman provincial division of Iraq. Shahrizor was a district of rugged mountains; its Kurdish population was composed mostly of pastoral tribes that were sometimes forcibly led to settle down as agriculturists by the Ottomans. Shahrizor also formed part of a belt of Kurdish villages that demarcated the frontiers of Mosul Province, the most important town in northern Iraq (Khoury 1997, 32).

In theory, the administrative model followed at Mosul by the victorious Ottomans was to serve for the whole of Iraq, as indeed it had served for other newly conquered Ottoman provinces elsewhere in the empire. In practice, there was a wide divergence between how Mosul, Baghdad, and Basra were taxed and administered. For example, in northern Iraq, the sultan's political adviser, a Kurdish shaykh by the name of Idris al-Bidlisi, struck a deal with local tribal commanders in Mosul: They were to keep the Safavid army at bay in return for political and economic compensation. But it was only in 1534, under Sultan Suleyman's reign (r. 1520–66), that Mosul was recognized as sufficiently secure that a new Ottoman governor could be appointed over the city. It was then that the full panoply of Ottoman fiscal and administrative law was introduced in the city and its countryside. A system of land grants (*ziamets, timars,* and *khass*) was established in the city and its environs, which were contracted out to military commanders and local notables for the provision of troops and the organization of the administration and economy. Mosul was also restructured administratively, becoming the chief province (*eyalet*) responsible for all other administrative districts in the region; the province itself now stretched all the way to the Persian frontier (al-Jamil 1999, 46).

Mosul's commercial worth to the empire was gauged by its role as a granary for the provisioning of Ottoman troops. Dina Khoury notes as much, saying, "[F]or the city of Mosul, the Ottoman conquest marked the beginning of commercial prosperity" (Khoury 1991, 60). The city's population increased, new professional elites from neighboring districts migrated to Mosul as settlers, religious scholars were brought in by the Ottomans to preach Hanafi (Sunni) Islam, and customs dues rose, further proof of the development of an affluent lifestyle. This prosperity was to continue throughout the 16th and early part of the 17th centuries. Yet Mosul was never to become the large and dominant center that Baghdad was. In fact, its situation as one town among many, surrounded by an agricultural belt of villages, was only changed in the 17th century when "the Ottoman wars with the Safavids transformed Mosul and some of its hinterlands into supply centers for the armies of the region as well as a clearinghouse for the disbursement of funds for the fortresses of the region" (Khoury 1997, 25).

In most histories of early Ottoman Iraq, the separation between Mosul and the rest of the Iraqi provinces is overly accentuated. Because Mosul was not geographically part of Ard al-Sawad (the alluvial territories of south-central Iraq that went under the name of "the black earth" in Islamic historiography) but part of the northern strip of al-Jazeera, and because it remained rather more firmly tied to Ottoman control than other cities, it is sometimes considered to be a province apart and isolated from Baghdad, Basra, and the country in between. This impression is belied by the fact that Mosuli trade was firmly tied to southern Iraq and eastern Syria in the Ottoman period. In fact, relations between the three major urban centers of Iraq—Mosul, Baghdad, and Basra—were strengthened under Ottoman rule.

The Ottoman Incorporation of Baghdad (Central Iraq)

Although the conquest of Iraq was accomplished in 1534, stability and security eluded the Ottomans at first so that it was Baghdad's misfortune (and Mosul's and Basra's as well) to be subject to a shaky political climate from the early 16th century onward. After the first Ottoman occupation of the city (1534), there were 89 years of peace and then war broke out again, with Baghdad besieged and finally conquered by Safavid shah Abbas in 1624. The Iranians ruled the city until 1638, when a massive Ottoman force led by Sultan Murad IV (r. 1623–40) finally recaptured the city for good. In the years of the first Ottoman occupation and the Safavid interregnum, however, a number of developments took place in the city and its neighboring districts that merit a sustained study.

Sultan Suleyman the Lawgiver (also known as the Magnificent) entered Baghdad on December 31, 1534, defeating the Safavid contingent, whose commander fled upon the Ottomans' approach. Shaykh Mani ibn Mughamis of Basra (the son of the local ruler), plus other district shaykhs such as those of the al-Jazeer, al-Gharraf, al-Luristan, and al-Huwaiza, traveled to Baghdad to pledge their loyalty to the sultan and to demand succor from the Portuguese (Ozbaran 1994, 125). After praying at the main Sunni shrines in Baghdad, Suleyman set about reconstructing the physical infrastructure in the province. He is known to have ordered the construction of a dam in Karbala and major water projects in and around the city's countryside. But he is also known to have instigated attacks on Twelver Shia, considering them to be a fifth column and in the pay of the Safavids.

Meanwhile, in Baghdad, a new governor was appointed and the creation of a defense force for the town envisaged; it was to be composed

A miniature of Sultan Suleyman the Lawgiver (also known as Suleyman the Magnificent), ca. 1560; he defeated the Safavids in 1534, gaining Baghdad and, later, southern Iraq (Giraudon/Art Resource, NY)

of 1,000 foot soldiers and another 1,000 cavalry. More significantly, a new administrative law and taxation regime was instituted that differed from the *timar* system of land grants established in Mosul, in which an elite of *sipahis*, or cavalry officers, was made responsible both for the military and financial expenses of their district. In Baghdad (and Basra), a different system entailed salaries being paid out to the provincial governors, either from Istanbul or from the provinces themselves. The *beylerbeyi* (governor) of the city had to dispatch a fixed sum of money to Istanbul called the *irsaliye,* after deducting the military and administrative expenses of the province from its proceeds. Baghdad, like Basra, was sometimes called a *salyane* province (a province in which the governor received an annual salary). Interestingly, *salyane* provinces have usually been associated with difficult or obdurate provincial administrations or were provinces where sometimes neither the governor nor the notability was seen as completely loyal to the Ottomans.

A case in point is the story of the Baghdad governor, who was instrumental in inviting the Safavid occupation of Baghdad in 1623–24. It all started when the governor, a usurper called Bakr the Subashi ("police chief," in Ottoman Turkish), called for Shah Abbas's (r. 1588–1629) help in defeating a pro-Ottoman rival, an action that he would soon regret. Having finally reestablished control of Baghdad, the Safavid shah was not going to allow for any potential Sunni disobedience. He immediately began a campaign to exterminate all those who had stood by Bakr, the latter only being saved after his son pleaded for his life; in fact, "during the Safavid reconquest of Iraq, Sunnis were massively persecuted and the shrine of [the 12th-century holy man] Abdul-Qadir al-Gailani in Baghdad damaged" (Cole 2002, 19). It took another 15 years for the Ottomans finally to defeat their enemy. Ottoman historians recount that among the first actions of the victorious sultan Murad IV upon his entry into Baghdad were to repair the damage done to Sunni shrines, rebuild Baghdad's city walls, and install a governor with authority over 8,000 Janissaries (slave-soldiers who formed an elite guard for provincial governors).

But while much ink has been spilled over the religious controversy that supposedly fueled the Ottoman-Safavid conflict throughout the 16th century, other reasons for the struggle to control Iraq are mostly passed over in silence. One obvious reason for continued Ottoman-Safavid hostilities was Iran's desire to export its silk by way of Ottoman lands. Although by the 15th century a large quantity of Iranian silk was steadily supplying Ottoman silk weavers in Bursa (northern Anatolia), the Ottomans were not always anxious to allow Safavid penetration of their newly unified markets. Trying to deprive the Safavids of revenue, they "arrested a number of Iranian silk merchants in Bursa and forcibly sent them to Istanbul and Rumeli" (Mathee 1999, 20). Then a customs blockade was established against Iranian products; paradoxically, it ruined Bursa's own income because customs dues on Iranian silk plummeted, causing a crisis in town. Cut off from this lucrative route, the Iranians then tried to fight the Portuguese in the Gulf over control of the silk route to India. However, initial steps at a rapprochement between Safavid Iran and the Portuguese in the Gulf did not make a great difference in Iran's export of silk to the Indian Ocean region. But, starting from the late 16th century, the commodity became attractive to European merchants, and as Iranian profits rose, they partially offset the Safavid losses on routes through Ottoman territory.

It has been claimed that the difference between the Ottoman and Safavid strategy for Iraq was that the latter chiefly focused on control of the Shii shrine cities of Kadhimain, Najaf, and Karbala and the monopoly of the pilgrim traffic to those cities. The Ottomans, on the other hand, wanted to create a large sea-based empire not only to complement their territorial possessions but also to link the heartland of Anatolia to the Gulf, Indian Ocean, Red Sea, and Mediterranean. Baghdad would be the axis around which these trade networks would hinge. However, as has just been shown, trade was also an important motivator for Safavid designs over Iraq. This becomes even clearer in 1639, a year after Sultan Murad IV recaptured the city from the Safavids, when a peace treaty was signed that gave the Ottomans control over Iraq. The Treaty of Zuhab ended the military conflict between the two large land empires, but it also opened up new avenues of peaceful Safavid interaction with the Ottomans, one of which was the pursuit of commercial gain. Henceforward, Iranian silk was to traverse the Ottoman Empire with little encumbrance.

The Ottoman Incorporation of Basra (Southern Iraq)

Basra was vital to Ottoman strategy because of its central location and its well-situated port. Before the Ottoman takeover of the city in 1546–49, the other great naval power, the Portuguese, had already cast a covetous eye on it. After their capture of Hormuz in 1514, an important trading emporium on the Gulf, Basra was deemed to be but one element, albeit a fundamental one, in the Estado da India's growing empire. Bordering the Shatt al-Arab, and with direct access to the Gulf and Arabian sea, the port was not only a natural harbor but a meeting place for merchants, sailors, and agents of every kind. From the earliest times, Basra's reach had extended to the Indian Ocean, East Africa, and even China; in the sixth century, sailing craft put out to sea carrying horses on board for Ceylon (Sri Lanka) (Fattah 1997, 160). The latter commodity was only to grow in significance as time went on. Basra's ties with the greater region were to become its chief calling card, and when, much later on, the Ottomans were able to control the chief access routes to the region, they chose to use Basra as a linchpin and point of departure for their commercial empire.

Basra's obdurate tribal leadership (from the Muntafiq confederation of tribes), however, wanted nothing to do with the Portuguese; they easily controlled the town as well as the periphery, and they brooked no outside interference. The Portuguese, however, did not waver from their goal; having made vast inroads in coastal India and the Gulf, they may have thought that Basra would not mount a difficult challenge. In 1529, the Portuguese sent two brigantines and a force of 40 soldiers to overpower the local ruler of Basra, only to have their intervention add to the unsettled state of affairs in the Gulf. While the ruler of Basra, Shaykh Rashid ibn Mughamis, was defeated and became the subject, if only nominally, of the Portuguese Crown, his surrender was only a temporary respite in the long, drawn-out war between local tribal elements in southern Iraq and the great seafaring powers of the Portuguese and, later, Ottoman Empires.

At about the same time that the Portuguese were attempting to control access in the Gulf and Indian Ocean, the Ottomans were planning a maritime strategy of their own, in which the traditional ports of Yemen and southern Iraq would complement the Ottomans' hold on the Gulf and Indian Ocean. It took over 20 years, but Sultan Suleyman's naval forces finally accomplished the goal. After attacks on Yemen and western India, the Ottoman naval fleet struck the Portuguese positions in the Gulf, eventually occupying Basra on December 26, 1546 (Inalcik and Quataert 1994, 337). Basra, like Baghdad and Mosul, thereafter entered the Ottoman ambit; a military commander was appointed to run the port, its tribal leaders were graced with titles (and compensated with gold), and by 1558, the construction of an Ottoman naval fleet to guard Basra's approaches was well under way. As in Baghdad, however, Basra's tribal leadership was not awarded *timars,* or the classic landholding grants bestowed upon Ottoman cavalrymen in the core empire in the early centuries of Ottoman rule. The speculation of scholars is that Basra was too precarious a climate to support an orderly tax regime in the early years of Ottoman incorporation.

Even so, most of the standard histories of the Ottoman occupation of Basra do not gloss over the fact that at first, neither Basra's local rulers nor Baghdad's, for that matter, easily settled down as subjects of the Porte. While the sultan's name was mentioned in the Friday prayers and

THE PORT CITY OF BASRA

Since its founding as a military encampment in 636, Basra has played an important role in Iraq's history. Its name in Arabic means "watching over," referring to its strategic importance in the early Muslim wars against the Sassanid Empire. Some contend the name is derived from the Persian word *bassorah* and refers to the convergence of the Tigris and Euphrates as well as smaller tributaries and creeks in the marshy region of the Shatt al-Arab. Because of its location, with canals running through it, Basra has been given the epithet of "Venice of the East." Basra was (and remains) an important center of trade during the 500-year rule of the Abbasids and the more than 300-year rule of the Ottomans. It was also the center of the late ninth-century Zanj slave revolt. Prior to the revolt Basra had been a cultural rival to Baghdad. It was the home of law, literary, and religious scholars, poets, writers, and Arab grammarians.

As did Baghdad, Basra went into decline after the Mongol invasion; in fact, the Mongols completely destroyed the original city. As a result, Basra rebuilt not on its own ruins but a little farther upstream. If anything, the rebuilt Basra became more important as a commercial center than its predecessor was. The rise of Ottoman naval superiority in the Persian Gulf and Indian Ocean ensured that Basra's commercial advantage would be made of use. From the late 17th century onward, as this superiority declined in the face of western European naval powers, notably Portugal and Great Britain, Basra was again the site of contention. Religious and political strife contributed to the city's decline. Furthermore, during the period of Mamluk rule in Iraq, 1750–1831, Basra became a subsidiary city (and province) to Baghdad. After the Ottomans reestablished their authority in Iraq, Basra became more autonomous within the empire.

Following the fall of the Ottoman Empire in the 20th century, and while under the so-called British Mandate, Basra's port was modernized. During World War II, the port was transferred from the British

his likeness minted on coinage (two traditional symbols of legitimacy in the Islamic world), and while the wily shaykh Rashid ibn Mughamis finally achieved his heart's desire and was confirmed as *beylerbeyi* (governor) of Basra, there is no escaping the conclusion that it was the indigenous inhabitants of the new Ottoman province that held the reins of power and not their titular masters. Rashid's son, Mani, succeeded

Known as the Venice of the East, Basra, at the time of this photo, ca. 1950s, was enjoying tremendous growth because of Iraq's burgeoning oil industry. (AFP/Getty Images)

to the Iraqis. And in the postwar years, Basra experienced a true renaissance generated by the growth of Iraq's oil industry. In these years, Basra became a major oil-refining center, as well as point of export. Its population increased from approximately 93,000 in 1945 to 1.5 million in 1977. In 1967, the University of Basra was founded.

his father, squabbled with the more pro-Ottoman shaykh Yahya, whom he was forced to give up his position to, only to witness the latter join up with yet another nominal subject of the Porte and attempt an insurrection against the Ottomans (Ozbaran 1994, 126). Although the Ottoman governor of Baghdad quelled that revolt, the trend is clear. Tribal shaykhs, on whom the Ottomans were first forced to rely, played the Ottomans against each other and sometimes won a brief respite from foreign overlordship as a result.

This said, the Ottomans doggedly continued with their pacification of Basra. In December 1546, they appointed an Ottoman commander, Bilal Pasha, to head the province. He received a set income per year and was in charge of about 2,200 troops. Since the Ottomans had not yet completed their shipyard in Basra, Suez (in Egypt) became the naval base they used to attack the Portuguese. They spent the remainder of the 16th century attempting to wrest total control of the Gulf from their enemies, having great success in Yemen in 1538 but failing dismally in Bahrain in 1552. Nonetheless, while the Ottomans' naval attacks against the Portuguese in the Gulf and Indian Ocean failed to dislodge the latter's hold on Hormuz, the most important trading center in the Gulf, their land armies blocked Portuguese access to the Red Sea. And their control of Basra, shaky though it may have been at times, allowed them direct contact with Aleppo on the land route north and, with it, the burgeoning trade of the eastern Mediterranean.

Conclusion

For the Ottomans, Iraq held the same importance it had held for their Byzantine and Roman predecessors: It was an essential crossroads for trade. It was important enough to grant areas such as Baghdad and Basra a kind of special dispensation with regard to administering finances to the empire. But, as in the time of the Seleucid, Sassanid, and Roman Empires, Iraq during the Ottoman domination was also a proxy battleground for foreigners. This time, the battle was fought between the Sunni Ottomans and Shii Safavids, and their warfare was theological as well as economical in nature. However, these two empires were not the only players in the area.

The 16th century marks the beginning of the entry of European trading companies in the Gulf and Indian Ocean, a development that was to cause major changes in the regional trading system of Iraq, Arabia, and the Gulf. However, in the 16th century, foreigners were not yet the unrivalled masters of the region that they would become later on. No matter who the foreign occupier was and how successful he was in gaining his ends, in the end, it was the local tribal leader, seafarer, or merchant on whom he had to rely for help in attaining his goals.

6

IMPERIAL ADMINISTRATION, LOCAL RULE, AND OTTOMAN RECENTRALIZATION (1638–1914)

Early modern Iraq, as historians prefer to designate the entity consisting of four (later reduced to three) provinces of Iraq under Ottoman rule, can be said to have begun in the early 17th century and come to an end in the early 20th century. In those roughly 300 years, the Iraqi provinces went from a loosely knit collection of towns, villages, farming countryside, and desert oases to as near a centralized state as could be achieved under the circumstances. The provinces of Baghdad, Basra, and Mosul, while never cohering completely to form a united region fully subject to Ottoman rule, exhibited important elements of an "Ottomanized" culture and administration that tied it to Istanbul and hence to the empire as a whole. It has been noted that Ottoman control extended only to the towns and was completely disregarded in the tribal areas of Iraq, but that statement is not quite correct. In some periods, especially in the 19th century, even tribal leaders vied for Ottoman recognition, if only to trounce their rivals with important badges of legitimacy. In order to understand the contradictions, as well as the conformities, inherent in the nature of the Ottoman experiment in Iraq, an examination of the changing vision of Iraq's governors, landholders, religious leaders, traders, artisans, and military men is essential.

Iraq's society and government was characterized by competing tendencies: Within the provinces localism, autonomy, and the establishment of family rule were important developments that ran counter to the parallel development of a growing centralized imperial bureaucracy, with its attendant structures among local society. At different times in Iraq's history, one or the other propensity became more important but never completely won. Strong autonomous structures of rule and governance appeared in the 18th century in various parts of Iraq but never

125

materialized into outright independence, while military and political centralization of the Iraqi provinces became the norm in other periods yet could never quite endure in the face of submerged but ubiquitous localist currents. Sometimes compromise and coexistence was the order of the day; at other times, conflict and dissension threatened. The history of Iraq throughout those three Ottoman centuries, then, is the history of these competing trends and the trajectory of Iraqi society from a loose assemblage of tribal principalities built on unstable alliances with transit merchants and holy men to an early state system in which imperial structures and principles emanating from Istanbul were reinterpreted and adapted in the frontier lands of Iraq.

Unity Versus Localism in the Seventeenth and Eighteenth Centuries

Iraq in the 17th and 18th centuries exhibited latent social, cultural, and economic unities that were often obscured by the more violent disruptions caused by war, tribal raids, and rebel-led movements.

Ottoman-Persian Wars

The Ottoman-Persian wars that came to a temporary close with the signing of the Treaty of Zuhab in 1639 and the delimitation of the Ottoman-Persian frontier in Iraq continued to cast a pall over the northern part of the country. Both the provinces of Shahrizor (Iraqi Kurdistan) and Mosul were to suffer continuous blows in the Persian campaigns to regain lost territory, most especially in 1730. Meanwhile, Nadir Shah (r. 1736–47), an adventurer of Afghan origin who had usurped the throne of Persia in 1736, thus ending the Safavid dynasty, besieged Baghdad in 1743. A treaty in 1746 between the Ottoman Empire and Persia reaffirmed the 1639 border, but these periods of peace were always short lived and, on the whole, almost inconsequential. One of the gravest military campaigns against Basra took place in the latter part of the 18th century. In 1776, Persian commander Karim Khan Zand, who had taken control of Persia in 1747 after Nadir Shah's assassination, took advantage of a civil war in Baghdad to occupy Basra. With Baghdad in the throes of its own internal strife, Zand's deputy had a free hand to rule the southern province for three long years. He was finally forced to evacuate his army after a southern-based tribe of Basra, the Muntafiq, inflicted a severe defeat on his army and chased it out of southern Iraq.

126

Tribal Campaigns

Besides the military offensives launched by the Ottomans and the Safavids and their successors, all of which took place within Iraq, tribal campaigns seriously disrupted the country. Historians generally agree that as a result of drought, overpopulation, and the struggle over scarce resources, a radical shift occurred among Arab tribes in the peninsula from the 17th century onward. This shift resulted in the migration of large tribal confederations from Arabia to Iraq.

Thus, from about 1640 onward, the large Shammar tribe, a collection of many sections and clans, began its push northward toward more hospitable climes. The Shammar were originally part of a Yemeni tribe, the Tay. The Tay moved north from Yemen in the late second century B.C.E. and settled in the mountainous Najd region of what is now Saudi Arabia, where they became camel herders and horse breeders. In pre-Islamic times, the Tay had made incursions into both Iraq and Syria during times of drought. The exact date varies according to the source, but sometime in the 16th century, the tribe began prominently using the name *Shammar,* for an early tribal leader. The Shammar raided Baghdad in 1690 but also migrated into Iraq during other periods of drought. The Shammar would become one of the most powerful tribes in Iraq, with its power extending into the 21st century. The Shammar were followed by other notable tribes such as the Anayza (a subsection of which, the Uteiba, founded Kuwait City early in the 18th century, while another branch produced the Sauds) and the Bani Lam. Like the Shammar, the Bani Lam are descended from the more ancient Tay tribe and also migrated into Iraq from Najd. They settled primarily in the region of the Lower Tigris.

Naturally enough, the struggle for power between the new arrivals and the tribes already established in Iraq created chaotic and unstable conditions across the region. From the early 18th century onward, the new governors (commanders of the *sipahis,* or cavalry corps) of the Iraqi provinces, sent out from Istanbul and educated at palace schools, came to grips with the situation. Having been charged with a centralizing mission to retake Iraq for the empire, the Baghdad governors Hassan Pasha (r. 1702–24) and his son Ahmad Pasha (r. 1724–47) set about imposing law and order by defeating the tribes, where possible, and co-opting their leaders. The history of this struggle is well documented in the Iraqi chronicles of the period, which are replete with accounts of Ottoman commanders attacking the tribes from Kurdistan to Basra. Occasionally, the Ottomans found the tribes useful and formed brief alliances with them during their wars against the Persians.

The Provinces of Baghdad and Basra

From 1702 to 1747, with one brief interruption, the *sipahis* assumed control of Baghdad and, much later on, of Basra on behalf of the Ottoman Porte. The governors of Baghdad in that period, Hassan Pasha and his son Ahmad Pasha, began their careers fighting off Persian offensives in the Iraqi provinces, while themselves attacking Persian forces deep in Persian-controlled territory, such as Kirmanshah and Hamadan. By 1736, however, the Ottomans, and their representatives in Iraq, were in full retreat. Nadir Shah's campaigns against Mosul and Baghdad threatened the entire edifice of Ottoman Iraq, and it was a great relief to Iraqis of all classes and backgrounds that a peace treaty was finally signed. In the uneasy conditions that persisted after the end of hostilities, Ahmad Pasha continued his father's mission to pacify Iraq internally, if only to centralize "the more efficient collection of provincial taxes" (Fattah 1997, 35) for the national treasury. Paradoxically, by attacking the troublesome tribal shaykhs of the south and east, Ahmad Pasha not only attempted to rationalize revenue-gathering operations through the imposition of more government-friendly tribal leaders (who could act as tax collectors for their districts) but sought to enlist their support as allies of the government itself. This was because one of the chief conundrums of Iraqi history throughout the centuries of Ottoman rule was that no local government—whether of Baghdad, Mosul, or Basra—could survive for long without tribal auxiliaries. Until the town became stronger than the countryside—a development that only occurred in the latter part of the 19th century, and this largely as a function of a better-trained army and the settlement of the nomadic tribes—no governor could hope to have eliminated the tribal threat completely unless through temporary alliances with the paramount shaykhs. This said, government attacks on refractory tribal elements were always a feature of the ongoing landscape of Iraq.

Mamluk Dynasty

Hassan Pasha and Ahmad Pasha, however, are primarily remembered for a longer-lasting development that marked their tenure in power. As inheritors of a patrimonial Ottoman tradition that emphasized the conversion of Christian youths from the southern Caucus, who were either captured in battle or sold to Ottoman commanders by their kinfolk, Hassan Pasha and Ahmad Pasha began to import young Georgian boys by the hundreds to Baghdad to reproduce the same imperial system. These "slaves of the sultan," later called *mamluk* or *mamalik* (literally "owned," in Arabic) were taught to read and write in several languages, follow the Islamic religion, and train in the martial arts at palace schools. They staffed the various regiments, households, and extended family networks of important army commanders, the first being those of Hassan Pasha and Ahmad Pasha themselves. Eventually, this Mamluk elite (shorthand for a number of different military households that grouped the military commander's immediate family and extended, non-family units in a patron-client relationship) became the law of the land. From 1750 to 1831, a dynasty of Mamluks ruled Baghdad, then Basra (making it a subsidiary of the former), and, later on, developed strong ties to Mosul, all the while officially representing the Ottoman sultan.

This Mamluk elite and the state that it created have variously been seen either as the vanguard of an independent Iraq, which was aborted by the renewed Ottoman push to recentralize the province, or the vestiges of a neopatrimonial state in which the Iraqi Mamluks tried to reproduce the institutions of the imperial household now under challenge in Istanbul itself (Nieuwenhuis 1982, 182). The Mamluks tried to balance the two trends. For instance, the annual revenue demanded of the provincial governments of Baghdad and Basra by Istanbul was almost always sent on time. With the exception of the Mamluk governors Suleyman Abu Layla (r. 1748–62) and Umar Pasha (r. 1764–75), who sent little or no revenue to Istanbul, most of the Mamluks were circumspect in their accounts with the Porte. Had they been the advance guard of an independent state, the money would presumably have been spent at home. On the other hand, certain Mamluk pashas divided into factions and led fierce battles against one another, all in the pursuit of an undiluted, quite possibly sovereign authority. Even as the Ottoman sultan sent diplomats to Baghdad to try to persuade the rebellious Mamluks of Istanbul's prior claim to Iraq, or, at other times, launched military offensives against the Mamluks to abolish the *pashalik* once and for all, the Mamluk pashas were forging countrywide alliances with tribes, merchants (urban and rural), and religious leaders (*ulama*) both to remain in power and to advance their case against the Porte's.

The bulk of their support rested on detachments of Janissaries and local militias composed of the Lawands and Kurds, even though in times of lax governmental supervision, they were often instigators of trouble in Baghdad or Basra. (The Janissaries were elite infantry soldiers educated and trained both in Istanbul and in Baghdad; even though they were known as the sultan's "slaves," they enjoyed many privileges and were also paid for their services.) However, even though the Mamluks relied on government troops led by the heads of the

Janissary contingents, they needed Arab tribal support, in part because they could not quite defeat the tribes and rule supreme on their own. During the 18th century, this increasing reliance on local support for the Mamluks became quite apparent. As Nieuwenhuis concluded:

> During the 17th and increasingly so in the 18th centuries, provincial government changed in character. The ruling elite increasingly concentrated themselves in towns with control extended to small areas of the surrounding countryside. Governors and high officials were increasingly recruited locally, as were military forces. Provincial government became somewhat less dependent on the interests of the Empire, as more attention was given to local interests (Nieuwenhuis 1982, 171).

The most important Mamluks were Suleyman Abu Layla, Suleyman the Great (r. 1780–1802), and Dawud Pasha (r. 1817–31). The first is a significant figure because he reconstituted the Mamluk system of military households by replenishing the supply of Georgian youths from their home region. As a result, he was able to force Ottoman acquiescence to his rule. The second and third, however, were the dynamic movers of a dynasty that had developed not only province-wide backing but the support of regional interests as well.

Suleyman the Great is so called because he was one of the best governors of his time and held in high esteem by Arabs as well as Europeans, a rare achievement (Abdullah 2001, 72). While still only a deputy governor in Basra, he staved off a Persian army for 13 months, only being forced to surrender the city when the promised reinforcements did not arrive from Baghdad. One of the faults of Mamluk rule was its inability to establish a formal line of succession. As a result, factionalism and power plays within the Mamluk class in Baghdad often worked to Mamluk disadvantage elsewhere. Such was the case with Basra. After the Persian occupation of Basra in 1776–79, Suleyman was imprisoned, only to reemerge after the death of the Persian khan and the withdrawal of the Persian forces from Basra. After taking over the leadership of Basra, Suleyman made a successful bid for the Baghdad governorate. It was under Suleyman the Great's rule that the provinces of Basra (which included the port city that went by that name) and Shahrizor, only recently liberated from the Persian army, were joined to Baghdad. Henceforth, under new administrative arrangements, the Mamluks were to rule both Baghdad and Basra.

Suleyman the Great's military entanglements were, for the most part, of an internal nature. He had to reconstruct his own palace guard to take control of Baghdad and then to defeat rebellious tribal chiefs who were threatening large areas of central and southern Iraq. For the first task, Suleyman Pasha set about reorganizing the Georgian guard that had provided the effective force for his Mamluk predecessors. The Janissary regiments (the "imperial" troops) had grown rebellious and were attempting to further weaken Mamluk sources of power. In 1780, Suleyman imported about 1,000 Georgian youths, trained and equipped them, and gave them ultimate responsibility for the defense of the capital; the Janissaries, meanwhile, were banished to areas outside Baghdad. On the other hand, in 1787, when the Muntafiq tribe allied itself with others and marched on Baghdad, Suleyman Pasha drew them down to southern Iraq and smashed their forces in a resounding victory.

Dawud Pasha, the last of the Mamluks, was extraordinary in another way. While also excelling in military pursuits and administrative method, he possessed the added gift of intellectual acuity. Under his rule, religious scholars, professors of law, and historians made the pilgrimage to Dawud's court in Baghdad, where he sponsored an intellectual revival that was second only to that witnessed under the first *sipahi* commanders of Iraq, Hassan and Ahmad Pasha (Fattah 1998, 71). The latter had built mosques and schools and provided new employment opportunities for Sunni scholars from Baghdad and its periphery, inviting them to join in the cultural revitalization of the city. Dawud followed Ahmad's example (it is estimated that he built more than 26 new mosques and schools); however, contrary to Ahmad, he joined in the deliberations of scholars and professors of law on an equal footing. This is because he had completed all the stages of religious education incumbent upon a scholar and could discuss religious doctrine with the best of the Islamic clergy. After he was deposed in 1831, following a full-scale rebellion against the empire, Dawud was pardoned by the sultan and lived out the rest of his days as a pious Muslim in one of Islam's holiest cities, Medina.

Dawud, however, is primarily important because he ruled Baghdad and Basra with an iron fist while also starting a reform movement in military and economic affairs. His reforms centered on creating a standing army of 20,000 troops, trained by a French adviser, who integrated the Janissaries and Palace Guard into one defense force. To complement this transformation, Dawud also established a munitions factory and other weapons-related plants (Abdullah 2003, 90). Dawud also carried out several systematic raids on Iraqi tribes that were impairing the government's control over Iraq.

SHIFTING EMPIRE WITHIN AN EMPIRE

The Mamluks are a rare example in history of slaves rising to power and, in the case of Egypt, ruling over their former masters. The Mamluks (in the singular form the word in Arabic means "owned") came from the Caucasus, primarily Georgia, and Turkic areas north of the Black Sea. They were not a monolithic group; those who ruled Egypt came from different provinces than those who attained power in Iraq. Youths from Turkic areas in the Caucasus and Central Asia were first enslaved in the ninth century and used by the Abassid caliphate in Baghdad. Converted to Islam, they became members of the cavalry in the caliph's army, whereupon their status was initially somewhat vague. Within the army, Mamluks lived a segregated life, which probably aided their rise to power.

The Mamluks came to Egypt in the 12th century during the reign of Salah al-Din (Saladin). By the 13th century, the Mamluks had become so entrenched in Egyptian state affairs (these being usually wars of succession) that they managed to insinuate themselves beyond the point of indispensability. Through a marriage alliance, they in turn became the Egyptian ruling dynasty, known as the Bahris. Thus, when the Mongols attacked Iraq and sacked Baghdad, the Egyptian Mamluks were able to give refuge to those who had escaped. When the Mongols turned southward (without Hulegu, who had returned east on the death of the great khan), they were defeated by a Mamluk army

The Province of Mosul

A similar development took place in Mosul with the emergence of autonomous family rule: While largely contesting Ottoman rule, the local dynasty was also subordinate to Ottoman ideology. Between 1726 and 1834, one family more or less became the law of the land in Mosul Province. The Jalilis were a local family from Mosul, whose members became Ottoman *valis* (also spelled *walis*), or governors, and were duly rewarded with land (*iltizams*, essentially "state" property that was granted to officeholders to defray their costs in office and to bring revenue to the state). Eventually the Jalili family (which consisted of 15 separate households) was able to transform state land into private property (*mulk*). They and several other important landholding families with whom they had developed alliances were able to further increase from Egypt at the Battle of Ain Jalut in Palestine in 1260. Throughout the 13th and into the early 14th century, the Mamluks enjoyed military success against the Mongols. In the 14th century, the Bahri Mamluk dynasty was replaced by the Burji ("tower") Mamluk dynasty. These were mainly Circassians. Mamluk rule in Egypt lasted until 1517, when they were defeated by the Ottoman army; however, the Mamluks continued to be an important force in Egyptian affairs until the early 19th century, when they were massacred by the forces of Muhammad Ali.

Elsewhere in the 13th century, the Mamluks established a dynasty in India that lasted from 1206–90. As in the case of Egypt, the Mamluks had made themselves militarily and administratively indispensable. When the sultan died, Qutb-ud-din Aybak (r. 1206–10) fended off a number of rivals to claim the throne for himself. His first capital was at Lahore, but he later moved it to Delhi. In all, there were 11 sultans, one of whom was a woman, during the dynasty's 84 years. This was about par for the course for Mamluk rule, which seemed to be subject to dynastic strife wherever it reigned.

Iraq, then, was the final power base of the Mamluks. Their internal power struggles so undermined their hold on the provinces that even the very much weakened Ottoman Empire was able to reassert its authority. Ironically, one of the last Mamluk fighting forces fought for Napoléon Bonaparte in numerous battles in the Middle East and Europe in the late 18th century and early 19th century, including the Battle of Austerlitz. This is ironic because it was the Mamluk defeat of French crusaders in the 13th century that had launched their bid for power in Egypt.

their considerable wealth and power through taxing or renting land from cultivators throughout the greater province. As landowners, and no longer landholders, they invested in land and began developing a system of commercialized agriculture that, in the Jalilii case, was to underpin their costly wars and their "pacifications" of tribal and/or village communities.

The system that the Jalilis and other notable families put in place relied on the growth of commercial crops such as olives, grapes, or other fruit in groves and farms; the investment in watermills (and the lands watered by them) in the countryside; and, above all, the promotion of regional trade with Baghdad and Basra as well as the region of Kurdistan and northern Syria (Khoury 1991, 157–158). As with the Mamluks, the Jalilis also became patrons of religious learning and invested in a literary and cultural revival that provided support to Mosul's religious establishment, as well as its historians, poets, and litterateurs. Among the most important religious notables to emerge in Mosul was the Umari family, some of whose members joined the Jalili-led provincial government in important administrative and financial posts. For example, Uthman al-Umari (1721–70) was an administrator (in Mosul as well as Baghdad) but was also a poet and a belle-lettriste (*adib*, in Arabic). Meanwhile, a cousin of Uthman's, Amin al-Umari (1738–88), was a professor of law and a historian. An even greater historian was Amin's brother, Yasin (1745–1820), who wrote 17 historical chronicles (Kemp 1981, 310).

Historian Dina Khoury makes the point that the Jalilis and the Umaris, like several other large families in Mosul, staked their prominence on extended family networks, or households, which, in the Umari case, combined intellectual and administrative influence with some financial resources. The Jalilis, on the other hand, were among the richest proprietors of Mosul; they also held a monopoly on military force, which compelled respect (Khoury 1997, 114–133).

The Province of Shahrizor

Iraqi Kurdistan came under Ottoman rule in 1550, and its leading families, represented by their *mirs* (Kurdish tribal chieftains or princes), became the advance guard for the Ottomanization of northwestern Iraq. Granted plots of land (*timars*) by Istanbul in return for bringing out the cavalry in times of war, Kurdish chieftains made expedient alliances with the Arab and Turkmen population in the region to buttress their power. From the mid-16th century onward, the frontier arrangements between the early Ottoman commanders and the *mirs* remained more or less the same, except during the wars between the Safavids and the Ottomans, when some Kurdish tribes would change sides and resettle on either side of the border, precipitating the migration of tribes from Ottoman Iraq to Safavid Iran or vice versa. The Kurds were always in a precarious position, because they were susceptible to the power of rival empires; living as they did in the borderlands between Iraq and Iran, they were often manipulated to fight for one side or another.

There were many tribal families of great influence in the Kurdish highlands, as well as *sufi* (mystic) brotherhoods led by leaders of some of the greatest Islamic fraternities (*turug*) in Islamic Asia, such as the Qadiri and Naqshbandi. For our purposes, the Baban family of southern Kurdistan serves as a useful example with which to describe 17th-

and 18th-century northern Iraq. With a few exceptions, in which rival leaders of the Baban emirate, or principality, switched sides and became Persian vassals, the Baban princes were usually Ottoman allies from the mid-16th to the 19th century. Exceptionally for Kurdistan, the Baban emirs received the Ottoman title of pasha (the highest military rank) in the 17th century and were large landholders, holding sway over hundreds of villages as well as the tribal countryside through their deputy governors and district chiefs. The tribal peasantry, meanwhile, was as oppressed as any other in the region.

Because the Babans had been an independent dynasty at the time of the Ottoman conquest in the mid-16th century, they possessed a certain cachet that distinguished them from other Kurdish *mirs*; however, that distinction was more often theoretical than real. The Babans, like other Kurdish dynasties, were not a politically stable unit. Family members often conspired against one another and, on some occasions, even fought drawn-out battles against rival members, often instigated by Persian guile. Sometime after 1787, one of the Babans, Suleyman, built the definitive capital for his fief and named it after himself. Today, Suleymaniya functions as the focus of southern Kurdistan. In the early 19th century, traveler and diplomat Claudius James Rich described Suleyman Baban's administration as a miniature of the Ottoman court: It had a prime minister (a hereditary office), several court officials with ceremonial roles, a guardian of the harem, an astrologer-astronomer, and a master of the horse (Bruinessen 1992, 172). The latter was an important post dating back to the Roman Republic, *magister equitum*. As the title declares, its holder was responsible for royal and/or military horses in an empire or kingdom, not a small post in the age before mechanized military. The master of the horse held close council with the emperor or king, but today, where it still exists, it is largely a ceremonial position.

Private Property and the Rise of a New Class

Certain developments became more pronounced in the provinces of Iraq in the 17th and 18th centuries, and these developments brought forth a more "localized" class. Among the most important was the system by which revenue was assessed and collected for the state; this changed dramatically, and with it, so did the whole tenor of provincial-imperial relations. This was most marked in Mosul (where land grants to cavalry commanders were introduced more systematically than in the other provinces), but its effects were noticeable everywhere else.

In the wake of Suleyman the Lawgiver's sweep into northern Iraq, it had been the case that certain field commanders were given the task of supplying the Ottoman Empire with men and matériel; because this system was prone to abuse, however, it was changed soon after Murad IV's entry into Baghdad in 1636. Henceforth, revenues were auctioned out to a tax farmer whose primary purpose was to collect not only the initial expenditure spent to buy the title of *multazim* (a contractor who had the cash to buy the right to tax the rural worker) from the state but to amass additional sums from the peasant in the form of sometimes illegal taxes. The *iltizam* system, whereby property was contracted out to taxed farmers to raise revenues for the state, became general practice throughout the empire, including the provinces of Iraq. Eventually, it brought to power a number of influential landholders and merchants, such as the above mentioned Jalili and Umari families in Mosul, who began to trade with Europe and to grow cash crops for sale outside the Ottoman Empire.

A third form of land grant made its appearance in the 18th century; the *mailkane,* or grant for life, presaged the beginning of inherited private property in Iraq and gave added impetus to the changes already manifest in the period. Those changes sprang from the near-monopolization of the produce of agricultural estates and the novel investment in trade by new classes of agrarian and commercial interests, whether Mosuli notables, Kurdish chieftains, heads of Mamluk military households, or, eventually and most significantly, tribal shaykhs.

Regional Trade

The trend to provincial autonomy and local dynastic rule was accompanied by regional linkages and interaction across provinces, sects, ethnicities, and backgrounds, and this happened most of all in trade. Regional networks based on long-distance commerce traded across far-flung districts, bartering, buying, and selling goods in market towns and ports all over the region. In the 18th century, everything from horses to wood and tea was exchanged, sold, or paid for by credit, from Arabia to northern and southern Iraq, southwest Persia, and western India. Family firms sent sons and nephews to financial and economic centers such as Bombay (present-day Mumbai, India), Aleppo (Syria), or Basra to corner the market in pearls, grain, or coffee. Credit was extended for long maritime voyages to East Africa or India; partnerships in prized commodities such as Arabian horses soldered associations between Indians from Bombay and Iraqis from Basra. Regional trade networks brought together disparate communities never before linked in history;

rural tribesmen in Hail (northern Arabia) sold to Arab or Persian merchants in Baghdad or Basra, who in turn shipped their goods on Kuwaiti ships piloted by Indian sea captains and crewed by African sailors.

Basra was the major fulcrum for all this regional trade. Its port served as a conduit for goods imported and exported by merchants from central Arabia, western Persia, and northern Syria. Indians and Afghans lived either in the Shii shrine cities of Iraq, or in semi-permanent merchant communities throughout the region. Armenian and Jewish merchants were the richest traders in Basra, equal only to the big Chalabi shipowners and merchants of the India trade. Faced with all this transient wealth, Mamluk governors tried hard to siphon part of it away to Basra's coffers; for instance, some of Basra's governors tried to corner the Basra-Aleppo caravan trade, much to the disenchantment of Basra's merchant community, which was forced to pay extra dues in the process. Meanwhile, Basra's governors often forced merchant houses to "loan" the local government money or extorted other tariffs in other coercive ways.

Basra's trade, and by extension that of Baghdad and districts west as well, was not only threatened by rapacious governors. It also fell prey to invading armies. Throughout the 17th and 18th centuries, trade suffered from wars and the chronic instability of the region. The biggest catastrophe to the trade of southern Iraq was the three-year occupation of Basra in 1776–79 by the Persian ruler Karim Khan Zand. Until Karim's death in 1779, his brother Sadiq Khan diverted Basra's trade to Persia, thereby weakening Mamluk control of the port. Grain shortages in certain areas sparked famines; the great rivers of Iraq flooded at the wrong times, devastating agriculture; booms in certain commodities were followed by busts; and smuggling and contraband were rife. But, significantly, trade continued even in wartime, and traditional routes and markets were not eclipsed so much as they were reproduced elsewhere, continuing to bolster the fragile unity between town and country, tribal shaykh and urban merchant (Fattah 1997, 19–41). However, due to plagues and further reroutings of trade channels, the merchant capital Basra entered a period of decline by the end of the 18th century, from which it was only to revive in the early 20th century, when the British took over Iraq and made Basra their chief entrepôt in the region.

Relations with the British

By the beginning of the 18th century, Great Britain was not only the rising power in the Gulf and Indian Ocean, but its representatives in Istanbul, Basra, and Baghdad commonly intervened forcefully in the local politics of the region. This was largely because of the importance of British trade to the region, especially to the port city of Basra, whose merchant community, no less than its governor, was dependent on the arrival of large trading ships from British India, as well as the hundreds of smaller trading vessels that monthly or weekly docked at Basra's harbor. There is even some evidence that shows that certain Mamluk pashas were only confirmed in power as a result of British influence with Istanbul. In fact, British authority became so significant that it is estimated that "[D]uring the last three decades of Mamluk rule (i.e., down to 1831), hardly any *mutassalim* (deputy governor) of Basra could maintain office without British support or consent" (Nieuwenhuis 1982, 82).

One of the incentives for trade on the part of British residents (the precursors to British ambassadors in the 20th century) in Baghdad and Basra was that up to the mid-19th century, British consular officials also functioned as representatives for the East India Company, the most important commercial establishment in the region at the time. As such, they were allowed to trade on their own account and oftentimes monopolized certain commodities, much to the chagrin of the local merchant class. This and their sometimes excessive political interference in matters of state often made them unpopular, to the point where they had to be reined in by their superiors. Such, for instance, was the case of Claudius James Rich, the resident in Baghdad from 1808 to 1821, and an inveterate traveler and sometime ethnographer of Kurdish tribes. Because he stepped on too many toes, especially those of the powerful Dawud Pasha, he got into hot water both with his superiors and the Mamluk governor. As evidence that Dawud's writ ran farther than Rich's, the pasha rescinded some of the commercial privileges (called the Capitulations) granted to foreign merchants by the sultan, seized British goods, and "made Rich prisoner in his own Residency" (Nieuwenhuis 1982, 83).

On the other hand, not every British resident was as obtuse as Rich. There is evidence that Samuel Manesty, the East India Company agent in Basra (1784–1812) as well as British representative, got along relatively well with Suleyman the Great; however, the relationship deteriorated as a result of a fierce dispute between Manesty and the deputy governor, ostensibly over murder accusations of a British-protected Armenian merchant (Abdullah 2002, 183).

Intellectual and Cultural Affinities

The provinces of Iraq (Baghdad, Basra, Shahrizor, and Mosul) were also united by longstanding intellectual and cultural affinities. Legions of Arab, Kurdish, and Turkmen scholars had graduated from the same religious schools and attended the same pious circles devoted to teaching the Qur'an, prophetic sayings, jurisprudence, grammar, and exegesis; they had sat at the feet of the most notable professors of the period and received certificates of scholarly merit. Some of them even traveled abroad in search of knowledge; whether they traveled to the holy cities of Mecca and Medina or to Egypt or India, scholars from Iraq mixed with each other and the larger Islamic learned fraternity, read the same books, studied the same curricula, argued over the same doctrinal or theological questions, and created unities in thought and behavior that cemented ties over long distances. Although Iraq's religious and literary leadership became increasingly entwined with the governing classes of the three provinces over time, the Iraqi scholars, or *ulama,* who served the state were never completely associated with it; the bonds of learning and the circles of knowledge that they had passed through made the *ulama* far readier to identify with a particular professor of law or student of religion than with the government of the moment. Thus, the leadership of the learned community could never be taken for granted by the government; while many of them became subservient to the state, the majority strove for autonomy in all intellectual and rational pursuits.

The Shii Shrine Cities of Iraq: Kadhimain, Najaf, and Karbala

Historically, the complexity of Iraqi society's main groupings—Arab Sunni, Arab Shia, Turkmen, and Kurds belonging to the two Muslim sects as well as to Christianity and Judaism—are both admixtures of ethnicity and religion and separations based on such. This has been compounded over the centuries by both Sunni and Shii conversions. Essentially, the Kurds, in the north, are and have historically been overwhelmingly Sunni. Arabs, both Sunni and Shii, occupy cities and towns throughout Iraq, though Baghdad and the area to the west and north came to be a densely populated Sunni region. Shii populations, which became a majority in Iraq during the 18th to 20th centuries, tended to be most dense in the south, and, indeed, the Shii holy cities of Najaf and Karbala are located south of Baghdad. A third holy city, Kadhimain, was at this time a separate entity, just north of Baghdad, but by the 20th century, it became incorporated as a suburb of the sprawling capital.

Najaf, located 100 miles (160 km) south of Baghdad, is the center of Shii power in Iraq and probably the holiest city in Shii Islam. It is revered as the burial site of the fourth caliph and first imam, Ali. It is also the site of one of the largest, if not the largest, cemetery in the world, which includes the tombs of several revered community leaders. Karbala, approximately 50 miles (78 km) northwest of Najaf and 60 miles (100 km) southeast of Baghdad, was the site where Husayn ibn Ali and his companions were slain. Traditionally, Shiis make twice-yearly pilgrimages to the city. Kadhimain, an early important Shii city, is the burial site of both the seventh and ninth imams, Musa al-Kazim (d. 799) and his grandson Muhammed al-Jawad (d. 835). Shii activity is centered on the al-Kadhimain Mosque, built in 1515. While these and other Shii holy cities never lost their spiritual significance, their importance vis-à-vis other Shii holy cities waxed and waned. For example, in

The domes and minarets of the important Shii mosque al-Kadhimain in Baghdad, built in 1515 (Werner Forman/Art Resources, NY)

the 19th century, the city of Qum in Iran, home to a shrine for Fatima, daughter of the Prophet, replaced Najaf as the preeminent city of Shii Islam.

This tension between Iranian and Iraqi Shiism was played out in other important aspects of the sect as well, the most basic being that two schools of thought predominated in the Shii world community: One legal interpretation, associated with Isfahan (Iran), preached a more activist social role for Shii clergy and went under the name of Usulism; the other, more conservative strain, found mainly in Iraq and Bahrain, was labeled Akhbarism. Basically, the difference centered on the amount of power allowed the class of jurisprudents, or legal scholars, in any Shii shrine city to interpret the holy law. The Akhbaris confined themselves to a reading of the Qur'an and the sayings of the prophet Muhammad and the imams, while the Usulis "insisted that the consensus of the jurisprudents could also serve as a source of legal judgment, as could the independent reasoning (*ijtihad*) of the jurist" (Cole 2002, 66). Because of a number of damaging blows to Iranian Shiism in the 18th century, including the invasion of an Afghan army, a large migration of Shii scholars to Iraq ensued. By 1779, Usulism had made vast inroads in the Iraqi shrine cities and, from Najaf and Karbala, was even brought to India.

The implications of this intra-Shii dispute on the development of Shiism in Iraq was immense. According to historian Juan Cole, Shiism in Iraq developed from a quietist current to a more activist one at precisely the same time as more localist movements were coming to the fore in the rest of Iraq as both the Ottoman Empire and the "vassal state" were in decline (Cole 2002, 77). With the rise of the Usuli school of law, a central tenet of which was the right of the *mujtahid* (a person qualified to interpret and give opinions regarding Islamic law) to represent "the absent Imam and [serve] as exemplars for lay believers" (Cole 2002, 77), local alliances between not only religious scholars but representatives of secular authority, such as leaders of tribes and bosses of town quarters, made their emergence.

The Nineteenth Century: An Uneven Centralization and the Co-optation of Local Elites

At the beginning of the 19th century, the northern provinces of Iraq (Mosul and Shahrizor) were still under autonomous family rule, while the Mamluks governed the central and southern provinces. But in the

1830s, a combination of the plague, the flooding of the Tigris, and an Ottoman army at the gates of Baghdad brought down the last of the Mamluks, Dawud Pasha. A short time later, the Jalilis of Mosul were also dislodged, as were the Babans of Shahrizor (ca. 1850). Henceforth, Istanbul sent a steady stream of governors to reclaim the provinces of Iraq. The history of the mid-19th century onward in Iraq is largely that of the interaction between a centralizing state and a society still autonomous in its philosophy and traditions.

This period in Ottoman history is characterized by a series of Western-influenced reforms, prompted by edicts called *tanzimat* ("regulations," in Turkish) that were promulgated in 1839 and 1859. New standing armies were raised; land laws went into effect reorganizing land tenure, production, and revenue; a new administrative map was created that reordered provinces on a more "efficient" basis; and local municipal governments were reorganized to include previously marginalized groups, such as Christians, Jews, and other minorities. It has often been stated, somewhat incorrectly, that as a result of these provisions, the provinces of the Ottoman Empire underwent a process of rapid "modernization." The Tanzimat era is generally seen as the period in which reforms associated with European modernity were adapted and applied, first, to Istanbul and its surrounding region and, later on, to both European and Arab provinces of the Ottoman Empire. But, as many recent studies have shown, this so-called Westernization was often only a gloss on ongoing, internal developments within the empire itself. Much of the "new" thinking was not so much the result of an overt application of European models but a continuous sifting of different paradigms to reshape a state and society in the throes of an internal transformation.

The Reform of the Army

The principal reform associated with the Tanzimat era was the reorganization and reconstruction of the army. Internal transformation had been the rallying cry of Ottoman reformers for quite some time. Prior to the early 19th century, the Ottoman army consisted of imperial troops, the bulk of which were Janissary regiments. The latter had infiltrated the trade and industry of Istanbul as well as the European and Arab provinces, creating local alliances that often ran counter to the wishes of the central government that they were supposed to serve and obey. On a couple of occasions, the Janissaries had even staged coups and dislodged the sultan himself. The Janissary threat had become so great that their doom seemed almost foretold; when Sultan Mahmud II extinguished them through wholesale slaughter, he signaled the rise of a more centralized military force completely under his command.

This new force, the Ottoman standing army, was trained and advised by Westerners, who founded new military schools and pushed for European arms, tactics, and strategy (Inalcik and Quataert 1994, 766). While it took almost half a century to materialize, a tighter, leaner army was established that went on to win several major battles in the early phases of World War I.

In the provinces of Iraq, the army was reorganized, and new military and civilian schools were established as a result; the latter's emphasis on languages and the hard sciences was somewhat of a radical departure from the traditional *kuttab,* or Islamic school, stress on religious and literary subjects and rote learning. But here again, the core principles of army discipline, effective training, and loyalty to the corps took a long time to materialize. In the last quarter of the 19th century, the Sixth Army, based in Baghdad, was considered to be one of the empire's least successful military units (Longrigg 1953, 38) simply because there was never enough money or matériel to hold it together. Composed of two divisions of infantry, a cavalry division, and artillery regiments, the army was made up of conscripts, many of whom could buy their way out of service through a military "tax." Entire sectors of Iraqi society escaped the military in this way, while those soldiers who remained were often unruly and spelled trouble for the army command.

In 1910–11, however, a strong governor in Baghdad, Nazim Pasha (1848–1912), who had also been named the commander of the army, attempted to whip the army into shape. Nazim Pasha's zeal in reforming the Sixth Army awakened British alarm. His emphasis that no expense be spared in this attempt to turn the ramshackle army into a fighting force made him a competitor to watch. Meanwhile, the British consul received disturbing reports of huge guns being brought in to revitalize Ottoman defenses and the daily and nightly training of troops. To top it all off, Nazim Pasha embarked on furious campaigns against the Iraqi tribes, creating much dissension in Baghdad, particularly since he attempted to defeat the tribes in one fell swoop, strongly testing his unprepared troops. Eventually, he was recalled to Istanbul because of heavy British pressure. Still, Iraq's Sixth Army performed very well in World War I, inflicting a huge defeat on the British in Kut in 1916, only to be routed at the end of the war.

Local Government Councils, Schools, New Printing Presses, and Newspapers

Prior to the mid-19th century, no local governing councils had existed in Iraq outside the shaykh's tent or the Ottoman governor's palace. After the Tanzimat edicts, an administrative council was established for each provincial capital. Headed by the *vali*, or provincial governor, it grouped appointed and elected members; for the first time, the latter consisted of Christians and Jews. Side by side with administrative reforms, civilian schools were created that taught a different curriculum, including military training, and followed novel philosophies. By introducing military training at an early stage and incorporating the hard sciences, geography, and foreign languages in its curriculum, the *rushdiya* (middle school) and *idadiya* (high school) school system in Iraq opened up different avenues for its student population.

Under Midhat Pasha (r. 1869–71), the first printing press was introduced in Iraq. This made possible the first state newspaper, *al-Zawra*,

Courtyard of the palace of the Ottoman governor of Baghdad in the late 19th century, during the period when the Tanzimat edicts had gone into effect (Library of Congress)

which was originally published in Ottoman Turkish but was later turned into a bilingual edition. Among its many editors was the sober Islamist intellectual Shaykh Mahmud Shukri al-Alusi (1857–1934), whose great reputation as a reformist scholar endowed the newspaper with a crusading ethos. Among his many editorials were those that castigated late Ottoman authorities for neglecting Islamic places of worship and pious foundations.

Forty years later, under less stringent censorship rules (brought on by the Constitutional Revolution in Turkey in 1908), a number of Iraqi as well as foreign-owned papers made their appearance. About 36 papers and magazines were published in Iraq by Iraqis before the collapse of the Ottoman Empire in 1918. For example, the outstanding weekly *al-Riyadh* began publication in 1910. Owned by Suleyman al-Dakhil, who is considered to be the first journalist-editor from Najd (central Arabia) to own and publish a newspaper, it was put together in Baghdad, due in no small part to the fact that Arabia and Iraq had long been linked by cultural, economic, and social ties. Although it only lasted four years, *al-Riyadh* published original and path-breaking reports on central Arabian tribes and dynasties and courted the Ottomans by openly appealing to them to intervene against British schemes in the Arabian Peninsula.

Al-Riyadh was only one of the many newspapers published at the turn of the 20th century. Other Iraqi-owned newspapers of note were *al-Raqib,* published by the crusading journalist Abdul-Latif Thunayan, and *Sada Babil,* owned and operated by the Christian intellectuals Dawud Sliwu and Yusif Ghanima. Echoes of those papers continue today. For instance, *al-Nahda* was established by Ibrahim Hilmi Umar and Muzahim Amin al-Pachachi in 1913. *Al-Nahda* lives on today because al-Pachachi's son, Dr. Adnan al-Pachachi, established a paper under the same name in 2003. (It was one of the most sober and well-researched papers published in Baghdad after 2003.)

The Land Law of 1858

Under the Ottomans, the area of south-central Iraq, known in Islamic history as al-Sawad, had become the home of many displaced tribes of Najdi origin, such as the Shammar and the Bani Lam, who had migrated from Arabia to Iraq from as early as the 17th century. Throughout the 18th to the last part of the 19th centuries, Ottoman governors tried several different strategies to tame the nomadic and semipastoralist tribes. Because the usual tactics of attacking tribal camps and suppressing select tribal leaders proved to be short-lived policies, Ottoman pashas and military commanders were eventually drawn to the strategy of tribal settlement on collectively held tribal lands. The notion was that sedentarization would produce stability, and stability would equal peace and prosperity.

The story of reform is usually associated with the arrival in Baghdad of the *vali,* or governor, Midhat Pasha in 1869. However, even earlier reformist *valis* introduced, for example, river steamers in 1855 (preced-

Arabs from Baghdad Province in traditional clothing. The man on the left (with shield) is wearing traditional Shammar clothing. (Library of Congress)

ing those of British firms) and augmented the fleet in 1869. Evidence also suggests that governors had already begun reviewing and attempting to overhaul the land system in Iraq before Midhat's arrival. With his accession to power in Iraq, however, the review and overhaul began in earnest.

Iraqi governments in Baghdad, Basra, and, to a lesser extent, Mosul faced large problems with regard to the agricultural sector throughout the 18th and early 19th centuries. First was the problem of the instability of revenue collection; although tribal lands were theoretically administered for the collective benefit of the tribe, the paramount shaykh had wide latitude in the use and disbursement of agricultural revenue. Throughout the period in question, tribal shaykhs were sometimes patronized by the state but more often warred upon. This was because in order to secure revenue for the state, either the shaykh paid out taxes willingly or was forced to do so through military coercion. Because of the erratic nature of revenue collection, therefore, the state never became truly solvent.

A second problem, alluded to earlier, was the fact that by the middle of the 18th century, "whatever the formal title of the land—*miri* [state lands], *mulk* [land privately owned], or *waqf* [endowments]—much of it was in fact under private control [and] much of the *miri*-land was treated as the private property of high officials or of members of influential families" (Nieuwenhuis 1982, 112–113). Thus, the second factor inhibiting the state's economic well-being was the permanent alienation of lands formally under state title. As a result of these two factors, both of which undercut the state's income, government reform of land tenure and production became an urgent proposition.

Midhat Pasha's first act was "to replace the piecemeal policies of his predecessors with a program of land registration and tax reform which, he hoped, would increase production, encourage nomadic settlement, raise revenues, and destroy the power of the tax farmers and tribal sheikhs all in one go" (Owen 1981, 185). The goal of the Land Law, promulgated in 1858 in Istanbul but applied only much later in Iraq, was to secure the land for those who actually cultivated it, but the tribal peasants for whom it was legislated attached no importance to private property and the greater majority even suspected that land registration schemes were a government ploy intended to list conscripts for the new army. Many shaykhs and urban merchants were more perspicacious, however, and registered formerly communal lands under their own names; after Midhat's departure in 1871, some *sanads,* or title deeds, were even auctioned off to the paramount shaykh's own family and allies (this happened in the Muntafiq districts of south-central Iraq), reversing Midhat's original intent to reward the cultivator and not his patron with title deeds.

Land registration failed its original constituency because it was undertaken with little cognizance of the facts on the ground; the idea that lands were communally held yet subject to the influence of the paramount shaykh was not something that had been anticipated in the law. Moreover, as time went on, the whole registration scheme became politicized; because registration brought with it economic power, the local governments began to use it in ways to further their political agendas. Thus, they awarded title deeds to tribal leaders who did their bidding, and disenfranchised those with whom they had complaints. Also, the drawing of new borders around tribal districts by administrative fiat caused turmoil in the districts themselves; so many title deeds were sloppily recorded that they became the cause for litigation later on. But perhaps the most important development of the new reordering of land and property ownership in late 19th-century Iraq was the rise of a new landed class of tribal shaykhs and urban merchants and moneylenders. This last, loosely defined strata was to become the new elite of the early 20th century, with whom the Ottomans and, later on, the British had to deal and, more important, placate at various critical junctures of the country's history.

Trade and Transport: The British Dimension in Local Affairs

The Tanzimat reforms were not the only factors to reshape Iraq in the 19th century. By the 1830s, a number of developments, both internal and external, had combined to radically affect Iraqi trade. In 1811–12, the Ottoman-Egyptian army under Ibrahim Pasha, son of the viceroy of Egypt, Muhammad Ali, had begun its Arabian campaign; eventually, it was to defeat the remnants of the once powerful Saudi state that had kept much of the Gulf, Arabia, and southern Iraq in its thrall. No longer threatened by the Saudi monopoly on regional trade, whether on land or by sea, merchants from the area were able to jump back into the fray, their networks revitalized, their prospects bright. In the early 1830s, however, the British had begun to make important inroads in the Gulf region. After the 1821 truce with the local principalities on the Arab side of the Gulf and their even more assured control of the sea route to India, the British became the unchallenged masters of Indian Ocean trade. Henceforth, regional merchants, whether Indian, Persian, or Arab, had to tread softly with the new power in their region; as a result of this new state of affairs, the more clever merchants made their peace early with the British presence in Iraq and the Gulf and became mediators between the latter and local society.

In Iraq proper, this meant that although foreign trade became the chief monopoly of British ships and British-affiliated merchants, local trade—the trade carried on in small boats on the twin rivers and camel caravan in the interior—remained under local hands. This made for a risky enterprise for the British. The British shipping company of Lynch Bros., for example, finally introduced its two steamers on the Tigris in 1862–65 but required the services of a soldier to make the journey from Baghdad to Basra, and from there to Bombay, in complete security. Still, a small but gradual increase in Iraq's seaborne trade to India occurred at that time, and Iraqi goods—dates, wheat, barley, and even live horses—were transported in greater numbers to India and Europe. It was only with the opening of the Suez Canal in 1869, however, that there was an exponential growth in Iraqi trade. From 1870 to 1880, for instance, the value of exports rose from £206,000 to £1,275,000 (Owen 1981, 182).

Between 1900 and 1913, Britain accounted for nearly half of Iraq's imports and a quarter of its exports (Owen 1981, 276). Based on the tonnage of ships alone, it was also by far the most important shipping power in the Gulf and Indian Ocean, reaching 137,000 tons a year, whereas local craft only carried 12,500 tons. Finally, it is calculated that in 1913, 163 British steamers arrived yearly in Iraq (Owen 1981, 276).

This raft of figures would be impressive on its own were it not for the fact that British supremacy was not only based on commercial power but on military influence as well. By 1914, at the start of World War I, Britain was the most important naval power in the world, a fact underlined in the Gulf and Iraq by its unstated supremacy on these shores.

The Shii Shrine Cities of Iraq Revisited

At the beginning of the 19th century, the Shii shrine cities of Najaf, Karbala, and Kadhimain continued under the spiritual influence of religious scholars, the *maraji al-taqlid* (*marja al-taqlid,* sing., "the source of emulation"; a religious leader of such erudition that individual Shiis follows his teachings), or the *mujtahids* (Islamic legal authorities). But beginning in or around the 1780s, changes had occurred in Najaf and Karbala that brought external influence to bear on the cities' social, economic, and political composition. The first had to do with what has been called the remission of "Indian money" to the shrines, especially those in Najaf and Karbala. Briefly, the Oudh Bequest, set up by the

Shiis ruler of Awadh (Oudh) in British-controlled India, channeled close to £10,000 a year to the leading Shii clergy in Iraq. Spent on badly needed infrastructure projects, such as canal building and irrigation works, as well as for money contributions to the leading *mujtahids,* the bequest cemented ties between Najaf, Karbala, and northern India. After the British annexation of Awadh in 1856, when the bequest began to be distributed by the British agent in Baghdad on behalf of the nawab of Awadh, it further shored up ties between the shrine cities and the British. However, because of the complicated situation of the Shii cities, in which autonomy movements were played out against the background of imperial Ottoman centralizing rule and rival Persian and Indian influences, little concrete change was affected between the Shii leadership and British economic and political interests in Iraq.

The second change occurred with the imposition of a more centralized administration in Karbala. Up to the early 20th century, all of the shrine cities of Iraq were in theory administered by Ottoman governors and tax collectors and kept in check by Ottoman troops. By the 1820s and 1830s, however, the localization of power had affected more than the religious clergy; it had brought about the emergence of a class within a class of merchants and city "bosses" who had usurped power from the older landholding families and begun to control the city's wards. This "mafia" (to use Juan Cole's terminology) consisted of youth gangs, small merchants, and laborers, with the occasional vagabond journeyman or thief thrown in.

The unique status of Karbala, with its self-governing hierarchy of clergy, landholders, and urban gang leaders, irked the Ottomans. After repeated military feints against the city, which had become dangerously independent in Ottoman eyes, the governor of Baghdad, Najib Pasha, sent an army to conquer Karbala and bring it back within the Ottoman fold. In January 1842, the die was cast. Breaching a strategic wall of the city, the Ottoman army attacked. After a fierce fight in which more than 5,000 of Karbala's forces were killed while only 400 government soldiers lost their lives, the Ottoman troops succeeded in reining in the local elements and conquering the town and its environs. On January 18, Najib Pasha entered Karbala and made straight for the sanctuary of Imam Husayn, where he and his military commanders prayed and gave thanks. After that, the governor spelled out the dimensions of Karbala's defeat: A Sunni governor was appointed over Karbala, Sunni judges were sent to the city to administer the court system, and a Sunni preacher was brought in to lead the Friday prayers, at which the Ottoman sultan's name would be ritually mentioned as a symbol of dominion (Cole 2002, 118).

While Karbala's fire was extinguished and its spirit broken, the structure of Ottoman power remained a facade. By the early 20th century, all the city's powerbrokers—the local mob leaders, smaller clergy, and merchants—had returned to assume their places in the great game of autonomous rule versus renewed imperialism in the context of late Ottoman Iraq.

Conclusion

By the turn of the 20th century, the Iraqi provinces had become more closely linked under late Ottoman rule. While the greater incorporation of the provinces into a more tightly centralized and demarcated region brought with it closer identification with the notion of "Iraq" as a common homeland, the country's population was not uniformly Ottomanized as a corollary of that identification. Certain elites emerged that recognized their affiliation with the greater empire, but they did so on a vastly different basis than before. The starting point for the reinforced ties between the provinces and the center was now based on a revised interpretation of what it meant to be an Ottoman citizen. No longer seen as subjects but as full-fledged members in a pluralistic Islamic empire, some Iraqis took up a wider Ottoman affiliation because it promised a fairer deal between equal citizens in the greater Ottoman realm. The ideology of Ottoman citizenship also tied in to the greater representation of national, ethnic, and religious minorities in the empire, particularly Christians and Jews, a factor that initially may have inhibited the wholesale adoption of an "Osmanli" nationality by its Arab-Muslim adherents.

Although reformist *valis* had successfully begun to implement ideas that would radically restructure the provinces, those ideas required time to fall into place. Even so, several reforms had begun to impact the country in the latter years of Ottoman rule. First were the military reforms that reorganized the Sixth Army and made it a competent fighting force capable not only of defending the country but of instigating well-planned offensives in wartime. Second, military and civilian schools had begun to cut into the huge illiteracy rate; the most promising military cadets were given scholarships to join the military and administrative colleges in Istanbul. Many of them returned as avowed Turkophiles. Third, with the introduction of the first official newspaper in Iraq, *al-Zawra* in 1869, the floodgates of newspaper and magazine publication were opened wide, bringing in their wake better-informed audiences who sparked lively discussions in coffeeshops and *majalis* (literary salons presided over by important patrons). Meanwhile, the private initiative that established literary and cultural clubs catering to Muslims, Christians, and Jews also spawned charitable organizations such as orphanages and small training programs for the poor.

By the 1900s, too, the influence of the more sharia-minded, literalist religious leadership had waned, even as the more spiritual Sufi brotherhoods had strengthened under imperial patronage. Religious schools that provided the basics of an Islamic education to young boys (and some girls) had lost their appeal; modern Jewish and Christian schools and missions had begun to attract not only children from their own community but, later on, Arab Muslims as well. In the south and center, a great movement of re-Islamization took place incorporating the tribes and urban communities that lived on the peripheries of the Shii shrine cities of Najaf and Karbala. This movement inculcated the principles of a renewed Shii mission among the roaming, as well as settled, population of greater Basra. In the 1880s, Sultan Abdulhamid II took notice and proposed the dispatch of Sunni preachers and the institution of schools to combat the upsurge of Shii reeducation of both the settled and tribal population. Meanwhile, a large, well-organized, and militant mystic brotherhood, the Naqshbandiya fraternity, emerged out of Kurdistan, eventually spreading into every corner of Islamic Asia.

The latter part of the 19th and early part of the 20th centuries are also associated with the institution, by government as well as private agents, of large technological and economic projects such as the establishment of steamship companies, the telegraph, a tramway in Baghdad, and the misnamed Baghdad-Berlin Railway, which actually extended to the Gulf. The opening of Baghdad's first "European" artery, later to be called Rasheed Street, was planned in the waning days of the empire; it was the first straight street between north and south and entailed numerous negotiations between Ottoman *valis,* merchants, British consuls, and shippers before it finally materialized. Meanwhile, a more pronounced effort to renovate and streamline the port of Basra so that it would provide more capacity for larger ships was begun but not finished by the time of World War I.

Late Ottoman Iraq was a work in progress that would remain unfinished for a variety of factors, some of them being the overall lack of trained administrative personnel, the ready availability of funds, and the wherewithal to put ideas into practice. Good *valis* had great ideas that they initiated with gusto but that languished when the financing

A railroad construction camp on the Baghdad-Berlin Railway, which actually extended from Baghdad to the Persian Gulf, in the first decade of the 20th century (Library of Congress)

stopped. Agricultural projects were started, literacy gained pace, streets were widened, and infrastructural schemes were set in motion. But it was too little, too late. Whatever the desires of reformist governors were in theory, in practice the last years of Ottoman Iraq were years of lost opportunities and unfulfilled expectations on the part of the government and the people alike.

7

BRITISH OCCUPATION AND THE IRAQI MONARCHY (1914–1958)

Allied with Germany and Austria-Hungary as the Central Powers during World War I (1914–18), the Ottoman Turks were defeated, and as a result, the empire was overthrown internally. Iraq came under British occupation. The occupation was later modified to a British Mandate, and Britain was tasked by the League of Nations to guide Iraq's transition to independence. Iraq attained full independence in 1932 and joined the League of Nations as a sovereign state, even though Britain retained a proprietary interest in Iraq's development. From 1932 to 1958, the country was ruled by a monarchy originally from the Hashemite family in the Hijaz (western Arabia). In 1958, a bloody coup overthrew the monarchy and installed the first of many republican regimes.

Although most histories of the nascent Iraqi state confine themselves to a strictly political narrative, it is worth noting that the era of the Iraqi monarchy also saw the beginnings of cultural and social movements of great originality and depth. All of these movements coexisted in a burgeoning political era when, at least under the monarchy and in the first few years of the republic, explorations in freedom and literary, artistic, and cultural self-expression were anchored in broad social and economic engagements that arose out of the working conditions and economic situations of the majority of Iraqis. This chapter will explore these themes briefly.

The British Campaign Against the Ottomans in Iraq and the Birth of the Mandate (1914–1920)

The story of Iraqi independence begins, paradoxically enough, with its incipient development under colonialism. World War I saw the

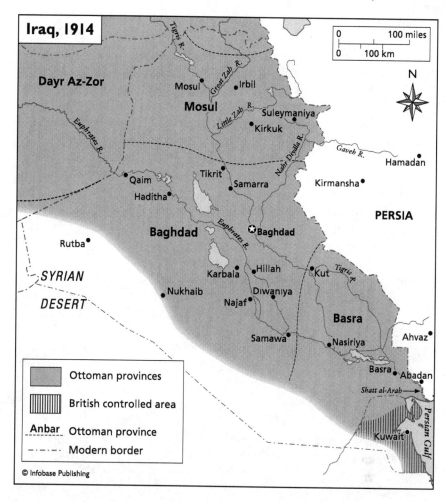

Iraq, 1914

Dayr Az-Zor

Tigris R.

Great Zab R.

Mosul • Irbil

Mosul

Little Zab R.

Suleymaniya

Kirkuk •

Nabr Diyala R.

Gaveb R.

Hamadan •

Tikrit •

Samarra •

Kirmansha •

PERSIA

Qaim •

Haditha •

Euphrates R.

Rutba •

Baghdad

Euphrates R.

Baghdad

SYRIAN

DESERT

Nukhaib •

Karbala •

Hillah •

Kut •

Tigris R.

Najaf •

Diwaniya •

Basra

Samawa •

Nasiriya •

Ahvaz •

Basra • Abadan

Shatt al-Arab →

Persian Gulf

Kuwait •

Ottoman provinces

British controlled area

Anbar Ottoman province

— · — · — Modern border

© Infobase Publishing

emergence of two military alliances, one comprising Britain, France, and Belgium; the other, Germany, Austria, and Ottoman Turkey. However, Britain and France fought on two fronts: Europe and the Middle East. Britain's interest in the Ottoman Empire and the greater Middle East as a whole had been nurtured for more than a century. On the strategic front, the British coveted Iran, Iraq, and the Gulf because they acted as a buffer to British India by protecting India's western flank. Economically, British interests in Iran grew in direct correlation to the rise of Iranian oil production. Meanwhile, sightings of oil in northern Iraq confirmed that the territory had great potential value in the future. For those reasons, the British (and the French) were intent on striking wartime deals with Arab and Middle Eastern allies to subvert Ottoman influence from within, thus achieving their political and economic objectives in the process.

Certain sectors of Iraqi society were affected by Arab nationalism; they sought independence from Ottoman rule especially after the Young Turk period saw a revival of a pan-Turkish ideal that minimized Arab contributions to the empire. The Young Turks' program was a European-influenced reform movement against the autocratic rule of Sultan Abdulhamid II begun in the late 19th century and that culminated with the Revolution of 1908, which centered on restoring the constitution and involved nationalist army officers. During the war, the class of notables of the Arab provinces of the Ottoman Empire largely stayed on the sidelines if they did not actively side with the Ottomans. Only a small but influential class of intellectuals, Arab officers trained at Ottoman military schools, and key members of the landholding and merchant class attempted to work actively for change. Making expedient alliances with the British and French, they began an inchoate but eventually united movement to win independence from the Ottoman Empire. Knowing their weaknesses and relying on the strengths of other countries, Syrians, Iraqis, and Hijazis negotiated both with the British and the French in order to receive arms, money, and training to defeat their Turkish overlords. The Arab Revolt, spurred on by a Hijazi notable descended from the House of the Prophet, Sharif Hussein bin Ali (1855–1931), became the chief symbol of anti-Ottoman resistance in 1916, which spread from Arabia to Syria to what was to become Transjordan. Significantly, the major group in support of Sharif Hussein's campaign against the Turks was drawn from the Iraqi-born Ottoman officers who had seceded from the army to join his ranks.

It was the British attack on southern Iraq, however, that galvanized the Ottoman front in the East. The British completed the first stage of the war against Ottoman Turkey after Indian Expeditionary Force "D" occupied Basra on November 22, 1914. Having secured the access routes to the Abadan oilfields in southwest Iran (in which the Anglo-Persian Oil Company had a big stake) and reassured their Arab shaykh allies in the Gulf of their commitment, the British then decided to take on the capital, Baghdad. Lulled into complacency by the Ottomans' lack of a serious defense of Basra, the British War Office, India Office, and Foreign Office gave conflicting advice to their general command in the field to continue upriver and invest the Iraqi capital as soon as possible. Much to British chagrin, the Ottomans rallied; at the famous battle of Kut, the Ottoman army surrounded the British forces of Major General

Charles V. F. Townshend and besieged them for 140 days until the latter, depleted of resources and on the edge of starvation, surrendered unconditionally on April 29, 1916.

Eventually, a new British commander, General Sir Frederick S. Maude, began a painstaking attempt to retake central Iraq, and his patience and skill produced results. Defeating hastily called tribal armies and plotting his strategy with care, Maude and his forces entered Baghdad as a "liberating" army on March 11, 1917. After he died in Iraq of cholera, Maude's place was taken over by yet another British general who continued to push northward. Despite the armistice with Ottoman Turkey, which came into effect on October 30, 1918, the British were able to bully the Ottoman general in northern Iraq to withdraw his troops from Mosul after the end of hostilities. Although Mosul's status within Iraq was not legally settled until 1924, the British incorporated the city within their rapidly expanding sphere of control in a de facto sense. By 1918, the British had occupied most of the country from south to north and east to west the Ottomans had been defeated, and Iraq was now on the cusp of a new era.

Despite British military successes, however, their political problems had just begun. During the Mesopotamia campaign, a civil administration for Iraq was established in pacified areas. Based on the Indian administrative model, it was tempered by indirect control, a novelty that did not sit well with many British administrators, accustomed as they were to the direct government of the Indian masses (Sluglett 1976, 16–17). U.S. president Woodrow Wilson's Fourteen Points for a new world order (first promulgated before the U.S. Congress in January 1918 and then at the 1919 Paris Peace Conference) and his focus on the right of self-determination had rendered outright imperialism an archaic and immoral practice. Points 5 and 12 of Wilson's program directly affected British policy in the Middle East. Point 5 declared: "A free, open-minded, and absolutely impartial adjustment of all colonial claims, based upon a strict observance of the principle that in determining all such questions of sovereignty the interests of the populations concerned must have equal weight with the equitable claims of the government whose title is to be determined." More specifically for Iraq, point 12 stated: "The Turkish portions of the present Ottoman Empire should be assured a secure sovereignty, but the other nationalities which are now under Turkish rule should be assured an undoubted security of life and an absolutely unmolested opportunity of autonomous development." Thus, British administrators were forced to revise their road map to Iraqi rule.

British troops march into Baghdad on March 11, 1917, more than a year and a half before the surrender of the Ottoman Empire. (The Granger Collection, NY)

GENERAL SIR FREDERICK S. MAUDE'S PROCLAMATION TO THE PEOPLE OF BAGHDAD, MARCH 11, 1917

General Maude's proclamation upon his entry in Baghdad has been published and republished several times since it was first read in 1917. Especially in the wake of the Anglo-American occupation of Iraq in 2003, it has been invoked by newspaper columnists, historians, and ordinary readers alike to depict the folly of going to war to occupy another country of which the colonizer knows nothing and making extravagant promises only to break them all, one by one. It reads in part:

> . . . [O]ur armies do not come into your cities and lands as conquerors or enemies, but as liberators. . . . [Y]our citizens have been subject to the tyranny of strangers . . . and your fathers and yourselves have groaned in bondage. Your sons have been carried off to wars not of your seeking; your wealth has been stripped from you by unjust men and squandered in different places. It is the wish not only of my King and his peoples, but it is also the wish of the great Nations with which he is in alliance, that you should prosper even as in the past when your lands were fertile . . . but you, people of Baghdad . . . are not to understand that it is the wish of the British government to impose upon you alien institutions. It is the hope of the British government that the aspirations of your philosophers and writers shall be realized once again, that the people of Baghdad shall flourish, and shall enjoy their wealth and substance under institutions which are in consonance with their sacred laws and with their racial ideals. . . . It is the hope of the British people . . . that the Arab race may rise once more to greatness and renown amongst the people of the Earth. . . . Therefore, I am commanded to invite you, through your Nobles and Elders and Representatives, to participate in the management of your civil affairs in collaboration with the Political Representative of Great Britain . . . so that you may unite with your kinsmen in the North, East, South and West in realising the aspirations of your Race.

Source: Quoted in Robert Fisk, "The West Has Been Liberating the Middle East for Centuries: Will We Never Learn?" *The Independent,* March 7, 2003.

The two chief administrators in Iraq in the 1920s were Sir Percy Cox and Arnold Talbot Wilson. Both of them were gradually converted to the idea that indirect rule meant a form of Iraqi participation, however symbolic. Yet, their conversion had taken far too long. In 1920, shortly after the mandate for Iraq was awarded to Britain by the League of Nations, a large-scale, well-organized, and devastating uprising took the British completely by surprise.

Iraq was a restive place and becoming even more so under an arrogant and unfeeling British administration that, in Wilson's words, had characterized Iraqi leaders seeking independence as a "handful of ungrateful politicians" (quoted by Lewis in Metz 1990, 34). And while Britain's assorted enemies in the country were not politically integrated by any stretch of the imagination, individual leaders were quick to realize that combating the new foreign overlord required extraordinary and unprecedented measures. One of these measures entailed the active solidarity of all Iraqis against the colonizer. And so, in the years just after World War I, anticolonialist secret societies sprang up in Najaf, Karbala, Kut, Hillah, and, most important, Baghdad. In Najaf was Jamiyat an-Nahda al-Islamiya (the League of Islamic Awakening), whose members included tribal leaders, journalists, landowners, and *ulama*. A second organization was al-Jamiya al-Wataniya al-Islamiya (the Muslim National League), whose purpose was to prepare the people for widespread rebellion. The Haras al-Istiqlal (Guardians of Independence) was a Sunni-Shia coalition made up of *ulama*, teachers, civil servants, merchants, and military officers. Thus, when the uprising came about Sunnis, Shiis, and some Kurds, townsmen and farmers, tribesmen, army officers, and civilians came together in a historic mass movement against British rule. In Iraq, at least, the 1920 revolt has become the stuff of legend. It had as its backbone the Shii *mujtahids* (clergy) of the holy cities of Najaf and Karbala, especially Grand Ayatollah Mirza Muhammad Taqi Shirazi (d. 1920), who inspired the tribes of the mid- and Lower Euphrates with a fatwa (legal opinion), as a result of which Iraqi tribesmen rose against the British, pitting their overwhelming numbers against the military superiority of the Royal Air Force (RAF). It was not an equal match. Many Iraqis were killed, and it is reported that it was in this period that the first use of poison gas against tribesmen was approved by the British command (Abdullah 2003, 129). Meanwhile, pockets of ex-Ottoman officers, all of Iraqi origin, engaged the British at battles such as that of Tel Aafar in northern Iraq. Finally, in an unprecedented show of solidarity, Sunnis and Shiis prayed at each other's mosques in

Baghdad, and nationalist poetry spread like wildfire in both the urban and rural districts.

The uprising of 1920 cost the British an inordinate amount of money (almost £40 million) and incurred heavy British and Indian casualties. Partly as a result of Parliament's disquiet at the level of fatalities incurred, as well as Britain's fraying alliances in Iraq itself, a quick about-face became imperative. An appointed council of Iraqi notables headed by the elderly shaykh Abdul-Rahman al-Gailani, the head of the ashraf (descendants of the Prophet) and a respected Sunni religious scholar, was hastily put together after intense consultations between the British and select Iraqis. Surprisingly, the majority of the members of the new provisional government were Sunni; in fact, as political historian Charles Tripp notes, "one feature of the new state structures which became immediately apparent was the absence of any Shi'i appointees to senior administrative positions, save in the 'atabat (holy cities)" (Tripp 2000, 45).

In fact, the reliance of the British on the Sunni ex-Ottoman officers and notable class to the detriment of the Shii majority in Iraq became the pattern followed by Iraqi governments for 83 years. But this lopsided arrangement was not yet recognized as a definitive blueprint for Iraq in 1921, and the broad cohesiveness of Iraqi sects and ethnicities continued to be manifest in a united political platform. For instance, both Sunnis and Shiis called for an Arab Islamic state governed by a monarch bound by a constitution. Eventually, they got their wish in the person of emir Faisal bin al-Hussein (r. 1921–33), the second son of Sharif Hussein bin Ali, leader of the Arab Revolt in 1916. At the Cairo Conference in 1921, convened by the colonial secretary, Winston Churchill (1874–1965), and attended by two Iraqi participants (Jaafar al-Askari, the minister of defense, and Sasun Hasqail, the minister of finance), agreement was reached on offering the throne of Iraq to Faisal bin al-Hussein. Formerly king of Syria but expelled from that country by the French in 1921 (France had received a League of Nations mandate over Syria and Lebanon), Faisal was seemingly the best choice for the post. Scion of the House of the Prophet, active participant in the Arab Revolt, and a man who had come to terms with the British presence in the Middle East, he was also the candidate that most Iraqis allied with British-controlled Iraq seemed to prefer. Although the single-question referendum that legitimized him in power was obviously manipulated (it was claimed that 96 percent of Iraqis approved of Faisal as king), this did not stop the British juggernaut, and Faisal became king of Iraq on August 23, 1921.

The Iraqi Monarchy and the Mandate (1920–1932)

After the 1920 revolt, the British and the Iraqi governing elite realized that a new arrangement had to be worked out between the two countries to placate independence activists as well as to give Britain a patina of legitimacy in the country. The treaty signed by the new Iraqi government and Great Britain on October 10, 1922, in essence restated the mandate. The "obligations" of each country tilted heavily in Britain's favor. Iraq agreed to respect the rights of foreigners, including foreign missionaries, and to cooperate with the League of Nations. Britain agreed to respect Iraqi sovereignty while at the same time acting as adviser on military matters, foreign and domestic, including judicial policies, and, of course, the economy. It provided for Iraqi control of defense matters but tacked on a military clause that required that Britain would continue to train and equip the Iraqi military and retain its military bases throughout the country. Britain was also to prepare Iraq for entry into the League of Nations. The terms of the treaty were to last for a period of 20 years, though they were open for revision. The treaty was met with hostility by the Iraqi press, which after the uprising was anything but acquiescent, and this temporarily hindered ratification by Iraq's Constituent Assembly, as it did not want to appear to be simply a "rubber stamp" for the British. On April 30, 1923, an amendment to the as-yet unratified treaty was signed by both parties that reduced the period of the treaty's enforcement from 20 years to four. Nevertheless, the Constituent Assembly only ratified the treaty on June 11, 1924, after Great Britain threatened to put the matter before the League of Nations, of which Iraq was not yet a member and which had mandated British sovereignty over Iraq in the first place.

The Constituent Assembly needed only one month to discuss the draft of Iraq's constitution, known as the Organic Law. It was approved in July 1924 and signed by King Faisal I on March 21, 1925. The Organic Law went into effect the day after the king signed it. It created a constitutional monarchy (meaning in one sense that it added itself to the status quo) with a parliamentary form of national government. The national legislature was to be bicameral: The Senate was made up of members appointed by King Faisal, while members of the House of Representatives were elected to four-year terms. Suffrage was strictly reserved for men.

In the aftermath of the 1920 uprising, three political parties came into being in Iraq. One of these represented those essentially Sunni Iraqis in power, and the other two—the Watani (Patriotic) and Nahda (Awakening) Parties, both formed by lay Shiis—were opposition parties. All three, however, were nationalistic and devoted to Iraqi independence. When independence was achieved in 1932, the parties disbanded as members transferred their allegiance to other parties and blocs that had formed around social and economic questions.

Building an Iraqi Army

After the 1920 insurrection, the growth of an Iraqi army was deemed essential from the British perspective, for not only had the rising demonstrated the folly of putting British troops in harm's way when local forces could be relied on to do the job themselves, but the Iraqi elite itself clamored for an army as a symbol of independence, however curtailed that independence was in reality. At the Cairo Conference in 1921, it was thought that a strong army could take over from the British in a mere four years; this proved to be a serious miscalculation. A national army was established only after several years of great perseverance and resolve on the part of Iraq's fledgling military elite. Throughout, the focus on conscription proved to be particularly contentious; one side, composed of the adherents of a centralizing state, promoted conscription as a tool to incorporate tribesmen into national service; the other, comprised of representatives of Iraq's various sects and ethnicities, worried that conscription would be used to further an antiminority agenda. The British also opposed conscription as "beyond the meager financial resources of the Iraqi government" and feared that tribal rebellions in the provinces would likely draw the RAF into the fray. Many Iraqis viewed British resolve to stay neutral in the matter as a further means of keeping their country dependent on Great Britain (Tripp 2000, 62).

King Faisal's Role

Other than British colonialist influence, the Iraqi nation-state that came into being largely bore King Faisal I's imprint. Early photographs of him in Arab dress portray a man with aquiline features and a grave demeanor, a man who, for many Iraqis and Westerners alike, came to personify majesty in every sense of the term. Faisal so embodied the characteristics of Arab nobility and tribal valor that he never failed to impress Western writers and observers who met him and came to know him well. But Faisal impressed Arabs and Iraqis as well, for these and other reasons. Originally a man without a country, he came to exemplify the best that his new country could offer: intelligence, patience, reserve, and steely determination. Even his foibles (he was seen by some early observers as

King Faisal I (Library of Congress)

too compliant and self-serving in the face of the British) were later interpreted in a different light by revisionist scholars. An important historian of Iraq, the late Hanna Batatu, claimed that Faisal understood his own limits and that of his adopted country so well that, contrary to first accounts of his rule, he knew when to jab and when to feint, as a result of which he "never danced to British piping" (Batatu 1978, 332).

Faisal's political balancing act came perilously close to being death defying. He had to contend with many different factors, most of which were at cross-purposes with one another. First was his duty to Iraq, a country so diverse in its social, ethnic, religious, and sectarian composition as to be practically unmanageable. Every community had its demands, and not all of them sat well with neighboring ethnicities or sects. By and large, Faisal I relied on two broad constituencies—the ex-Sharifian officers (mostly veterans of the 1916 Arab Revolt led by Faisal's father, Sharif Hussein bin Ali, they were graduates of the Ottoman Military College) and the mostly Shii tribal leaders of the mid-Euphrates—and acted as a mediator between the different interests of both. While not completely representative of the country he came to govern, those two groups came to be seen as the pillars of the regime and survived Faisal's death. Finally, other than the satisfaction of internal demands, Faisal had to contend with the British and their imperial pursuits in Iraq. Having no real support base when he arrived in the country, and dependent on the financial largesse of first the British high commissioner, Sir Percy Cox, and then Lieutenant Arnold Wilson, Faisal had to navigate dangerous shoals to bolster his weak position.

The Ex-Sharifian Officers

The ex-Sharifian officers on whom Faisal depended were, for the most part, men of lower-middle-class backgrounds who had entered the

FRONTIER QUESTIONS

One of the thorniest problems in early 20th-century Iraq was the frontier question. Because the demarcation of borders involved claims on economic resources (mineral wealth, groundwater reservoirs, or even entire villages) as well as movable assets (tribes and their flocks of sheep, for instance), they were difficult to delimit with precision. Appended below is a description of the Iraqi-Syrian frontier, historically one of the least problematic from Iraq's perspective.

> The boundary which separates Iraq from Syria is in theory determined by the Anglo-French Boundary Convention of 1920, but the Commission provided for the Convention to trace the boundary line has not yet in fact come into being, and the actual frontier of the territories administered respectively by Iraq and Syria has for purposes of convenience been left approximately as it was before the signature of the Convention. Thus Iraq has continued to administer the whole of Jabal Sinjar (what is now Iraqi Kurdistan) while on the Euphrates the boundary fixed in May 1920 by the British Government of Occupation and the Arab Government of Syria has been adhered to, leaving to Syria the Iraq half of the village of Albu Kamal and a strip extending seven miles to the south.
>
> The administrative frontier runs for the whole of its length through deserts without settled habitation, but two great nomadic [tribes], the Shammar and the 'Anizah roam over the area of which it traverses, the Shammar to the east of the Euphrates, the 'Anizah mainly to the west, the frontier line cutting through their grazing grounds. The tribesmen, unaccustomed to an artificial boundary, pay scant attention to it. Shammar or 'Anizah sheikhs do not seek a passport when they wish to visit one of their kindred on the other side of the border which is at best vaguely known, nor, if the object of the expedition be hostile, do they hesitate to raid an enemy who has recently become the subject of another state. Nevertheless, when convenient, the frontier may be put to service. Unwonted activity on the part of Government officials in the collection of the sheep and camel tax, or the pursuit of criminals, may point to the advisability of "seeking pasturage" in the adjacent country while, if the favor of government seems likely to fall permanently below the highwater mark of expectation, there is always the possibility of a change in nationality by the mere shifting of the black tents into a region where those in power may be more generously inclined.

Source: Annual Reports by His Majesty's Government to the Council of the League of Nations, 1921–32, Baghdad: Government Printing Press, n.d, p. 40.

Ottoman Military College in Istanbul in the late 19th and early 20th centuries in the hopes of attaining high rank in the army after their graduation. Batatu estimates that there were 300 of them and that they could roughly be divided into two elements: those who had joined Sharif Hussein bin Ali in the Arab Revolt of 1916 and those who later on attached themselves to his son, Faisal, when the latter established his first royal court in Damascus (Batatu 1978, 319). Despite this seeming unity, they were not a monolithic group. The ex-Sharifian officers who became Faisal's righthand men were only four: Jaafar al-Askari, the first minister of defense; Nuri al-Said, many times prime minister under the monarchy; and Ali Jawdat al-Ayyubi and Jamil al-Madfai, who also became government ministers under Faisal I and his son Ghazi I.

The ex-Sharifian officers were Sunni, but not all of them were Arab. Still, their natural proclivities were to support an Arab and Iraqi nationalism that often ran counter to British policy. This was paradoxical; the ex-Sharifian officers, quite like King Faisal I, owed their positions to the fact that they represented an Iraqi elite that the British could do business with. In fact, unlike a number of other personalities in the country, the ex-Sharifian group was essential to British policy because they were considered to have imbibed modern ideas of government and administration and were, by and large, the product of a secular background. This may not have completely been the case with the Shia, who were even less monolithic than the ex-Sharifians and represented different trends and philosophies.

The Shii *Mujtahids*

Faisal's relations with the leadership of the Shii shrine cities were troubled from the start. Even though he tried putting his best foot forward with them, the attention showered by Faisal on the *mujtahids* was not completely reciprocated. For example, Sayyid Mahdi al-Khalisi and Sayyid Muhammad al-Sadr only gave him conditional pledges of allegiance (Nakash 1994, 77). Although a Shii consensus had emerged very early after the 1920 revolt that favored the choice of a (Sunni) Hashemite for the throne of Iraq, Faisal's close relationship with the British made some of the Shiis uneasy. When the leading *mujtahids* decided to raise the stakes by issuing *fatwas* banning the participation of Shiis in the elections of 1922, the die was cast. Since most of the important *mujtahids* of the time were nationals of Iran, "the government introduced an amendment to the existing Law of Immigration on June 9, 1923 permitting the deportation of foreigners who were found engaging in anti-government activity" (Nakash 1994, 82). To

A street in Karbala, 1932. By then, the Shii leadership had consolidated its hold on the city and come to terms with the Sunni monarchy. (Library of Congress)

preempt being arrested, the nine leading *mujtahids* fled to Iran, leaving the field wide open for the Arab-born clergy to take their places. This they did, signaling the return to the government fold of a number of important Shii spiritual leaders who were intent not only on producing a rapprochement with the monarchy but also on consolidating their domestic positions vis-à-vis the resurgent Iraqi Shii leadership in Najaf and Karbala.

The Shaykhs of the Mid-Euphrates

Although historian Yitzhak Nakash believes that the failed revolt of 1922–23, which led to the voluntary exile of an important section of the Shii leadership of the Iraqi shrine cities, "symbolized the decline of Shi'i Islam in Iraq and its rise in Iran in the 20th century" (Nakkash 1994, 88), the situation may not have been that dire. There was, for instance, Faisal's relationship with the wealthy Shii property owners in the tribal south. The big tribal shaykhs in the mid-Euphrates region had long been seen by both the British and, later on, Faisal I, as a bulwark against the petty concerns and interests of the antistate faction, particularly the rising intelligentsia in the towns. The British reversed the parceling of tribal lands among various sections of particular tribes that had been instituted by the Ottomans in the latter part of the 19th and early 20th centuries to weaken the power of the shaykhs. The British consolidated the hold of the paramount tribal shaykh on what had been communal tribal property by pushing for various land laws that privileged the ruling tribal stratum. Among the most important were laws that bolstered the individual ownership of land in the hands of big shaykhs. This was to grow into a near-British obsession; various British officials rationalized the growth of private property in the tribal domains as a law and order issue. The important shaykhs were made not only responsible for agricultural output destined for the world market but also the guardians of order in the countryside. After independence in 1932, the Iraqi government continued this policy by introducing land laws that reorganized the land tax so that it became a tax only on a certain number of basic goods brought to market; it became, therefore, a tax on consumption. As a result, from 1932 onward, the tribal shaykhs, which as a group became privy to an obscene amount of land, paid little or no taxes at all (Batatu 1978, 105).

The British relied on the landed shaykhs for a number of reasons, not all of which were shared by Faisal I. First, certain British officials, such as Lady Gertrude Bell (1868–1926), the Eastern secretary to the high commissioner, held a romanticized vision of them as the "backbone" of the country. In the 1920s and 1930s, those ideas were part and parcel of the ordinary European's view of the Arab, for the concept of the "noble savage" still held sway among British officialdom. Second, the British thought that "[the shaykh] was the readiest medium at hand on which [the British] could carry on the administration of the countryside" (Batatu 1978, 88). Because the British had been sorely tested in the 1920 insurrection, putting severe strain on the Exchequer (British treasury), they needed a local cadre of officials to fund, police, and administer the backcountry of Iraq. And while an army had been instituted, and the mostly Assyrian Christian staffed "Iraq levies" were considered a significant, if secondary, military force operating under British command, tribal militias were thought to be equally important adjuncts to Iraq's defenses. However, the British opposed national conscription (though the Assyrian levies were more or less conscripts), which would have incorporated tribesmen into national service; even the most pro-British members of Faisal's government realized that it was a policy designed to diminish the effectiveness of the one legitimate national fighting force in the country, the Iraqi army.

Moreover, the tribal shaykhs were given seats in parliament by government fiat; Batatu estimates that in 1924, "out of the 99 members who made up the Iraqi Constituent Assembly . . . no fewer than 34 were shaykhs and aghas [Kurdish chieftains]" (Batatu 1978, 95). The Tribal Criminal and Civil Disputes Act, incorporated into the Iraqi constitution of 1925, further strengthened the shaykhs' power as an identifiable bloc by enshrining tribal custom in law. But it was only after Iraq's independence in 1932 that the shaykhly class came into their own, and they began to use parliament to legislate further economic gains and press for policies that ultimately resulted in "highly concentrated landholdings and a huge inequality in land distribution" (Haj 1997, 34).

Besides the wealthy tribal strata, however, there were other constituencies that were fast amassing land and power in Faisal's Iraq. First, northern "pump pashas," men of merchant and landholding background who invested in mechanical pumps to reclaim agricultural land, began to make their appearance in the mid-1920s. They were encouraged by a law that offered tax incentives to entrepreneurs who could resuscitate unclaimed state lands, and more than 1 million acres were brought into play by the middle of the 20th century. Second, entrepreneurial capital began to be invested in industries, amongst them textiles, construction, and agribusinesses such as date processing. But, as Samira Haj notes, because of a number of structural problems, Iraqi industries remained "small and fragile and confined to light consumer industries" (Haj 1997, 74). Nonetheless, a new class of mercantile and industrial interests, some landed, some not, had definitely begun to make its appearance in the 1930s. Even after Faisal I's death in 1933, the Iraqi state, personified by Faisal's successors, Kings Ghazi I and Faisal II, continued to rely on a narrow sector of the populace that formed the pillars of state rule, the ex-Sharifians and the tribal shaykhs. However, by relying on this narrow stratum, the state marginalized groups and parties for which there was not much affinity at the top. Among the most important were the Kurds.

The Kurds

One of the foremost scholars on Kurdistan, Martin van Bruinessen, notes that in the 1920s and 1930s, Kurds formed 23 percent of Iraq's population, or 2–2.5 million people (Bruinessen 1992, 14). Of course, this was not a static figure; because of the permeability of frontiers and the immigration of Kurds from Greater Kurdistan, the figures can only be taken as an approximation. However, with the end of World War I and the demarcation of Iraq's borders, Kurds living in Iraq were forced to become more Iraq centered.

The story behind the inclusion of the Kurds in the new state is one of oil, intrigue, and a diverted nationalism. By the war's end, the Kurdish districts of Kirkuk, Irbil, and Suleymaniya had been occupied by British forces. Administratively, they came under the Mosul *vilayet* (government), even though the Kurds saw themselves as a race apart. Influenced by Wilsonian ideals of self-determination, just like many of the occupied populations of the Arab Middle East and heeding the calls of Kurdish intellectuals in European exile, the Kurd leadership in Iraq hoped for independence and a state of their own. The Treaty of Sèvres (1920), which partitioned the Arab Middle East, did in fact provide for the creation of an autonomous Kurdish state, but it was rejected by Kemal Ataturk (1881–1938), the Turkish leader. The Treaty of Lausanne (1923), which was finally signed after torturous negotiations between Britain and Turkey, ratified the assimilation of Mosul into British-controlled Iraq but failed to address the creation of a Kurdish nation.

The fact that Mosul possessed oil was an open secret, even though Lord George Nathaniel Curzon (1859–1925), the chief negotiator at Lausanne, vehemently denied that fact in Parliament. The British desire for "an empire on the cheap" (a colonized territory that cost them little or nothing) made it imperative that Mosul be included in Iraq. The Kurdish question, such as it was, came as a distant second; in the lengthy negotiations with the Turks at Lausanne, there were even proposals to split Iraqi Kurdistan and then cede the northern Kurdish districts to Turkey, in part because those districts possessed no oil (Mejcher 1976,

137). One is forced to conclude that one of the strongest reasons for the British consideration of southern Kurdistan within Iraq stems from the fact that its inhabitants lived in the oil-rich areas of Mosul *vilayet*.

A League of Nations commission set up to look into Turkish claims on the province of Mosul suggested in 1925 that the *vilayet* should remain within Iraq. But it added the proviso that "the Iraqi state should recognize the distinctive nature of the Kurdish areas by allowing the Kurds to administer themselves and to develop their cultural identity through their own institutions" (Tripp 2000, 58–59). This was a proviso that Kurdish notables periodically took up with the British as well as the new Iraqi government. Although a Local Languages Law was passed by the assembly, making Kurdish one of the state languages of Iraq, there was not much incentive either on the part of the British or the Iraqi authorities to accentuate ethnic differences at a time when an all-inclusive, national ideology was being promoted instead. The league also suggested that the period of enforcement of the terms of Anglo-Iraq Treaty, which had been reduced from 20 years to four, now be extended to 24 years as a way of ensuring protection for the Kurds. Although hesitant to do so, Iraq's National Assembly ratified the treaty in January 1926.

As a result of this British strategic decision to include ethnic and linguistic minorities within a state not of their own choosing, the ambivalence of the Kurdish position became more pronounced. While some Kurdish *aghas* settled down in Iraq, others exploded in open rebellion. Even before the Treaty of Sevres was passed, many small "disturbances" (to use a British euphemism) had already occurred in the Kurdish regions. Perhaps the best known was the insurrection of Shaykh Mahmud al-Barzanji (1878–1956) of Suleymaniya. In May 1919, Shaykh Mahmud, previously the British-appointed governor of his district, declared the independence of Kurdistan; because he could not rally enough followers from other Kurdish tribes to mount a credible offensive against the British, however, southern Kurdistan was retaken, and Shaykh Mahmud was thrown in jail. A larger debacle took place in northern Kurdistan in 1931. The Iraqi army was actually forced to retreat under Shaykh Ahmad al-Barzan's attack (he and his tribe were against the imposition of conscription in the Kurdish region); only the help of the RAF was able to turn the tide and restore Iraqi authority in the area.

The Monarchy from 1932 to 1958

By 1929, two things were evident regarding Iraq's political situation: The dual system of a mandated government was not going to work, and

Iraqi nationalists would never be satisfied with the treaty as it stood. In fact, the Iraqis had had their fill of treaties with Great Britain. Yet another one, more favorable but still short of the nationalists' demands of independence, had been presented to Iraq's assembly in December 1927. It was never ratified by the Iraqi government, which in 1929 was led by Nuri al-Said as prime minister. Furthermore, public opinion in Britain was beginning to sour on the whole idea of the mandate. Subsequently, the British sought to remedy the circumstances with yet another treaty. Signed on June 30, 1930, this treaty acknowledged an independent Iraq with complete sovereignty over its internal affairs. As it was a treaty (as opposed to a capitulation), Great Britain was to remain a close ally and "support" Iraq in case of the threat of foreign aggression. Because of that provision, Britain was allowed to maintain military bases near Basra and west of the Euphrates River. The terms of the treaty were to last for 25 years and go into effect as soon as Iraq became a member of the League of Nations as an independent state. That occurred on October 3, 1932.

Despite treaty terms that sounded as though Iraq and Great Britain were in alliance as full partners, the issue of British military bases in

Rooftops of Iraq's capital city, Baghdad, three days after gaining independence from Great Britain on October 3, 1932 (Library of Congress)

Iraq would fester in the post-mandate era. The first treaty signed by the new Iraqi government in 1922 provided for Iraqi control of defense matters within the space of four years but tacked on a military clause that required Britain to continue to train and equip the Iraqi military, as well as retain its military bases throughout the country. That treaty was succeeded by two others, also regulating Iraqi-British affairs, mostly to British advantage; it was the third treaty signed at Portsmouth in 1948 that led to fierce nationalist, socialist, and populist agitation in the country and became the prelude to the rejection of British military tutelage once and for all.

While the monarchy cultivated local allies from every ethnic, sectarian, and economic group that it could and all of Iraq's kings tried to remain on very good terms with the principal families, tribes, and religious aristocracies of the kingdom, Iraq was not fully a representative state. Perhaps the one monarch who really tried to bridge the sectarian, ethnic, and political divisions in the early years was Faisal I. According to Batatu, Faisal went out of his way to associate the Shia with the new state and to ease their admission into government service; among other things, he put promising young Shii members through an accelerated program of training and afforded them the chance to rise rapidly to positions of responsibility. He also saw to it that the Kurds received an appropriate quota of public appointments (Batatu 1978, 26).

Later on, under Faisal's successors, Ghazi I and Faisal II (the latter was too young to rule, except through his uncle, the regent Abdulillah), the monarchy paid lip service to the policy of pluralism and inclusion, but Iraq's minorities and its aggrieved Shii majority were not often brought into consultations with the government. This became clearer after Faisal I's demise, when the underrepresentation of the Shia in parliament as well as in the judiciary and the push to pass the National Defense Bill in 1934 creating a strong national army, aroused fears both among the Shia and the Kurds that the slight window of opportunity afforded them in the embryonic state of the 1920s was fast shutting down.

Even before that came about, the Shia and Kurds had had reason to fear the new government. One of Iraq's minorities, the Assyrian Christians, was the first to test the strength of the new regime and feel the backlash of its power. Living in and around Mosul, the Assyrians had felt a measure of security during the period of British mandatory rule, but once that was eliminated, they sought new guarantees of protection. During summer 1933, with Faisal I in Europe and the Assyrians clamoring for autonomy, and following deadly clashes between the former Assyrian levies (whom the British had not disarmed) and the Iraqi army, the government unleashed the army, which massacred approximately 300 Assyrians. In this, they were assisted by the Kurds, who also looted Assyrian villages. The king, who was ill with heart problems and seeking treatment in Europe, returned to Iraq, but it was too late to do anything but assuage the concerns of the League of Nations and the British. After the incident, Faisal returned to Switzerland to seek medical treatment but died of a heart attack in Berne on September 8, 1933, less than a year after Iraq had gained independence. The new country's fledgling institutions—a professional army, a bicameral parliament, political parties, and a moderately free press—survived until the end of the monarchical period but in flawed form. Save for the elite, institutions of representative government never really took root in the country. Quite to the contrary, for many national groups, loyalty to the Iraqi state was cultivated on the level of personalized ties, and relations between the emergent state and its constituents were shaped first and foremost by the growth of political patronage. Much later on, in the 1970s and 1980s, the state assumed impersonal and bureaucratic features that marked its gargantuan hold on the ordinary Iraqi citizen. But even then, personal networks of power managed to circumvent weak state institutions.

King Ghazi I, Regent Prince Abdulillah, and the Growing Instability of the Iraqi State

After King Faisal's death, the institutions of state power, grafted a decade before under British occupation, were redeveloped and began to take on forms of their own. As with many newly formed nation-states in the 1920s to 1960s, the trappings of power in Iraq were "indigenized" and developed local momentum. Among the chief formative institutions of the country was the army. The policy of conscription gradually gave rise to an army that grew from 12,000 in 1932 to 43,000 men in 1941 (Tripp 2000, 78). The seeds for a powerful and politicized officer corps were planted during that time period, the rise of which would play an enormous role in Iraq's future state building. Although Faisal I had promoted the idea of a national army as a counterweight to divisive tribal tendencies, the pan-Arab platform that army officers espoused created problems with those minorities and sects at odds with that particular philosophy. Instituted by Faisal I as a force for unity, the army gradually became an ideological instrument that alienated important forces in the country.

Moreover, Iraq from the 1930s to the 1950s exhibited certain fault lines that were only to grow in severity as the years wore on. First, as has been noted, was the preponderance of a propertied tribal strata in the National Assembly, promoting its interests over all others. The various tribal laws enacted on the shaykhs' behalf, first by the British and, later on, by the independent monarchy, only served to buttress them in power, while reserving the most wretched future for the masses of landless, impoverished tribesmen and peasants who suffered under the shaykhs' whims. Second, the fabled prize for which the British had occupied Iraq from north to south—oil—did not generate large profits until the late 1950s, and those profits, when they arrived, largely went to insulate the state from popular pressures. As a result of the economic disparities and social inequalities characteristic of Iraq in the 1940s and 1950s, widespread discontent against the state and its representatives increased during this period, spawning large nationalist and socialist or communist movements that grew explosive with time.

King Ghazi's brief reign (r. 1933–39) and the period of the regency (1939–58, during which Prince Abdulillah ruled as regent for Faisal II) saw several important developments. Chief among them was the consolidation of various strongmen in power, the most important of them being King Faisal I's boon companion, the many-times prime minister Nuri al-Said. The latter quickly developed into the most forceful politician of his age, seating and unseating parliaments and planning Iraq's foreign policy in the face of Arab nationalist pressure, Iranian and Turkish designs and subterfuge, and sometimes obdurate British policy. Meanwhile, a continuously expanding Iraqi army, staffed by nationalist generals, held to its own vision of Iraq's future. The conflicting visions of the civilian leadership of Iraq and that of the army generals eventually created an unstable political atmosphere and a ripe climate for coups d'état, the first in 1936, the second in 1941, and the third, and most tragic of all, in 1958.

The 1936 Coup d'État

In the 1930s, a number of disgruntled, mostly urban-based groups began to propagate ideas of social and economic reform of the Iraqi state, calling for a more equitable distribution of resources and more say for junior members of the bureaucracy, as well as the intelligentsia and workers' movements. In particular, they railed against the strangulation of the economy by the reactionary class of tribal landlords in parliament. Socialist-leaning factions, such as the Ahali group, competed for public attention alongside the newly reorganized Iraqi Communist Party. More important were the parties that held power or would soon hold it. In 1931, the al-Shaab (People's) Party joined forces with the Watani Party to form Hizb al-Ikha al-Watani (Patriotic Brotherhood Party). A mixture of Sunnis and Shiis, the Ikha Party was also close to the Nahda Party. This alliance would propel Ikha leader Yasin al-Hashimi to the premiership. Nevertheless, developing in a climate of heavy government repression against Shii-led movements in the tribal countryside as well as Kurdish rebellions in the north, they gave voice to antigovernment measures against both the disenfranchised urban and the rural populations of the country.

In October 1936, the first of Iraq's many coups took place against the reigning government of the day. General Bakr Sidqi (1890–1937) undertook the coup, which resulted in the naming of a new prime minister, Hikmat Suleyman (1889–1964), Sidqi's ally. (Suleyman, as interior minister, had issued the order to attack the Assyrians; Sidqi was the general who had carried out the order.) The ousted government of Yasin al-Hashimi had made so many enemies that it was said that even King Ghazi secretly approved of the changeover. Suleyman formed a government that brought in many Ahali members and a greater number of Shiis than had previously been the practice in Iraqi governments (Tripp 2000, 89); he also named General Sidqi chief of the general staff. Suleyman was an Iraq nationalist who was eyed with suspicion by the more pan-Arab officer corps. When he embarked on modest attempts to redistribute Iraq's land resources, he found himself the object of virulent hostility on the part of Iraq's landholding elites. This, plus the growing resentment against the dictatorial tendencies of Sidqi, and Sidqi's eventual murder by elements of the army, led Suleyman to resign in 1937. Subsequently, one of the ex-Sharifian officers close to King Faisal I, Jamil al-Madfai, took the reins of power.

The 1941 Coup d'État and the Second British Occupation

The demise of Bakr Sidqi, instigated by a powerful clique of Arab nationalist army officers, known as the Golden Square, brought the army into politics and changed the tenor of civilian-military relations. Henceforth, all nonmilitary politicians would have to heed the army. When the al-Madfai government resigned in 1938, largely because it was considered suspect by the officer corps, the veteran politician Nuri al-Said stepped in, but even he had to be circumspect in his relations with the army. Al-Said's prior public announcements on Palestine, in which he tried to broker a resolution during the Palestinian general strike of 1936 that would "bring all sides together . . . within the framework of a larger Arab federation of the Fertile Crescent, led by the Hashemite dynasty" (Tripp 2000, 97), provided him with the Arabist aura that satisfied the Golden Square. The death in 1939 of King Ghazi in an automobile accident projected al-Said even more firmly in power, since his experience was seen as a valuable asset to the young regent, Prince Abdulillah, who was chosen as the protector and adviser of the infant Faisal II (Tripp 2000, 98–99).

When World War II (1939–45) broke out, the British put pressure on al-Said to "sever diplomatic relations with Germany, to intern all Germans, and to give whatever assistance Great Britain would require under the terms of the [Anglo-Iraqi] Treaty" (Tripp 2000, 99). But Iraq's deliberate neutrality throughout the war soon gave way to a more nationalistic, anti-British stance, which eventually brought into power Rashid Ali al-Gailani, himself allied to members of the Golden Square. In April 1941, as a result of civilian encroachment on what was seen as army prerogatives, the Golden Square, together with General Amin Zaki, the acting head of the general staff, moved against civilian politicians and, eventually, the monarchy itself. As the army took over Baghdad, the regent, joined by loyal politicians such as al-Said, al-Madfai, and Ali Jawdat al-Ayyubi, left for neighboring Transjordan.

Rashid Ali's government was immediately challenged by the British; they believed they had the justification to land troops in Iraq, although the clause in the Anglo-Iraqi Treaty they depended on was ambiguously worded. In the event, they did land troops in Basra. Spurred on by the officers of the Golden Square, Rashid Ali sent Iraqi troops to counter the British deployment. A short but bitter war erupted, which the British won in May. With the defeat of Rashid Ali's government, the regent and al-Said were once again welcomed to Baghdad. In 1942, al-Said's government declared war on the Axis and put on trial three of the four army officers who most represented the Golden Square; they were executed, although Rashid Ali al-Gailani escaped to Germany and later on made his way to Saudi Arabia.

The Portsmouth Treaty

Back in power, Nuri al-Said set about reordering Iraqi politics, serving as prime minister throughout most of the war years. He was succeeded by Hamdi al-Pachachi and Tawfiq al-Suwaidi. It was during these years that democratic influences took hold in Iraq, especially during the extremely brief premiership (February 23–June 1, 1946) of al-Suwaidi, who in a flurry of liberal activity "ended martial law, closed the al-Faw

Prince Abdulillah, serving as regent, opens the Iraqi parliament in 1942; behind him is Prime Minister Nuri al-Said. (Library of Congress)

detention camp, lifted press censorship, introduced a new Electoral Law, . . . [and] permitted political parties to form once again" (Tripp 2000, 114). At this time, the two most important political parties were al-Hizb al-Watani al-Dimuqrati (National Democratic Party, or NDP) and Hizb al-Istiqlal (Independence Party).

One of the most important events in the 1940s was the renegotiation of the Anglo-Iraqi Treaty of 1930, and it was al-Said's political ally Salih Jabr (Iraq's first Shii prime minister) who took upon himself the delicate task of setting down the final dates for the British withdrawal of its armed forces from Iraq and the rescinding of its bases. Negotiated in secret, for fear of Iraqi popular wrath, the treaty signed at Portsmouth on January 15, 1948, did, in fact, set a timetable for British withdrawal—1973 (which was 15 years past the expiration date of the 1930 treaty)—but hedged it with a clause that stated that in case of war, the British could return and take occupancy of "their" bases (Tripp 2000, 120). When the story came out, Iraqis were predictably outraged. The treaty was abandoned after 20 ministers resigned, street protests took over the capital, and Iraqi security forces shot at demonstrators, causing further anger.

The fury unleashed by the Portsmouth Treaty brought together a number of political parties such as the NDP, the Communist Party, and the Baathists (members of the Arab nationalist Baath Party). The same constellation of political groupings were to gain in strength throughout the next decade. In July 1958, they became significant players in the postmonarchy age.

Arab Nationalism, Iraqi Nationalism, and the Question of Palestine

There were many issues that defined postwar politics, the most important of which was the role of "the Arab nation" during the postcolonial age. The Palestinian question was but one aspect of that issue. From as early as 1936, when nationalist agitation for an Arab Palestine spread across all classes and social forces in Iraq, and throughout the 1940s and 1950s, when mass popular movements took up the slogan of "Palestine Is Arab," the question of Palestine dominated politics, unseated governments, and contributed to the large revolutionary social movements that eventually brought about the monarchy's demise. Still, overall, the Palestinian question came second to the conditions in Iraq and the larger Arab nation.

Generally speaking, there were three political groups that vied for the honor of supporting the Palestinian issue in Iraq: the Communist Party, the socialist parties represented by the old Ahali movement, and the Arab Baath Socialist Party. Other institutions, such as the army, were also profoundly torn by the loss of Palestine in 1948 and, at certain periods, espoused broad nationalist sympathies, later on kept in check by the prime minister and the palace. But there were substantial differences in how the question was raised by different Iraqi parties at different times.

In May 1947, Soviet foreign minister Vyacheslav Molotov called for "an independent, dual, democratic, homogeneous Arab-Jewish state" (Batatu 1979, 597). This was a radical departure for the Soviet Union, which had long championed the cause of an Arab Palestine, and correspondingly threw the Iraqi Communist Party (ICP) leadership in total panic. Emerging out of internal Soviet interests, the statement nonetheless bewildered the Iraqi Communists. Eventually, after a year of internal struggle, the ICP threw its weight behind an Arab-Jewish state, thus accepting the principle of partition that had been severely criticized by the Arab countries, only to find that it had fallen into a trap of its own making. The USSR repudiated its own statement some years later, and the ICP followed suit, but not before it had caused grave dissension among different publics in the Arab world, including Iraq.

The Arab nationalist parties were less rigid and more general about their support for Palestine (tending to conflate it in the 1930s and 1940s with neocolonialist machinations in general). The Palestinian cause was central because it was an Arab cause and not primarily because it was an example of the injustices brought about by "the capitalist-imperialist system" on a peasant economy. Even though the economic and political ramifications of Zionist migration in Palestine had long been recognized, the nationalist parties thought Palestine was, first and foremost, an Arab nationalist issue. As such, it struck a chord with the newer parties in the nationalist constellation.

The Arab Baath Socialist Party was born in Syria in or around 1941; it did not have great success in Iraq until 10 years later. By 1951, its supporters were ranked in the hundreds. By that time also, it had come under the leadership of Fuad al-Rikabi, who, together with the Baath parties of Syria, Jordan, and Lebanon, formed a National Front. This front came together with the Communists and other nationalist parties in Iraq around two central issues: They resisted the Baghdad Pact, an alliance of Great Britain, Turkey, Iran, Pakistan, and Iraq formed in 1955 to block the Soviet Union from expanding into the Arab world; and they supported Egyptian president Gamal Abdel Nasser's nationalization of the Suez Canal, the artificial waterway that linked the Mediterranean Sea with the Red and Indian Seas. Since its completion in 1869, the canal had been run by the Suez Canal Company, in which Great Britain held a majority stake. The National Front began calling for the end of Nuri al-Said's (eighth and final) government, the withdrawal of Iraq from the Baghdad Pact, the abolition of martial law, and the pursuit of "positive neutralism," the cold war policy that came to Iraq from Egypt via Syria in which countries not aligned with either the West or the Soviet Union (or China) used their neutralism to further their national aims. The die was cast. When al-Said's government finally did fall in May 1958, the revolution was but a couple of months away.

Oil and the Development Board

Oil became an important issue in the political struggles of the 1950s, whether between Iraq and the West or, increasingly, as the subtext between Iraqi governments and the people. Until then, oil production had not affected Iraq's economy in a substantial way. International capital funded and therefore controlled the Iraq Petroleum Company (IPC), investing millions of dollars to develop the oil industry in Iraq but usually purchasing what it needed for such a task from Western companies. And except for the construction of the industry's infrastructure, it required relatively few workers; it is estimated that "between 1929 and 1953, Iraqi oil workers represented no more than 2.7 percent of the total non-agricultural labor force" (Haj 1997, 71). Few of the profits stayed in Iraq, too. However, a coup in Iran in 1951 that brought the popular nationalist Muhammad Mossadeq to power led to the nationalization of the Anglo-Iranian Oil Company (AIOC). Encouraged by these events, Iraqi national-ist parties demanded an immediate renegotiation of the IPC's agreement with the major Western companies working in Iraq. Under popular pres-sure, the Iraqi government of the day was able to compel an increase in production and a 50-50 profit share but failed to drastically overhaul the whole system, as the nationalists had wanted. Nationalization of Iraq's oil resources was to remain but a dream to be realized only much later on.

The IPC's royalties, never very large in the 1930s and 1940s, now grew substantially. The government and its advisers sought to har-ness this windfall by investing oil revenues in development projects throughout the country, and so the Development Board was born. The board was granted 70 percent of Iraq's oil revenue earnings to plan nationwide projects. A critical look at those projects shows that most of them were in the agricultural sector, while only a smattering benefited industry, always very weak in Iraq. The agricultural projects focused on flood control, land reclamation, and water storage; although impor-tant for the infrastructure of agricultural lands as a whole, they were long-term projects that did not provide immediate returns. In Iraq in the 1950s, this was not good enough. They also appeared to primarily benefit the class of tribal proprietors rather than the impoverished and landless majority, whose concerns were daily taken up by the various nationalist, socialist, and communist parties in the country. The latter had long promoted the idea that a small elite of landed shaykhs and gentry were diverting the country's riches into their coffers; the large agricultural schemes envisaged by the Development Board only proved the opposition's claims and buttressed that popular perception.

Education and Culture under the Iraqi Monarchy (1921–1958)

The early years of nation-building experienced an unfolding panorama of literary and artistic currents. The history of education, too, contributed its fair share of development to the emergence of progressive politics in the country, especially with regard to women's issues. Thanks to the burgeoning publication of countless autobiographies of the monarchist era, ranging from political (and sometimes self-serving) accounts to a genre of urban literature that can only be termed as stories of the city, we are now in a position to substantiate the political histories with a more nuanced view of Iraqi educational and cultural activity during the period of the monarchy.

Education and Its Impact on Women

The development of education for Iraqis of both genders began even before Iraq came under British rule, but because a public education was a complete novelty for females, it affected women perhaps more than men. By 1921, 21 schools for girls were in operation throughout the country, with an attendance of 2,500. The Dominican Sisters opened up a girls' school in Baghdad with almost 1,000 students; though most of their pupils were Christian, a number of Muslim girls began to attend as well. In 1924, meanwhile, some schools were assigned the task of opening a training class for women teachers, especially in Mosul and Baghdad. In that same year, several secondary schools for boys were opened, but girls had to wait until 1925, when the first American private high school for girls was opened, under the auspices of the church-sponsored United Mission of Mesopotamia (Longrigg 1953, 169).

By 1950, tremendous strides had been taken in the education both of men and women. The fact that instruction was free and primary education was made compulsory undoubtedly accelerated the process. Nearly a third of the 6,000 primary teachers in government schools were women, as were a similar proportion among teachers at higher levels (Longrigg 1953, 390). In 1950 alone, it was estimated that 200,000 children were being educated in Iraq, a statistic that went some way toward countering the nationalist parties' slogans that the British-influenced educational system in Iraq was elitist. High school graduates could apply to enter a range of schools such as the Law School, the Engineering College, the Royal College of Medicine, the College of Agriculture, and several schools of arts and sciences and the fine arts.

Education did prepare women to meet different expectations, but for a long time, it barely made a dent in their social emancipation. In the early 1920s and 1930s, becoming secular in Iraq was a difficult proposition for girls as well as their families, especially when it meant a direct attack on fundamental symbols of tradition, the head scarf (hijab) and the black cloak Iraqi women wear when they step outside of the house (*abaya*). And in the popular perception of the time, the education of girls went hand in hand with the lifting of the veil. The struggle over the lifting of the *hijab* and *abaya* consumed a ferocious energy, on the part of those opposed to its withdrawal as well as on the part of others who fought for its extinction. "The revolution over the *hijab*," as one Iraqi woman phrased it, consumed a great deal of ink and paper, because it was mostly fought out in the embryonic Iraqi press. Among the chief detractors of the *hijab* and *abaya* were two very famous Iraqi poets, Jamil Sidqi al-Zahawi (1863–1936) and Maruf al-Rusafi (1875–1945), who went head to head with the "reactionary" group of scholars, editorialists, and newspaper columnists in the mid-1920s to hammer out a feminist charter, calling for the eradication of the *hijab* and *abaya* because it was "a false guardian" and imprisoned women in fear. In any event, the social and religious custom of wearing a *hijab* and *abaya* was discontinued over time, and by the 1940s, most Iraqi women (in the cities, at least) went bareheaded to their schools, universities, and offices.

Poetry and Free Verse

In order to understand the transformations in Iraqi culture throughout the period of the monarchy, we must begin with poetry, that indispensable window onto the Iraqi soul. As early as the 1920 revolt, poetry was used to express conflicting emotions. Using traditional form and structure but expressing new themes, Iraqi poets unleashed a torrent of revolutionary rhetoric that stirred their audiences to national unity. In classical Arabic poetry the meter (*wazn*), which was codified in the eighth century, is based on the length of syllables. Each line (*bayt*, sing.; *abyat*, pl.) is divided into two half-lines (*shatrayn*). The rhyme (*qafia*) is basically determined by the last consonant of a word, and it is the pronunciation, not the writing, of the word that counts. Lebanese scholar Philip Hitti in 1936 describes the effect on the audience as follows: "No people in the world, perhaps, manifest such enthusiastic admiration for literary expression and are so moved by the word, spoken or written, as the Arabs. Modern audiences in Baghdad, Damascus and Cairo can be stirred to the highest degree by the recital of poems, only vaguely comprehended, and by the delivery of orations in the classical tongue, though it be only partially understood. The rhythm, the rhyme, the music, produce on them the effect of what they call 'lawful magic' (*sihr halal*)." (quoted in Chejne 1969, 5). On the one hand, one of the most famous poets of the revolt, Muhammad Mahdi al-Basir, wrote and declaimed his poetry in public spaces (usually mosques), becoming famous for poems about national sacrifice and the notion of *al-watan* (the homeland or nation), that all-encompassing category that upheld a higher ideal than that espoused by narrow sectarian or ethnic divisions (Tramontini 2002–03, 175). On the other hand, the poet Sayyid Habib al-Ubaydi al-Mosuli used poetry not only to celebrate the nation but to promote an aggressive anti-Westernization, going so far as to accuse the British in Iraq of being "an enemy dressed like a friend . . . [who] is nothing but a fraudulent intruder" (Tramontini 2002–03, 178).

Leslie Tramontini believes that this two-sided articulation, or what she calls an "us/them" dichotomy, was prevalent throughout the nationalistic poetry of the 1920s. One of Iraq's greatest poets, Muhammad Mahdi al-Jawahiri (1900–97) reflected that duality throughout his long life but also surpassed it to become the voice of countless generations of Iraqis, aspiring through him to capture, in the words of Saadi Simawe, the "holy trinity . . . [of] homeland, liberty and beauty" (Simawe 1997, vii). Unlike many of his more revolutionary colleagues, al-Jawahiri remained a neoclassical poet who throughout his life, infused the classical structure of Arab poetry with new themes. A prolific writer both of poetry and prose (he became a journalist after a short stint as King Faisal I's court poet), al-Jawahiri's works were collected in a *diwan* (anthology) in 1973, covering 50 years of his poetry. In 1992, by then an elderly man in his early 90s, al-Jawahiri electrified Jordanian television audiences with a ringing recital of a poem originally written for the then-regent of Iraq, Abdulillah; standing ramrod tall before King Hussein of Jordan, while wearing his trademark *araqchin* (white skullcap), al-Jawahiri recited the same poem, now in the Jordanian king's honor, without forgetting a single line or missing a beat.

But was Iraqi verse only about big themes of patriotism, resistance, sacrifice, and rebirth? An important school of Iraqi poets thought differently. The pathbreaking works of the poets Nazik al-Malaika (1922–2007), Badr Shakir al-Sayyab (1926–64), and Abdul Wahhab al-Bayyati (1926–99) still manage to attract an enormous following in the Arab world. Al-Malaika's first poetry collection, *Ashiqat al-layl* (Lover of the night) was published in 1947. Since that time, she has become one of the most celebrated poets in the Arab world, principally because she pioneered the writing of *tafila* (free verse), a pioneering step in Arab literature. The structure of Arab verse up to that time had been constrained by classical form and orientation. In addition, al-Malaika was a brilliant critic, who not only wrote rigorous expositions of the works of Arab authors but also translated several Western books into Arabic.

Al-Sayyab, the "Poet of the 1958 Revolution" who had suffered repression during the final years of the monarchy (at one point he was forced into exile in Kuwait), was also a proponent of free verse. His 1960 book, *Rain Song*, is considered one of the major works of modern Iraqi poetry. Like al-Sayyab, al-Bayyati was forced into exile in the 1950s, returning to Iraq after the overthrow of the monarchy in 1958. Under subsequent governments, he alternately served as a cultural attaché, was exiled, or was simply a traveler who liked to return home. He published 25 collections of poetry between 1950 and 1998, a good deal of it dealing with his contentious relations with the various Iraqi governments. At the time of his death in Damascus, he was again in exile, having been stripped of his citizenship by the government of Saddam Hussein.

Iraqi Art

A great Iraqi sculptor, Muhammad Ghani Hikmat recalls that had it not been for the support of the Iraqi state in the 1940s, he would never have had the opportunity to travel to Italy to perfect his skills (conversation with the author, Amman, July 2004). His comment and the recollections of many other talented artists from Iraq point to the systematic support granted to artists in the royalist era. As a result of this backing, the fine and plastic arts witnessed a rapid development that few Arab countries could match. In fact, even today, Iraqi art possesses a cachet in neighboring countries that verges on reverence.

That the Iraqi government of the day realized the innate genius of several painters and sculptors of the period and sent them abroad to study is only one half of the equation. The other half is that those same artists came back to revitalize the local Iraqi scene, after which nothing was the same. The first and best-known artists of the period, Faiq Hassan (1914–92) and Jawad Salim (1921–61), blazed a path that was followed by several outstanding artists of their generation. Hassan is remembered for his trademark paintings of wild stallions; Salim, for his massive mural in a Baghdad square of the Iraqi people unchained.

After World War II, Hassan and Salim formed a group called la Societé Primitive, influenced as they were by French impressionism. Later on, the group came simply to be known as the Pioneers (al-Ruwwad). Among its fluctuating membership were several great painters of rural Iraq, among them the surgeon Khalid al-Qassab (1924–2004). Artists such as Hassan, Salim, al-Qassab, and Hikmat took inspiration from the light, color, and texture of Iraq itself and reinterpreted the history and culture of their native society in broad strokes and bold shades, exhibiting their works all over the world.

Detail of the Monument of Liberation by Jawad Salim, located in Tahrir Square in Baghdad (AP Photo/Hadi Mizban)

Conclusion

On July 14, 1958, Brigadier General Abdul-Karim Qasim overthrew the monarchy, setting in motion a series of developments that led to the massacre of nearly all of the members of the Hashemite royal family. The survivors were the king's aunt, Princess Bedia, and the regent Abdulillah's wife, Princess Hiyam, whose fabled escape from the palace after the slaughter of the royal family is a story still recalled by exiled royalists.

The revolution of 1958 brought to an end 37 years of nation-building that had begun with the initial colonial era followed by a period of independence constrained by both domestic and external factors. Although the new nation-state quickly developed an internal coherence of its own, it was never able to surmount the fatal flaws that were tacked on from the very beginning. For reasons of their own, both the British and the nascent monarchy had chosen to rely on a minority of landowners and ex-military officials to steer the ship of state, disregarding in the process the diversity and complexity of the Iraqi experience. Although King Faisal I had tried very hard to make of Iraq a state representative of all its people, later governments clung to a narrower vision of what it meant to be an Iraqi. A unitary state was not a foregone conclusion, but it became so after politicians and military officers jettisoned the trappings of the liberal constitutionalist order they had once subscribed to. The issues of Arab nationalism, Iraqi nationalism, and the question of Palestine also added their weight to the legitimacy of the Iraqi state. Meanwhile, the glaring discrepancies and downright injustices in social, economic, and political conditions paved the way for a revolution of massive proportions so that when it finally came, it destroyed a weak, well-meaning state order that had already been hijacked by reactionary elements among the army and the propertied classes.

8

THE GROWTH OF THE REPUBLICAN REGIMES AND THE EMERGENCE OF BAATHIST IRAQ (1958–1979)

After the revolution of 1958 toppled the monarchy, Iraq went through several years of instability, as the early republican regimes struggled to maintain their hold on the country's fractious population. Abdul-Karim Qasim's government was itself overthrown in 1962, and the political ideology that he had espoused—Iraqi nationalism—made way for pan-Arabism, the movement inspired by Egyptian president Gamal Abdel Nasser. Eventually, an offshoot of Arab nationalism—Baathism—became the dominant party ideology of its day. This chapter will discuss the tumultuous years of 1958–79, the social, political, and economic developments that marked those years; and the sociopolitical groundwork laid for the eventual rise to power of the Baathist regime of Saddam Hussein.

The First Republican Regime (1958–1963)

When Brigadier General Abdul-Karim Qasim (1914–63) took power in 1958, his regime attempted to show that there was a fount of goodwill for the new government. While the royalists seethed at the massacre of the Hashemite family and Britain and Jordan made threatening noises about invading Iraq, a substantial majority of Iraqis came out in the streets in the first few days of the revolution to voice hopes that Qasim's coup augured better times. According to political historian Charles Tripp, much of this public enthusiasm was stage-managed by the Communists and other national parties in Iraq (Tripp 2000, 149–150). Still, to the poor peasant and the city intellectual, no less the Kurdish laborer and the small Shii trader, Qasim's coup d'état could not have come at a better moment. Burdened by disproportionate taxes, oppressed by absentee landlords, and chafing under discriminatory policies against ethnic and sectarian groups, many Iraqi individuals and communities hoped that the revolutionary fervor of the disparate factions in power would lift them out of their misery and provide them with a better life.

Qasim's revolutionary government, which included representation by all of the major political blocs except the Communists, promised a national agenda in which feudal relations in the countryside would be dismantled; country-wide programs tackling poverty, health, and literacy would be promoted; ethnic and sectarian divisions abolished; and economic development, reenergized. Furthermore, a three-man Sunni-Shii-Kurd Sovereignty Council was to fulfill the ceremonial functions of the head of state. But from the very beginning, the revolution began to devour its children: The latent split between Iraqi nationalists and pan-Arabists became real; the jostling between parties relying on mass

A celebratory crowd in Baghdad days after the overthrow of the monarchy by a coup led by Brigadier General Abdul-Karim Qasim (AP Photo/hg)

membership and the other more traditional political factions came out in the open; and Iraq's fragile economy could not withstand the radical reorientations imposed on its agricultural, commercial, or industrial bases.

Iraqi Nationalism Versus Arab Nationalism

From the very first, unresolved ideas of identity and political allegiance roiled the revolutionary leadership. Qasim, in the beginning a man of little ideological conviction (Batatu 1978, 808–809), soon became a believer in Iraqi nationalism. Meanwhile, the number-two man in the revolutionary government, Colonel Abdul-Salam Aref (1921–66), worshipped the Arab nationalist leader of Egypt, Nasser, and wanted at once to unite Iraq with the United Arab Republic, the union between Syria and Egypt that had been formed on February 1, 1958, under the leadership of Nasser and the Arab Socialist Baath Party. One of the founding members of the Arab Socialist Baath Party, Michel Aflaq (1910–89), arrived in Baghdad soon after the coup. With his message of Arab unity, he fanned the flames even further. While initially lending support to the idea of Arab unity, Qasim eventually fell back on his particularist ideology, Iraqi nationalism. Supported by the greatest populist movement in the country, the Iraqi Communist Party (ICP), he began a campaign to unseat the main proponent of the pan-Arab campaign in Iraq, Colonel Abdul-Salam Aref. Aref was the face of the Iraqi Free Officers, the group of military leaders of which Qasim was initially a member and without whose support there would have been no coup. The Free Officers looked toward Egypt for their ideology as well as their name. (President Nasser had been one of the original Free Officers, along with Anwar al-Sadat, that initiated the coup that overthrew the king of Egypt, Farouq.) That ideology was pan-Arabism (sometimes identified as Nasserism), but in 1958 pan-Arabism for Iraq would have amounted to domination by Egypt, and to a lesser extent by Syria, in the United Arab Republic, as its most junior member.

The Iraqi nationalists' alarm at the rapidly changing turn of events owed to several reasons. Samira Haj has argued that the economic base for many of the ministers and influential power brokers in Qasim's regime lay in commercial and industrial interests (Haj 1997, 112–117). For the most part, they represented the interests of national capital, which would have been swamped by competition with Syrian and especially Egyptian industries, the latter having undergone a period of expansion after the Egyptian revolution of 1952. Moreover, the Iraqi

The first session of Iraq's republican cabinet on July 22, 1958. From left: Colonel Abdul-Salam Aref, deputy prime minister; Brigadier General Abdul-Karim Qasim, prime minister; and General Naguib el-Robey, chairman of the Sovereignty Council; the others are unidentified (AP Photo/Bag. H.)

Communist Party, which could easily manipulate the Iraqi "street" into demonstrating against any government of the moment if the latter pursued objectives inimical to the ICP's interests, was against union because it also feared that the more "progressive" Iraqi bourgeoisie would be subsumed within that of Egypt's. Finally, it is important to remember that Arab nationalism sat uneasily with Iraqi Kurds, and its pan-Sunni component displeased some, if not all the Shiis.

Aref's removal soon became expedient, if not necessary, to Qasim's survival. A month and a half after the July revolution, Aref was dismissed from his position in the cabinet and sent abroad to act as Iraqi ambassador to the German Federal Republic. At the same time, Arab nationalists in the government and in the ministries and departments were sacked, with Iraqi nationalists taking their place. When Aref made a surprise return to Baghdad in October 1958, he was immediately arrested and "charged with plotting against Iraq and the life of Qasim, its leader" (Haj 1997, 118). He was convicted of treason and originally sentenced to death but later pardoned—a decision that Qasim would regret.

THE KURDISH QUESTION FROM 1958 TO 1963

One of the key questions bedeviling the Qasim government was what policy to institute toward the Kurds. As it so happened, this was exactly the same question posed by the Kurds themselves with respect to the new regime. An important Kurdish communist activist by the name of Aziz al-Hajj, whose account is translated and reproduced below, explains at some length why some Kurds at first welcomed the overthrow of the monarchy in 1958 then lived to rue the day. Elated that the new provisional constitution emphasized that Kurds were equal partners with the Arabs in Iraq, the Kurds initially were strongly pro-Qasim. But three years after the 1958 revolution, as Kurdish gains began to slip away, the almost inevitable friction between the two major ethnic groups in Iraq—Arabs and Kurds—again began to mount, and by 1961, the Kurds were once more in full-fledged revolt against the central government.

> [The Constitution said:] "The Iraqi state is based on the cooperation between all citizens and the respect of their rights as well as their freedoms, the Arabs and Kurds are considered partners in this nation, and the constitution safeguards their national rights within Iraqi unity as a whole." Still, article 2 of the same constitution stated that "Iraq is a part of the Arab nation," a provision regarded warily (or with reservations) by the Kurds.
>
> Another great gain in favor of the Kurdish people was the return after the revolution of (the legendary Kurdish rebel leader) Mulla Mustafa al-Barzani to great honors [in Iraq] as well as the return of hundreds of the Barzani [tribal members] who had been refugees with him in the USSR. [In addition], many Kurdish newspapers and magazines of different political orientations were published, the Kurdish Democratic Party [KDP] was officially established in early 1961, and a government department was instituted to teach the Kurdish language. . . . Relations between al-Barzani (who had become the head of the KDP) and Qasim were so strong that al-Barzani stated that he was but a soldier in Qasim's army. . . . The important gains of the July revolution for the Kurds [consisted of] a new political climate in the first year

Social and Economic Developments

During the same month the Qasim regime ushered in a major revolutionary decree, a new agricultural law, the Policy of Agricultural Reform *of the revolution [which made clear that the country would no longer] tolerate the forced unity of Arabs and Kurds in one nation-state but instead rely on the creation of new currents of reciprocal cultural exchange, in which the Kurds strongly supported Qasim's government, and the KDP condemned any separatist pronouncements, to the point where separation from Iraq was seen as deleterious to the Kurdish people itself. . . .*

But in 1961, elements of tension began to accumulate and to mature rapidly in the Kurdish region, and this stemmed from 1) the chauvinist/racist mentality of most of the ruling military clique, and the reliance on one person in power; 2) the need of the regime to distract the Iraqi people from accumulating economic and social problems, especially the calls for democracy and 3) imperialist plots, especially that of oil companies, as well as plots of [Iraqi] reactionary groups and Iranian government elements. As a result of this . . . [a double strategy was formulated against Arab-Kurdish unity]. Iranian-supported Kurdish landowners [in Iraq], who were against any form of government-instituted land reform, declared an armed rebellion in the first half of 1959, but it failed in the face of Kurdish Communist groups and the Iraqi army. . . . Second, Arab reactionary groups in Iraq, including Arab nationalists and chauvinist/racist elements in the army and government kept up their hostility against the Kurds. . . .

On the field, the fire of repression was directed this time against the KDP and its leadership, [so that] the activities of the government department responsible for teaching Kurdish were frozen, some reactionary newspapers began a poisonous campaign against the Kurds, Kurdish was neglected in official government ministries in the Kurdish region . . . and the government embarked upon a series of steps to abandon the industrial, architectural, and agricultural [potential] of the Kurdish provinces (for instance, the sugar factory in Suleymania was discontinued, as were the factories for socks and underclothes in Irbil) and Kurdish papers and journals were stopped. The government also [began a campaign] of mass imprisonment and execution of Kurdish nationalist elements.

Source: Dr. Aziz al-Hajj. *Al-qadiya al-Kurdiyya fi al-Iraq: Al-tarikh wa al-afaq.* (The Kurdish question in Iraq: History and the future). The Arab Institute for Research and Publications, Beirut, 1994, pp. 27–31).

(in Arabic, al-Islah al-Zirai). The law set out to reform, if not dismantle completely, the huge landed estates that had been the mainstay of tribal as well as urban landlords:

> *[It] imposed ceilings on individual holdings (618 acres in irrigated areas, 1,236 acres in rainfall areas) and promised that the sequestrated land would be redistributed to landless fellahin [tribal peasantry] in plots of about 20–40 acres each. In addition, cooperatives were to be set up and new contracts, more beneficial to the peasants, were introduced to regulate relations between landlords and their tenants and sharecroppers (Farouk-Sluglett and Sluglett 1987, 1990, 76).*

It has been argued that although this law was viewed in retrospect as a radical change by the landowning classes themselves, for the urban migrants and the sharecroppers in the fields, it was seen as far too "reformist" and "mild" (al-Khafaji 2004, 191). In fact, there is a certain school of thought that believes that, in practice, Qasim's revolutionary land decree was far less extreme than that laid out in his own pronouncements on the subject and that provisions for compensation as well as the retention of certain properties by landlords was designed to "possibly even lead them [landowners] to become auxiliary allies within a reformed nation" (Haj 1997, 121). The ICP saw the law as too conciliatory to the class of landed proprietors and totally insensible to the interests of the agriculturists in the countryside; although the party initially continued its support for the regime, eventually the ICP-dominated peasant societies were brought out in the streets of Baghdad to function as a powerful lobby in favor of harsher regulations against the landed classes. Furthermore, as the historian Thabit Abdullah has shown, while "almost all who lived off agriculture owned some land" in 1971 (Abdullah 2003, 160–161), the reforms affecting agriculture sharply curtailed its production so that whereas the agricultural sector represented 17 percent of GNP in 1960, by 1980, the figure had dropped to 8 percent.

Qasim's regime also attempted to protect the nascent Iraqi industrial sector. While some writers have inserted quotation marks around the term *industrial* in the belief that the sector was so underdeveloped that it could barely stand on its own and tottered in between trade and agriculture, both of which it relied on heavily (Haj 1997, 130), some light industries did well under the Qasim government. Oil extraction and the manufacture of soap, cloth, woolen textiles, and leather profited from tax exemptions, tariffs, and bans on foreign imports. Economic nationalism also dovetailed with the government's very popular Law No. 80, which "confiscated 99.5% of the [Iraq Petroleum Company's] concession land" (Abdullah 2003, 161). The concessions had been granted in 1952 to encourage the IPC to develop production in the unexploited territories. Law 80, proclaimed by the Iraqi government in December 1961, took back almost all of the concessionary territory without compensation to the IPC. A justification for the takeback was that the IPC had done nothing with the territory. The IPC was also seen as an exploiter of Iraq's most precious natural resource and a company that withheld profits that were the Iraqi peoples' birthright: The majority of profits originally went to the company's international investors, and even after 1952, only 50 percent went to Iraq. The move was logical; a dearth of government revenue necessitated an improvement of the terms agreed with the IPC in 1952. However, despite the passage of the law, the IPC immediately turned the tables on the government by initiating a go-slow policy in the fields that it controlled, depriving the Iraqi state of much-needed income. The issue of which sector—the government or the oil companies—was the ultimate arbiter of oil policy in Iraq was only to be resolved under the government of Saddam Hussein in the early 1980s.

The Shawwaf Revolt of 1959

The agricultural law of October 1958 helped escalate the struggle between Arab nationalists and Iraqi nationalists, culminating in the bloody events of March 1959 in Mosul. Colonel Abdul-Wahhab al-Shawwaf, commander of the Fifth Brigade in Mosul, Iraq's third-largest city, lent his name to a major revolt against Qasim's regime; the revolt, generally speaking, allied landowning tribal shaykhs of the Shammar tribe to Arab nationalist parties against the Communist-led popular quarters of the city. Although the latter were numerically inferior to the combined weight of the nationalists and conservative landowners, they were able to find support in certain elements of the armed forces, the artisans in the city, and the agriculturists of the Christian villages surrounding Mosul (Batatu 1979, 870–879). There was also some belated support for the Arab nationalists from Egypt and Syria, but in the end, it did not prove conclusive. The causes for the Shawwaf revolt have variously been attributed both to the institution of the new agrarian law (which threatened the large landholdings of shaykhs and notables in the northern region) and to the assault on Arabism, a principle held dear by many of the Free Officers who had instigated the 1958 revolution.

On March 8, 1959, the main Mosul radio station broadcast a manifesto in the name of Colonel Shawwaf declaring Qasim a traitor and castigated in vociferous terms the anti-Arab nationalist forces for bringing about the social, economic, and political ruin of the country.

THE RED "MENACE"

One of the best historians of Iraq, Khalil Ibrahim Hussayn (affectionately dubbed "Reuter" by his friends for his incomparable breadth of knowledge), wrote an excellent but highly partisan account of the Shawwaf revolt. Himself a member of the Free Officers, the Arab nationalist grouping that came to power in 1958, his book illuminates the seemingly insidious way in which the Communists took control both of Iraq's government apparatus and its organs of civil society. In the paragraphs translated and presented below, Hussayn's scorn for the Communists, as well as for Qasim's "weak" government, is scorching.

> The Iraqi Communist Party tried to model itself on the Russian Communist Party and its experience in the October Revolution of 1917 in creating resistance groups to its local enemies in the country as well as to foreign invaders . . . such as those instituted by the government of the Popular Front in Spain in 1936 in its struggle with Franco. That is why, one day after the revolution of July 1958 occurred, that is, on the 15th of July, the Political Committee of the ICP . . . published a special edition [of its paper] in which it broached the philosophy, politics, and rationale for the establishment of popular resistance. The leaders of the ICP met with Abdul-Karim Qasim and gave him a copy of their memorandum . . . and he supported them, thinking that he could manipulate them to realize his own goal of taking over the principle organs of the country . . . in his struggle with the Arab nationalists and the idea of Arabism, and after him the deluge!
>
> Anyone who reads the clauses of the memorandum will notice at once that the ICP's purpose was not to create popular resistance committees to help the army in its defense against Iraq's external enemies, should there be a foreign invasion, or a maintenance of the republican regime, but to create an organization that would serve as a popular base that could be used to rally for demonstrations, to attack other political parties, to supervise peoples' houses and to control their movements, and to insult [and abuse] them. . . .
>
> The Department of Military Intelligence [wrote] a report addressed to the leaders of the revolution [i.e., Qasim and his government ministers] . . . that the ICP undoubtedly aimed to create a communist army [without government oversight] that would be ultimately responsible to the communist leadership, which would make it a state within a state. It would also aim to establish a "red dictatorship" that would create fear and anxiety among the citizenry, and [provide the context] for armed resistance to other parties, and even the Iraqi army itself.

Source: Khalil Ibrahim Hussayn. *Thawrat al-Shawwaf fi al-Mosul, 1959* (The Shawwaf revolt in Mosul in 1959). Baghdad: Bashar Press, 1987, pp. 271–274.

Although the Arab nationalists were able to garner some rapid successes within the city, the communist-led counteroffensive was too strong; al-Shawwaf himself was killed in the early stages of the rebellion. Meanwhile, the Iraqi Air Force, under the command of progovernment forces, repeatedly hit the barracks of the Fifth Brigade, and tanks entered the city. The Arab nationalists, once a defiant force of opposition, were decimated one by one. The city descended into chaos as urban notables fought against tribesmen; Kurds, Yazidis, and Arabs joined opposing sides; and peasants and workers were executed for belonging to the Arab Socialist Baath Party by ICP sympathizers, who counted the working classes as invaluable allies. "The days of March" resulted in the execution and outright murder of hundreds of people and is still remembered as an indescribable bloodbath, topping even that of the July revolution.

Historian Hanna Batatu makes the excellent point that the massacres that took place over four days in Mosul arose out of a combination of ethnic and sectarian causes, as well as of class interests (Batatu 1979, 863–871). For instance, he notes that the conscripts of the Fifth Brigade, who were Kurdish, fought against their superior officers, who were Arab; Kurdish landed shaykhs sided with Arab landholding shaykhs against their own peasants; and in certain poor quarters of Mosul, Arab laborers supported Kurdish and Christian peasants against their own coreligionists. Overall, it was not the fragile sense of community, society, and state affecting Mosul that stands out in the 1959 revolt but the way that one party made expedient alliances over class, ethnicity, and sect to emerge as the supreme organization in the country. However, the rise to power of the ICP, whose sway now extended over the press, labor unions, and universities, eventually brought about the seeds of its own downfall, and the collapse of its alliance with Qasim's government.

Communists against Nationalists

The communist "tide" (dubbed in Arabic, *al-madd al-shuyui*) was a highly volatile period in Iraq's history that has yet to be properly documented. Briefly, it signaled the rapid ascension of the ICP to power and influence and the just as speedy dissolution of the Arab nationalist parties in the country. A purge of thousands of military officers and government ministers ensued, as Communists supplanted left-leaning, liberal, and traditionalist party members in office and in the army. By late 1959, the ICP numbered about 20,000 members, and its attendant professional associations and unions correspondingly attracted thousands of affiliates. A lawyer and member of one of Iraq's influential families confided to this writer that the atmosphere at Baghdad University was suffocating at the time; Communists periodically entered classrooms in full session or the university cafeteria to "kidnap" or openly attack students. The Communist paper *al-Ittihad al-Shaab* (The peoples' union) was thrust in the faces of students and professors alike and woe to those who dared to challenge it.

Some communists or "fellow travelers" have written riveting memoirs reflecting upon that time. A one-time member of the Central Committee of the ICP, Dhannun Ayyub was originally a schoolteacher from Mosul who became a newspaper editor and then, under Qasim, director-general of the Ministry of General Guidance (Wizarat al-Irshad al-Amma). As such, he was made responsible for the press, radio, television, and cinema in Baghdad. Claiming that he deplored the events of Mosul, and especially the brutal assassinations of noncommunists in the city, he was nonetheless initially seen as a procommunist sympathizer who staffed the ministry with members of the Communist Party. A reformer who dismissed more than 100 ministry employees in one week because of their purported inefficiency, Ayyub increasingly became a vocal defender of Qasim in his ongoing duel with the Egyptian president Nasser on Iraqi state radio (Ayyub 1984, n.p.). The dictum of "power corrupts" may well have applied to him. Ayyub, who by his own admission had now become a pro-Qasim partisan, parted ways with the increasingly vociferous Communists over ideology and tactics, only to be labeled a "renegade" and even an "Aflaqi" (a covert supporter of Arab nationalism, in reference to one of the cofounders of the Arab Socialist Baath Party, Michel Aflaq).

It was this tension between the ICP and the more traditionalist socialist/nationalist parties such as the National Democratic Party (NDP), the emergent Baath Party in Iraq, the Iraqi nationalists, and the pro-Qasim faction that set the scene for the revolution's first year. Qasim had watched with growing frustration as the Communists grew in strength, while other parties were marginalized; as a man who believed that political balance was essential to his survival, this was not a good omen. At first, he attempted to rein in the Communists or mollify them by turn with further appointments. However, after the Communists' responsibility for the horrifying events of Kirkuk in July 1959 became widely known—120 houses, stores, and cafés largely belonging to the Turkmen minority were burned to the ground, some with their occupants still inside, on the grounds that they belonged to members of an anticommunist ethnic minority—Qasim began to

Nationalists and other Iraqis publicly mock Egyptian president Gamal Abdel Nasser after he voiced support for the March 1959 Mosul uprising. (AP Photo/Jim Pringle)

arrest a number of powerful ICP leaders and to dismiss others from their government posts. This attempt to curb the ICP was cut short by a Baathist attempt on Qasim's life in October 1959 (one of the would-be assassins was a 22-year-old Saddam Hussein). Again, Communist fortunes rebounded, as the attention of the government switched to hunting down Baathist cadres to avenge the attempted assassination of "the Sole Leader," Qasim's sobriquet.

Islamic Movements among Sunnis, Shiis, and Kurds

It is often forgotten that at the height of Iraq's secularist "moment," religiously inspired movements jostled for Iraqis' attention as well. Among the most famous was the Daawa Party, a major Shii organization that emerged slightly before the 1958 revolution and whose rapid spread was helped, in part, by the clergy's worry that the ICP was making inroads among Iraq's Shii youth. Among the Sunnis in the 1940s and 1950s, the Muslim Brotherhood (MB), spreading out from Egypt, gained rapid ascendancy in Iraq. The MB also influenced the first Islamic organizations in Iraqi Kurdistan.

All three Islamic movements, as well as those that followed in their wake, essentially started as Muslim reformist currents that aimed at the education and spiritual regeneration of their followers. Only slowly were they politicized. In 1946, the MB in Egypt sent several preachers to neighboring Arab countries to spread the word of Islam. Shaykh Amjad al-Zahawi became the first head of the Society for the Salvation of Palestine; from that time onward, the MB in Iraq joined nationalist rallies against the Portsmouth Treaty signed in 1948 allying Iraq to Britain. The MB also concerned itself with educational activities and sermons and lectures at mosques inside Iraq. Their chief bugbear was the ICP, whose members were seen as apostates with whom no true Muslim would form an alliance. Unfortunately for them, under the Qasim regime, the Communists became very powerful and, in fact, targeted the Islamic parties, who went underground for a while. Generally speaking, even though the MB finally received permission to become a legal party, it continued to be severely restricted under the republican governments. The MB's quiet activism even led to charges of collusion with the state. In the Kurdish case, for instance, the MB was criticized by later Kurdish nationalists because it had not called for armed struggle against the "infidel" Baathist government of 1963, with its "heathen nationalism and racism on one side, and communist socialism on the other" (quoted by Shourush in Abdul-Jabar 2002, 178).

The Shii parties, however, had a longer history of Islamic resistance. As early as 1950, the Movement of Muslim Youth was established in Najaf; its example was followed by many other Shii groups, some of which grew in importance while others collapsed. A new and much more forceful movement called al-Daawa (the Call) was founded in 1957, established by eight clerics and lay scholars. Its initial inspiration was Sayyid Muhsin al-Hakim in Najaf, but later on, it attracted another important religious scholar, Sayyid Muhammad Baqir al-Sadr (1935–80). Because there was deep hostility to involving the Shii clergy in politics in the Shii shrine cities as well as elsewhere, the appeal of al-Daawa had to be buttressed by scholarly arguments. Al-Daawa members worked to rejuvenate religious education and to revive rites and practices that formed an integral part of Shii faith-based traditions. After 1967, al-Daawa, like other religious parties, was suppressed violently by the state. In general, observers note that the politicization of religious movements and the overwhelming support for resistance against the state among the rank and file occurred most visibly after the

1970s, as the Baath regime began to stoke sectarian and ethnic rivalries and persecute religious communities.

Iraqi Kurds in the Republic's Early Years

With the demise of the Hashemite monarchy, Kurdish nationalism in Iraq enjoyed a brief renaissance, though this was probably not foreseen by the generals, especially the Free Officers. The revolutionary government's more liberal attitude toward political parties allowed, among others, the Kurdistan Democratic Party (KDP) to emerge from the shadows. At this time, the KDP was led by Mulla Mustafa al-Barzani as the party's president, however al-Barzani's background and outlook, that of a guerrilla leader, was much different than that of the urban intellectuals who had chosen him to lead the KDP. As a result, intraparty rivalries, not to mention Kurdish tribal rivalries, occupied al-Barzani's attention in the late 1950s. All of this was to the benefit of General Qasim who was only too glad to pay lip service to Kurdish aspirations but preferred a weakened KDP (van Bruinessen 1992, 27).

As Qasim established his hold on the government, Iraqi nationalism became dominant over pan-Arabism, and this benefited the Kurds, who believed they had a better chance of achieving their own nationalist goals in an independent Iraq than if Iraq were part of the United Arab Republic. Furthermore, since Iraq was drawing closer to the Soviet Union, al-Barzani, in 1961, hoped to exploit this new friendship by asking the USSR to intercede on behalf of the Kurds. This the Soviets refused to do, and Qasim, perhaps angered at al-Barzani's perceived meddling, decided to foment further division among the Kurds by encouraging opposition tribes to rebel against al-Barzani.

In the end, the move backfired against Qasim. The Iraqi military was soon drawn into what had been an intertribal war so that by the end of 1961, the Iraqi army was battling the Kurds' determined insurrection. Qasim made another blunder vis-à-vis the Kurds when he outlawed the KDP. This played into al-Barzani's hands by forcing a number (though not all) of his tribal opponents to join the insurrection. Perhaps because the fighting was done in the north, in Kurdish territory, the army failed to defeat the Kurdish guerrillas. This added fuel to the anti-Qasim fires in Baghdad and led to his own political downfall and demise in 1963.

The Kuwait Question

Despite ICP criticism of Qasim's economic and social reforms as too reformist and limited to change the life of the poor, Qasim has gone down in Iraqi history as a champion of the poor. He was the first ruler of modern-day Iraq to envisage the housing of Baghdad's disadvantaged classes, establishing Revolution City (a large housing project later to be renamed Saddam City and eventually Sadr City). He was also a secular nationalist who spent funds on health and education and changed the law to ameliorate the legal situation of women with regards to marriage and inheritance. Moreover, he allowed the establishment of trade unions and tried his best to improve workers' conditions. Nonetheless, Qasim's increasingly erratic frame of mind, especially in the latter years of his rule, caused him to veer away from internal developments toward external, largely manufactured crises that had the power to aggravate the country's political stability. One such crisis occurred over Kuwait, making Qasim the second Iraqi ruler (after King Ghazi I in the 1930s) to threaten the emirate. Tragically, he was not to be the last.

In order to understand the context of Qasim's démarche on Kuwait, it is important to retrace some of Iraq's history in 1958. In the last year of the monarchy, Iraq and Jordan, prodded by the United States and the United Kingdom, had decided to form the Arab Federation to counteract the effects of the very popular United Arab Republic (UAR), the union between Egypt and Syria spearheaded by Egyptian president Nasser. Nasser had appealed to the Arab "street" over the heads of Arab governments to join the UAR and ensure Arab unity, a campaign that was ultimately directed at the pro-Western governments in the Arab world and their patrons. Iraq and Jordan were ruled by kings (and first cousins) descending from the Hashemite family, but other Arab countries with a pro-Western tilt were also invited to join. Iraq's prime minister under the Arab Federation was Nuri al-Said, an astute politician who realized that the federation needed additional members to gain international legitimacy. Because it seemed a useful exercise, with which the British initially found favor, Kuwait's shaykh was invited to Baghdad to discuss his country's membership in the Arab Federation. Kuwait was a British protectorate at the time, having ceded external sovereignty in 1899 in exchange for financial subsidies and military support to protect itself from Ottoman annexation. When the shaykh remained noncommittal about Kuwait's joining the federation, al-Said asked the British ambassador to intervene on Iraq's behalf. For good measure, he also proposed that the boundary line between Iraq and Kuwait could be settled if Kuwait were to join the federation.

But the British stalled, and the Iraqi monarchy's days were numbered. In July, the revolution overthrew the monarchy and with it, the Arab Federation. When Qasim became "the Sole Leader" of Iraq, the question of Kuwait had faded in the background. It only returned to the spotlight in 1960 after Kuwait requested that its two large neighbors, Iraq and Saudi Arabia, demarcate their common borders. Saudi Arabia agreed; Iraq refused. After Kuwait became independent from the British in 1961, Qasim sent the emir of Kuwait a frosty telegram without extending his congratulations, as was diplomatic usage (Khadduri and Ghareeb 1997, 64). Kuwait immediately saw the writing on the wall; this was confirmed when, four days after Kuwait became independent, Qasim declared at a press conference that "Kuwait was 'an integral' part of Iraq on the strength of their past historical links" (Khadduri and Ghareeb 1997, 65). Qasim's position, essentially the same as King Ghazi's had been, was that Kuwait had been part of the province of Basra during the Ottoman Empire and that its status as a British protectorate was never valid. Qasim then took the bold step of "announcing that he was appointing the ruler of Kuwait as *qaimaqam* of the district, subordinate to the governor of Basra" (Tripp 2000, 165).

On the strength of persistent rumors that Iraq's forces were concentrating near Kuwait, the emir of Kuwait immediately invoked Britain's pledge of assistance in case of external threats, and Britain obliged. On July 1, 1961, Britain landed 7,000 troops in the desert emirate, while Saudi Arabia dispatched 1,200 soldiers. Even the Arab League, founded in 1945 to further Arab policies and foster cooperation among Arab nations, of which Iraq was a founding member, spurned Iraq's explanation and sent 3,300 soldiers to defend Kuwait, a member since its independence. Between this and his ongoing clashes with the United Arab Republic, Qasim ended up diplomatically isolated from the rest of the Arab world. And even though the Soviet Union blocked Kuwait's entry into the United Nations in 1961, after Qasim's assassination in 1963, it changed its position and voted to admit Kuwait into the world body.

Qasim's Demise

Foreign debacles aside, Qasim's internal problems proved insurmountable and eventually led to his demise. In 1962, in the midst of a ferocious war against the Kurds led by Qasim's generals, members of the KDP sent out feelers to the Baath Party and other Arab nationalist groups, who remained influential within the army, stating that Kurds would lay down their arms once Qasim was overthrown (Tripp 2000, 168). At the same time, the Baathists continued to cement their ties with Arab nationalist parties and to work covertly with other political groups in their preparation for a coup against the government. On

A PERSONAL NOTE

Forty years later, on a journey to Baghdad after the 2003 war in Iraq, this author detected many traces of Qasim's still-powerful legacy. For instance, I could not help but notice a proliferation of signs and banners that had blossomed all over the capital. Many of them denounced the excesses of the Saddam Hussein regime; others castigated the Americans. But it was the red flags and symbols of the communist parties (at last count, there are three in present-day Iraq) that truly made a mark on the public consciousness; before the Shiite parties took up the challenge, and themselves began to spread the green and black banners of the imams all around Baghdad, it was the vanguard of the communist groups that reclaimed the streets of the capital in memory of their hero, Abdul-Karim Qasim. Qasim's name was everywhere, at times even commemorated with photographs and large red sashes on public monuments. He is still revered today not only by the communists but by an older generation of Iraqis who remember his compassion for the poor. This memory is so ingrained among certain groups that in the last national elections on January 30, 2005, a political party naming itself after Qasim confidently entered the fray, only to be defeated resoundingly without gaining a single seat in the National Legislature. Doubtless, it will reemerge one day when its prospects are better.

February 9, 1963, Qasim was overthrown and executed by members of the Baath Party, who had long despised his communist associations. He was defended to the last by the poor and disenfranchised members of the populace; according to Thabit Abdullah, "[I]ntense street battles continued for several days with the most stubborn resistance offered in the poor neighborhoods" (Abdullah 2003, 166).

Abdul-Salam Aref's Presidency (1963–1966)

After Qasim's death, his erstwhile revolutionary comrade-in-arms now turned bitter enemy, Colonel Abdul-Salam Aref, became head of the government. At first, Aref was an unrepentant Nasserite Arab nationalist who sought to coexist with Baathist elements in the army, air force, and government; in fact, Baathists held a majority in the National Council of the Revolutionary Command that held power in Iraq following the coup. Aref's vice president was the Baathist Ahmad Hassan al-Bakr (1914–82), and the most influential member of the government was Ali Salih al-Sadi, interior minister and secretary of the Baath regional command (al-Qiyada al-Qutriyya). Marion Farouk-Sluglett and Peter Sluglett have chronicled the horrifying first months of the coup in which the National Guard, a Baathist irregular paramilitary force under the command of Munther al-Wandawi, controlled the streets of the capital and indiscriminately arrested, imprisoned, and murdered the opposition, at first the Communists and later on any hapless bystander (Farouk-Sluglett and Sluglett 1987, 1990, 85–87). By the late summer of 1963, the uneasy political coalition that had brought Aref's Free Officers (Nasserites) into power had begun to show massive cracks, and al-Sadi and al-Wandawi's targets had switched from Communists to Nasserite Arab nationalists, represented by Aref himself,

Relying on a newly formed praetorian unit, the Republican Guard (at first staffed solely with soldiers from the 20th Infantry Brigade) as well as members of his tribe, the al-Jumayla, Aref moved to strengthen his position. Allying himself with disillusioned Baathists (Tripp refers to them as "conservative" Baathists who were horrified by the excesses of the left-wing elements of the party), Aref confronted the Sadi-Wandawi faction head on, leading to a decisive defeat of al-Sadi and his henchman, al-Wandawi, at the hands of units loyal to Aref. By November 1963, Aref had become the undisputed president of the Iraqi republic.

Thus came to an end the first attempt of the Baath Party to control Iraqi politics. Internal divisions (whether consisting of economic inequalities, sectarian distinctions, a tenuous ideological base, or military-civilian differences) had weakened the party and allowed its enemies to successfully challenge its fractured leadership. The brief one-year National Guard regime of terror under the increasingly unstable Sadi-Wandawi leadership effectively entrenched mob rule in Baghdad; unsurprisingly, it rapidly brought about its own demise. The Aref government that trounced the rebels was itself a patchwork affair, but it relied on a loyal tribal base, Aref's expeditious alliance with a few well-chosen men from Tikrit (a city on the Tigris River approximately 95 miles northwest of Baghdad) who represented the military wing of the Baath Party, and Arab nationalist groups that were more influenced by Nasser's political agenda in Egypt than Aref himself was.

To secure the loyalty of the latter, Aref indulged in symbolic gestures designed to buttress his Arab nationalist credentials. By 1964, and for a combination of factors (chiefly having to do with the souring relations between Egypt and Syria, which had ended their union in 1961), the moment for a revived United Arab Republic seemed to have passed, and

Egypt no longer held the same fascination for Arab nationalists in Iraq that it had in the past. Nonetheless, Nasserist thought still possessed a certain cachet in Iraq. It was therefore deemed wise to inaugurate a few symbolic "unity projects" recalling Aref's commitment to Nasserism:

> [These] were launched with great ceremony: a preliminary accord on unity between Nasser and 'Aref in June 1964, the establishment of a "unified political command" in December 1964 and the adoption of the eagle of the UAR as the national emblem of Iraq in 1965" (Farouk-Sluglett and Sluglett 1987, 1990, 95).

Following on the heels of these projects, Aref pursued the Egyptian example by nationalizing all banks, insurance companies, and the majority of Iraq's industries in July 1964. The nationalization of private enterprise was supposed to create a more efficient state-run industrial sector; in effect, it delayed it, because the country had not as yet developed a large enough pool of managerial talent that could run the new state companies. Capital flight also denuded the country of the necessary wherewithal to start afresh. As Tripp has pointed out, even though Aref's emulation of Egypt led to his impulsive nationalization decree, "the dominant feature of Iraq's economy, accounting for about one-third of its GDP, was neither agriculture nor industry, but oil" (Tripp 2000, 178). Consequently, negotiations were resumed between the Iraqi government (in the person of the oil minister) and the Iraq Petroleum Company in order to work out a fairer deal for the government. As a result of the negotiations that were concluded in June 1965, government oil revenues increased while the IPC received access to the off-limits territory. However, the IPC was not given exclusive access; the Iraq National Oil Company (INOC, organized in February 1964) also held such rights (Tripp 2000, 181).

Once firmly established in power, Aref purged his government of those who had helped him defeat the Sadi-Wanadwi regime. First to be eased out were the Baathists, whose representatives—Abdul Sattar Abdul-Latif, Hardan al-Tikriti, and Hassan al-Bakr—were either demoted or transferred as ambassadors abroad. The next to tangle with the Aref regime were the nationalists who followed Egypt's example; their supra-Nasserite loyalties had begun to irk the government, especially when their ill-conceived nationalization decrees led to the flow of capital outside the country and a corresponding rise in unemployment. The final blow came when the Nasserite air force commander, Aref Abdul-Razzaq, prime minister and minister of defense, attempted to lead a coup against his own government in September 1965 when Aref was outside the country; he was severely defeated by the Baghdad regiment under the command of Colonel Said Slaibi, Abdul-Salam Aref's kinsman, and the conspirators had to flee the country.

As a result, Aref's government fell back on its one loyal constituency, the al-Jumayla tribe. Abdul-Rahman al-Bazzaz (1913–73) became prime minister in 1965, and his brief civilian rule was one of the highlights of the Aref period. However, the government's dependence on narrow sectarian and tribal loyalties (the al-Jumayla were Sunnis, as, of course, was Aref) created hostility among the diversity of Iraqis, as did the earlier attempts to forge contentious alliances between various Arab nationalists, Baathists, and Iraqi nationalists. At the same time, the Kurdish war, which had temporarily come to an end in the first year of Aref's rule, began once more as the government decided it could not accept Kurdish nationalist demands. Finally, Aref's versatile use of the word *socialism* rankled the consolidated Communist party, resulting in the resumption of a communist-termed "violent" struggle against the regime by some party factions. In 1966, however, Aref's death as a result of a helicopter crash obviated the need of the government to resolve these and other problems that continued to plague the country.

Abdul-Rahman Aref's Presidency (1966–1968)

After the obligatory period of mourning, Abdul-Salam's older brother, Abdul-Rahman Aref (1916–2007), also an army officer, was elected to the presidency, edging out al-Bazzaz, who had become temporary president following the younger Aref's death. By all accounts, Abdul-Rahman Aref was less competent and certainly less charismatic than his brother, but he epitomized continuity and a certain style of governing that relied heavily on the powerful personal and tribal networks that had sustained Abdul-Salam's later rule. However, the Kurdish war was in full swing and negotiations with the IPC were at a delicate stage. The IPC was now in clear competition with the INOC, especially after the latter had signed "an agreement with a French group of companies to exploit areas from which the IPC had been excluded" (Tripp 2000, 189). Thus, Abdul-Rahman Aref's new government faced a grim scenario at first.

Under al-Bazzaz, who had stayed on as prime minister, the Kurdish war ground to a halt after a 12-point program recognizing both Kurdish and Arab national aspirations to Iraq was promulgated. Al-Bazzaz offered an amnesty to the Kurds and recognized Kurdish as an official language of Iraq. This promising window of opportunity was dashed by Aref's own military command, the leaders of which were suspicious of ethnic binationalism (Kurdish-Arab) in Iraq. Al-Bazzaz resigned, and a new government under Naji Talib once again began to make threatening noises against the Kurdish leadership of Mulla Mustafa al-Barzani. Meanwhile, Aref's reliance on the Republican Guard, with its core al-Jumayla constituency, and his diffident style of governing, created a vacuum that officer groups exploited with great agility.

Added to this was Aref's less aggressive actions against the Baath Party (either out of a desire for reconciliation or the mistaken belief that the Baathists could no longer pose a problem to him), and his decision to maintain Iraqi neutrality during the Six-Day War in 1967 pitting Egypt, Syria, and Jordan against Israel left him in a precarious position. Street demonstrations, many of them violent, occurred in Baghdad and other cities and towns throughout Iraq in the wake of Israel's victory in the brief war. The Baathists, who generally vied with the Communists for control of the streets, did not seize the opportunity. Since 1966, a kinsman of Ahmad Hasan al-Bakr, Saddam Hussein (1937–2006), had been reorganizing the Baath Party militia. During the rioting of the summer of 1967, Hussein further capitalized to strengthen the Baath Party. In addition, the officer corps harbored numerous factions opposed to Aref's policies, especially the neutrality during the Six-Day War, which many felt had humiliated the army and Iraq in the eyes of fellow Arabs. By 1968, familiar foes had come together to plot the demise of the Aref government, finally succeeding in dismantling an ineffectual government with virtually no bloodshed.

The Baathist Government of 1968–1979 and the Ascent of Saddam Hussein

The overthrow of the Aref government was led by the Baath Party in Iraq. Baathist thought had come late to Iraq. It first developed in Syria in the interwar years as a national liberation movement both against the French and the older Syrian urban notable class. After World War II, it developed into a mass political movement with several distinctive features: It was pan-Arab (its members believed that all the postwar Arab states appearing in the aftermath of colonialism were really part of the greater Arab nation), socialist (they believed Arab wealth was for the Arab people), and anti-imperialist (Farouk-Sluglett and Sluglett 1987, 1990, 88–89). In Iraq, Baathism did not become an important strand of thought until the mid-1950s; even as late as the 1958 revolution, the party had only attracted several hundred members. In fact, the Slugletts make the point that the main difference between Baathism in Iraq and in Syria was that the movement in Syria grew out of an original synthesis between Christian and Muslim intellectuals that was very much part of the specific social, cultural, and political makeup of the country, whereas in Iraq it never really put down roots in the larger context of Iraqi society (Farouk-Sluglett and Sluglett 1987, 1990, 91).

Throughout the Qasim and Aref years, the Baath Party in Iraq went through a series of transformations that taken together paved the way for its ultimate seizure of power in 1968. Interior Minister Ali Salih al-Sadi created a militant brand of Baathism in 1959 and was eventually brought to heel by Abdul-Salam Aref; the "conservative" wing of the Baath Party, including Hardan al-Tikriti and Ahmad Hassan al-Bakr, first allied itself with the Aref regime, then was summarily demoted and shunted from power by that same government. Ultimately, the Baath Party, no less than any other mass movement in Iraq, was forced to go into hiding as a result of Abdul-Salam Aref's increasingly severe attempts to consolidate his power. The party never completely spoke with one voice or acted in a concerted way in this period; from 1963 to 1968, party members formed cliques within cliques that often relied on personal, tribal, and geographical ties in order to solder a precarious unity. So long as it projected an Arab nationalist outlook that drew recruits from various corners of the country, Baathist ideology was sufficiently vague and adaptable to accommodate a number of disparate elements of the Iraqi population. As a result of this flexibility and lack of internal rigidity, some Baathist cliques remained on speaking terms with the governments of both Abdul-Salam Aref and his brother Abdul-Rahman Aref.

The July 1968 Coup d'État

After Abdul-Salam Aref's demise, Abdul-Rahman Aref, in a half-hearted attempt to widen his circle of power, brought back elements of the Baathists into government consultations. Over time, the Baathists were able to return as a powerful political force. In July 1968, they exploited an opening created by infighting within the regime and, with the aid of important members of the officers corps, including leading generals in the Republican Guard, struck, taking over the headquarters of the 10th Armored Brigade, the Ministry of Defense, and the radio station. On July 17, Baghdad awoke to a new regime, led by President Ahmad Hassan al-Bakr. On the next day, a core governing group made up entirely of army officers and called the Revolutionary Command Council (RCC) effectively became the face of the new government; it would become the main instrument holding together the Iraqi government from 1968 onward. From the very beginning, the RCC was controlled by the Tikriti, Sunnis not only allied by region but by kinship, all belonging to the Talfah clan. These kinsmen included Ahmad Hassan al-Bakr and Saddam Hussein, who were solidifying their hold on the Baath Party. But first, the Baath Party had to solidify its hold on Iraq. In the days after the coup, the Baathists found themselves precariously sharing power with the officers who had assisted them, a circumstance they feared would lead to their own downfall. To counteract that possibility, the more politically astute al-Bakr and Hardan al-Tikriti outmaneuvered and co-opted their military allies so that by July 30, 1968, the government of Iraq was solely in Baathist hands.

When the Baathists came to power, they did not have wide support in the country; however, in the early 1970s, they were able to enact large social and economic programs that gained them favor with the most disaffected elements of society, including peasants, youth, and trade union members. There were also political forces that needed to be neutralized through temporary political alliances. In general, there were four challenges that the Baathist government faced. The first concerned the control of the Baath Party and the insinuation of men loyal to al-Bakr and Hussein in various branches of the party and other organs of state. Saddam Hussein clawed his way to the top, eventually becoming vice president of the RCC. During the subsequent years, he continued to methodically secure his political base in the party either through the elimination of cadres or individuals who stood in his way or through the co-optation of others, such as the recruitment of new members to the RCC who were loyal to him. This strategy also necessitated the rebuilding of new patronage networks answering only to him. Eventually, those developments instigated the expansion of the *mukhabarat* (intelligence) state and the creation of separate but competing security agencies to defend the president and thwart various enemies, at home or abroad.

The second and third challenges had to do with creating a temporary peace between the Baathists and, on the one hand, the Communist Party (which retained popularity among certain elements of the population) and, on the other, the Kurdish leadership, with its demands for regional autonomy and its on-again, off-again alliances with the shah of Iran, Israel, and the Americans. The fourth and last challenge emanated from the leadership of the Shii learned community, the *hawza*. Under the reinvigoration of its clerics, especially Sayyid Muhammad Baqir al-Sadr, as well as others, the *hawza* mounted a formidable challenge.

The Nationalization of the Oil Sector and Its Consequences for the Iraqi Economy

One of the developments that most lent stature to Saddam Hussein and ensured that he would be catapulted into national politics as the key political actor in the country had to do with the nationalization of oil. Conforming to a strong national desire to be independent of Western influence, the government nationalized the IPC's operating fields in June 1972. Among those fields nationalized by the 1972 decree was the Kirkuk concession, discovered in 1920 and up to that period, still the basis for much of Iraq's oil production (Yergin 1991, 584). The chief reason for the nationalization of oil had to do with the IPC's stranglehold on the Iraqi economy. Iraq needed the revenues from more oil than the IPC was prepared to pump, and since oil production was nearly completely controlled by the IPC, the Iraqi government had to augment its revenues from oil by bringing other fields online, preferably with different partners and on better terms. To embark on ambitious development programs, Iraq was prepared to risk the wrath of the IPC by asking the Soviet Union to help develop another large oil field, Rumaila, located in southern Iraq and in Kuwait. It was Hussein who went to Moscow to initiate talks that culminated in the Iraq-Soviet Treaty of Friendship and Cooperation, signed in April 1972, as well as a number of trade agreements (Tripp 2000, 208).

In 1975, the government takeover of the oil industry was completed, to much popular acclaim. Overnight, the Baath regime now controlled

Saddam Hussein in 1975, the year the Baathist regime completed the nationalization of Iraq's oil industry (AP Photo/Zuhair Saade)

211

vast sums of money, calculated by the Iraqi expert Abbas Alnasrawi to have been in the realm of $521 million in 1970 and upward of $26 billion in 1980 (Alnasrawi 2001, n.p.). It was, in Alnasrawi's words, "Iraq's prosperous decade."

Oil earnings became one of the most important factors undergirding Iraq's relations with the Arab and Islamic worlds and with the West. Ominously, 40 percent of that revenue went toward the buying of armaments from Western (mostly French) and Soviet suppliers, with that figure further increasing at the onset of the Iran-Iraq War (1980–88). Just as significantly, oil revenues gave a sizable boost to the Iraqi economy. In the years between the nationalization of all of Iraq's operational oil fields and the eruption of the Iran-Iraq War, the high price of oil financed the large-scale growth of the health, education, and public works sectors and made construction one of the prized occupations of the burgeoning middle class. Because of the vast amounts of money at its disposal, the Iraqi government expanded social services, increased spending on development, recruited more men into the army, and augmented the sum of its currency reserves to about $40 billion. By the late 1970s, oil formed 98 percent of the country's exports, prompting the growth of total state investments, which rose from 72 million dinars in 1968 to 1.2 billion dinars in 1975 (Salucci 2003, 2005, 76).

One of the outcomes of the rise of oil revenues was the growth of the Iraqi middle class. Although this class was heavily dependent on the state and included a number of different sectors (state employees of nationalized industries, state-affiliated rural landowners, and a cadre of professionals, such as teachers and medical personnel), it was a vital source of administrative talent and managerial expertise. Interestingly, the phenomenal growth of private construction firms far outstripped the expansion of state industrial or agricultural concerns. Although construction firms—of which the most prominent emerged in Baghdad, Tikrit, Najaf, and Basra—depended on government projects funded by oil money, they were also important to the realization of ambitious development projects requiring foreign expertise. This was especially the case from 1970 onward, when the government contracted with large Western multinationals to buy and set up petrochemical plants and new transportation systems (Farouk-Sluglett and Sluglett 1990, 238–250). Thus, the

new totalitarian, single-party system succeeded in promoting a state-run industrial sector, mobilizing and developing social services, reducing unemployment and providing better chances for the rising middle classes, which grew from 34 percent of the urban population in 1968 to more than 50 percent in

1980. General prosperity and progress in social and economic development were palpable indeed (A. Jabar in Potter and Sick 2004, 126).

State investment in the social sector also brought about important gains. In the late 1970s, the Iraqi state pushed aggressively to promote universal literacy, claiming, by the end of the 1980s, to have reached an astounding literacy rate of 95 percent, up from approximately 55 percent in the late 1970s. The Iraqi commitment to raising the literacy rate resulted in the expansion of the educational system in the 1970s, especially in the larger cities. For example, technical education increased three-fold since 1977, to more than 120,090 students in 1986. Baghdad University, with its different campuses, had 34,555 students in 1988, Mustansiriya University attracted 11,686 students, and the University of Technology served 7,584 students. Universities in Basra, Mosul, and Irbil (Iraqi Kurdistan) "enrolled 26 percent of all students in higher education in the academic year 1983–84" (al-Hariri 1988, n.p.). This was all the more impressive because education, including higher education, was for the most part free, and up to 1982, many postgraduate students and professors were sent to study abroad on government scholarships and fellowships (Watenpaugh et al, 2003, n.p.).

Oil revenues were also plowed into the health sector; medical care was free. By 1988, Baghdad had more hospitals than any other city in the country, approximating nearly 37 percent of the total. Rural clinics were also set up by the state, in which medical residents had to serve up to four years before returning to their hometowns. Finally, social security, workers' compensation, and pensions were regularly paid to retirees and elderly people.

However, the almost total reliance on the state left large sectors of the Iraqi economy, both public and private, wide open to governmental manipulation. More significantly, under the government of Saddam Hussein, the confiscation of fortunes and the imprisonment and sometimes execution of Iraqi merchants, industrialists, and heads of private construction firms occurred with a depressing regularity. As a result, political as well as financial insecurity continued to dog the Iraqi middle class well throughout the 1970s and 1980s.

The Communist Challenge

In 1968, when the Baathist government headed by al-Bakr came to power, the Iraqi Communist Party still had influence in the larger cities of Iraq. Although its membership had dwindled because of arrests, imprisonment, and executions, the ICP retained a solid base among workers' groups and coalitions of students and women's associations. However, a new political generation, made up of surviving veterans and younger political strategists who had risen through the ranks, was divided over which strategy to espouse. One group advocated the unleashing of social revolution through the creation of a mass urban party, while the other promoted the pursuit of a massive educational campaign in the countryside to pave the way for radical change. But there was little that the Communists could do in the late 1960s; the ICP's leadership was largely based in Iraqi Kurdistan, away from the real center of power, and its base was fragmented, with many of its members in hiding or languishing in prison.

It was at this juncture that the newly ascendant Baath Party, hoping to bolster its revolutionary credentials as well as to create a rapprochement with the USSR, asked the Communist leadership to join it in a National Progressive Front. The invitation put the Communists in a quandary. Though recognizing the anti-imperialist influence of Baathist doctrine, they were not at all taken in by its antidemocratic practices (Salucci 2003, 2005; 60). And while relations between the Communists and the ruling Baathist clique strengthened as a result of the 1972 nationalization of the Iraqi Petroleum Company, the promotion of a new land reform decree, and the USSR's openly supportive ties to the government, the Communists were not completely immune from the Baathist rule of terror. Alternately imprisoning and torturing ICP members while pledging undying friendship to the Communist leadership at the same time, Baathist "persuasion," by means subtle or overt, eventually brought the ICP into a tactical alliance with the government, an action which the Communists were later to regret.

Entering the National Progressive Front in 1973, the Communists were immediately confronted with having to support the 1974–75 war against their erstwhile allies, the Kurdish people and their chief, Mulla Mustafa al-Barzani. Meanwhile, the once-impregnable Communist hold on peasant cooperatives, women's and students' associations, and labor unions was being challenged by the Baathists, even as Communist cadres were increasingly being thrown in jail or liquidated.

The Kurdish Predicament

After a 1969 speech in which the cofounder of the Arab Socialist Baath Party in Syria, Michel Aflaq, stated that the party had no reservations with regard to Kurdish autonomy, President al-Bakr began a series of confidence-building moves to allay Kurdish suspicions of the Iraqi central government. Secret negotiations between al-Barzani and the vice president of the RCC, Hussein, ensued. According to a veteran observer of Kurdish affairs, Edmund Ghareeb,

> [t]he March 1970 Agreement ... was one of the most extraordinary accords reached between a government and its Kurdish opponents. This agreement recognized Kurdish identity, an admission that the Iraqi peoples consisted of two nationalities, Arab and Kurdish ... autonomy was promised to the Kurds within four years in a Kurdish region made up of the areas where they formed a majority [and] the Kurdish language was given official status ... [plus] a Kurdish vice president and five Kurdish ministers were to be appointed to the government (Ghareeb in Inati 2003, 171–72).

Moreover, reconstruction in Kurdish areas was to begin at once. Kurdish leaders pledged to hand over their heavy weapons and stop being allies of foreign governments. The Kurds under al-Barzani broke their links with Iran, the principal supplier of arms and matériel to the Kurdish side.

In retrospect, the March 1970 agreement was significant because of a number of factors. First, it granted the Kurds far more than they had ever been given by any previous Iraqi government. Second, it was negotiated by that most intractable of politicians, Saddam Hussein, whose flexibility on the terms of the agreement was considered even then an unparalleled act of statesmanship.

Barely a year later, an attempted assassination of Mulla Mustafa al-Barzani took place, with the Kurdish leadership suspecting that it had been ordered by none other than Hussein himself. To make matters worse, the regime began moving Arabs, initially Christians but later on other components of Iraqi society, to Kirkuk. This policy of making Kurds a minority in a city they coveted further stoked Kurdish resentment; it was also totally contrary to the 1970 agreement, in letter and spirit.

By the early 1970s, the Baath Party was reaching out to leftist parties to garner legitimacy in its fight against foreign interests; in order to wean itself away from the multinational oil companies, Iraq began to cement its ties with the USSR. In 1973, as a result of the breakdown of the agreement in all but name, al-Barzani repudiated it and made plans to defend his hard-won gains in northern Iraq. The Slugletts suggest that one of the consequences of Iraqi rapprochement with the Communist Party and the Soviet Union was that the shah of Iran, alarmed at Iraq's newfound stability, rushed to bolster the Kurds with arms and material help (Farouk-Sluglett and Sluglett 1990, 151). In fact, Mulla Mustafa "quickly established ever more cordial relations, overt and covert, with the three archenemies of Iraq—Iran, Israel, and the United States" (Izady in Potter and Sick 2004, 79). Abandoning his former protector, the USSR, al-Barzani met with Henry Kissinger, the U.S. national security adviser, who assured him that the United States would stand by him in his efforts to win Iraqi Kurdistan's independence (Sluglett and Sluglett 1987, 1990, 159). The upshot of these conversations was a peremptory move away from the March Agreement of 1970 and a resumption of war in 1974.

The war between the Kurdish *peshmergas* (guerrillas) and the Iraqi army was costly both in men and matériel. While the Kurdish forces were able to attract a large number of Kurdish partisans to their side and were able to hold off the much larger Iraqi army for a considerable period, the Iraqi side doggedly kept up its operations in the north. The Kurds received antiaircraft systems and 122-mm guns from Iran, tying them more firmly within the Iranian orbit, while Iranian jets bombed Iraqi positions on the Kurdish front, threatening that the conflict would escalate into a full-blown war between Iraq and Iran (Sluglett and Sluglett 1987, 1990, 169). The Iraqi treasury was fast being depleted, and the central government's position was so dire that Iraq's foremost ally, the USSR, tried to intervene to stop hostilities.

Finally, at the all-Arab Rabat Summit bringing to an end the October war of 1973 (also known as the Ramadan War, in which Iraq joined Egypt, Syria, and Jordan in a war against Israel), King Hussein of Jordan was successful in getting the Iraqis and Iranians to talk. The Algiers Agreement of 1975 concluded between Iran and Iraq solidified Saddam Hussein's position. A permanent demarcation of the Iran-Iraq boundary, an issue that had bedeviled both countries for centuries, was agreed to. The boundary was established at the *thaiweg*, a median line measuring the deepest part of the Shatt al-Arab, a 120-mile long river that flows by the important trading ports of Basra in Iraq and Abadan in Iran. With the signing of this agreement the Kurdish independence movement lost its military and economic lifeline:

> Within forty-eight hours of the signature of the Agreement, the Iranians removed their 155 mm field guns, and the Kurdish resistance collapsed; the Iranians even threatened to join the Iraqis in a combined attack on the Kurds if the latter refused to accept the terms of the Agreement (Sluglett and Sluglett 1987, 1990, 170).

Confrontation with the Shii Learned Community

The Baathist regime was extremely wary of the *marjaiyya's* ("the sources of emulation," the most learned of the Shii clergy) hold on the Iraqi Shia, as well as its transnational links with the Shii clergy in Iran. This suspicion was amply returned in kind by the students and scholar-preachers of the Shii shrine cities. From as early as 1968, the latter had begun a series of strikes and protests in Najaf aimed at curtailing government intervention in Shii affairs. The religious leadership had long been alarmed by the continued growth of Communist influence in the shrine cities and the spread of communist doctrine among disaffected Shii youth. To bring Najafi youth back into the fold, a number of *mujtahids,* or Shii scholars, began a counteroffensive. Among the most prominent leaders of this movement was an important theoretician and activist in Najaf, Ayatollah Sayyid Muhammad Baqir al-Sadr (1935–80), who wrote two books and one unpublished manuscript on the theory and practice of philosophy, economics, and society in Islam, as well as numerous tracts on Islamic law and banking.

In 1969, in the wake of the confrontation over the establishment of a university in Kufa, Imam Ali's historic capital, the government began to arrest a number of important community leaders who had backed the university's establishment, which Baathists saw as a threat to their control. In 1977, al-Sadr, one of the founders of the militant Islamic party al-Daawa, led a large demonstration against the Baath in the holy month of Muharram in which thousands of Shiis in Karbala and Najaf participated, deeply shaking the regime. In fact throughout the 1970s, al-Sadr was arrested several times and thrown in prison, the last time along with his sister Bint al-Huda and other activists (Mallat 1993, 7–19). At about the same time that al-Sadr was being harassed by agencies of the security state, the government began its policy of forced transfer of hundreds of Iraqi Shii families, ostensibly of Persian origin, to Iran; the nightly roundups and hurried collection of individuals and groups was to accelerate with the outbreak of the Iran-Iraq War. On April 1, 1980, members of the clandestine Daawa Party attacked Tariq Aziz, then a rising government official, at Mustansiriya University. Although Aziz survived, the regime immediately took its revenge on al-Sadr by executing him, along with his sister. According to Eric Davis, the spiraling violence between the government and its opponents in the Shii holy cities could have been averted but for government mistrust of traditional Shii autonomy in their own internal affairs: "It was not that organizations such as al-Da'wa were that powerful but rather that they represented oppositional poles around which the discontented Shi'a could potentially organize" (Davis 2005, 190–191).

Conclusion

On the eve of the Iran-Iraq War, the government's perturbed relations with leftist organizations, the Kurdish leadership, and the Shii community signaled festering domestic problems that spelled ominous trouble ahead. The war was not only to test severely Iraqi society throughout the long eight years of its duration but also to consume all the advances that had marked "Iraq's prosperous decade." Moreover, it is wise to remember that while many Iraqis today consider the 1970s a golden age, the affluence and abundance of those years were not evenly distributed. Alongside the thriving middle class existed a number of groups that were isolated from the general prosperity because they were deemed of marginal importance to the state. For example, although state investment was plowed into the rural sector, at least in the early 1970s, agriculture, like industry, did not experience the same boom as the construction sector. Moreover, while the hold of the old landowning class was shattered, a new class of Baathist-allied landlords replaced them soon after. Throughout this decade of prosperity, warning signs of dissidence and revolt troubled the equanimity of the state and its by now all-powerful leader, Saddam Hussein. And so, on the eve of one of the most draining military conflicts, the Iran-Iraq War, a confrontation that was to presage a cycle of endless war thrust upon Iraqi society, the state decided to confront its critics, to co-opt those it could, and to silence the rest.

9

THE RULE OF SADDAM HUSSEIN AND THE DIFFICULT LEGACY OF THE MUKHABARAT STATE (1979–2003)

From 1979 until 2003, Saddam Hussein ruled supreme, controlling the country through different institutions, most of them linked to the *mukhabarat,* or "intelligence," state, which he helped develop. Power also remained firmly tied to an elite composed of family members and tribal supporters. From 1980 to 1988, the Iraq-Iran War exacted a huge toll; the country's resources were stretched to the maximum, and its people were drained, because of the hemorrhage of casualties at the front and the air raids on Baghdad and Basra. One of the consequences of the war was that the regime amassed a foreign debt so staggering that it teetered on bankruptcy. In the two-year interlude between the Iran-Iraq War and the invasion of Kuwait in 1990, the regime deployed the army against its internal enemies, especially the Kurds. In the aftermath of the Persian Gulf War and the defeat of Iraq by an international coalition force, the world was stunned to see the swift retribution meted out to insurrectionists by a still-intact Iraqi army in the southern and northern parts of the country. After the imposition of a devastating array of sanctions on the country, the most severe ever devised by the international community (supported in whole or in part by the United States and the United Kingdom), Hussein's government grew ever more defiant, manipulating the embargo to reward allies and friends. After September 11, 2001, U.S. president George W. Bush galvanized the United Kingdom and other countries to attack Iraq and to occupy the country. We are still facing the consequences of this move today, a move that was decried by the United Nations as illegal. As of this writing, the U.S. Army is still stationed in Iraq, fighting a growing and deadly insurgency.

The Mukhabarat State

The growth of Saddam Hussein's power occurred in conjunction with the creation and rapid expansion of an interconnected system of military and civilian intelligence agencies directly answerable to the president. The intelligence and security organizations Hussein created from as early as 1968 onward were designed as institutions of state control and became the vital building blocks of the *mukhabarat* state that supported his later rule. In the early years, as vice president of the Revolutionary Command Council (RCC), Hussein's primary task had been to serve as President Ahmad Hassan al-Bakr's chief enforcer; Hussein had been the man who arrested and ordered the assassination of a number of the country's political forces, including Communists, Nasserites, and lapsed Baathists. Alternately wooing or imprisoning and executing Communist as well as "radical" Baathists leaders, al-Bakr and Hussein were able to purge all those independent elements that could pose a threat to the new regime. Relying on men of Tikrit, Bakr and Hussein's birthplace, Hussein recruited kinsmen he could trust and eventually positioned them to be subordinate to him on the RCC, the security organs of the state, and in the Baath Party itself.

The controlling aspect of the Iraqi intelligence network went by the formal name of Jihaz al-Mukhabarat al-Ama (General Directorate of Intelligence) and held a power in Iraq similar to that of the KGB of the former Soviet Union: It collected information both externally and internally and held the power of arrest. Rooted in precursor Baathist security and intelligence organizations led by Hussein, the Mukhabarat was divided into three bureaus—political, administrative, and "special"—that contained a combined 28 directorates whose purviews included electronic surveillance, secret operations, counterintelligence, propaganda, surveillance, and military industrial security. There were also four directorates concentrating on Iraq's four main regions. These were located in Mosul, Basra, Ramadi, and Karbala. Considering the enormous power such a position held, Hussein took care to place the leadership of the Mukhabarat in the hands of a Tikriti, usually a close family member.

While skillfully balancing different elements within the country through co-optation and financial incentives, Hussein also relied on patronage networks (especially those emanating from within his own family and clan), tribal loyalties, and the power of the purse in maintaining authority. But overall, it was the security agencies that ensured the early detection of potential coup plotters, counteracted internal resistance, planned and carried out action against foreign countries or leaders, and protected the president from enemies near and far. The result was an oppressive system that sustained and privileged Saddam Hussein's rule for 35 years. "It is estimated that between twenty thousand and thirty thousand people [most of whom were Communists] were arrested in the period 1979–81 . . . while hundreds 'disappeared' or were killed" (Salucci 2003, 2005, 64).

A PRISONER'S STORY: 13 YEARS IN SADDAM HUSSEIN'S JAILS

An array of human rights abuses—including arrests and imprisonment without trial, forced expulsions, torture, summary executions, and ethnocide—were leveled against the government of Saddam Hussein starting well before the war in 2003. After the U.S. occupation of Iraq, those charges reached a crescendo. This is the story of one famous prisoner of the regime.

Ata Abdul-Wahhab was a Baghdad-based lawyer and judge from a well-known Arab Sunni family who went on to become a diplomat at the United Nations and, in 1957, personal secretary to King Faisal II and Prince Abdulillah of Iraq. After the revolution of July 1958 took place, Abdul-Wahhab became a businessman. In that capacity, he visited Kuwait in 1969 to establish an insurance company. It was while he was in Kuwait that he was seized by Iraqi intelligence agents, bundled into the trunk of a waiting car, and sent to Baghdad. There, he was imprisoned in the terrifying Palace of the End (Qasr al-Nihaya), one of the palaces of the last monarchs of Iraq, which had been turned into a prison. Repeatedly tortured by Iraqi authorities over many months and placed on death row for five years, his sentence was finally commuted to solitary life imprisonment. His brother Zaki Abdul-Wahhab, however, who had been imprisoned alongside him, was executed in 1970. In 1982, Ata Abdul-Wahhab, by then imprisoned in the infamous Abu Ghraib, was finally freed. The following are translated excerpts of his autobiography, recounting his 13 years of incarceration.

(continues)

A PRISONER'S STORY: 13 YEARS IN
SADDAM HUSSEIN'S JAILS (continued)

[Abdul-Wahhab's book] A Lineage of Clay . . . began its days in Abu Ghraib prison's death row in Baghdad in the 1970s. It passed through several stages until it was completed 20 years later in Beirut. It was not published then . . . and the reason for that is that the third section of the book, which was written outside of Iraq, discusses a severe ordeal which began with my kidnapping from one country to another, then torture in Qasr al-Nihaya (the Palace of the End) for a period of eight months. Then followed the decree of execution and the passage of five and-a-half years in solitary on death row, after which the sentence of death was reduced to imprisonment without parole and then it ended with my release from jail after 13 years. . . .

The solitary cell on death row consists of a small room with a toilet, and a steel door, which opens onto a large space surrounded by many other cells, either empty or filled, and guards who regularly check up on death row inmates to see what they're doing patrol that space. Because the toilet was in the cell, it was permissible to cover the entry with a curtain made of blankets or other coverings found in the cell, and that was to produce [a space to retreat to] while performing one's daily needs. Those were the only minutes one could retreat from people.

I used to cover the whole toilet area to lengthen my retreat. At first, I stayed for a short time, mindful that the prison guards might take notice at this strange behavior. When no one seemed to object, I took a longer time until slowly, slowly I spent several consecutive hours [in the toilet area] doing what I wanted, with the prison guard thinking that I used to spend all those hours in the squatting position on the floor toilet. . . .

In that cell, cell no. 2, surrounded by tens of cells, and which I occupied because it was empty by coincidence, I spent many

The Iran-Iraq War (1980–1988)

In late 1979, an Islamic revolution occurred in Iran that toppled the regime of the Western-supported shah Muhammad Reza Pahlavi (1919–80)—who subsequently left the country along with his family and closest aides—and brought to power the Shii religious leader Ayatollah Ruhollah Khomeini (1902–89). The revolutionaries who took over the government consisted of theology students, members of the bazaari class (traders and shopkeepers), and representatives of some secular political groups, some of whose leaders had been arrested under *years, and behind that [toilet] curtain which cut me off from view, I wrote a great deal. Everything I wrote, I concealed in the folds of my blanket or underneath the bed. I wrote long letters to my family and friends; I translated many English-language classics, and I wrote poetry. And all of this became the first section of A Lineage of Clay. . . .*

The prisoner on death row, squatting in his individual cell all day and night, is faced with an enormous emptiness, which threatens him with collapse. I had to find a way to occupy this emptiness so that I would defeat it, before it defeated me. The first way was to continue thinking night and day, so that I could while away the long barren days and nights. This was in the first stage when I was not allowed books, paper, or pens. My primary support came in the form of a [renewed] belief in God, passing from doubt and a belief in nature and man, to faith in the Creator based on the rational premise that everything in existence has a meaning that is waiting to be discovered. This sufi [or mystical] thinking in that terrible emptiness ran through my mind in smooth succession, without fear of the ultimate end so that I recalled past events rationally, being helped by the enormous amount of time on my hands. The result was that this continuing monologue brought about great peace of mind, leading to an immunity from instability and a steadfastness in front of the abyss, as well as the realization of a program of thought that developed slowly, incrementally, day after day. I developed various practical ways to resist this emptiness. It has been said that fear of the unknown leads to cleaving to God. This is true. But I want to say that this was not what led me to believe, because ever since my release from prison in 1982, my faith has not been shaken until today, and here I am writing in 2003.

Source: From Ata Abdul-Wahhab. *Sulalat al-tin* (A lineage of clay). Amman: Arab Establishment for Studies and Publications, 2004, pp. 561–562, 565–566.

the shah. In the chaotic postrevolutionary situation that unraveled the Pahlavi monarchy as quickly as a woolen sweater, conditions seemed ripe for outside intervention, particularly by Iran's neighbors, if not by the United States. It was Baathist Iraq that struck the first blow, sparking a crisis that was to weaken the Baathist government irretrievably.

The Iran-Iraq War of the 1980s was the longest and costliest war ever fought between the two countries. It was truly a war without a winner. Besides the devastating losses incurred on both countries' armies, air forces, and navies, the bombings of the important oil-refining towns of the Shatt al-Arab, and the lingering aftermath of poison gas attacks and air raids on both civilians and soldiers, the war was also prolonged by political entanglements and alliances that contributed to the appalling destruction on both sides. Finally, there was the ideological component: Both Iraq and Iran used their incipient state medias (and, on Ayatollah Khomeini's part, weekly sermons) to project messages of invincibility and righteousness based on interpretations of either pre-Islamic annals (Iraq) or Islamic history (Iran).

The war started on September 22, 1980, after repeated border skir-mishes. Whether those were sufficiently provocative to draw in the Iraqi army, history must be the final judge. An Iranian scholar has con-sidered them less confrontational than the shah's arming of the Kurdish rebellion in the 1970s, but that is clearly only one opinion (Bakhash in Potter and Sick 2004, 22). It does seem fairly obvious, however, that several factors played into Saddam Hussein's timing in launching the war. One was the turmoil in Iran as a result of the spreading grip of the Islamic revolution on the country as a whole. The shah's hasty depar-ture, the collapse of the once-powerful Iranian army and the execution of its top leadership, the factional struggles taking place in Iran's politi-cal establishment, and the revolutionary zeal that eventually brought on the American hostages crisis roiled the country. The country was isolated internationally and seemed weak.

Second was the desire on Hussein's part to abrogate the Algiers Treaty so as to return Iraqi sovereignty to both sides of the Shatt al-Arab waterway. Many observers in Iraq believe that for Hussein, the agreement had been a temporary truce and not a definitive compact. Finally, it must be noted that the Iraqi command structure harbored unrealistic expectations for immediate victory. It severely miscalculated Iran's strength and was confronted with an unexpected determination of Iran's Revolutionary Guards to fight on.

Stages of the War

The war developed over several stages. The first stage involved Iraqi air and land attacks on several positions in west and southwest Iran. These were initially rebuffed. Meanwhile, six divisions crossed into Iran and occupied Khuzistan, Khorramshahr, and Abadan, the last of which was the site for Iran's southern oil fields. After seizing a considerable strip of territory, Iraq fully expected that Iran would surrender, but the Iranians refused, commencing an uneven counteroffensive against the Iraqi army that eventually brought about the recapture of Abadan in 1981.

The second stage began with the Iranians overrunning Iraqi lines and launching a large campaign on Iraqi territory, near Basra. The Iraqis soon repulsed them. Three major human wave campaigns then took place, in which the Iranians suffered a large number of casualties. Eventually, the ground war settled into a war of attrition that lasted from 1984 until 1987. During those years, Iraq repeatedly employed chemical weapons against Iran; the war on cities and long drawn-out sieges on population centers became the order of the day. The war was also internationalized when both sides started attacking merchant shipping in the Persian Gulf so as to prevent supplies from reaching the opponent. Eventually, the United States entered the war on the side of Iraq, initially supplying intelligence and aid. When Kuwait, which bore the brunt of the "Tanker War," as this phase of the hostilities was called, petitioned the international community for help, the United States and the Soviet Union both offered assistance (as a way of protecting their own vested interests) in 1987. The U.S. Navy then began protecting any tanker in the area flying the Stars and Stripes, an important signal to the Iranians of superpower intent. In May 1987, the worst assault of the war on a U.S. warship occurred when the USS *Stark* was accidentally attacked by an Iraqi plane. While this caused some diplomatic problems, the United States basically shrugged off the mistake to focus its enmity on Iran. U.S. military assistance to Iraq during the war amounted to destroying Iranian oil platforms in the Persian Gulf, sinking Iranian gunboats, and the "accidental" downing of an Iranian airliner, for which the United States paid an indemnity.

Also in the dwindling days of the conflict, the external war made way for the internal one. In an act little publicized by the parade of high U.S. officials visiting Hussein in the latter days of the war, it is believed that the Iraqis used poison gas against the Kurds at Halabja in March 1988, a town then controlled by Iranian troops and Kurdish guerrillas. The massacre of hundreds of civilians went unnoticed for several years until a forceful campaign by human rights activists brought it to the world's attention. Finally, after years of stalemate and reversal in which thousands of people perished and the two capitals, Baghdad and Tehran, had been attacked with missiles, Ayatollah Khomeini made his famous speech in which he compared accepting a cease-fire to drinking poison. This ushered in an end to the war, which took place on August 20, 1988, when both sides agreed to abide by UN Resolution 598.

The War's Effects on Society

In Iraq, and undoubtedly in Iran also, the end of the war came as a tremendous relief to civilians and soldiers alike. The enormous cost in human and material losses had taken a grave toll on society. Iraqis had witnessed a vast amount of suffering, borne somewhat unfairly by conscripts' families and the poorer elements in society. Many Iraqis were still imprisoned in Iran; many more had died. On top of the human toll, numbering in the hundreds of thousands, the Iraqi economy was in shambles. Economics professor Abbas Alnasrawi (among others) has calculated that the Iraqi regime started the war flush with oil money, only to end it eight years later badly in debt (Alnasrawi 2001, n.p.). In 1980, Iraq's oil income was calculated at $26.1 billion; by 1988, the government could only muster $11 billion to lift the country out of its economic crisis. Moreover, Hussein had contracted a vast amount of debt owed to Kuwait, Saudi Arabia, and the Gulf States. Posing as a champion of the Arabs and the defender of the "Eastern gate" of the Arab world, he had demanded and received billions of dollars to continue the war. By the first decade of the 21st century, after U.S.-led coalitions had twice invaded Iraq, Baghdad's coffers were virtually bare,

Iraqi prisoners of war return home via the al-Munthiriya checkpoint on the Iran-Iraq border on September 30, 1999, more than a decade after the end of the Iran-Iraq War. They came back to a country whose people continued to suffer the cost of that war, the subsequent ill-fated Kuwait invasion, and international sanctions. (AP Photo/Jassim Mohammed)

prompting many of its creditor nations to cancel all or part of Iraq's debt.

Ideological vilification had entered the vocabulary of both countries. In Iraq, war propagandists, of whom Hussein was perhaps the most versatile, had crafted a pastiche of pre-Islamic, Islamic, and Arab slogans to inspire and "educate" the masses so that they could support the war effort. The Iranians were depicted as "Magians" (al-majus, the pre-Islamic term for the Persian population in Iran). The entire war was called "Saddam's Qadisiyya," in reference to the site of the famous battle of 673 in which the Islamic armies had routed the Persian Sassanians. One of the canniest ways this propaganda campaign was carried out was through state television and the radio. This author remembers that in 1981, Iraqi government television frequently showed the president touring the outlying villages of Baghdad. Invariably, at the end of each tour, his present to Iraqi farmers and villagers was a television set for each household, thus cementing the state media's hold on the ordinary Iraqi.

The Baathist focus on a mix of ideology and patronage to serve the ruling clique's interests during the Iran-Iraq War has received its most elaborate treatment in the recent work of political scientist Eric Davis. Davis argues that the return to history to bolster the state's position during the war did not begin with the conflict itself but appeared well before it (Davis 2005, 176–199). In the boom years of the late 1970s, Saddam Hussein was personally involved in the instrumentalization of history, both as a discipline and as a call to arms for the ordinary Iraqi. The state introduced a systematic overhaul and reinterpretation of historical memory to mobilize consent and prompt popular support for the Baathist-sponsored understanding of both the past and the present. Through the use of Mesopotamian myths, folk symbols, poetry conferences, archaeological fieldwork, the institution of museums, and the expansion of state-produced history journals, the government drove home the point that it was maintaining and resurrecting asala (authenticity) as the watchword of "Iraqi Pan-Arab thought. For the Ba'th, authenticity is first and foremost about creating and policing cultural boundaries" (Davis 2005, 171). For example, the state used allusions to the Shuubiyya as a tool to discredit Iran and by extension Iraqi Shia and all other groups that opposed Arab nationalism. Shuubiyya had been a movement in early Abbasid Iraq dominated by Persian scribes and litterateurs that protested the privileged position of the Arabs within Islam and demanded equality for all Muslims.

In Iran, on the other hand, overtly Islamic symbols were employed to maintain popular support. According to political scientist Farideh

Farhi, "[T]he emphasis on Shi'i values, Shi'i generated epic aspects of the war, mourning, opposition to existing values in the city, martyrdom, action as opposed to words, purity and devotion, and spiritual rewards in the afterlife [became] the most important elements of the culture of war propagated by the war machine in Iran" (Farhi in Potter and Sick 2002, 104). In both countries, the symbolic vocabulary used during the war was retained in the postwar situation, partly so that the immense sacrifices on both sides could be manipulated for political gain and national consolidation.

Prelude to the Invasion of Kuwait

The Iraqi invasion of Kuwait caught the world largely by surprise. However, a combination of historic reasons and developments following the end of the Iran-Iraq War led to the Iraqi regime's rash attack on its Arab neighbor. Iraq had long complained of its limited access to the sea, and its need for deepwater anchorage in the Persian Gulf. Several years before the beginning of the Iran-Iraq War, Iraqi claims to the disputed islands of Warba and Bubiyan had made for an uneasy relation with Kuwait, which considered the islands Kuwaiti and indispensable to its defense. The contention between the two countries over the islands had been ongoing for decades. In 1988–90, Iraq continued to press its demands for a reappraisal of its border agreement with Kuwait, in which the contested islands figured prominently. Agreement was never reached, although various démarches over the question continued to occupy both governments for some time. Undergirding the Iraqi argument over Kuwait was the historical claim to the emirate made by royalist and republican regimes in Iraq from at least the early 20th century onward, which has always failed to elicit support from the international community.

At the same time that the government was addressing itself to the historic Iraqi demand for wider access to the Gulf coast, its extreme anxiety for cash created further tension with oil-producing states. In the wake of the war with Iran, Iraq's debts, particularly those incurred with Saudi Arabia and Kuwait, had soared to an all-time high; subsequently, various Iraqi emissaries had tried to impress upon Kuwait that its big neighbor to the north required further loans to regain its stability, but they were rebuffed out of hand. Worried that the overproduction of oil by several OPEC (Organization of Petroleum Exporting Countries) member states was reducing the value of the one commodity that Iraq could manipulate, Saddam Hussein also tried to coax the Kuwaitis, no less than the Saudis, to agree to raise the price of oil to $25 a barrel at the OPEC meeting in November 1989. Although Saudi Arabia and the United Arab Emirates seemed to have agreed to the Iraqi proposal, Kuwait initially refused it, only reluctantly accepting the idea some time later (Khadduri and Ghareeb 1997, 87). Finally, Iraq argued that Kuwait had begun slant drilling in the south Rumaila oil field claimed by Iraq, though the field was in both Iraq and Kuwait. This argument, first enunciated by Saddam Hussein, was later developed in more detail by Izzat al-Duri, the Iraqi representative at various conferences called to address the matter. Reiterating what Hussein had asserted before him, al-Duri baldly stated that economic warfare was being waged against his country. As a result of all these issues, the different perceptions of what the Gulf States owed Iraq, and what constituted a permanent Iraq-Kuwait border became major sticking points, first, at the Arab summit in Baghdad and later on, at the more exclusive meeting in Jiddah, Saudi Arabia, both in 1990.

While all this activity was taking place in Arab capitals, Hussein began to send out feelers to the Americans. Anxious to probe the U.S. reactions to his quarrel with Kuwait, he sat down with April Glaspie, the U.S. ambassador to Iraq. The transcript of the meeting later released by the Iraqis (there were at least two transcripts of the conversation, one published by the Americans), has become the stuff of history. In subsequent interpretations of the meetings, various observers have been quick to point out that Glaspie had given Iraq the "green light" to go ahead in its military intervention in Kuwait. Equally vociferously, U.S. officials denied that Glaspie's instructions reflected anything of the sort, with Glaspie herself noting in her testimony before the Foreign Relations Committee of the U.S. Senate in 1991 that whatever transcript had been produced by the Iraqis was fabricated, if not in whole, at least in part. As of early 2008, the State Department has never published the details of the encounter, so whatever really took place at that fateful meeting can only be conjecture. But in Hussein's mind, the die was cast. On August 2, 1990, eight days after Glaspie's meeting with the Iraqi president, Hussein's massed troops on the Iraq-Kuwait border invaded Kuwait.

The War Over Kuwait and Its Aftermath

After five Iraqi military divisions entered Kuwait, occupying the entire country in 24 hours, the United States, the United Kingdom, various member states of the United Nations, and a passel of Arab governments

THE GENERALS ARE THE LAST TO KNOW

An Iraqi journalist and one-time editor of the Iraqi daily *al-Jumhuriyya* (The republic) who fled into exile in 1992, Saad al-Bazzaz, wrote a deeply damaging book on Saddam Hussein's conduct during the war on Kuwait. Entitled, *al-Janaralat Akher Man Yalam* (The generals are the last to know), it depicts an Iraqi army thrown into war devoid of leadership, whose military command was literally apprised of the invasion of the emirate just three days before its occurrence. In a fascinating and troubling section, the author details the different military plans Hussein's coterie concocted to keep the invasion a secret until the bitter end.

The idea of the invasion of Kuwait was instrumental in reviving Ali Hussein al-Majid's fortunes [Saddam Hussein's cousin, the infamous Chemical Ali, so called because of his use of chemical weapons against the Shii inhabitants in southern Iraq] which he had lost after the president became angry at him after the embarrassment caused by the financial scandal incurred by his nephew Thair Abdul-Qader Suleiman and the nephew's in-law (Thair was married to the former Iraqi president Ahmad Hassan al-Bakr's daughter). This had forced the president to expel Thair from the [Special Security] Forces, which protected the president, and to throw him in jail. [Thair] also went on state television where he was denounced as a thief who had exploited his relationship with various high officials. Ali Hussein [al-Majid] was accused of using his nephew's offices as a cover for his financial misdeeds without prior authorization from the President. By June 1990 [Ali Hussein

went into high alert. While the United States and its European allies made plans to coerce Iraqi withdrawal from Kuwait, largely through the United Nations, some Arab states sought an "Arab solution" to negotiate the departure of Iraqi troops. This last proposal was completely superseded by the rapidly unfolding events on the ground. While protesting Iraq's flagrant invasion of a fellow member state of the United Nations, the United States sponsored a push to punish Iraq, as a result of which "Iraqi and Kuwaiti assets were frozen, the UN Security Council imposed a total economic and trade embargo on Iraq, and Iraq's only oil export pipelines through Turkey and Saudi Arabia were promptly cut" (Tripp 2000, 253). With the adoption of UN al-Majid] was about to lose his local government position; however, Saddam thought that he would be one of the few who could be trusted [in the affairs] of Kuwait.

So in July 1990, [al-Majid] was invited to attend the limited meeting [on Kuwait] in which, for the first time in the history of Iraq, two military plans were drawn up. The first was called Plan A, the second Plan B, to limit the dimensions of the military activity aiming to occupy Kuwait or part of it. Plan A called for the control of the islands of Warba and Bubyan and the line of the border up to 30 or 50 kilometers deep. Plan B called for the occupation of all of the Kuwaiti territory and islands. Plan A was considered the operative plan until July 29, 1990. That is when Iraqi military Intelligence reports stated that there were no preparations for military conflict [in Kuwait] and that "the US does not have enough troops near Kuwait to abort any large-scale plan to occupy the whole of Kuwait. That is why Plan B was chosen on July 29, 1990. . ."

In those [few] hours, the Iraqi political command (composed entirely of the members of the Revolutionary Command Council and the Regional Command of the Baath Party) only held one meeting where the president made several comments on the impending conference in Jiddah, in which the vice president, Izzat Ibrahim, was going to meet with the Kuwaiti crown prince, Shaykh Saad Abdullah al-Sabah. The president skirted the issue of a military plan but he said, "We shall see what happens in Jiddah and then proceed accordingly" so that when the participants to the conference left, they had no inkling whatsoever that the order to occupy Kuwait had already been formulated, no matter what was going to take place in Jiddah.

Source: Saad Al-Bazzaz. Al-janaralat akher man ya'lam (The generals are the last to know). London: Dar Al-Hikma, 1996, pp. 46–50.

Resolution 678 authorizing force, war came a step closer. Indeed, an international coalition of 30 countries had formed, and was preparing to attack Iraq and eject it from Kuwait. On January 16, 1991, the United States–led coalition began its offensive, eventually leading to the massive bombing of both Iraq and Kuwait and the chaotic withdrawal of the Iraqi army from the Kuwaiti theater. Offensive operations ended on February 28 following Iraq's announcement that it would fully accept all UN resolutions passed since its invasion of Kuwait. One of the events widely reported at the time but now almost forgotten was the U.S. strafing by air of hundreds of Iraqi army stragglers as they left Kuwait on foot or in impounded vehicles.

Almost immediately after the disorganized exit of the army from Kuwait, a wave of rebellions erupted in the north and south of Iraq. In both Iraqi Kurdistan as well as the deprived regions of southern Iraq, soldiers and deserters, community leaders, as well as leaders of pro-Iranian Islamic militias fought the remnants of the Iraqi government throughout Iraq; only in Baghdad was the population too dispirited and leaderless to make a stand. Even though U.S. president George H. W. Bush had encouraged Iraqis to take matters into their own hands, the Americans offered no assistance at all. Indeed, the U.S. Army, stationed in Nasiriya (south-central Iraq), made no move to help the insurgents, some of whom approached U.S. troops demanding their intervention. The memory of this bitter event is still alive among many Iraqis to this day.

Meanwhile, in April 1991, the Republican Guard reasserted control and suppressed the rebellions, creating a large-scale exodus of Kurdish refugees to Iran and Turkey and of mostly Shii Arabs to Saudi Arabia. The government also embarked on a ferocious campaign of extermination of rebel-led areas, in which countless people died. The Iraqi army, under the heavy-handed direction of Hussein's cousin "Chemical" Ali Hussein al-Majid, occupied the Shii shrine cities and terrorized their inhabitants. The Kurdish region, somewhat better placed to resist the advances of the Iraqi army, was nonetheless subjected to heavy fighting in the aftermath of the rebellions. Kirkuk, an important symbol for the Kurds, was quickly recaptured as the Iraqi army beat down the challenge in the north. According to Eric Davis,

> The intifada [mass uprising] was brutally repressed, especially in the south, where an estimated 20,000 to 100,0000 people were killed. SCUD missiles and artillery shells were fired into the city of Karbala and many young Shi'i men were arrested and never seen again. Following the intifada, the Iraqi regime began to drain the southern marshlands, one of the world's most pristine ecological preserves, to prevent its use as a guerilla haven. By the late 1990s, in one of the twentieth century's most serious ecological crimes, this area had been all but totally destroyed. Meanwhile, Baathist repression intensified, with repeated executions of army officers accused of plotting against the regime (Davis 2005, 231).

Iraqi forces later withdrew from the north under threat of U.S. military action, and UN Security Council 688 was passed, "which called for Iraq to end its repression of its own population" (Tripp 2000, 258). The United States, United Kingdom, and France created protected havens, first in the north—where the inhabitants were a mix of Arabs (Sunni,

Shia, and Christian), Kurds, Turkmen, and tiny minorities of Yazidis and Shabak—and later on in the south, largely populated by Arabs of Shii background (with pockets of Arab Sunni communities in Zubair and Basra). Patrolled by U.S. aircraft, which unilaterally attacked the country's air defenses and regularly interdicted Iraqi aircraft from flying in Iraqi airspace, the havens created the beginnings of a self-confident regional autonomy, particularly in Iraqi Kurdistan. Later endowed with a regional government in which the Kurds were the majority partner (the others were the Turkmen and Arab Christian groups), the northern haven became the headquarters of a flourishing economy, funded and otherwise supported by international organizations from Europe as well as the United States.

The Impact of War and Sanctions on Economy and Society
UN Resolutions 661 and 687

The embargo imposed on Iraq by the United Nations four days after the Iraqi invasion of Kuwait was supposed to hold Saddam Hussein's government in check and prevent it from ever threatening its neighbors again. Resolution 661 prohibited all UN members from buying oil from Iraq and from having virtually any other commercial, financial, or military dealings with the country. "[S]upplies intended strictly for medical purposes and, in humanitarian circumstances, foodstuffs" were exempted from the resolution. After the war had ended, UN Resolution 687, passed on April 3, 1991, established the conditions of a cease-fire. It created the UN Compensation Fund to compensate countries, corporations, and individuals that had suffered from the Iraqi invasion of Kuwait, its assets coming from 30 percent of Iraqi oil export revenues. (By 2001, the fund had paid billions to satisfy Kuwaiti claims. As of this writing, this money is still pouring into Gulf coffers, albeit at a reduced percentage, even after the U.S. occupation authorities purportedly lifted sanctions on Iraq as soon as they had entered Baghdad in April 2003. In January 2008, Iraqi vice president Tariq al-Hashemi appealed to Kuwait to reach "compromise solutions" to Iraq's war reparations debt.) Furthermore, Iraq was to pay 5–10 percent of the revenues received from oil for UN operations in Iraq, and 13 percent for the Kurdish autonomous zone in northern Iraq. Peter Pellett, a professor in the Department of Nutrition at the University of Massachusetts at Amherst who joined three missions by the UN Food and Agriculture Organization (FAO) to Iraq in the 1990s, has calculated that the north received 50 percent more aid than south-central Iraq, which meant that "in practice, only about one-half of the original revenue from oil sales [was] available for food and humanitarian supplies for the almost 18 million people dwelling in the area administered by the Iraqi government" (Pellett in Arnove 2002, 191).

The economic sanctions remained in effect for 13 years and were meant to make Iraq also comply with another part of Resolution 687, which called for "the unconditional acceptance, under international supervision, of the destruction, removal or rendering harmless of [Iraq's] weapons of mass destruction, ballistic missiles with a range over 150 kilometres, and related production facilities and equipment [as well as] provide for the establishment of a system of ongoing monitoring and verification of Iraq's compliance with the ban on these weapons and missiles." As a result of the conditions set by 687, the UN weapons monitoring and verification agency, United Nations Special Commission on Iraq (UNSCOM), began its first chemical weapons inspection on June 9, 1991. It remained in Iraq until 1998 when U.S. president Bill Clinton, relying on UNSCOM reports from the field, claimed that Hussein's regime had still not come clean on weapons of mass destruction (WMD) and was being unusually duplicitous about where it was hiding them; this followed after months of tension between the weapons monitoring team in Baghdad and Iraqi government officials. A four-day bombing campaign of Iraqi sites by the United States and United Kingdom, code-named "Desert Fox," followed. Having been warned to evacuate by the United States a couple of weeks earlier, UNSCOM decamped in December of that year, but not before leaving telltale signs of espionage and breaches in security. It had long been suspected that UNSCOM team members had been working for various foreign intelligence organizations, including the United States and Israel. According to Tareq and Jacqueline Ismael,

> These accusations repeated by the Iraqi regime throughout the crisis and resolutely denied by UNSCOM chief Richard Butler were confirmed when, on 7 January 1999, the US government admitted its intelligence agents had posed as weapons inspectors to spy on Iraq. This admission was further confirmed when, on 23 February 1999, the CIA admitted that it had been in Iraq posing as weapons inspectors for a number of years. The admission saw UNSCOM disbanded, UNMOVIC [United Nations Monitoring, Verification and Inspection Commission] founded and undermined the ... credibility of the United Nations as an impartial arbiter (Ismael and Ismael 2004, 25).

Humanitarian Crisis

While those monitoring activities were taking place, ostensibly to force the dismantlement and destruction of Iraqi WMDs, and as U.S. air surveillance became more acute, firing on Iraqi targets at will, the world slowly learned of the catastrophic consequences of the imposition of sanctions on Iraq. A series of detailed UN reports—chiefly conducted by food and agricultural organizations such as the FAO World Food Program (WFP) and humanitarian agencies such as the United Nations International Children's Emergency Fund (UNICEF), United Nations Development Program (UNDP), and World Health Organization (WHO)—investigated the state of nutrition and health in postwar Iraq. The results were sobering. According to Peter L. Pellett,

> [T]he Security Council's decision to maintain sanctions despite the destruction of Iraq's civilian infrastructure during the Gulf war and the inability, until 1996, of Iraq and the council to agree on humanitarian exceptions, led to a sharp increase in hunger, disease and death throughout Iraqi society, especially among women, children, and the elderly. The population of Iraq, which formerly enjoyed some services comparable to those in the West, has suffered terrible hardship because of the sanctions. In effect, the population moved from the edge of first-world status to poor, third-world status with staggering speed (Pellett in Arnove 2000, 185–186).

The UN reports were complemented by other groups such as the Harvard Study Team (later renamed the Center for Economic and Social Rights, CESR), one of the most comprehensive sources for the gradually worsening conditions in Iraq. Launching the first investigation of postwar conditions in the country, the CESR sent a team to Iraq in April 1991, one month after the war. Its subsequent international mission in September 1991 employed 87 experts and thoroughly assessed the socioeconomic conditions on the ground, noting the deteriorating conditions of health and welfare in Iraq. The CESR observed:

> [T]he economic and social disruption caused by the Gulf Crisis has had a direct impact on the health conditions of the children in Iraq. Iraq desperately needs not only food and medicine but also spare parts to repair basic infrastructure in electrical power generation, water purification and sewage treatment. Unless Iraq quickly obtains food, medicine and spare parts, millions of Iraqis will continue to experience malnutrition and disease. Children by the tens of thousands will remain in jeopardy. Thousands will die (CESR 1991, n.p.).

The clincher came in CESR's statement, "[B]ased on these interviews, it is estimated that *the mortality rates of children under five is 380% greater today* than before the onset of the Gulf Crisis." Moreover, in an omen of things to come, CESR noted that due to lack of spare parts and equipment that was nearing obsolescence, electricity generation had fallen dramatically, while again because of the lack of spare parts and the fact that sanctions had severely cut off the importation of chlorine, the operational capacity of water treatment plants had been considerably degraded. This resulted in "a profoundly negative impact on public health, water and wastewater systems, agricultural production and industrial capacity" (CESR 1991, n.p.).

Throughout the 1990s, CESR survey teams, along with UN agencies and other nongovernmental organizations (NGOs), chronicled the growing calamity in Iraq. Partly because of the outcry over the ongoing humanitarian catastrophe in Iraq, the United Nations came under pressure to modify the sanctions. Under the oil-for-food agreement, which Iraq finally agreed to in 1996, the Iraqi government was initially allowed to sell $2 billion worth of oil every six months to buy supplies for its people; however, the crisis continued. In 1996, the CESR published its most forceful report yet, recommending that the UN Security Council "modify the oil-for-food deal to remove the limits on oil revenues for humanitarian needs . . . adopt alternatives to comprehensive sanctions on Iraq and in future cases [and] establish a clear legal framework to govern Security Council sanctions" (CESR 1996, n.p.). The CESR was also the first organization to arrive at the figure, later developed in more detail by UNICEF, that "if the substantial reduction in child mortality throughout Iraq during the 1980s had continued throughout the 1990s, there would have been half a million fewer deaths of children under five in the country as a whole during the eight year period 1991 to 1998" (Information Newsline 1999). Meanwhile, the Security Council's own humanitarian panel concluded that a steep degradation of living standards had taken place in Iraq, affecting health, the distribution of food, the expansion of infrastructure, and the growth in education. "[I]nfant mortality rates in Iraq were among the highest in the world, low infant birth weight affected at least 23% of all births, chronic malnutrition affected every fourth child under five and only 41% of the population had regular access to clean water" (Global Policy Forum 2002, n.p.).

In 1998, the limit set in 1996 for the oil-for-food program was raised to $5.2 billion and finally removed altogether in 1999. However, the heavy restrictions that had been placed on the distribution of oil revenues, including the proviso that 30 percent would be paid into the UN

Growing up under the sanctions: Baghdad schoolchildren in 2000, the year after restrictions in the oil-for-food program were finally lifted (AP Photo/Jassim Mohammed)

Compensation Fund, remained in place even as the UN lifted the cap on Iraq's oil exports.

Economy and Society in the 1990s

After 13 years of sanctions, two devastating wars, and decades of social and economic damage arising out of misguided developmental objectives and the militarization of the economy, internal as well as external pressures on the Iraqi economy began to sorely affect the family structure, education, public health, and livelihood of millions of Iraqis. This author participated in an oral history project in Amman, Jordan, in 2005 in which mostly elderly Iraqis, longtime residents, and new arrivals, agreed to be interviewed. For many Iraqi interviewees, the sanctions era was only the culminating development of many years of war with Iran, in which social and economic problems arising during the Iran-Iraq War, such as galloping inflation, industrial stagnation, lack of employment opportunities, and massive rural-to-urban migration, were accelerated during the 1990s, further crushing an already traumatized population. During the sanctions era, the dinar was devalued even further, decimating salaries and retirement benefits. Iraqis had to work two or three different jobs and had to sell their possessions to make ends meet. Iraq's health system, one of the best in the Middle East, broke down, as did its educational structure. Small wonder, then, that the majority of respondents in the oral history project characterized the sanctions era as nothing short of total war.

The lack of books, medicine, musical instruments, pencils, or even new, reliable tires for the family car, all examples of imports stopped by Committee 661 (the committee established by the UN Security Council to monitor the implementation of sanctions imposed on Iraq), brought communication to a standstill. Worn-out tires killed people as surely as a bullet. Minds starved of learning lost energy. New and rapidly spreading cancers required novel drugs, of which there was none. The sale of family heirlooms and furniture, down to the doors of houses in some cases, by Iraqis needing to augment their debased state salaries, crushed the human spirit. New markets grew up in city streets catering to the demand of secondhand goods. Al-Mutannabi, the street of the booksellers, was only the most famous. School attendance dropped precipitously, with school-age children now claiming the streets as their sources of livelihood, and hawking and peddling became some of the most conspicuous trades in large cities such as Baghdad. The Iraqi professional class, largely having run out of their savings and unable to make ends meet because of the pittances they received as salaries, left the country in droves. And the public health crisis accelerated, as departing doctors made way for young and relatively inexperienced interns who, for the first time in decades, had to handle maladies that had once been thought to have been wiped out in Iraq, specifically malnutrition, diphtheria, and cholera. The spread of daytime robberies, unheard of in Baghdad until the mid-1990s, destroyed trust. The extortion of government officials and the rising levels of corruption raised the ordinary Iraqi's instinct of self-preservation to a new level. The Baathist regime continued to pamper some, if not all, of its military personnel (conscripts fared badly while commanders of the Republican Guard regiments were well taken care of). The sanctions era, I was told over and over again, turned Iraqis into machines in which, as one elderly respondent told me, "we lost the memory of being human." Significantly, most of the interviewees noted the existence of an external and internal embargo; to Iraqis, the first was imposed by the United Nations and the second, by the Iraqi government, which, with some notable exceptions, preyed on Iraq and its long-suffering population.

Workers in an antibiotics factory located outside Baghdad in the late 1990s. The sanctions following the Kuwait invasion created food and medical shortages in Iraq. (AP Photo/Jassim Mohammed)

The Rise of Resistance to the Baathist Regime and the Emergence of External Opposition

From the mid-sixties onwards, movements of religious reform and political resistance began to emerge in Iraq. In 1979, after preliminary clashes escalated between the government and the first Shii political party in Iraq, al-Daawa, resulting in the execution of the charismatic Daawa leader, Ayatollah Muhammad al-Sadr, as well as the persecution of his followers, the movement was not to be heard of again until it surfaced as a somewhat reluctant member of the Supreme Council of the Islamic Revolution of Iraq (SCIRI). Known thereafter by its initials, SCIRI was an Iranian-founded and Iran-based umbrella organization grouping three important Iraqi Shii clerical groups: the Marjaaiyya group under Muhammed Baqir al-Hakim, the Daawa group, and an independent coalition of Shii political activists (International Crisis Group 2007, n.p.). The three groups pledged to oust Saddam Hussein's regime through military and political means and to replace it with an Islamic government. Although Daawa organizers broke off relations with SCIRI almost immediately, the Daawa party continued its campaign of resistance and acts of subversion against the regime until its members were massively hunted down and all but destroyed by Baathist governments in the 1970s and 1980s. Still, the party survived under the leadership of various splinter groups until 2003, after which it regrouped to become an influential member of the American-influenced ruling class.

SCIRI, meanwhile, went from strength to strength. Funded and trained by the Iranians, its leaders (from the influential Hakim family) adopted the controversial Khomeinist ideology of the *wilayat al-faqih* which stipulated that the chief jurisprudent in Shii Islam can take on the role of a guardian jurist and that in the absence of the Hidden Twelfth Imam, the clergy should rule. Although some influential clerical members of the Daawa party had campaigned to turn this issue into a major plank of the party, it was not a doctrine that was easily accepted by the rank and file of Iraqi Shiis, many of whom were followers of the quietist school of Shii thought. Nonetheless, after the Daawa party seceded from SCIRI, that same question was taken up by the Hakim family and became a defining principle for SCIRI-associated Iraqi exiles in Iran and later on, in Iraq itself. SCIRI also created a militia, the Badr Brigade, which carried out attacks across the Iranian border into Iraq. Funded, trained, and armed by the Iranian regime, it was estimated to have recruited 10,000 fighters by the late 1990s (Cole 2003).

Kurdish resistance movements had also long been rife in Iraq. Unlike those of the Shii opposition, however, the Kurds were able to stake out an important position after the 1991 war. While Iraqi government campaigns had accelerated the tempo of Iraqi military incursions into the Kurdish region at the end of the Iran-Iraq war in 1988, the Kurdish rebellion in the wake of the first Gulf war, much like the Shii uprisings in the south and center of Iraq, set into motion a number of significant developments. First was the massive refugee crisis which occurred after the flight of thousands of Kurds to Turkey. Confronted with the approach of Iraqi troops into the still-fragile enclave of Iraqi Kurdistan, thousands of Kurds fled to the Turkish border in the rain and snow. Faced with a quandary in part generated by an international outcry, Coalition forces (the United States, the United Kingdom, and France) ultimately backed the creation of an autonomous Kurdish region in northern Iraq. As a result of the protection offered them by the creation of the "no-fly zones," Kurdish rebel leaders metamorphosed into incipient statesmen, with the Kurdish Democratic Party (KDP) leader Massoud Barzani controlling Irbil in the north and the head of the Patriotic Union of Kurdistan (PUK), Jalal Talabani, ensconcing himself in Suleymaniya, in the south. In June 1992, a Kurdish parliament opened its doors in Irbil, and in October of that same year, the Iraqi Kurds formed a Kurdish federal state.

However, this progress was not to last, as the leadership of the northern and southern districts of Iraqi Kurdistan continued to eye each other with suspicion. As a result of this mistrust, two parallel administrations emerged in the autonomous Kurdish region, and conflicts over territory and revenue eventually led to open warfare in December 1994. The war between the Kurdish chieftain, Barzani, and his more urbane rival, Talabani, was to continue until 1996, with thousands of Kurds killed in the process. Eventually, U.S. intervention brought about the end of the war, but relations remained tense for many months afterwards.

The Kurds "formally declared their desire to become part, in a post-Saddam Iraq, of a federal state . . . this aspiration became a standard plank of the Kurdish parties' political program as they engaged with the non-Kurdish Iraqi opposition groups, especially the Iraqi National Congress of Ahmad Chalabi, which accepted federalism as the solution to the Kurdish question" (International Crisis Group 2003, n.p.). The Iraqi National Congress (INC) was formally inaugurated in Vienna in June 1992 when the two Kurdish leaders, Barzani and Talabani, joined almost 200 Iraqi delegates from opposition groups to create a coalition to fight the Baathist leadership in Baghdad. Massively funded by the United States, the INC grouped parties of various ideological stripes, including SCIRI stalwarts, retired military officers, and Kurdish partisans. The INC, however, was dealt a strong blow when Iraqi troops overran its base in Salahuddin (Iraqi Kurdistan) in 1996; it is estimated that 200 of the INC's men were captured and killed by the Iraqi forces and 2,000 arrested (Katzman 1998, n.p.).

Prelude to the U.S. Invasion of Iraq

In the early months of the U.S. presidency of George W. Bush, foreign policy began to coalesce around an anti-Iraq strategy that pitted hard-line neoconservatives (neocons) against pragmatic realists in the administration. The initial phase of this policy was confined to financial support to the INC and to increasing the air strikes begun during the Clinton administration. However, the differing opinions within the Bush administration resulted in a temporary stalemate regarding U.S. policy toward Saddam Hussein. The stalemate was broken on September 11, 2001, with the terrorist attacks on the World Trade Center in New York City and the Pentagon outside Washington, D.C.

(as well as a failed attempt in which an airliner crashed in a field in Pennsylvania). The U.S. government publicly identified al-Qaeda as the group behind the attacks, a terrorist group that had close ties with Afghanistan's Taliban leadership. On October 7, 2001, U.S. and British bombers targeted Taliban forces and al-Qaeda strongholds within Afghanistan in support of insurrectionary ground forces from the so-called Northern Alliance (various Afghani warlords who made common cause against the Taliban). Kabul, the capital, was one of the targets. The purpose of the invasion was to capture al-Qaeda leader Osama bin Laden and to overthrow the Taliban. In 2002, U.S. ground forces joined in the invasion. The Taliban was quickly overthrown, although most of the leadership escaped to the mountainous frontier region that bordered Pakistan, while bin Laden and other al-Qaeda leaders were never captured, having escaped initially to the mountains of Tora Bora, near the Khyber Pass in eastern Afghanistan. It is believed that the brief truce in fighting, ostensibly to allow al-Qaeda fighters to surrender their weapons, in reality allowed bin Laden and other high-ranking members of the organization to escape. Nevertheless, by early 2002, the United States and its allies were firmly in control of Afghanistan, although by 2006, Taliban influence and insurrection would rise again.

With the comparatively easy "success" of the Afghanistan phase of the "war on terror" under their belts, the neocons, the advisory group toward which President Bush leaned, were in the ascendant. In the annual State of the Union speech, delivered on January 29, 2002, President Bush linked Iraq, Iran, and North Korea "and their terrorist allies" in what he called an "axis of evil" (White House 2002), thus playing on two 20th-century historical ideas: the Axis powers of World War II (Germany, Italy, and Japan) and the more recent vintage "evil empire" as President Ronald Reagan had characterized the Soviet Union in the 1980s. The press picked up on the phrase, and the notion was planted that all three countries were direct threats to U.S. security, though, of course, the three countries were not allied (in the case of Iraq and Iran far from it). Referring to Saddam Hussein in the same State of the Union speech, Bush declared, "This is a regime that has something to hide from the civilized world" (White House 2002).

What Hussein was hiding, the Bush administration claimed, was WMD. This (mis)information was allegedly given to the Central Intelligence Agency (CIA) by the INC. Hussein denied such claims, but the warlike rhetoric coming from the United States, not to mention the October 2002 joint congressional resolution that authorized U.S. military force in Iraq, prompted him to agree to allow weapons inspectors back into Iraq. Thus, as per the unanimously passed UN Security Council Resolution 1441, the UNMOVIC, headed by Swedish diplomat Hans Blix, began inspecting sites in November 2002. Although the inspectors found no WMD, the United States remained adamant. An anxious Hussein, according to the account by journalist Michael R. Gordon and General Bernard E. Trainor, after consultations with the RCC, military advisers, and members of the Baath Party, announced that Iraq had no WMD and "called on several select officials to confirm his disclosure. Iraq's defense minister, Sultan Hashim Ahmad al-Tai, told U.S. interrogators after the fall of Baghdad that many of the generals were stunned by the news. . . ." According to Deputy Prime Minister Tariq Aziz, morale "plummeted" (Gordon and Trainor 2006, 118). However, the Bush administration was not about to publicly take its sworn enemy at his word, no matter who confirmed that word.

In February 2003, U.S. secretary of state Colin Powell (who had been chairman of the U.S. Joint Chiefs of Staff during the Persian Gulf War) addressed the United Nations General Assembly, with "evidence." Though Powell failed in his attempt to gain UN sanction for the invasion, the United States and Great Britain decided to push on with it. Powell's so-called evidence was later proven false, but by then the war was on. Whether faulty intelligence was at the heart of the claims or administration pressure on the CIA to produce intelligence that would justify the claims has yet to be completely decided.

Both Great Britain and the United States took care to involve Iraqi opposition leaders in exile. Conferences were held in London and Washington, D.C., in late 2002 and early 2003. On February 25, 2003, less than a month before the outbreak of hostilities, there was an opposition meeting held in Salahuddin in Iraqi Kurdistan. On the meeting's agenda was whether to form a government in exile and the possibility of a provisional government after the fall of Hussein, which the United States opposed. Nonetheless, the Salahuddin conference did create the Leadership Council composed of Ayad Allawi, Massoud Barzani, Ahmad Chalabi, Abd el-Aziz al-Hakim, Adnan al-Pachachi, and Jalal Talabani.

The coalition President Bush put together to fight in Iraq included Great Britain, Spain, Italy, and Poland, among others, although notably France, Germany, Russia, and China opted not to join and even criticized U.S. policy. By far, the brunt of the fight, both with troops on the ground and weaponry, was borne by the United States, with heavy British assistance. A month before the invasion a worldwide antiwar rally in more than 800 cities and involving between 6 million to 10 million people took place. Yet, just prior to the war, nearly three-quarters of U.S. citizens favored invasion, an even higher percentage believing that Iraq was linked with al-Qaeda. All last-minute attempts at diplomacy were bound to fail.

The administration's policy was also motivated by another development: Much to Western chagrin, the international air embargo on Iraq had all but collapsed in 2002, with Russian, Arab, and other flights regularly touching down at Baghdad airport after an absence of 12 years. Diplomats and traders began arriving in Baghdad, with ambitious business deals in their pockets; their appearance was usually preceded by a cargo of humanitarian supplies, which were presented to the "Iraqi people." A Baghdad trade fair in that same year drew large crowds of international businessmen. Meanwhile, the Arab League invited Iraqi diplomats to attend the first meeting in a decade; however, a rapprochement between Iraq and Kuwait, highly touted in the Arab press, never fully materialized.

At a highly publicized forum that year Secretary General Kofi Annan warned that "the UN was in danger of losing the debate in the court of international public opinion regarding its responsibility for the humanitarian crisis, 'if we haven't already lost it'" (Ismael and Ismael 2004, 26). To deflect the growing clamor for an end to the embargo, the United States and United Kingdom introduced "smart," or targeted, sanctions to the United Nations as replacement for the previous comprehensive sanctions (Ismael and Ismael 2004, 34). But, as antisanctions activists pointed out, the changes were largely procedural in nature. Besides changing the system by which Iraq imported goods, Security Council Resolution 1409 tried to abolish the smuggling of commodities into Iraq in return for cheap oil, which was going on quite openly outside the oil-for-food program (Campaign Against Sanctions on Iraq 2003, n.p.). However, this failed because too many Western allies in the Middle East region were profiting handsomely by the deal.

Conclusion

For 20 years, even as he enjoyed near absolute power, Saddam Hussein's regime was in a constant state of decay. Like many an autocrat before him, Hussein sought to bolster his authority by deflecting attention away from Iraq's numerous problems, first with the Iran-Iraq War of the 1980s and then with the invasion of Kuwait. However, these merely accelerated the centrifugal forces that were pulling on Baghdad. While

Iraq's military disasters led to insurrections that were brutally put down, the corruption of the Baathist regime played a large role in spurring on inevitable social and political forces that would destroy Hussein's Iraq.

The Kurds proved resilient in resisting Baathist brutality, and the Arab tribes were equally resilient in adapting to the times. Indeed, their paramount shaykhs seemed to all but outmaneuver Hussein at the bargaining table. Hussein's ambiguous attitude toward Islam was primarily an attempt to prevent his being outmaneuvered by the Iranian ayatollahs, but in doing so, he gave legitimacy to the Iraqi ayatollahs, who were no longer willing to acquiesce to the regime. However, it was the exiled opposition, whose influence in the West was far greater than its influence within Iraq (where many of the exiled leaders were distrusted), which kept up the anti-Hussein drumbeat throughout the 1990s and into the 21st century. Their propaganda played well enough in London, Washington, D.C., and elsewhere to bolster the sanctions against Iraq that would, themselves, play a role in the paranoia that would lead to yet another war.

10

THE WAR IN IRAQ
(2003-2008)

By the end of February 2003, it was obvious to the world that a U.S.-led coalition was intent on invading Iraq. The stated goal was twofold: remove Saddam Hussein from power and recover his supposed cache of weapons of mass destruction. While a good deal of the world opposed the idea of regime change by military intervention, many Iraqis supported it. Leaders who had been living in exile in London and Washington, D.C., had actively sought such an outcome, and some had even assisted the United States in making its case.

Within Iraq, the mood was more cautious. Certainly, the removal of Hussein would be welcomed by Shii Arabs as well as Kurds since both groups had suffered greatly during his rule, especially in the wake of the Persian Gulf War. Moreover, there were some Sunni groups and tribes whose opposition to Hussein had made their positions tenuous. Many tribal shaykhs had benefited greatly under Hussein, who practiced a kind of government subsidy that in effect purchased tribal loyalty. How ought they react to the upcoming invasion? As it turned out, in many cases, they expected business to resume to normal, even without Hussein in power. Furthermore, there had already been assassination and coup attempts against Hussein. These had all failed. Who was to say this latest threat would succeed?

Another reason for the caution was that no one was sure what to expect after the fall of the Baathist regime. Would the Sunnis retain their position as mandarins of Iraqi society? Would the Shiis finally have a say in the government, respective of their majority status? And what of the Kurds? Was their longtime dream of Kurdistan about to come true? Or, would they enjoy an autonomy on par with Arab Iraq? No one stopped to ponder these questions in the rush toward war early in 2003. And as civil society broke down in the weeks and months after the coalition invasion of Iraq, the answers became muddled in insurgent and sectarian violence. Old hatreds flamed anew, even as the infrastructure of Iraq burned. Within a year those who may have looked upon the coalition forces as liberators, no longer did so. Yet, despite the ongoing disaster, and to its credit, Iraq managed to forge a new government, federal in nature, parliamentary in practice. The country had taken its first step toward recovery.

The First Phase of the War

With an overwhelming majority of the American public and the U.S. Congress behind armed intervention in Iraq, not to mention a sizable percentage of the American people falsely believing there had been a connection between Hussein and the September 11, 2001, terrorist attacks (thus linking the upcoming invasion with the U.S.-declared "war on terror"), the Bush administration and the Labour government of Prime Minister Tony Blair in Great Britain were confident of a quick and successful invasion of Iraq. On March 18, 2003, Bush issued an ultimatum to Hussein ordering the Iraqi dictator and his two sons, Udai and Qusai, to leave Iraq, giving them a 48-hour deadline to honor the ultimatum. Though he was offered sanctuary in Bahrain (as reported by China's Xinhua News Agency), Hussein appeared on Iraqi television in military uniform and announced his refusal to leave Iraq. The next day, the United States jumped the gun on the president's deadline when it bombed the compound of Hussein's sons in a Baghdad suburb, where it was mistakenly thought they were meeting with their father and other Iraqi leaders. Instead, civilians, including a child, were killed, thus becoming the first "collateral damage" of a war that had yet to begin.

The invasion of Iraq, dubbed Operation Iraqi Freedom by forces of the "Coalition of the Willing," as the mostly U.S. and British multinational force was called, took place on March 20, 2003, from staging areas primarily in Kuwait. The original invasion plan had called for simultaneous attacks from the north as well as the south, but Turkey refused permission for coalition troops to amass in its territory. The attack, with simultaneous aerial bombing and ground force assault (as opposed to the Persian Gulf War where weeks of bombing preceded the ground war), was termed *shock and awe*. With history in mind, the British were charged with securing and occupying Basra and the surrounding area, while U.S. forces swept northward for the assault on Baghdad. This northward push was called Operation Cobra II, after General George S. Patton's Third Army breakout from Normandy in

1944 during the liberation of France, the original Operation Cobra. Within two days, forces were halfway to Baghdad, but it was not until April 9, that the capital was formally under U.S. control. By then, fighting in northern Iraq (with Kurds aiding the coalition forces) had begun. This was the second prong in the original attack plan; part of its mission was securing the Kirkuk oil fields, which was fairly easily accomplished. With the British in the south securing the Rumaila fields and the U.S. forces securing Kirkuk, there were far fewer oil well fires than had occurred in the Persian Gulf War.

The fall of Baghdad brought home the realization that Hussein was no longer in power, yet he had managed to escape capture, as had his sons. Others in the Iraqi leadership, however, had not. Deputy Prime Minister Tariq Aziz surrendered to U.S. forces on April 24, after formally handing over the reins of government to the coalition forces. In search of Saddam Hussein, coalition forces had pushed toward his hometown of Tikrit, which had become the final major city to fall to coalition forces on April 14. While the Battle of Tikrit yielded Hussein's political and clan stronghold, it failed to uncover the deposed leader. Nevertheless, the Pentagon declared an end to major military operations. At that point, the (subsequently) estimated number of Iraqi

The fall of Saddam Hussein. American troops help topple a statue of the former dictator in Palestine Square on April 9, 2003, the day coalition forces formally took control of Baghdad. (AP Photo/James Nachtwey)

WERE THE WEAPONS INSPECTIONS MERELY A RUSE?

In his account of his role in the search for weapons of mass destruction in Iraq, Hans Blix pointed out how the U.S. government in the weeks before the onset of hostilities, tried to portray him as an obstructionist—not to the inspection, but to the invasion.

> My refusal . . . to assume that items "unaccounted for" might exist displeased some people in Washington. On March 2 the New York Times reported "a senior administration official" as saying that "the inspections have turned out to be a trap. . . . We're not counting on Blix to do much of anything for us." And further: Blix had issued defiantly ambiguous pronouncements and was now "more interested in pleasing all sides than stating the facts" that Iraq had prohibited weapons, and that I did "not want to go back to Sweden and be the cause of a war." The criticism was evidently based on the conviction that U.S./UK evidence was conclusive and that my only reason for not swallowing it hook, line and sinker was that I would not want to be seen as easing a Security Council vote authorizing war.
>
> The same article further reported that there was every hope in the Washington administration that the votes for the [UN] resolution [authorizing the invasion] could be obtained, "but decreasing hope that Mr. Blix will be a help in rounding them up." Getting the UN votes authorizing the war was the main U.S. preoccupation. That the professional inspectors, who had by then visited many hundred sites based on intelligence tips, and analyzed many thousands of documents, had not come to confirm U.S./UK assertions was apparently not an overwhelming concern of the administrations.
>
> . . . Arguing against the French proposal to intensify inspections by tripling the number of inspectors, [U.S. secretary of defense] Donald Rumsfeld was quoted in the International Herald Tribune as saying that if you need inspectors to determine if Iraq is complying, then one or two would do. In other words what was needed was judgment, not inspection. The war was seen as certain and the adoption of the resolution endorsing it desirable but not indispensable (Blix 2004, 215–216).

casualties was between 4,900 and 6,375, according to CBS News. Those figures were subsequently revised upward.

On May 1, 2003, President Bush, in a staged television event, landed in a jet fighter aboard the aircraft carrier USS *Abraham Lincoln,* which was in the process of returning to its home port of San Diego from the Persian Gulf. The president, who emerged from the jet in a flight suit and helmet with a banner declaring "Mission Accomplished" in large letters as a backdrop, said, "The battle of Iraq is one victory in a war on terror that began on September 11, 2001, and still goes on." He also stated in reference to al-Qaeda that "no terrorist network will gain weapons of mass destruction from the Iraqi regime, because that regime is no more." Thus, in declaring victory, the president had reiterated two falsehoods: that Iraq possessed WMD and that Hussein was in alliance with bin Laden.

The Coalition Provisional Authority

With the notion of regime change firmly in their minds, the war planners, as had many others, posited a golden Iraqi future once Hussein was deposed. But they gave little thought as to how to go about building such a golden future. Many felt that with the downfall of the Baath Party would come a U.S.-assisted democracy that would reflect the pluralism of Iraqi society. Outwardly, this appeared so. Approximately a month and a half before the invasion, President Bush decided to leave the reconstruction of Iraq in the hands of the Pentagon, thus making Secretary of Defense Donald Rumsfeld a major player in the postwar scenario. To handle this, the Office for Reconstruction and Humanitarian Affairs (ORHA) was established and headed by retired general Jay Garner. Despite Garner's military credentials, ORHA had little acknowledgment or support from the military after the fall of Baghdad. And though it seemed to be the working arm of the neocons back in Washington, it never got its programs off the ground. On May 22, 2003, the U.S. and British-sponsored United Nations Resolution 1483 authorized the Coalition Provisional Authority (CPA) to ease Iraq's transition to democracy and, while doing so, carry on the reconstruction of the country. The United States reserved the right to name the head of the CPA, and Rumsfeld chose L. Paul Bremer whom President Bush earlier in the month had named U.S. envoy to Iraq. The establishment of the CPA, with its power "to exercise executive, legislative, and judicial powers" (Hashim 2006, 18), lent credence to charges that the United States and United Kingdom were now occupying powers. It also superseded ORHA, which became a department of the CPA. Yet either way, ORHA or the CPA, Iraqi reconstruction and postwar governance was done through the neocon prism within the U.S. Department of Defense.

While the CPA was the real power in post-Hussein Iraq, it was cloaked by the 25-member Governing Council. The council was composed to reflect Iraq's ethnic and sectarian populations: "The Shi'a as a group would hold a slim majority . . . Kurds and Sunni Arabs would each have a roughly equal share of 20 percent of the seats," and "minorities such as the Turkomen and Christian communities would need to be represented." There were also political affiliations to consider: Islamists, Kurdish parties, secularists, and liberal democrats, among others (Allawi 2007, 164). Among the members of the Governing Council were those who had made up the Leadership Council, but at least one member of the Governing Council had been associated with the Baath regime: Aquila al-Hashemi had been connected with Deputy Prime Minister Aziz. She was shot on September 20, 2003, and died three days later, never having made it to the UN General Assembly with a delegation of her colleagues, who were hoping to convince the United Nations to grant international recognition to the Governing Council (and thereby undercut the power of the CPA). Her assassination was dismaying evidence of how the insurgency was expanding.

The insurgency took many people by surprise, but it was only one aspect that showed how poorly prepared the CPA was. The CPA underestimated the amount of damage that was done to Iraq's infrastructure by the invasion, which combined with, in the words of former postwar finance minister Ali A. Allawi, the "advance state of decay" (Allawi 2007, 114) that Iraq had fallen into in the years after the Persian Gulf War revealed that immediate postwar plans by the neocons in Washington, D.C., as well as exiled Iraqis in London (of which Allawi was one) were woefully shortsighted. Another error was made early as the coalition forces, unable to prevent the breakdown of order in Baghdad (and elsewhere), failed to properly protect the files of the Baath regime, the exception to this being the Ministry of Oil. According to Allawi, these government files not only contained incriminating evidence against various Baath leaders but would have made future governance of Iraq easier (Allawi 2007, 115).

In many cities and towns, but especially Baghdad, looting and arson were for a time endemic to the overthrow of the regime. Food and other goods became scarce; public facilities were damaged if not destroyed. Securing proper health care became a problem as did procuring potable water and electricity. Naturally, a black market sprang up wherever there was a demand, and a good deal of stolen goods ended up in neighboring countries, a lot of it via Kurdistan. Cultural institutions were also hit hard by the war and its aftermath, the best-known incident of this being the looting of the National Museum of Iraq. Just after the fall of Baghdad in April 2003, an estimated 15,000 pieces—many of these artifacts from ancient Sumer—were taken from the museum (though approximately one-third of these have been recovered). There was also damage to archaeological sites by coalition helicopters. Among those sites damaged were the sixth-century B.C.E. temples of Nabu and Ninmah and the remains of a Greek theater dating back to the Seleucid Empire. The day after the National Museum was looted, the main building of the Iraq National Library and Archives was set afire, causing extensive structural damage. According to the library's director, Saad Eskander, "it is estimated the library lost 25 percent of its collection, including rare books, whereas the archive lost 60 percent of its collection, including invaluable Ottoman records" (Eskander 2006, n.p.). Eskander also mentioned that the republican archive was completely destroyed. While some U.S. officials' reactions echoed the worldwide shock at the looting and arson, others gave defensive responses for the failure to protect the national treasures. Overall, the looting, terror, and violence following the breakdown in security caused by the struggle and the aftermath of the fall of the capital was compared to the Mongol sack of Baghdad in 1258. Another concern that had unforeseen effects was the theft of weaponry and explosives that helped to arm the insurgents.

The Insurgency

After securing the oil fields, the search for Saddam Hussein became a top priority along with the search for WMD. Aside from the obvious political capital to be gained from the capture of Saddam Hussein, there was the matter of the incipient insurgency that was springing up against the coalition forces and the CPA. At this early stage, Baathist cells were among the insurgent fighters, and some of these cells were battling for the restoration of Hussein. It must be noted, though, that even then, they were a minority among the insurgents; the insurgency itself began as a Sunni attempt to retain its position in the new Iraq. Nevertheless, it was feared by some and hoped by others that Hussein might reemerge amid the chaos as a resurrected leader of all the opposition forces. In August 2003, a letter purportedly written by Hussein was broadcast by the al-Jazeera news network. As described by Ahmed S. Hashim, it "called upon senior Shi'a clerics to declare a *jihad* against the foreign presence in Iraq" (Hashim 2006, 130). Was it really Hussein calling upon some of his sworn enemies to further the insurgency? Or, by this time, was he merely a symbol, and a quickly fading one, of a desperate Baathist resistance, his name being the only one some thought could rally the country? No one knows for sure, but as Hashim points out, the move seems naive. Certainly, aiding and abetting Hussein was the furthest motive possible for Shii participation in the insurgency.

Hussein managed to elude capture for another four months after the controversial letter surfaced. But on December 13, 2003, he was discovered hiding in a hole on a farm near the village of Daur. When the image of the tired, disheveled former dictator was shown worldwide, many thought the coalition had accomplished its mission, especially with growing doubt, even from believers in the United States, of the existence of WMD in Iraq. However, the Bush administration was loathe to leave the country ripe for another Baathist takeover (or worse), declaring that a democratic government must be in place before the coalition pulled out of Iraq. This policy began to have immediate negative effects. Not only did it fuel antiwar movements in the United States and elsewhere, where Bush's motives for the invasion were always suspect, but it provided the paramount reason for broadening the insurgency. Although some may have thought the insurgency would fall apart with the capture of Hussein, it was, in Allawi's words, "only a blip on the insurgency's radar screen" (Allawi 2007, 242), especially since the insurgency itself would soon devolve into a civil war in all but name.

Four days before Saddam Hussein's capture, the Governing Council had passed the Special Tribunal law to try former regime members for their crimes. In the meantime, an interim government took over in Iraq and on June 30, 2004, took responsibility for all Baathist regime members under detention, including Hussein. Hussein languished in prison for nearly two years before he was brought to trial on October 19, 2005. The delay was partly due to indecision among the Iraqi judiciary as to whether the machinery of justice had the ability to handle such a case. Some members of the judiciary were concerned about personal safety, while still others rejected the notion of war crimes as being a rationale for doing the bidding of the coalition. U.S. meddling in the form of assisting in the removal of the chief executive of the Special Tribunal, Salem Chalabi, on trumped up charges further delayed Hussein's trial. Finally, on July 17, 2005, formal charges were brought against him (and seven codefendants) in regard to the massacre of 148 people in

Dujail, a town on the Tigris River in northern Iraq in 1982, following an attempted assassination of Hussein. The charges also included the torture of numerous other people and the illegal arrests of 399 people, all resulting from the same incident.

The assassinations of members of Hussein's legal team and the attempted killings of other members offered proof of the chaos into which Iraq had fallen. The trial was, in fact, held inside the so-called Green Zone, the safe U.S.-protected area of Baghdad, which gave the Special Tribunal the aura of an American-prompted court. The trial lasted until November 5, 2006, when Hussein was found guilty of crimes against humanity and sentenced to death. The verdict was upheld on appeal to the Iraqi Supreme Court of Appeals. Hussein was hanged on December 30, 2006.

Sunni Resistance

By the time of Hussein's conviction and execution, the Iraqi insurgency was bordering on civil war. It had its origins in the makeup of Iraqi society and its history, which the CPA seemed to be either ignorant of or willfully ignoring. At any rate, the insurgency began almost from the fall of Baghdad. Not only were there the expected Baathist cells, but also non-Baathist and even anti-Baathist Sunnis who, as members of the oligarchy that had ruled Iraq, with intermittent exceptions, since the days of the Abbasids, opposed the CPA and even the Governing Council and who sought to retain their hold on Iraq's authority. As Hashim has noted, these Sunnis sought to hold on to their identity as leaders of Iraq, a goal the Bush administration misunderstood. Nevertheless, the majority of Sunnis who ultimately joined the insurgency were not initially opposed to the coalition forces, since they did not know at the time how long the forces would remain in Iraq.

A case in point is the Dulaimi tribe, some of whose members more than 10 years earlier had tried to oust Hussein and who were now involved in the fighting against the coalition. Their experience symbolized part of what went awry for the CPA's reconstruction plans. During the Baathist regime, the Dulaimi and other Sunni Arabs had worked within the government, later opposing it on political grounds. They assumed that when the regime fell, they would fill the power vacuum. However, it was the CPA that filled that vacuum, until such time that a new Iraqi government could be put in place. And any new government, if it was to be truly democratic or at least have the appearance of being such, would naturally reflect the makeup of Iraqi society, the majority being Shii. Thus, a Sunni motive for the insurgency was a barely disguised power play.

Another problem the war planners failed to anticipate and with which the CPA and every subsequent Iraqi government had to deal was the tribal reactions to the sudden loss of government subsidies. Tribal identity, revived and strengthened in the previous decade by such largesse, was also an impediment to a peaceful governmental transition once the bribes stopped coming. Many youthful members of the tribes, whether urban or not, drifted into the insurgency.

With civil authority in the hands of the CPA and to a far lesser extent the Governing Council, religious leaders, both Sunni and Shii, had more influence than they had enjoyed under Hussein, as both government authorities recognized that the majority Shiis would not return to their quiescent past in Iraq. Many called for a renewed unity between Sunni and Shia. Some issued warnings that the occupation of Iraq ought to be short otherwise hostilities might erupt; others preached war against the coalition forces from the outset. All of this went unheeded by the CPA and the military.

The flashpoint for the insurgency was not the looting and arson in Baghdad but an occurrence in the city of Fallujah in Anbar Province. (The area west of Baghdad that included the cities of Fallujah and Ramadi, the provincial capital, came to be known as the "Sunni Triangle.") The U.S. government and some media outlets painted Fallujah as a hotbed of Hussein loyalists, but as Hashim points out, "in the early days of the occupation many leading residents of Fallujah rejected the clandestine call of the deposed Iraqi leader to 'escalate jihad against the occupation forces'" (Hashim 2006, 24). However, when U.S. troops arrived and occupied some of the municipal buildings and schools in the city center, the residents began demonstrating. The turning point came when a demonstration on April 28, 2003, in front of one of the schools turned violent, resulting in the deaths of 15 people and the wounding of another 65 (other sources give higher figures). Another demonstration soon after that one resulted in the deaths of three more civilians and the wounding of 17 U.S. soldiers. From May 2003 onward, insurgents in Fallujah stepped up attacks against U.S. forces so that "by the end of summer, the people in Fallujah were openly boasting that they were in outright rebellion against the occupation" (Allawi 2007, 169). The coalition forces, but primarily the United States, now found themselves involved in a situation that they had not prepared for in advance. The insurgency soon spread to cities and towns north of Fallujah on the Euphrates River, including burning down the occupied municipal buildings in Hit and drive-by shootings aimed at U.S. troops in Ramadi. More and more Sunni imams began to preach jihad against the coalition and not just in the so-called Sunni Triangle. However, during that first summer of the war, central Iraq was the focus of the insurgency, though American and British politicians, the military, and even the CPA were all in denial of the actual situation as it deteriorated in Iraq.

By August 2003, it had become impossible to maintain such a stance, as two bombings in Baghdad not only caught the world's attention but the second one raised the specter of al-Qaeda inside Iraq where previously there had been none. The first, on August 7, was a car bomb that killed 18 people at the Jordanian embassy; Jordan had granted asylum to two of Hussein's daughters. The second attack, on August 19, was by a suicide bomber who drove a truck into the Canal Hotel, site of the UN headquarters in Baghdad. Among the 22 people killed in the attack was the esteemed diplomat Sérgio Vieira de Mello, the UN special representative of Secretary General Kofi Annan whose task was to help form the interim Governing Council. Vieira de Mello had been in Baghdad since June 2. For the time being, the United Nations remained in Iraq despite the tragedy, but a second bombing in the hotel's parking lot (on September 22) convinced the secretary general to evacuate all but a few staff members from the country. Ali Allawi's reasoning for insurgents' targeting the United Nations was that "attacking it would drive home the insecurity and violence in the country" (Allawi 2007, 171). A main goal was to discredit the U.S. reconstruction efforts, which made workers, especially foreign reconstruction workers, important targets for the insurgents. Other targets included water mains, oil pipelines, NGOs, and Iraqis who were working with the coalition (Hashim 2006, 34).

Since the coalition forces had demobilized the Iraqi army—which had been one of the reasons for discontent in Fallujah where a good proportion of the young men had been in the military—many of those with military experience soon gravitated to the insurgency, bringing their expertise with them. The overall effect was that the insurgency not only expanded but took on a more disciplined aspect, and by the end of the year, even the CIA had come to the realization that the insurgency was daily gaining support among the general population (Hashim 2006, 34).

Shii Resistance

The year 2004 saw the evolution of the Shii involvement. If the insurgency was complicated enough in its origins and its ongoing hostilities,

Shii participation eventually brought Iraq to a state of civil war. While the two most influential Iraqi Shii leaders took different approaches to the occupation, they were both opposed to foreign rule in their country. One of these was the cleric Moqtada al-Sadr, son of the murdered grand ayatollah Muhammad Sadiq al-Sadr. Moqtada al-Sadr inherited the populist Shii movement built by his father and turned it into a potent force following the fall of the Baathist regime. In April 2004, al-Sadr called on his Mahdi Army to defend their fellow Shiis from the occupation and from the CPA's allies among the Iraqi security forces. The Mahdi Army soon had control not only of Sadr City (a section of Baghdad) but the cities of Basra, Kufa, Najaf, and Nasiriya. It also

Because of the stubbornness of Grand Ayatollah al-Sistani in demanding elections to a national assembly as a prelude to a fairer Iraqi constitution, the Transitional Government came about in January 2005. In the weeks prior to the election, al-Sistani's image was a reminder of Shii resurgence in post-Baathist Iraq. (AP Photo/Alla al-Marjani)

provided an effective counterbalance to Sunni aggression. The strength of his militia was to be a major factor in al-Sadr's political influence in the coming years.

In Najaf, Grand Ayatollah Sayyid Ali al-Sistani had been plotting a different oppositionist course for more than a year. Although he ordered an end to criminal activity and revenge killings, he also ordered "the *ulema* of Iraq not to accept any positions of administrative or executive responsibility in any layer of government" (Allawi 207, 168). Al-Sistani also called for elections for a national assembly that would then write Iraq's new constitution. This was a response to Bremer's technocratic proposal that the new constitution be drawn up by Iraqi experts. Al-Sistani, perhaps, feared that Shii concerns would be underrepresented by these experts, or perhaps the oligarchic nature of Bremer's proposal struck him as hypocritical of the coalition's stated intentions for the invasion. More important, though, al-Sistani was interested in preserving the Islamic nature of Iraq in the new government, and this contradicted the secular democracy the Bush administration and the CPA had in mind for Iraq. When his followers asked him for a religious ruling on the idea of the CPA's panel of experts to write the Iraqi constitution, al-Sistani replied six days later:

> Those forces have no jurisdiction whatsoever to appoint members of the Constitution preparation assembly. Also there is no guarantee either that this assembly will prepare a constitution that serves the best interests of the Iraqi people or that it expresses their national identity whose backbone is sound Islamic religion and noble social values. The said plan is unacceptable from the outset. First of all there must be a general election so that every Iraqi citizen who is eligible to vote can choose someone to represent him in a foundational Constitution preparation assembly. Then the drafted Constitution can be put to a referendum. All believers must insist on the accomplishment of this crucial matter and contribute to achieving it in the best way possible (quoted in Allawi 2007, 204).

The words of Grand Ayatollah al-Sistani carried so much weight they could not be ignored. Yet Washington, London, and the CPA sought a solution that was, in their eyes, a compromise. What came to be known as the November 15 Agreement (in which al-Sistani's representatives did not participate) called for caucuses that would send members to a transitional assembly. Of the agreement's five basic provisions, this was the most contentious. The other four provisions called for the drafting of a constitution, a decision on the status of the coalition forces in Iraq, restoration of Iraqi sovereignty by June 30, 2004, and new elections for an Iraqi federal government—the Kurds insisted the new government be federal—by December 31, 2005. Al-Sistani opposed the November 15 Agreement because it made no provision for elections to the transitional assembly, not to mention the method by which the new Iraqi constitution would be created. His veiled threats did not dissuade Bremer or the CPA from a little arm-twisting of their own; the Governing Council ratified the agreement, while the CPA did more than a little backroom lobbying "to raise the spectre of a Shi'a dominance of the political system" (Allawi 2007, 216).

Interim Government

From Washington and London's perspective, there was still reason to fear a split in the Governing Council, with Shii members supporting al-

Sistani's position. Thus, by early 2004, the United Nations was back in Iraq (an advance team arrived on January 23); Secretary General Annan, despite initial reluctance, agreed to send a larger UN team, led by Special Envoy Lakhdar Brahimi, to help mediate the situation. Despite Shii contentiousness, Iraqi sovereignty was achieved on schedule when the CPA handed over power to the Iraqi Interim Government on June 28, 2004. The Interim Government was headed by Ayad Allawi, who was, ironically, a former member of the Baath Party who had resigned in the mid-1970s when Saddam Hussein was consolidating his power. His anti-Hussein, pro-Western stance gained him covert funding from the United States and Great Britain. In 1990, Allawi had founded the Iraq National Accord, which became a strong political party in the post-Hussein years.

Although he was elected by the outgoing Governing Council (of which he was a member) to serve as prime minister of the Interim Government, it was clear to many in Iraq that Allawi was Bremer's choice. As such, his government did not hold much water among the people. As the months wore on, the insurgency stepped up its attacks, not only against coalition forces but against Iraqi police and security forces as well. Allawi himself was the target of an assassination attempt on April 20, 2005, as a price had been on his head since the previous summer. With the exception of the Kurds, by 2004, the insurgency had mass appeal throughout Iraq. The original impetus to the insurgency was the simple Iraqi desire for self-government, now that Hussein and the Baathists had been removed. Many Iraqis viewed the coalition as an impediment to this goal; the Shii imams were especially suspicious of the CPA and even members of the Governing Council who had returned from exile. As steps progressed toward the Interim Government, which would alter Iraq's historical political dynamic, sectarian hatreds mingled with the desire to oust the coalition. With neither trusting a political system that seemed imposed from above, Sunnis and Shiis began battling each other, as well as coalition forces, in order to further their own causes.

Another unplanned aspect of the downfall of Hussein was the extent to which foreign mercenaries, usually Sunnis, joined the battle against the coalition, though not always with the blessing of the native insurgent leadership. The most notorious of the foreign insurgents was undoubtedly the Jordanian Abu Musab al-Zarqawi, the leader of al-Qaeda in Iraq, who further muddied the already confusing goals of the insurgency by expanding the violence from one that seemingly sought to drive the coalition forces out of Iraq to a sectarian civil war. (Al-Zarqawi died as the result of a U.S. air strike on June 7, 2006.) Iran countered this influx by surreptitiously sending arms to fellow Shii in Iraq.

Meanwhile, the fact that Sunnis and Shiis, except in a few isolated instances, were not united in their hostility to the coalition worked in the coalition's favor; however, the sectarian violence placed the coalition in the crossfire. The U.S., British, and other coalition troops now found themselves fighting without the clear-cut purpose the invasion had provided, other than to put down the insurgency. But at times, the insurgency was not the reason for the violence, especially when terrorists bombed mosques and other gathering places.

The Formation of a Government

Amid all the chaos in Iraq—the insurgency, the sectarian violence, the looting, the influx of foreign insurgents, the wrecked economy, and the assassinations—the task of forming a government went on. The Iraqi Interim Government under the pro-Western prime minister Allawi lasted from June 28, 2004, until May 3, 2005. During his brief watch, Allawi oversaw the January 30, 2005, elections to the National Assembly, which took place despite the fact that a majority of the Sunni Arab parties boycotted the election and threats of terror, especially from al-Zarqawi. In all, 275 representatives were elected, the vast majority from two parties supported by Shiis. It was the National Assembly that on April 28, 2005, voted in the new Transitional Government (as per the Law of Administration for the State of Iraq for the Transitional Period, Iraq's working constitution at the time) by choosing the men who would fill the key positions.

The Transitional Government

After some wrangling, the National Assembly struck a balance with Iraq's three main groupings (Sunni, Shia, and Kurds) as well as the realities of the political apportionment of the assembly itself. The result was the election of Jalal Talibani as president and Adil Abdul Mahdi and Ghazi al-Yawar as vice presidents, all three of whom were elected by a two-thirds majority. They comprised the Presidential Council. The Presidential Council then named Ibrahim al-Jafaari as prime minister, who in turn was elected by the National Assembly with a two-thirds majority. As president, Jalal Talibani served as head of state and military commander (in addition to heading the Presidential Council), while the prime minister was head of government. INC leader Ahmad Chalabi was named one of three deputy prime ministers. Former prime minister Allawi now led the opposition.

From the outset, the Transitional Government was in crisis mode. In light of the assassination attempt on Allawi the previous month and the increased violence from insurgents and terrorists, the new government took a hard line against the fighters. Thousands were arrested in Baghdad alone. One result of the new government dealing with intense violence was that "the demarcation between militias and the formal police and special security units became increasingly blurred" (Allawi 2007, 421). This led to the increased politicization of the security forces. The war had also created disarray in the petroleum and electricity industries, which the insurgency targeted daily, especially after the January 2005 election of the National Assembly. The chaos within the energy sector continued throughout the entire term of the Transitional Government, which could only practice triage (repairs of damages) as the violence escalated. The effect was that Iraqis, especially in the capital city of Baghdad, faced ever decreasing energy output.

Less visible but important for Iraq's long-term stability were the problems of Iraq's budget and debt. At the time of the fall of the Baathist regime, Iraq's debt totaled more than $130 billion, a good deal of it dating back to the Iran-Iraq War of the 1980s. The debt was classified into four categories, with the largest amount owed, more than $50 billion, to Saudi Arabia ($39 billion), Kuwait ($8 billion), the United Arab Emirates, and Qatar. During the term of Prime Minister Allawi's Interim Government, another of the four categories of Iraq's creditors, the Paris Club (consisting of various Western nations and Japan), agreed to cancel 80 percent of Iraq's $40 billion debt, though the majority of the debt forgiveness ($20 billion) was tied to Iraq's negotiations with the International Monetary Fund. As for the budget, Allawi acknowledged that "the central problems . . . were the twin issues of revenue generation and . . . large, untargeted entitlement and subsidy programs" (Allawi 2007, 429). Both of these problems were the direct result of a wrecked economy that neither increased oil production nor a "quick fix" cash influx would repair. As a result, public subsidies, especially to the oil industry, were reduced, petroleum prices were increased (with a $500 million "safety net" for the poor), $1 billion block grants to the provinces were set aside, as were $500 million to capitalize regional development banks, and $300 million to support the families of Baathist victims (Allawi 2007, 431). Predictably, rioting followed the December 18, 2005, implementation of price increases on petroleum products, but the increases remained in effect.

The Transitional Government captured the world's attention with the ratification of the Iraq constitution on October 15, 2005, by national

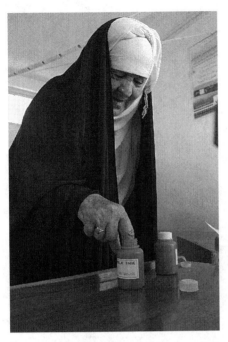

A woman prepares to vote on the referendum for Iraq's constitution, October 15, 2005. The constitution passed, thus paving the way for Iraq's permanent government. (AP Photo/ Mohammed Hato)

referendum and the subsequent elections of December 2005. In the former, it was declared that 63 percent of Iraqis voted in the referendum and that 78 percent of these favored the new constitution. However, the vote was actually closer than that because the referendum was not a straight up and down majority vote. It was decided beforehand that even if a majority of Iraqis favored the draft constitution, if three of Iraq's 18 provinces voted against the constitution by a two-thirds majority or greater, then not only would the constitution have to be redrafted, but the National Assembly would be dissolved (since the National Assembly had passed the draft constitution for referendum vote) and new elections set. Despite sectarian differences, with most Arab Sunnis opposing the draft constitution, only two of the provinces, Salahad-Din and al-Anbar, both heavily Sunni, voted against the draft constitution by the stipulated two-thirds. With the passing of the draft constitution, Iraq became a federal nation, a move pushed by the Kurds. The Presidential Council announced soon after the referendum that new legislative elections (under the auspices of the new constitution) would be held on December 15, 2005.

The Permanent Government

The December election for the new Iraq Council of Representatives attracted approximately 70 percent of Iraq's registered voters who chose from lists of parties and coalitions rather than specific candidates. Furthermore, a minimum of 25 percent (or 69 seats) of the 275 seats to the council were dedicated to women. As with the referendum two months earlier, far more Sunnis turned out to vote than had been the case with the January 2005 election for the National Assembly, which most Sunnis believed was unfairly stacked against them. The result, confirmed on February 10, 2006, was a more balanced legislature. The United Iraqi Alliance (UIA), a Shii coalition, still led the lists with 128 seats—of these the Sadrist Movement was allocated the most seats in the coalition, 28—but this was a net loss of 12 seats from the National Assembly. The second highest number of seats, 53, went to another coalition, the Democratic Patriotic Alliance of Kurdistan, but it too suffered a net loss from the number of seats it held in the National Assembly. The biggest gains went to the Sunni and Sunni-led coalitions. The Iraqi Accord Front and the Iraqi Front for National Dialogue, both of which were unrepresented in the National Assembly, received 44 and 11 seats, respectively. This placed them third and fifth among the coalitions on the Council of Representatives.

POLITICAL PARTIES AND COALITIONS OF THE PERMANENT GOVERNMENT

Since Iraqis were not voting for specific candidates in the December 2005 elections, coalitions among the more than 50 political parties became important to garner more votes. Of the various coalitions, the most important were the United Iraqi Alliance (UIA), a Shii coalition; the Democratic Patriotic Alliance of Kurdistan; the Iraqi Accord Front, a Sunni coalition; the Iraqi Front for National Dialogue, a Sunni-led but mixed coalition; and the leftist Iraqi National List. Like many political coalitions, there was bickering among the parties (especially the UIA) and various amounts of fracturing. The coalition parties at the time of the formation of the permanent government included the following:

United Iraqi Alliance

- Supreme Council of the Islamic Revolution in Iraq (SCIRI), which later changed its name to Supreme Islamic Iraqi Council (SIIC), led by Abdul Aziz al-Hakim
- Islamic Daawa Party, led by Nouri al-Maliki
- Sadrist Movement, led by Moqtada al-Sadr

(continues)

POLITICAL PARTIES AND COALITIONS OF THE PERMANENT GOVERNMENT *(continued)*

- Islamic Virtue Party, led by Abdulrahim al-Hasini
- Islamic Daawa Party—Iraq Organization, led by Abdul Karim al-Anizi
- Badr Organization, the militia of SCIRI, which was a separate member of the coalition but has since been folded into the Iraqi military and security forces

Democratic Patriotic Alliance of Kurdistan

- Kurdistan Democratic Party, led by Massoud al-Barzani
- Patriotic Union of Kurdistan, led by Jalal Talibani
- Kurdistan Workers Party
- Kurdistan Communist Party—Iraq, led by Kamal Shakir
- Islamic Group Kurdistan, led by Ali Bapir
- Iraqi Turkmen Brotherhood Party, led by Walid Sharika

Iraqi Accord Front

- Iraqi Islamic Party, led by Tariq al-Hashemi
- Iraqi National Dialogue Council, led by Khalaf al-Ulayyan
- General Council for the People of Iraq

Iraqi Front for National Dialogue

- Iraqi National Front, led by Saleh al-Mutlaq
- National Front for a Free and United Iraq, led by Hassan Zaydan
- Iraqi Christian Democratic Party, led by Minas al-Yusufi
- Democratic Arab Front, led by Farhan al-Sudayd
- Sons of Iraq Movement, led by Ali al-Suhayri

In addition, the Iraqi National List, led by Ayad Allawi, included 16 parties and small coalitions, such as the Iraqi Communist Party, the Assembly of Independent Democrats, the People's Union, the Arab Socialist Movement, the Iraqi Republican Group, and Allawi's Iraqi National Accord.

Numerous other parties sprang into being either in the late Hussein period or after his downfall representing monarchists; leftists not in the Iraqi National List, including three other communist parties and the Green Party; smaller Sunni and Kurdish parties; and Turkish, Yazdi, and Assyrian Christian blocs. The only political party banned by Iraqi law was the Baath Party.

The various coalitions went into caucus to decide how best to put forth their candidates for the government posts. Notably, there was a split within the UIA over who should be put forth as prime minister (that the prime minister would be a Shii was a given considering the number of seats held by the Shii coalitions). Ibrahim al-Jafaari actually won a UIA vote but in the end fell to political machinations, including behind-the-scenes pressure by the United States, which feared his closeness to the Sadrist Movement, now demonized by the coalition. The wrangling lasted until late April, when Nouri al-Maliki, a member of the Daawa Party (which was part of the UIA coalition) was chosen as a compromise candidate. In keeping with the form of the constitution, on April 22, 2006, al-Maliki was designated by President Jalal Talibani, himself reelected by the Council of Representatives on April 6, 2006, and sworn in the next day. The reelection of Talibani, a Kurd, was testament to the increased influence the Kurds now enjoyed in Iraq. Al-Malili was sworn in as prime minister on May 20, 2006, the day the new government took over.

Besides security and sectarian violence, the most urgent problems facing Iraq's government were the wrecked economy, the decreased energy output, massive food shortages, and a shattered health care system. In the years since taking power, the government received massive amounts of foreign aid to help offset these problems, but it also took steps of its own to alleviate them. Oil continued to be Iraq's main export, but other industries showed signs of either slow revival or birth. These accounted for about 15 percent of Iraq's exports. Iraq's main imports were food and medicines, showing in that respect that little had changed from the sanction days. Prior

Prime Minister Nuri al-Maliki of Iraq addresses the UN General Assembly on September 26, 2007. Al-Maliki, leader of the Shii Daawa Party, became Iraq's first prime minister under the constitutional permanent government on May 20, 2006. (AP Photo)

265

to the government's taking control, only a little more than half of all Iraqis had access to potable water, but several water projects were subsequently undertaken, including a new canal to supply drinking water to Basra. However, the water crisis in Baghdad had not been alleviated five years after its fall to coalition forces. The Iraqi government also encouraged foreign investment not only in the usual oil industry sector but also in the electricity sector, hoping to give impetus to an industry nearly shut down by the war and the insurgency.

By 2008, neither the government nor foreign aid had been able to repair Iraq's broken health-care system. Doctors, nurses, and other health-care workers continued to flee the country as part of the Iraqi diaspora, while the rebuilding of hospitals and clinics was behind schedule. The emigrations and the high numbers of those leaving the health-care field in Iraq meant that Iraq had only about one-quarter of the number of health-care workers it had prior to the invasion. Poor water and frequent electrical blackouts contributed to the problems. A Reuters article by Luke Baker cited a report by the health organization Medact, which pointed out that only 4 percent of the $18 billion Iraqi reconstruction fund was slated for health care. While the report suggests an increase in government involvement, others have blamed the government, particularly the health ministry, for its failure to alleviate the problem.

Further complications for Iraq's government arose in 2008. Foremost among these was the insurrection of the Mahdi Army, the Shii militia controlled by Moqtada al-Sadr. Six months after the British forces departed from Basra in September 2007 (at the time perhaps the most stable city in Iraq) the Mahdi Army, bolstered by the surreptitious delivery of arms from Iran, not to mention Iranian president Mahmoud Ahmadinejad's March visit to Iraq, began an insurgency in Basra that was a direct threat to Shii Prime Minister al-Maliki's rule. Nevertheless, al-Maliki traveled to Basra as a sign of support for the Iraqi security forces and the civilians. The insurgency lasted until the end of April.

Late in April al-Sadr threatened war against Iraqi and U.S. forces, but after the defeat of the Mahdi Army in Basra and retaliations in Sadr City, the Shii neighborhood of northern Baghdad, he agreed to a (fragile) cease-fire on May 11. The victory not only boosted the morale of the Iraqi security forces but solidified al-Maliki's position among the Sunnis and Kurds. Al-Maliki thereupon turned his attention to Mosul, the stronghold of the Sunni al-Qaeda in Iraq. Four months earlier he had promised to rid the city of the group, and on May 14, repeating his successful Basra strategy, he traveled to Mosul to take charge of the military operations in Iraq's third-largest city.

Conclusion

It will take years before all of the facts regarding the buildup to the invasion of Iraq are made public (if ever), but the U.S. motive of regime change is undeniable. Equally undeniable is that many Iraqis suffered under the Baathists, primarily Shiis and Kurds. A third undeniable fact is that the nation of Iraq has suffered on an unprecedented scale in its history as a result of the invasion and poor planning for the aftermath of the overthrow of Saddam Hussein. From the Arab Iraqi perspective, the aftermath has been far worse than the invasion. Only the Kurds have truly benefited in the post-Hussein era, having their plan for a federalist Iraq accepted and one of their leaders, Jalal Talibani, twice elected president.

Five years after the U.S.-led coalition invasion, Iraq lay in ruins, wracked by war, terrorism, and sectarian civil war. The number of refugees approached 4 million, or 16 percent of the total population, split nearly evenly among those who fled the country and those who were displaced within Iraq. It is believed that 40 percent of Iraq's middle class had fled. More than 600,000 people had died as a result of violence since the March 2003 invasion, and the majority of these deaths occurred after the fall of the Baathist regime. Health care in Iraq is in shambles, and in a conference held in Baghdad in December 2007, it was revealed that as many as 5 million Iraqi children had been orphaned, accounting for nearly 35 percent of the child-age population.

A World Public Opinion poll titled "The Iraqi Public on the U.S. Presence and the Future of Iraq," conducted by the Program on International Policy Attitudes and released on September 27, 2006, revealed that "seven in ten Iraqis want U.S.-led forces to commit to withdrawal within a year," and that "an overwhelming majority believes that the U.S. presence in Iraq is provoking more conflict than it is preventing." Six in 10 Iraqis also supported attacks on U.S. forces as part of a perception that the United States planned to build permanent U.S. military bases in their country. Overall, the poll revealed that Iraqis favored the central government and even favored the continued training of their security forces by the U.S. military. Prime Minister al-Maliki was the only Shii leader favored by Kurds and some Sunnis as well as Shiis. However, public opinion of other Shii leaders and many issues were split along sectarian lines, with Kurds generally in agreement with Sunni Arabs. A 2007 BBC poll showed that the percentages of those Iraqis opposing the coalition's presence in Iraq rose to 78 percent, and the percentage who thought the coalition's presence was making things worse also increased. Essentially, these polls revealed the hopes and frustrations of the Iraqis and their desires to settle their own problems with foreign assistance, but not interference.

POSTSCRIPT

When U.S. troops entered Baghdad on April 9, 2003, it was after a relatively easy victory over the Iraqi army and irregular militias. Immediately, U.S. leaders in charge began to disestablish the remnants of the Iraqi state. One of the first edicts passed on June 17, 2003, by the new "viceroy," Paul L. Bremer III, was the dissolution of the Iraqi army. Other pronouncements on the same date annulled the Ministries of Defense and Information and began the process of "deBaathification," which was supposed to eradicate by the root all the ideological, political, and security excesses incurred under 35 years of Baathist rule in Iraq. The hope was that, by dismissing thousands of Baathist professors, government officials, and army officers, any national government following in the wake of the U.S. military administration would begin with a clean slate. But it was not so simple. Undeterred by thousands of years of history, the Americans blundered into a country of which they knew virtually nothing. Their comeuppance was to begin almost immediately.

The U.S. plan for postwar Iraq, such as it was, was based on a radical blueprint worked out partly in secret by neoconservative ideologues in the Bush administration, with the aid of fellow travelers in American right-wing think tanks and select members of the Iraqi opposition in exile (Naomi Klein, 2004). According to this blueprint, Iraq, the "failed state," was to be the theater for a massive restructuring exercise that would jettison the *dirigiste* command economy, dismantle the trappings of the authoritarian state structure, and open wide the doors to the benefits of an untrammeled free market. Although Bremer immediately signaled his intention to aggressively conform to this agenda, several events conspired to waylay his strategy.

One important reason why the blueprint did not immediately materialize was the American disregard for history, especially Iraq's own. This allowed the administration to concoct a pastiche of traditions and principles, mostly imbibed from British rule in Iraq in the period between 1917 and 1932. For instance, it believed that the greatest army in the world could easily control the country on its own and that a military institution sufficed to run the country. However, exactly as had happened under the British, the administration was soon forced to change at least the externals of this plan (even under Bremer's civilian administration, the army still ran a significant part of the operation). After months of pretending that he could govern Iraq alone, however, Bremer was ultimately forced to bring the Iraqis into government, circumscribed though it was by lack of real power and sovereign control. The Governing Council was appointed by Bremer on July 13, 2003; it was composed of 25 members from different ethnic, confessional, and linguistic groups. Again, in direct imitation of the seemingly easily tradable "traditions" of the first Iraqi government under British occupation, in which the elderly Shaikh Abdul-Rahman al-Gailani took on the post of prime minister, the equally venerable Sayyid Muhammad Bahr al-Ulum (an 80-year-old former exile) became the most influential voice on the council. The sole difference, of course, and this was an important change, was that al-Gailani had been a Sunni Muslim and Bahr al-Ulum is a Shii.

Exactly as had happened under the British, revolts began to brew. While not attaining the momentum of the Iraqi uprising of 1920 against the British, on a piecemeal basis, these revolts made the United States very uncomfortable. In fact, the burgeoning Iraqi insurgency; the seemingly endemic corruption in the first contracts awarded to big American multinationals; the lackadaisical attempts to fix electricity, sewage, and water plants; the skyrocketing rate of unemployment; the indiscriminate arrest and imprisonment of random (and, quite frequently, innocent) civilians that the American troops had come to liberate; and the arrogance of the Coalition Provisional Administration's bureaucrats with regard even to their Iraqi allies created the conditions for a national emergency. While at first the Americans were fortunate that no two sects or parties made common cause against the occupation, by the beginning of 2006, the situation had become so dire that almost 2,200 U.S. service personnel had been killed (the number of Iraqis who died was a state secret, but independent sources, most notably the British *Lancet* study of October 2004, put the figure at close to 100,000 *civilians* dead).

Quickly taking a page out of British colonialist strategy in Iraq, and egged on all the while by the most influential Shii ayatollah in Iraq, Sayyid Ali al-Sistani, the Americans pushed forward national elections as the solution for a free and independent Iraq. In January 2005, several million Iraqis braved bombs and indiscriminate violence to vote for their parties' choice of candidates. The "mandate for change" (in President George Bush's terminology) ushered in a Shii majority led by a political coalition grouping powerful religious parties with a smattering of secular groups. Meanwhile, a referendum on an Iraqi constitution in October was passed, not to everyone's satisfaction. In December 2005, Iraqis went to the polls again, to elect a permanent four-year government. After several months of wrangling, the political stalemate produced by Shii negotiations with the Kurds and Sunnis suddenly was reversed, and an "independent" government was announced.

The rest, as they say, is history. From 2005 to 2008, the struggle to control Iraq occupied various parties—the U.S. administration in Washington, D.C.; the U.S. embassy in Baghdad; the U.S. army brass in Iraq; several U.S. contractors; the Iraqi government; the Iraqi army; armed militias of various hues and ideologies; political parties and citizens' fora; local neighborhood organizations; and several Arab and foreign governments—turning the country into a deadly combat zone, which even patchily applied "surge" strategies failed to tamp completely. Despite the decapitation of the Baath regime and the arrest, imprisonment, and execution of Saddam Hussein and many of his henchmen, it has been estimated that the United States and its Iraqi allies had fallen far short even of their own goals with regard to Iraq. Once again, the Americans' propensity to dispense with thousands of years of Iraqi history had led them astray, as a result of which their zeal to control Iraq's oil and to create of the country a strategic gateway to the entire region is still not entirely guaranteed. As of this writing, there is still no accord on oil policy or a Status of Forces Agreement to concretize the U.S. presence on Iraqi soil, and, should the opinion of a wide array of different local forces in Iraq be taken into account, there may never be.

In fact, judging from Iraq's past record, the only sure-fire guarantee seems to be that resistance movements to U.S. hegemony will grow as time goes by. From the first insurrections in Iraq against Umayyad rule to the civil war erupting in Baghdad as a result of the Persian annexation of Basra in the 1770s to the opposition movement spawned by the government signing of the Portsmouth Treaty in 1948, Iraqis have always rebelled at externally imposed diktats and foreign hegemony. And they will continue to fight foreign invaders until they leave the country once and for all, taking with them the patchwork agreements and piecemeal treaties the invaders once thought could govern the thousand-year-old nation of Iraq.

APPENDIX 1

BASIC FACTS ABOUT IRAQ

Official Name
Republic of Iraq (al-Jumhuriya al-Iraqiya)

Government
The constitution of Iraq was ratified by national referendum on October 15, 2005. It called for the establishment of a parliamentary democracy, divided into the executive, legislative, and judicial branches. The legislative body is the 275-seat Council of Representatives. There is also a vacant Federation Council, whose role and membership have not been defined. The executive branch consists of a president, who is head of state, and a prime minister, who is head of government. The president is chosen by the Council of Representatives. The prime minister is appointed by the Presidential Council, made up of the president and two vice presidents, but is ratified by the Council of Representatives. The cabinet consists of 34 ministers appointed by the Presidential Council and the prime minister and two deputy prime ministers. The judicial branch includes the Higher Judicial Council, Supreme Federal Court, Federal Court of Cassation, Public Prosecution Department, Judiciary Oversight Commission, and lesser federal courts.

Political Divisions
There are 18 governates, or provinces: Anbar, Basra, Muthanna, Qadisiya, Najaf, Irbil, Suleymaniya, Tamim, Babil, Baghdad, Dahuk, Dhi Qar, Diyala, Karbala, Maysan, Ninawa, Salahad Din, and Wasit.

Capital
Baghdad

Geography

Area

Iraq's total area is 168,754 square miles (437,072 km²), making it the 58th largest country in the world. Its total land area is 166,859 square miles (432,162 km ²). Iraq's water area is very small, only 1,895 square miles (4,910 km²).

Boundaries

Iraq is located in the Middle East. Jordan and Syria are to its west; Turkey is to the north; Iran is to the east; and Kuwait and Saudi Arabia border on the south. Iraq also has a small coastline on the Persian Gulf to the south.

Topography

Iraq is mostly an alluvial plain trisected by the Tigris and Euphrates Rivers. In the north and the northeast, bordering Turkey and Iran, are the Zagros Mountains. West of the Tigris River is desert, while the area in the southeast is marshy.

Climate

The majority of Iraq experiences cool winters and dry, hot summers. Winters are cold in the mountainous north. There can be heavy snow-fall in the north that leads to springtime flooding in central and southern Iraq.

Highest Elevation

The highest elevation is an unnamed peak in the Zagros Mountains that stands 11,844 feet (3,611 m) above sea level. The next highest peaks are Gundah Zhur at 11,831 feet (3,607 m) and Kuh-e Hajji-Ebrahim at 11,693 feet (3,595 m).

Demographics

Population

According to a July 2007 estimate, the population of Iraq is 27,499,638. Males account for 50.6 percent of the population; females, 49.4 percent. Children 14 years and younger make up 39.4 percent of the population; people aged 15 to 64 represent 57.6 percent; those 65 and older make up 3 percent of the population. The median age is 20 years: males, 19.9 years; females, 20 years. The total infant mortality rate is 47.04 deaths per 1,000 live births: For males, it is 52.73 deaths per 1,000 live births; for females, 41.07 deaths per 1,000 live births. Life expectancy at birth is 69.31 years: for males, 68.04 years; for females, 70.65 years. The growth rate is 2.618 percent.

Major Cities

Baghdad is the capital and largest city of Iraq, with a population of 5,904,000 (2007 estimate). According to the 2003 census taken by the Ministries of Trade and Planning, the populations of Mosul and Irbil were approximately 1,100,000 each, while Basra's population stood at 825,000, as was the population of Suleymaniya. Kirkuk's population stood at 600,000 inhabitants; Najaf, 500,000; Karbala, 475,000; Nasiriya, 400,000; and Ramadi, 300,000 inhabitants. The invasion and subsequent insurgency and sectarian violence have obviously skewered these cities' populations beyond normal projections.

Language

Arabic is the official language of Iraq, though Kurdish is the official language in the Kurdish regions. Other languages spoken in Iraq are Assyrian and Armenian.

Religion

The overwhelming majority of Iraqis, 97 percent, are Muslim, which is the official religion. Shia account for between 60 and 65 percent of the population; Sunni are 32 to 37 percent. The majority of the remaining 3 percent are Christian.

Economy

Gross Domestic Product

The 2007 estimate of Iraq's GDP was $55.44 billion.

Currency

Iraq's currency is the dinar. As of mid-May 2008, one U.S. dollar was equal to 1,199.5 dinars. This continued the dinar's steady gain from a low point of 1,890 to the dollar in the second half of 2003.

Agricultural Products

Iraq's chief crops are wheat, barley, rice, vegetables, dates, and cotton. Sheep and poultry are also raised for consumption.

Minerals

Iraq has the second-largest proven oil reserves in the world (after Saudi Arabia). Other minerals are natural gas, rock sulfur, phosphate, stone, and gypsum.

Industrial Products

The petroleum industry is by far the largest industry in Iraq. Other industrial sectors include chemicals, textiles, leather, construction materials, food processing, fertilizer, and metal processing.

Trade

Iraq's major export is crude oil, amounting to 84 percent of its total. It also exports other crude material, food, and live animals. Its primary export partners are the United States, where Iraq sends 46.8 percent of its exports; Italy, 10.7 percent; Canada, 6.2 percent; and Spain, 6.1 percent (as of 2006). The 2007 estimated value of Iraq's exports was $34.04 billion.

Iraq imports primarily food, medicines, and manufactured products. Its leading import partners are Syria, from which Iraq takes in 26.5 percent of its imports; Turkey, 20.5 percent; the United States, 11.8 percent; and Jordan, 7.2 percent. The 2007 estimated value of Iraq's imports was $23.09 billion.

APPENDIX 2

CHRONOLOGY

Iraq, the First Society (Prehistory to 539 B.C.E.)

ca. 7000 B.C.E.	Agricultural settlements established in what is now northern Iraq
ca. 5000 B.C.E.	Beginning of the Ubaid period, the first recorded settlement in what is now southern Iraq
ca. 3500–2334 B.C.E.	Rise of Sumerian cities, notably Uruk
ca. 3300 B.C.E.	Sumerians invent writing in the city of Uruk Akkadian Empire, located in northern Babylonia (what is now central Iraq), subsumes the Sumerian cities
2112–2004 B.C.E.	Akkadians are overthrown, and the Third Dynasty of Ur is established, also referred to as the Neo-Sumerian period
2017–1763 B.C.E.	Isin-Larsa period, named for the two city-states that predominated in what is now central Iraq
2000–1300 B.C.E.	Domestication of the camel allows for more mobility among the Arab tribes to the south
1894–1595 B.C.E.	The First Dynasty of Babylon (Old Babylonia)
1806 B.C.E.	Babylonian law is codified under Hammurabi
1595–1200 B.C.E.	Dark Ages of ancient Babylon
1170–612 B.C.E.	Assyrian Empire
625–539 B.C.E.	The Neo-Babylonian Empire
586 B.C.E.	Jerusalem falls to Nebuchadnezzar, Jewish exilic period begins

From the Persian Empire to the Sassanians (539 B.C.E.–651 C.E.)

ca. 550 B.C.E.	Persians under Cyrus the Great defeat the Medes

539 B.C.E.	Cyrus defeats the army of the last Babylonian king, Nabonidus; legend says the Jewish exilic period ends during Cyrus's reign
525 B.C.E.	Cyrus's successor, Cambyses, conquers Egypt
521 B.C.E.	Darius the Great assumes the Persian throne after Cambyses' death; he will reign until 486 B.C.E.
518 B.C.E.	Construction of Persepolis begins
490 B.C.E.	Athenians defeat the invading Persians at the Battle of Marathon
336 B.C.E.	Alexander of Macedon succeeds to the throne upon the death of his father, Philip; vows to continue Philip's campaign to liberate Greek cities under Persian control in Anatolia
333 B.C.E.	Alexander defeats the Persians at the Battle of Issus
331 B.C.E.	Alexander defeats Darius III at the Battle of Gaugamela in Mesopotamia; the way is now clear for him to take Babylon and, ultimately, Persia
330 B.C.E.	Alexander defeats Darius in a battle in Bactria; Darius is killed in the battle and the Persian Empire is subsumed into the Macedonian Empire; Alexander will continue his eastward conquest for another six years, halting only after the threat of mutiny by his soldiers
324 B.C.E.	Alexander returns to Babylon with the intention of making it his capital
323 B.C.E.	Alexander dies in Babylon
322–307 B.C.E.	Intermittent wars of the Diadochi (Alexander's successors); in the division of the empire, the Macedonian general Seleucus is given Babylonia, 312 B.C.E., from which the founding of the Seleucid Empire is dated
305 B.C.E.	Seleucus declares himself king and transfers the capital from Babylon to Seleucia on the Tigris River; his empire is at its zenith during his reign
238 B.C.E.	Arsaces I comes to power in Parthia in northeastern Iran; over the next 60 years Parthia conquers various eastern Seleucid provinces

ca. 171 B.C.E.	Mithridates the Great succeeds to the throne of Parthia
160–138 B.C.E.	Mithridates sets out on a war of conquest against outlying Seleucid provinces and the heart of the empire itself
ca. 129–64 B.C.E.	Seleucid Empire is reduced to a rump state in Syria, serving as a buffer between the Roman and Parthian Empires
113 B.C.E.	Upper Mesopotamia falls to the Parthians
69 B.C.E.	Parthia and Rome unite to attack the Seleucid Empire
53 B.C.E.	The Roman general Crassus attacks the Parthians but is turned back, thus begins 150 years of intermittent warfare between Rome and Parthia
114 C.E.	Roman legions under the emperor Trajan invade Parthia in a dispute over Armenian succession; Trajan's successor, Hadrian, will return all conquered territory to Parthia
198	Roman emperor Septimus Severus sacks the Parthian capital of Ctesiphon but returns to Rome
224	Ardashir I, an Iranian petty king, overthrows the Parthians and establishes the Sassanian Empire
260	Sassanians defeat Romans at the Battle of Edessa and capture the emperor Valerian
325–337	Sassanian Empire under Shapur II expands in Mesopotamia and Armenia
571	Birth of the prophet Muhammad
622	Muhammad flees Mecca for Yathrib (Medina), this is known as the Hijra (flight), or Hegira, and marks the beginning of the Islamic calendar
632	Muhammad dies
632–634	The Apostasy Wars pit the forces of Muhammad's successor, the first caliph, Abu Bakr, against rebellious tribes
634	First clashes between Sassanians and Arabs
640	Kufa settled by Arabs and Persian soldiers in revolt against the Sassanians
642	Arabs complete conquest of Iraq
651	Sassanian Empire falls to the Muslim caliphate

Iraq under the Umayyad Dynasty (651–750)

656	Ali ibn Abu Talib, Muhammad's cousin and son-in-law, becomes fourth caliph; many believe Ali should have been caliph upon the death of Muhammad and that the caliphate should descend from the family of Muhammad; this "party of Ali" becomes known as Shia
661	Ali assassinated in Kufa
680	Ali's son, Hussein, killed in battle against the forces of Umayyad caliph Yazid ibn Muawiya
750	Umayyad caliphate ends

Abbasid and Post-Abbasid Iraq (750–1258)

750	Abbasid dynasty established by Abu al-Abbas
762	Second Abbasid caliph, Abu Jaafar al-Mansur, chooses the site for his new capital, Baghdad
early ninth century	Bayt al-Hikma (the House of Wisdom) established in Baghdad
ca. 834	Samarra constructed to serve as the capital during the caliphate of al-Mutasim
869–883	The Zanj Revolt of slaves in southern Iraq
874	Shia Islam crystallizes into three main schools of thought: Twelvers, Ismailis, and Zaydism
892	Caliphate returns to Baghdad
945	Buyid (Buwayhid) Shia military regime established in Iran and Iraq; Abbasid caliphate reduced to a ceremonial post
1055	Seljuk Turks invade Iraq and defeat Buyids
1059–1157	Seljuk sultanate rules Iraq

Turkish Tribal Migrations and the Early Ottoman State (1256–1638)

1258	Baghdad sacked by Mongols under Hulegu Khan
1258–1336	Iraq ruled under the Il-khanids
1299	Osman declares his Anatolian principality independent of the Seljuk Turks, setting the stage for the establishment of the Ottoman Empire
1301	Osman defeats a Byzantine force near Nicaea

1326	Orhan, Osman's son and successor, captures Bursa in northwestern Turkey
1331	Orhan captures Nicaea
ca. 1336	Tamerlaine conquers Iraq
1337	Northwestern Anatolia completely under Ottoman control
1354	Orhan's son, Suleyman, captures territory on the European side of the Hellespont; the Ottomans push farther into the Balkans over the next 35 years
1453	Constantinople falls to the Ottomans
ca. 1500	The Safavids, Shia Muslims, consolidate power in eastern Anatolia, Azerbaijan, and Iran; their hostilities with the Sunni Ottomans exacerbate Sunni-Shia enmity
1534	Ottoman control of Mosul complete; first Ottoman occupation of Baghdad
1546–49	Ottomans lay siege to Basra
1624	Safavids capture Baghdad
1638	Ottomans retake Baghdad

Imperial Administration, Local Rule, and Ottoman Recentralization (1638–1914)

1639	Treaty of Zuhab temporarily ends Ottoman-Safavid hostilities
1690	Shammar tribe raids Baghdad
1702–47	Baghdad governors Hassan Pasha and his son Ahmad Pasha are charged by the Ottomans with retaking Iraq; they set about conquering the tribes and bring in Georgian Mamluks as imperial serfs
1736	Nadir Shah usurps the Persian throne ending the Safavid dynasty
1746	A treaty reaffirms the 1639 Ottoman-Persian border
1747	Persians occupy Basra
1750	Mamluks rule the governate of Baghdad and later Basra as a dependency of Baghdad
1776–79	Persians reoccupy Basra

1787	The south Kurdistan city of Suleymaniya is founded
early 19th century	British gain in influence in central and southern Iraq
1820s–30s	Erosion of clerical influence in Shii shrine cities
1831	Dawud, last Mamluk ruler in Iraq, deposed after attempted revolt against the Ottomans
1839	First Ottoman *tanzimat* (modernizing regulations) issued
ca. 1850	Kurdish rulers are ousted, and Ottomans take direct control of northern Iraq
1856	Second *tanzimat* issued; the new edicts allow for appointed and elected provincial administrative councils in Iraq
1862	British shipping begins on the Tigris River
1869	First printing press is introduced in Iraq, soon after the first state newspaper *al-Zawra* is published; about this time the Ottoman Land Law of 1858 is applied to Iraq to secure agricultural land for the cultivators; tribal peasants undermine the law
	Suez Canal opens in Egypt, Iraq's trade grows exponentially in the next decade
1880s	Sunni preachers are sent to Iraq by the Ottoman sultan to counteract the rising influence of Shii clerics
1900–13	Britain becomes Iraq's most important trading partner

British Occupation and the Iraqi Monarchy (1914–1958)

July–August 1914	World War I begins; Ottoman Empire aligns with Germany and Austria-Hungary against France, Great Britain, and Russia; this will pit the Ottoman against the British in Iraq
November 22, 1914	British forces occupy Basra
April 29, 1916	Ottoman force surrounds and defeats the British at Kut
March 11, 1917	British take Baghdad
October 30, 1918	Ottomans sue for peace almost two weeks before the Germans and subsequently with-

	draw from their strongholds in northern Iraq; almost all of Iraq is under British control
1920	League of Nations awards Britain a mandate to govern Iraq; the terms of the mandate lead Sunni, Shia, and Kurds to unite in revolt against British rule
August 23, 1921	Prince Faisal bin al-Hussein becomes king of Iraq
October 10, 1922	A treaty between Iraq and Great Britain restates the mandate in only slightly friendlier terms for Iraq
April 30, 1923	An amendment to the 1922 treaty reduces the terms of the agreement from 20 years to four
June 11, 1924	Iraq's Constituent Assembly ratifies the 1922 treaty between Iraq and Great Britain
March 21, 1925	King Faisal signs the Organic Law, Iraq's first constitution
1925	League of Nations commission decides the fate of Mosul: The city and province are to remain in Iraq
October 3, 1932	Iraq becomes an independent state and gains admittance to the League of Nations
September 8, 1933	King Faisal dies of a heart attack in Berne, Switzerland; he is succeeded by his son Ghazi
October 1936	First Iraqi coup replaces the prime minister but leaves the monarchy in place
1939	King Ghazi dies in an automobile accident; Prince Abdulillah is chosen as regent for the infant king Faisal II; Prime Minister Nuri al-Said secures his own position
	World War II begins with the German invasion of Poland on September 1
1941	Arab Socialist Baath Party is founded in Syria
April 1941	Anti-British military officers instigate a coup; Prince Abdulillah, Prime Minister al-Said, and other pro-British Iraqi politicians flee to Transjordan; Rashid Ali al-Gailani heads the government
May 1941	British land troops in Iraq as per Anglo-Iraqi Treaty; Rashid Ali al-Gailani sends Iraqi troops to fight the British, who win after a brief

	war; the regent and the politicians return to Baghdad
1942	Iraq declares war on the Axis (Germany, Italy, and Japan)
January 15, 1948	Portsmouth Treaty signed between Britain and Iraq extends by 15 years the period for British forces and bases to remain in Iraq
1952	Iraqi nationalists pressure the Iraq Petroleum Company for a 50-50 split of profits
July 14, 1958	Brigadier General Abdul-Karim Qasim overthrows the monarchy, setting up the Republic of Iraq

The Growth of the Republican Regimes and the Emergence of Baathist Iraq (1958–1979)

1957	Daawa Party is founded
1958	Qasim rejects overtures to have Iraq join the United Arab Republic (Egypt and Syria) in favor of Iraqi nationalism
October 1958	Qasim government promulgates a new agricultural law that calls for ceilings on landholdings and redistribution to the landless
March 1959	Colonel Abdul-Wahhab al-Shawwaf, commander of troops in Mosul, declares Qasim a traitor, with the backing of landowning shaykhs of Shammar tribe and Arab nationalists; the ensuing battle turns Mosul into chaos and pits Communists against Baathists
July 1959	Qasim begins arresting leaders of the Iraq Communist Party after Communists burn down 120 buildings in Kirkuk belonging to anticommunist Turkmen
October 1959	Baathist gunmen attempt to assassinate Qasim; one of the gunmen is 22-year-old Saddam Hussein
1961	Kurdish gains under Qasim erode, and friction between Kurds and Arabs erupts into revolt Law No. 80 confiscates almost all of the concession land owned by the Iraq Petroleum Company

July 1961	Britain lands 7,000 troops in the newly independent Emirate of Kuwait after Iraq begins massing troops on the border; Saudia Arabia sends 1,200 troops, and the Arab League sends 3,300
February 9, 1963	Qasim is overthrown and executed following Kurdish overtures the previous years that they would lay down their arms if Qasim were ousted; Colonel Abdul-Salam Aref heads the government
November 1963	Aref becomes undisputed leader of Iraq
February 1964	Iraq National Oil Company is organized
July 1964	Aref nationalizes banks, insurance companies, and the majority of industries
June 1965	Aref's nationalization policy forces the Iraq Petroleum Company to renegotiate its contracts with Iraq
September 1965	Prime Minister and Defense Minister Aref Abdul-Razzaq leads a failed coup
1966	President Abdul-Salam Aref dies in a helicopter crash; he is succeeded by his older brother, Abdul-Rahman Aref
June 1967	Iraq remains neutral during the Six-Day War that pitted Israel against Egypt, Syria, and Jordan; this decision leads to rioting in Iraq in which the Baath Party seizes the opportunity to gain the support of the military, which was embarrassed by the neutrality
July 17, 1968	Baathists overthrow Abdul-Rahman Aref; Iraq is now led by President Ahmad Hassan al-Bakr
1970s	Saddam Hussein gradually consolidates his positions within the Baath Party and the government
March 1970	Talks between Saddam Hussein and Kurdish leader Mulla Mustafa al-Barzani lead to an agreement recognizing Kurdish identity and promised autonomy for the Kurds within four years
April 1972	Saddam Hussein travels to Moscow to initiate talks that result in the Iraqi-Soviet Friendship Treaty
June 1972	The Baathist government nationalizes the operating oil fields of the Iraq Petroleum Company

October 1973	War between Israel and Egypt, Syria, and Jordan erupts again; this time Iraq joins in
1974	Hostilities between Kurds and Iraqis resume
1975	Nationalization of the petroleum industry complete

The Rule of Saddam Hussein and the Difficult Legacy of the Mukhabarat State (1979–2003)

1979	Dictatorship of Saddam Hussein begins
September 22, 1980	Onset of Iran-Iraq War
November 1982	The Shii opposition party the Supreme Council of the Islamic Revolution in Iraq (SCIRI) is founded in Tehran by Ayatollah Baqir al-Hakim
May 1987	USS *Stark* accidentally attacked by an Iraqi warplane in the Persian Gulf
March 1988	Iraqis allegedly use poison gas against Kurds in the town of Halabja
August 20, 1988	Iran-Iraq War ends
1988–90	Iraq presses for reappraisal of its border with Kuwait
August 2, 1990	Iraqi troops invade Kuwait
August 6, 1990	The United Nations imposes economic sanctions against Iraq; the sanctions last for 13 years
January 16, 1991	U.S.-led coalition begins its offensive (Operation Desert Storm) to liberate Kuwait
February 28, 1991	Iraq accedes to all UN resolutions passed since it invaded Kuwait; rebellions among the Shia in the south and the Kurds in the north soon break out
April 1991	The Republican Guard and the Iraqi Army reassert Baathist control
April 3, 1991	UN Resolution 687 requires Iraq to pay compensation to countries, corporations, and individuals that had suffered because of the invasion of Kuwait
June 9, 1991	The United Nations Special Commission on Iraq begins its first chemical weapons inspection
September 1991	Center for Economic and Social Rights (CESR) estimates that mortality rates for children under

	age five is 380 percent higher than before the Gulf crisis
1992	Coup is attempted by generals from the Sunni Dulaimi tribe
	Iraqi National Congress is founded in exile
1994	Saddam Hussein's secular Baathist regime embraces the trappings of Islam
1996	CESR report urges the UN Security Council to modify the oil-for-food plan and find alternatives to the crippling sanctions on Iraq
1998	Amount of oil Iraq can sell to purchase supplies for its people is raised from $2 billion every six months to $5.2 billion
December 1998	United States and Britain engage in four days of bombing various Iraqi sites
1999	Oil-for-food limits are eliminated altogether
January 7, 1999	U.S. government admits intelligence agents posed as weapons inspectors; the Central Intelligence Agency confirms this on February 23
February 18, 1999	Grand Ayatollah Muhammad Sadiq al-Sadr, founder of the Shii Sadrist Movement, is assassinated
January 29, 2002	In his State of the Union address, U.S. president George W. Bush identifies Iraq as being part of an "axis of evil," along with Iran and North Korea
October 2002	A joint U.S. congressional resolution authorizes the use of military force in Iraq
November 2002	A UN Monitoring, Verification, and Inspection Commission team headed by diplomat Hans Blix begins inspecting sites in Iraq
February 2003	U.S. secretary of state Colin Powell presents so-called evidence of weapons of mass destruction in Iraq
February 25, 2003	Iraqi opposition leaders meet in Salahuddin in Iraqi Kurdistan

The War in Iraq (2003–2008)

| March 18, 2003 | U.S. president George W. Bush issues a 48-hour ultimatum for Saddam Hussein and his sons |

	Udai and Qusai to leave Iraq; they are reportedly offered sanctuary in Bahrain but refuse
March 19, 2003	A U.S. air strike on a Baghdad suburb fails to eliminate the Husseins; 15 civilians are killed
March 20, 2003	The U.S.-led coalition invasion of Iraq, dubbed Operation Iraqi Freedom, begins
April 9, 2003	Baghdad falls to coalition forces; in the ensuing chaos, the National Museum of Iraq is looted and 15,000 pieces taken; the next day arsonists set afire the Iraq National Library and Archives; 25 percent of the library's collection and 60 percent of the archives are burned
April 14, 2003	Tikrit falls to coalition forces
April 24, 2003	Deputy Prime Minister Tariq Aziz surrenders to U.S. forces
April 28, 2003	The first stirring of the insurgency occurs with a demonstration in Fallujah that ends in violence
May 1, 2003	President Bush lands on the flight deck of the USS *Abraham Lincoln* to declare victory in Iraq
May 22, 2003	UN Resolution 1483 authorizes the Coalition Provisional Authority (CPA) in Iraq; it is headed by L. Paul Bremer
July 2003	The 25-member Iraq Governing Council is formed
July 22, 2003	Udai and Qusai Hussein are killed in a shootout with U.S. soldiers in Mosul
August 7, 2003	Car bomb kills 18 people at Jordanian embassy; Jordan had granted asylum to two of Saddam Hussein's daughters
August 19, 2003	A suicide bomber kills 22 people at the Canal Hotel, site of UN headquarters in Iraq; the United Nations pulls out of Iraq
December 13, 2003	Saddam Hussein is discovered hiding in a hole in the ground on a farm near the village of Daur
January 23, 2004	A UN advance team reenters Iraq to pave the way for a larger UN presence
April 2004	Insurgents kill and mutilate the bodies of four U.S. contractors in Fallujah

	Moqtada al-Sadr begins involving his Mahdi Army, the militant wing of the Sadrist Movement, in the insurgency
June 30, 2004	The Interim Government takes over in Iraq; the CPA relinquished authority two days earlier
October 2004	U.S. troops and Iraqi security forces attack insurgent strongholds in Samarra
January 30, 2005	Elections to Iraq's 275-seat National Assembly are held
April 20, 2005	Prime Minister Ayad Allawi of the Interim Government is the target of a failed assassination attempt
May 3, 2005	The Iraq Transitional Government replaces the Interim Government; five days earlier the National Assembly chose Jalal Talibani as president and Ibrahim al-Jafaari as prime minister of the Transitional Government
July 17, 2005	Formal charges are lodged against Saddam Hussein
August 31, 2005	A rumor of a suicide bomber causes a stampede among Shia pilgrims on the Bridge of Imams, killing more than 1,000 people
October 15, 2005	The Iraqi constitution is passed by national referendum
October 19, 2005	Trial of Saddam Hussein begins
December 15, 2005	Elections are held for the 275-seat Iraq Council of Representatives, which replaces the National Assembly; results are confirmed the following February
January 2006	Roauf Abd el-Rahman replaces Rizgar Amin, who resigned as judge in the Saddam Hussein trial
	Iraq issues its first international bond
November 5, 2006	Saddam Hussein is found guilty of crimes against humanity
December 30, 2006	Saddam Hussein is hanged
February 22, 2006	The Shii mosque al-Askari is bombed in Samarra
April 6, 2006	Jalal Talibani is reelected president of Iraq by the Council of Representatives

April 22, 2006	President Talibani designates Nouri al-Maliki as prime minister
May 20, 2006	The permanent government of Iraq takes control
June 7, 2006	Abu Musab al-Zarqawi, leader of al-Qaeda in Iraq, dies following a U.S. airstrike
June 14, 2006	Prime Minister al-Maliki announces Operation Together Forward, a new security plan for Baghdad; it ends in failure four months later
January 10, 2007	U.S. president Bush announces Operation New Way Forward, commonly known as "the Surge," which commits an additional 20,000 troops to the war
February–November 2007	Operation Fadh al-Qanoon to secure Baghdad
June–August 2007	Operation Phantom Thunder to combat al-Qaeda in Iraq and other insurgents
February 2008	Coalition forces fighting insurgents in Mosul
February 21, 2008	Turkish troops pursue Kurdish rebels into Iraq, Turks withdraw eight days later
March 2008	Sunni shaykhs agree to oppose al-Qaeda in Iraq
March 2, 2008	Iranian president Mahmoud Ahmadinejad visits Iraq
March 24, 2008	Fighting between Iraqi security forces and Mahdi Army in Basra
May 11, 2008	Moqtada al-Sadr agrees to a cease-fire

Appendix 3

Bibliography

Abdul-Jabar, Faleh, ed. *Ayatollahs, Sufis and Ideologues: State, Religion and Social Movements in Iraq.* London: Saqi Press, 2002.

Abdullah, Thabit. *Merchants, Mamluks and Murder: The Political Economy of Trade in Eighteenth Century Basra.* Albany: SUNY Press, 2001.

Abdul-Wahhab, Ata. *Sulalat al-Tin* (A lineage of clay). Amman, Jordan: Arab Establishment for Studies and Publications, 2004.

Abu Lughod, Janet. *Before European Hegemony: The World System, AD 1250–1350.* New York and Oxford: Oxford University Press, 1989.

Allawi, Ali A. *The Occupation of Iraq: Winning the War, Losing the Peace.* New Haven, Conn., and London: Yale University Press, 2007.

Alnasrawi, Abbas. "Oil, Sanctions, Debt and the Future." March 11, 2001. Campaign Against Sanctions on Iraq. Available online. URL: http://www.casi.org.uk/info/alnasrawi.html. Accessed December 14, 2007.

Annual Reports by His Majesty's Government to the Council of the League of Nations, 1921–32. Baghdad: Government Printing Press, n.d.

Arnove, Anthony, ed. *Iraq under Siege: The Deadly Impact of Sanctions and War.* Boston: South End Press, 2002.

Associated Press. "Iraqi Leader Takes Charge of Offensive in Mosul." New York Times Online, May 14, 2008. Available online. URL: http://www.nytimes.com/aponline/world/AP-Iraq.html?scp=2&sq=al-Maliki&st=nyt. Accessed May 14, 2008.

Ayyub, Dhannun. *Qissat Hayatuhu bi Qalamuhu* (His autobiography in his own words). Vol. 5. Vienna: Dialog Press, 1984.

Baghdadi, Shihab al-Din Abi Abdullah Yaqut bin Abdullah al-Hamawi al-Rumi, al-. *Mu'jam al-Buldan* (The dictionary of nations). Ed. Farid Abdul-Aziz al-Jundi. Vol. 1. Beirut, Lebanon: Dar al-Kutub al-Ilmiyya, 1990.

Baker, Luke. "Iraq Healthcare in Disarray, Report Says." Reuters. January 16, 2008. Available online. URL: http://www.reuters.com/article/latestCrisis/idUSL16828588. Accessed February 20, 2008.

Batatu, Hanna. *The Old Social Classes and the New Revolutionary Movements of Iraq: A Study of Iraq's Old Landed and Commercial Classes and of its Communists, Baathists and Free Officers.* Princeton, N.J.: Princeton University Press, 1978.

Berkey, Jonathan P. *The Formation of Islam: Religion and Society in the Near East, 600–1800.* Cambridge: Cambridge University Press, 2003.

Blix, Hans. *Disarming Iraq.* New York: Pantheon Books, 2004.

Bruinessen, Martin Van. *Agha, Shaikh and State: The Social and Political Structures of Kurdistan.* London: Zed Books, 1992.

Campaign Against Sanctions on Iraq. "Will 'Smart Sanctions' Alleviate the Humanitarian Problem in Iraq?" May 2003. Available online. URL: http://www.casi.org.uk/guide/smartsanctions.html. Accessed December 17, 2007.

Center for Economic and Social Rights. "Health and Welfare in Iraq after the Gulf Crisis." September 20, 1991. Available online. URL: http://cesr.org/node/517. Accessed December 17, 2007.

———. "UN-Sanctioned Suffering: A Human Rights Assessment of United Nations Sanctions on Iraq." May 1996. Available online. URL: http://cesr.org/node/396. Accessed December 17, 2007.

Chaudhuri, K. N. *Trade and Civilization in the Indian Ocean: An Economic History from the Rise of Islam to 1750.* Cambridge: Cambridge University Press, 1985.

Chejne, Anwar G. *The Arabic Language: Its Role in History.* Minneapolis: University of Minnesota Press, 1969.

Cole, Juan. *Sacred Space and Holy War: The Politics, Culture and History of Shiite Islam.* London and New York: I. B. Tauris, 2002.

———. "The Iraqi Shiites: On the History of America's Would-Be Allies." *Boston Review,* October–November 2003.

Colledge, Malcolm A. R. *The Parthians.* New York and Washington, D.C.: Frederick A. Praeger, 1967.

Dalley, Stephanie. *Myths from Mesopotamia: Creation, the Flood, Gilgamesh and Others.* Oxford: Oxford University Press, 1989.

Daryaee, Touraj. "The Persian Gulf Trade in Late Antiquity." *Journal of World History* 14, no. 1 (2003): 1–16. Available online. URL: http://muse.jhu.edu/journals/journal_of_world_history/v014/14.1daryaee.html. Accessed February 15, 2008.

Davis, Eric. *Memories of State: Politics, History and Collective Identity in Modern Iraq.* Berkeley and Los Angeles: University of California Press, 2005.

Donner, Fred. *The Early Islamic Conquest.* Princeton, N.J.: Princeton University Press, 1981.

Elbendary, Amina. "They Came to Baghdad." *Al-Ahram Weekly* Online, no. 634, April 17–23, 2003. Baghdad supplement. Available online. URL: http://weekly.ahram.org.eg/2003/634/baghdad.htm. Accessed May 30, 2008.

Enayat, Hamid. *Modern Islamic Political Thought.* Austin: University of Texas Press, 1982.

Eskander, Saad. "Prelude to Iraq National Library and Archives." Iraq National Library and Archives. Available online. URL: http://www. iraqnla.org/fp/News/news3.htm. Accessed January 22, 2008.

Farouk-Sluglett, Marion, and Peter Sluglett. *Iraq since 1958: From Revolution to Dictatorship.* London and New York: I. B. Tauris, 1987.

Fattah, Hala. *The Politics of Regional Trade in Iraq, Arabia and the Gulf, 1745–1900.* Albany: SUNY Press, 1997.

Fisk, Robert. "The West has been liberating the Middle East for Centuries; Will we never learn? *Independent,* March 7, 2003.

Frye, Richard N. "Byzantine and Sasanian Trade Relations with Northeastern Russia." *Dumbarton Oaks Papers,* Vol. 26 (1972), pp. 263–269. Available online. URL: http://links.jstor.org/sici?=0070-7546%281972%2926%3C263%3ABASTRW%3E2.   0.CO%3B2-R. Accessed February 15, 2008.

Global Policy Forum. "Iraq Sanctions: Humanitarian Implications and Options for the Future." August 6, 2002. Available online. URL: http://www.globalpolicy.org/security/sanction/iraq1/2002/paper. htm#summary. Accessed December 17, 2007.

Gordon, Michael R., and General Bernard E. Trainor. *Cobra II: The Inside Story of the Invasion and Occupation of Iraq.* New York: Pantheon Books/Random House, 2006.

Grainger, John D. *The Cities of Seleukid Syria.* Oxford: Clarendon Press, 1990.

———. *Seleukos Nikator: Constructing a Hellenistic Kingdom.* London and New York: Routledge, 1990.

Haj, Samira. *The Making of Iraq, 1900–1963: Capital, Power and Ideology.* Albany: SUNY Press, 1997.

Hajj, Aziz, al-. *Al-Qadiya al-Kurdiyya fi al-Iraq: al-tarikh wa al-Afaq* (The Kurdish question in Iraq: history and future). Beirut, Lebanon: Arab Institute for Research and Publications, 1994.

Hamshin, Ahmed S. *Insurgency and Counter-insurgency in Iraq.* Ithaca, N.Y.: Cornell University Press, 2006.

Hariri, Mokhless, al-. "Education." Library of Congress Studies: Iraq. 1988. Available online. URL: http://lcweb2.loc.gov/cgi-bin/query/ r?frd/cstdy:@field(DOCID+iq0045). Accessed December 13, 2007.

Hourani, Albert. *A History of the Arab Peoples*. Cambridge, Mass.: Harvard University Press, 1991.

Hussayn, Khalil Ibrahim. *Thawrat al-Shawwaf fi al-Mosul 1959* (The Shawwaf Revolt in Mosul in 1959). Baghdad: Bashar Press, 1987.

Inalcik, Halil. *The Ottoman Empire: The Classical Age, 1300–1600*. London: Wiedenfeld & Nicholson, 1973.

Inalcik, Halil, and Donald Quataert. *An Economic and Social History of the Ottoman Empire*. Cambridge: Cambridge University Press, 1997.

Ismael, Tareq Y., and Jacqueline Ismael. *The Iraqi Predicament: People in the Quagmire of Power Politics*. London: Pluto Press, 2004.

Inati, Shams, ed. *Iraq: Its History, People and Politics*. Amherst, N.Y.: Humanity Books, 2004.

Information Newsline. "Iraq Survey Shows 'Humanitarian Emergency.'" UNICEF. August 12, 1999. Available online. URL: http://www.unicef. org/newsline/99pr29.htm. Accessed January 17, 2007.

International Crisis Group, "War in Iraq: What's Next for the Kurds?" Middle East Report No. 10, March 19, 2003.

International Crisis Group. "Shiite Politics in Iraq: The Role of the Supreme Council." Middle East Report No. 70, November 15, 2007.

Jamil, Sayyar, al-. *Al-Takwin al-Arab al-Hadith, 1516–1916* (The modern foundation of the Arabs. 1516–1916). Mosul, Iraq: Ministry of Higher Education and Scientific Research, 1991.

Kafadar, Cemal. *Between Two Worlds: The Construction of the Ottoman State*. Berkeley: University of California Press, 1995.

Katzman, Kenneth. "Iraq's Opposition Movements," Congressional Research Service Report, March 26, 1998.

Khadduri, Majid, and Edmund Ghareeb. *War in the Gulf, 1990–1991: The Iraq-Kuwait Conflict and Its Implications*. Oxford: Oxford University Press, 2001.

Khafaji, Isam, al-. *Tormented Births: Passages to Modernity in Europe and the Middle East*. London and New York: I. B. Tauris, 2004.

Khoury, Dina. *State and Provincial Society in the Ottoman Empire*. Cambridge: Cambridge University Press, 1997.

Khurt, Amélie, and Susan Sherwin-White, eds. *Hellenism in the East: The Interaction of Greek and Non-Greek Civilizations from Syria to Central Asia after Alexander*. Berkeley and Los Angeles: University of California Press, 1987.

———. "Merchants and Trade in Early Modern Iraq." *New Perspectives on Turkey*, nos. 5–6 (Fall 1991).

Klein, Naomi. "Report—Baghdad Year Zero. Pillaging Iraq in Pursuit of a Neo-con Utopia." *Harper's*. 1 September 2004, 43.

Lapidus, Ira. *A History of Islamic Societies*. Cambridge: Cambridge University Press, 1988.

Lepper, F. A. *Trajan's Parthian War*. Oxford and London: Oxford University Press/Geoffrey Cumberlege, 1948.

Longrigg, Stephen Hemsley. *Four Centuries of Modern Iraq*. Oxford: Clarendon Press, 1925.

———. *Four Centuries of Modern Iraq*. Beirut, Lebanon: Librarie du Liban, 1953.

Mallat, Chibli. *The Renewal of Islamic Law: Muhammed Baqer as-Sadr, Najaf and the Shi'i International*. Cambridge: Cambridge University Press, 1993.

Mathee, Rudi. *The Politics of Trade in Safavid Iran: Silk for Silver, 1600–1730*. Cambridge: Cambridge University Press, 1999.

Nakash, Itzhak. *The Shi'is of Iraq*. Princeton, N.J.: Princeton University Press, 1994.

Niewenhuis, Tom. *Politics and Society in Early Modern Iraq: Mamluk Pashas, Tribal Shaykhs and Local Rule between 1802 and 1831*. The Hague, Netherlands: Martinus Nijhoff, 1982.

Oppenheim, A. Leo. *Ancient Mesopotamia: Portrait of a Dead Civilization*. Chicago and London: University of Chicago Press, 1977.

Owen, Roger. *The Middle East in the World Economy, 1800–1914*. London and New York: Methuen, 1981.

Ozbaran, Salih. *The Ottoman Response to European Expansion*. Istanbul, Turkey: Isis Press, 1994.

Postgate, J. N. *Early Mesopotamia: Society and Economy at the Dawn of History*. London: Routledge, 1992.

Potter, Lawrence, and Gary Sick, eds. *Iran, Iraq and the Legacies of War*. New York: Palgrave Macmillan, 2006.

Rauf, Imad Abdul-Salam. *Tarikh mashari' miyah al-shurb al-qadima fi Baghdad*. Baghdad: Dar al-Shu'un al-Thaqafiyya al-Amma, 2002.

Rawlinson, George. *The Seventh Great Oriental Monarchy*. London: Longmans, Green, 1876.

Robinson, Chase F. *A Medieval Islamic City Reconsidered: An Interdisciplinary Approach to Samarra*. Oxford: Oxford University Press, 2001.

Roux, Georges. *Ancient Iraq*. London: Penguin Books, 1992.

Sack, Ronald H. *Images of Nebuchadnezzar: The Emergence of a Legend*. London and Toronto, Canada: Associated University Presses, 1991.

Salucci, Illario. *A Peoples' History of Iraq: The Iraqi Communist Party, Workers' Movements and the Left, 1920–2004*. Chicago: Haymarket Books, 2005.

Saunders, J. J. *The History of the Mongol Conquests.* Philadelphia: University of Pennsylvania Press, 1971.

Setudeh-Nejad, Shahab. "Cultural and Cosmological Impact of Iranian Civilization in Vietnam and Peninsular Areas of Southeast Asia." N.d. Iran Chamber Society. Available online. URL: http://www.iranchamber.com/culture/articles/iranian_cultural_impact_southeastasia.php. Accessed February 15, 2008.

Shaban, M. A. *The Abbasid Revolution.* Cambridge: Cambridge University Press, 1971.

Simawe, Saadi, ed. "Modern Iraqi Literature in English Translation." *Arab Studies Quarterly* 19, no. 4 (Fall 1997).

Tramontini, Leslie. "If ever your sky narrows over me, O Fatherland: Some reflections on the nationalist discourse of the poets of the Iraqi *thawrat al-ishrin.*" In Beirut, Lebanon: Orient Institute, 2002–03.

Tripp, Charles. *A History of Iraq.* Cambridge: Cambridge University Press, 2000.

Van de Mieroop, Marc. *A History of the Ancient Near East, ca. 3000–323 BC.* Boston: Blackwell Publishing, 2004.

Watenpaugh, Keith, Edouard Méténier, Jens Hanssen, and Hala Fattah. "Opening the Doors: Academic Conditions and Intellectual Life in Post-War Baghdad." *Iraqi Observatory,* July 15, 2003.

White House. "President Delivers State of the Union Address." January 29, 2002. Available online. URL: http://www.whitehouse.gov/news/releases/2002/01/20020129-11.html. Accessed January 19, 2008.

Yergin, Daniel. *The Prize: The Epic Quest for Oil, Money and Power.* New York: Simon & Schuster, 1991.

Zettler, R. L. "Reconstructing the World of Ancient Mesopotamia: Divided Beginnings and Holistic History." *Journal of the Economic and Social History of the Orient* 46 (2003): 3–45.

APPENDIX 4

SUGGESTED READING

General

Bernhardsson, Magnus Thorkell. *Reclaiming a Plundered Past: Archaeology and Nation Building in Modern Iraq.* Austin: University of Texas Press, 2005.

Hunt, Courtney. *The History of Iraq.* Westport, Conn.: Greenwood Press, 2005.

Marr, Phebe. *The Modern History of Iraq.* Boulder, Colo.: Westview Press, 2004.

Polk, William R. *Understanding Iraq.* New York: HarperCollins, 2005.

Simons, G. L. *Iraq: From Sumer to Saddam.* New York: St. Martin's Press, 1994.

Iraq, the First Society (Prehistory to 539 B.C.E.)

Barton, George A. *The Royal Inscriptions of Sumer and Akkad.* New Haven, Conn.: Yale University Press/American Oriental Society, 1929.

Black, Jeremy, trans. *Literature of Ancient Sumer.* Oxford: Oxford University Press, 2004.

Dougherty, Raymond Philip. *Nabonidus and Belshazzar: A Study of the Closing Events of the Neo-Babylonian Empire.* New Haven, Conn.: Yale University Press, 1929.

Gilgamesh. Introduction by N. K. Sandars. London and New York: Penguin, 1972.

Glassner, Jean-Jacques. *The Invention of Cuneiform: Writing in Sumer.* Trans. and ed. Zainab Bahrani and Marc Van de Mieroop. Baltimore, Md.: Johns Hopkins University Press, 2003.

Grayson, Albert Kirk. *Assyrian Rulers of the Early First Millennium BC (1114–859 BC).* Toronto, Canada, and Buffalo, N.Y.: University of Toronto Press, 1991.

————. *Assyrian Rulers of the Third and Second Millennia* BC *(to 1115 BC)*. Toronto, Canada, and Buffalo, N.Y.: University of Toronto Press, 1987.

Kramer, Samuel Noah. *History Begins at Sumer.* Garden City, N.Y.: Doubleday, 1959.

Leick, Gwendolyn. *Mesopotamia: The Invention of the City.* London: Allen Lane, 2001.

Lutz, Henry Frederick. *Early Babylonian Letters from Larsa.* New Haven, Conn.: Yale University Press, 1917.

Oates, Joan. *Babylon.* London: Thames & Hudson, 1979.

Saggs, H. W. F. *The Greatness That Was Babylon: A Survey of the Ancient Civilization of the Tigris-Euphrates Valley.* London: Sidgwick & Jackson, 1988.

From the Persian Empire to the Sassanians (539 B.C.E.–651 C.E.)

Allen, Lindsay. *The Persian Empire.* Chicago: University of Chicago Press, 2005.

Bar-Kochva, Bezalel. *The Seleucid Army: Organization and Tactics in the Great Campaigns.* Cambridge and New York: Cambridge University Press, 1976.

Cook, J. M. *The Persian Empire.* New York: Schocken Books, 1983.

Dignas, Beate. *Rome and Persia in Late Antiquity: Neighbors and Rivals.* Cambridge: Cambridge University Press, 2007.

Fraser, P. M. *Cities of Alexander the Great.* Oxford: Clarendon Press, New York: Oxford University Press, 1996.

Ghirshman, Roman. *Persian Art, the Parthian and Sassanian Dynasties, 249 B.C.–A.D. 651.* New York: Golden Press, 1962.

Heckel, Waldemar. *The Conquests of Alexander the Great.* Cambridge and New York: Cambridge University Press, 2008.

Olmstead, A. T. *History of the Persian Empire.* Chicago: University of Chicago Press, 1959, 1966.

Rawlinson, George. *The Story of Parthia.* New York: G. P. Putnam's Sons, 1893.

Sherwin-White, Susan M., and Amélie Kuhrt. *From Samarkand to Sardis: A New Approach to the Seleucid Empire.* Berkeley: University of California Press, 1993.

Iraq under the Umayyad Dynasty (651–750)

Agha, Saleh Said. *The Revolution Which Toppled the Umayyads: Neither Arab nor Abbasid.* Leiden, Netherlands, and Boston: Brill, 2003.

Aslan, Reza. *No God but God: The Origins, Evolution, and Future of Islam.* New York: Random House, 2005.

Halm, Heinz. *Shi'ism.* Trans. Janet Watson and Marian Hill. New York: Columbia University Press, 2004.

Jafri, Husain M. *Origins and Early Development of Shi'a Islam.* London and New York: Longman, 1979.

Momen, Moojan. *An Introduction to Shi'i Islam: The History and Doctrines of Twelver Shi'ism.* New Haven, Conn.: Yale University Press, 1985.

Tabarī. *The History of al-Tabarī (Ta'rīkh al-Rusul wa'l Mulūk).* Albany: SUNY Press, 1985.

Trifkovic, Srdja. *The Sword of the Prophet: Islam: History, Theology, Impact on the World.* Boston: Regina Orthodox Press, 2002.

Waines, David. *An Introduction to Islam.* Cambridge and New York: Cambridge University Press, 2003.

Abbasid and Post-Abbasid Iraq (750–1258)

Baldick, Julian. *Mystical Islam: An Introduction to Sufism.* New York: New York University Press, 1989.

Chittick, William. *Sufism: A Short Introduction.* Oxford: Oneworld Publications, 2000.

Hanne, Eric J. *Putting the Caliph in His Place: Power, Authority, and the Late Abbasid Caliphate.* Madison, N.J.: Fairleigh Dickinson University Press, 2007.

Kennedy, Hugh. *When Baghdad Ruled the Muslim World: The Rise and Fall of Islam's Greatest Dynasty.* Cambridge, Mass.: Da Capo Press, 2005.

Lassner, Jacob. *The Shaping of Abbasid Rule.* Princeton, N.J.: Princeton University Press, 1980.

Wiet, Gaston. *Baghdad, Metropolis of the Abbasid Caliphate.* Trans. Seymour Feiler. Norman: University of Oklahoma Press, 1971.

Turkish Tribal Migrations and the Early Ottoman State (1256–1638)

Allsen, Thomas T. *Culture and Conquest in Mongol Eurasia.* Cambridge and New York: Cambridge University Press, 2001.

Amitai, Reuven, and Michal Biran, eds. *Mongols, Turks, and Others: Eurasian Nomads and the Sedentary World.* Leiden, Netherlands, and Boston: Brill, 2005.

Amitai-Preiss, Reuven. *The Mamluk-Ilkhanid War, 1260–1281.* Cambridge and New York: Cambridge University Press, 1995.

Imber, Colin. *The Ottoman Empire, 1300–1650: The Structure of Power.* New York: Palgrave Macmillan, 2002.

Inalcik, Halil. *The Ottoman Empire: The Classical Age, 1300–1600.* Trans. Norman Itzkowitz and Colin Imber. New York: Praeger Publishers, 1973.

Köprülü, Mehmet Fuat. *The Origins of the Ottoman Empire.* Albany: SUNY Press, 1992.

Manz, Beatrice Forbes. *The Rise and Rule of Tamerlane.* Cambridge and New York: Cambridge University Press, 1989.

Murphey, Rhoads. *Ottoman Warfare, 1500–1700.* New Brunswick, N.J.: Rutgers University Press, 1999.

Newman, Andrew J. *Safavid Iran: Rebirth of a Persian Empire.* London: I. B. Tauris; New York: Palgrave Macmillan, 2006.

Phillips, E. D. *The Mongols.* New York: F. A. Praeger, 1969.

Imperial Administration, Local Rule, and Ottoman Recentralization (1638–1914)

Davison, Roderic H. *Reform in the Ottoman Empire, 1856–1876.* Princeton, N.J.: Princeton University Press, 1963.

Fulanain. *The Marsh Arab, Haji Rikkan.* Philadelphia: J. B. Lippincott, 1928.

Heller, Joseph. *British Policy towards the Ottoman Empire, 1908–1914.* London: Cass, 1983.

Karpat, Kemal H. *The Politicization of Islam: Reconstructing Identity, State, Faith, and Community in the Late Ottoman State.* New York: Oxford University Press, 2001.

Karsh, Efraim. *Empires of the Sand: The Struggle for Mastery in the Middle East, 1789–1923.* Cambridge, Mass.: Harvard University Press, 1999.

Kasaba, Reşat. *The Ottoman Empire and the World Economy: The Nineteenth Century.* Albany: SUNY Press, 1988.

Khalidi, Rasid, et al., eds. *The Origins of Arab Nationalism.* New York: Columbia University Press, 1991.

Mansfield, Peter. *The Ottoman Empire and Its Successors.* New York: St. Martin's Press, 1973.

Weismann, Itzchak, and Fruma Zachs, eds. *Ottoman Reform and Muslim Regeneration: Studies in Honour of Butrus Abu-Manneb.* London and New York: I. B. Tauris, 2005.

British Occupation and the Iraqi Monarchy (1914–1958)

Fieldhouse, D. K. *Western Imperialism in the Middle East, 1914–1958.* Oxford and New York: Oxford University Press, 2006.

Haldane, Sir James Aylmer Lowthorpe. *The Insurrection in Mesopotamia, 1920.* London and Nashville, Tenn.: Imperial War Museum in association with Battery Press, 2005.

Jwaideh, Wadie. *The Kurdish National Movement: Its Origins and Development.* Syracuse, N.Y.: Syracuse University Press, 2006.

Khadduri, Majid. *Independent Iraq, 1932–1958: A Study in Iraqi Politics.* London and New York: Oxford University Press, 1960.

Lyon, Wallace A. *Kurds, Arabs and Britons: The Memoir of Wallace Lyon in Iraq, 1918–44.* London: I. B. Tauris, 2002.

Silverfarb, Daniel. *Britain's Informal Empire in the Middle East: A Case Study of Iraq, 1929–1941.* New York: Oxford University Press, 1986.

Simon, Reeva S. *Iraq between the Two World Wars: The Creation and Implementation of a Nationalist Ideology.* New York: Columbia University Press, 1986.

Simon, Reeva S., and Eleanor H. Tejirian. *The Creation of Iraq, 1914–1921.* New York: Columbia University Press, 2004.

The Growth of the Republican Regimes and the Emergence of Baathist Iraq (1958–1979)

Alnasrawi, Abbas. *The Economy of Iraq: Oil, Wars, Destruction of Development and Prospects, 1950–2010.* Westport, Conn.: Greenwood Press, 1994.

Caractacus (pseudonym). *Revolution in Iraq: An Essay in Comparative Public Opinion.* London: Gollancz, 1959.

Dann, Uriel. *Iraq under Qassem: A Political History, 1958–1963.* New York: Praeger, 1969.

Fernea, Robert A., and William Roger Louis. *The Iraqi Revolution of 1958: The Old Social Classes Revisited.* London and New York: I. B. Tauris, 1991.

Khadduri, Majid. *Republican Iraq: A Study in Iraqi Politics since the Revolution of 1958.* London and New York: Oxford University Press, 1969.

Niblock, Tim, ed. *Iraq, the Contemporary State.* New York: St. Martin's Press, 1982.

The Rule of Saddam Hussein and the Difficult Legacy of the Mukhabarat State (1979–2003)

Abdullah, Thabit. *Dictatorship, Imperialism and Chaos: Iraq since 1989.* London and New York: Zed Books, 2006.

Bengio, Ofra. *Saddam's Word: Political Discourse in Iraq*. New York: Oxford University Press, 1998.

Chubin, Shahram, and Charles Tripp. *Iran and Iraq at War*. Boulder, Colo.: Westview Press, 1988.

Freedman, Lawrence. *The Gulf Conflict, 1990–1991: Diplomacy and War in the New World Order*. Princeton, N.J.: Princeton University Press, 1993.

Gunter, Michael M. *The Kurdish Predicament in Iraq: A Political Analysis*. New York: St. Martin's Press, 1999.

Hiro, Dilip. *Desert Shield to Desert Storm: The Second Gulf War*. New York: Routledge, 1992.

Long, Jerry M. *Saddam's War of Words: Politics, Religion and the Iraqi Invasion of Kuwait*. Austin: University of Texas, 2004.

Mackey, Sandra. *The Reckoning: Iraq and the Legacy of Saddam Hussein*. New York: Norton, 2002.

Musallam, Musallam Ali. *The Iraqi Invasion of Kuwait: Saddam Hussein, His State and International Power Politics*. London and New York: British Academic Press, 1996.

Sponeck, H. C. Graf. *A Different Kind of War: The UN Sanctions Regime in Iraq*. New York: Berghahn Book, 2006.

Stansfield, Gareth R. V. *Iraq: People, History, Politics*. Cambridge: Polity, 2007.

Workman, W. Thom. *The Social Origins of the Iran-Iraq War*. Boulder, Colo.: Lynne Rienner Publishers, 1994.

The War in Iraq (2003–2008)

Agresto, John. *Mugged by Reality: The Liberation of Iraq and the Failure of Good Intentions*. New York: Encounter Books, 2007.

Byman, Daniel. *Things Fall Apart: Containing the Spillover from an Iraqi Civil War*. Washington, D.C.: Brookings Institution Press, 2007.

Cockburn, Patrick. *The Occupation: War and Resistance in Iraq*. London and New York: Verso, 2006.

Hallenberg, Jan, and Håkan Karlsson, eds. *The Iraq War: European Perspectives on Politics, Strategy and Operations*. London and New York: Routledge, 2005.

Herring Eric. *Iraq in Fragments: The Occupation and Its Legacy*. Ithaca, N.Y.: Cornell University Press, 2006.

Hersh, Seymour. *Chain of Command: The Road from 9/11 to Abu Ghraib*. New York: HarperCollins, 2004.

MacDonald, Charles G., ed. *Kurdish Identity: Human Rights and Political Status*. Gainesville: University Press of Florida, 2007.

Packer, George. *The Assassins' Gate: America in Iraq.* New York: Farrar, Straus & Giroux, 2005.

Rieff, David. *At the Point of a Gun: Democratic Dreams and Armed Intervention.* New York: Simon & Schuster, 2005.

Riverbend (pseudonym). *Baghdad Burning: Girl Blog from Iraq.* New York: Feminist Press at CUNY, 2005.

———. *Baghdad Burning II: More Girl Blog from Iraq.* New York: Feminist Press at CUNY, 2006.

Sjoberg, Laura. *Gender, Justice, and the Wars in Iraq: A Feminist Reformulation of Just War Theory.* Lanham, Md.: Lexington Books, 2006.

U.S. House of Representatives Committee on Oversight and Government Reform. *The Impact of CPA Decisionmaking on Iraq Reconstruction.* 110th Congress, First Session. Washington, D.C.: U.S. Government Printing Office, 2007.

Woodward, Bob. *State of Denial.* New York: Simon & Schuster, 2006.

INDEX

Page numbers in *italic* indicate illustrations. The letters *c* and *m* indicate a chronology entry and a map, respectively.